Johann Sebastian
Bach
and
Liturgical Life in Leipzig

Eastward view of the interior of St. Thomas Church before its 19th-century restoration.
Source: R. Petzoldt, *Johann Sebastian Bach: Das Schaffen des Meisters im Spiegel einer Stadt*
(Leipzig, 1950), following p. 48.

Johann Sebastian Bach

and

Liturgical Life in Leipzig

Günther Stiller

Translated by
Herbert J. A. Bouman
Daniel F. Poellot
Hilton C. Oswald

Edited by
Robin A. Leaver

Publishing House
St. Louis

A translation of *Johann Sebastian Bach und das Leipziger gottesdienstliche Leben seiner Zeit.*
Published in Berlin, Germany, 1970.

Used by permission of Evangelical Publishing Co., Berlin.

Copyright © 1984 Concordia Publishing House
3558 S. Jefferson Avenue, St. Louis, MO 63118-3968
Manufactured in the United States of America.

Library of Congress Cataloging in Publication Data

Stiller, Günther.
    Johann Sebastian Bach and liturgical life in Leipzig.

    Translation of: Johann Sebastian Bach und das Leipzig gottesdienstliche Leben
seiner Zeit.
    Bibliography: p.
    Includes index.
    1. Bach, Johann Sebastian, 1685-1750. 2. Lutheran Church— Germany (East)—
Leipzig—Liturgy—History—18th century. 3. Church music—Lutheran Church.
4. Church music—Germany (East)—Leipzig—18th century.
I Leaver, Robin A. II. Title.
ML410.B1S853 1984   783'.092'4   84-5842
ISBN 0-570-01320-8

1 2 3 4 5 6 7 8 9 10 PP 93 92 91 90 89 88 87 86 85 84

Contents

Abbreviations
of Frequently Cited Sources

AG   *Allerhand Geschichte, die Neue Kirche betreffend, so von Ao 1699 an dahin Ao...zugetragen* (Manuscript notes, 1699— 1739).

Ag   *Agenda: Das ist, Kirchen-Ordnung, Wie sich die Pfarrherren und Seelsorger in ihren Ämtern und Diensten verhalten sollen* (Leipzig, 1712). The basic content appears unchanged in all editions published between 1647 and 1771.

BD   *Bach-Dokumente, herausgegeben vom Bach-Archiv Leipzig*, supplement to NBA ed. W. Neumann and H.-J. Schulze (4 vols.; Leipzig and Kassel, 1963—1979).

BG   *Bach-Gedenkschift 1950 im Auftrag der Internationalen Bach Gesellschaft*, ed. K. Matthai (Zurich, 1950).

BiThü   *Bach in Thüringen: Gabe der Thüringer Kirche an das Thüringer Volk zum Bach-Gedenkjahr 1950* (Berlin, 1950).

BJ   *Bach-Jahrbuch*, published by the Neue Bachgesellschaft (1904—).

Blu   *Friedrich Blume, "Outlines of a New Picture of Bach," Music and Letters* 44 (1963): 214—27.

Bn   *Bildnisse der sämmtlichen Superintendenten der Leipziger Diöces*, lithographic reproductions of original portraits by C. E. A. Paalzow, with brief biographical sketches by F. G. Hoffmann (Leipzig, 1839).

BR   *The Bach Reader: A Life of Johann Sebastian Bach in Letters and Documents*, ed. Hans T. David and Arthur Mendel (New York, 1966).

BWV   Wolfgang Schmieder, *Thematisch-systematisches Verzeichnis der musikalischen Werke von J. S. Bach* [Bach-Werke-Verzeichnis] (Leipzig, 1950).

ChV   *Chronologisches Verzeichnis der Evangelisch-Lutherischen und Reformierten Prediger in Leipzig von 1539 bis 18—...* (Manuscript notes, 1539—1864).

Gb   Christian Gerber, *Historie der Kirchen-Ceremonien in Sachsen* (Dresden and Leipzig, 1732).

Jau. I   Reinhold Jauernig, *"Johann Sebastian Bach in Weimar," BiThü*, pp. 77—85.

Jau. II   Reinhold Jauernig, *"Johann Sebastian Bach in Weimar," JSBiThü*, pp. 49—105.

JSBiThü *Johann Sebastian Bach in Thüringen: Festgabe zum Gedenkjahr 1950* (Weimar, 1950).

KB *Kritischer Bericht* of *NBA*.

KM Walter Blankenburg, *Kirche und Musik: Gesammelte Aufsätze zur Geschichte der gottesdienstlichen Musik*, ed. E. Hübner and R. Steiger (Göttingen, 1979).

L *Leiturgia: Handbuch des evangelischen Gottesdienstes*, ed. Karl Ferdinand Müller and Walter Blankenburg (5 vols.; Kassel, 1954—1970).

LA 1723 *Das jetzt lebende und florirende Leipzig* [Leipzig Directory] (Leipzig, 1723).

LA 1729 *Kern des ietzo florirenden Leipzigs* [Leipzig Directory] (Leipzig, 1729).

LA 1735 *Kern des ietzo lebenden Leipzigs* [Leipzig Directory] (Leipzig, 1735).

Leu*Gsch* Hans Leube, *Die Geschichte der pietistischen Bewegung in Leipzig* (Dissertation, Leipzig, 1920).

Leu*Ref* Hans Leube, *Die Reformideen in der deutschen lutherischen Kirche zur Zeit der Orthodoxie* (Leipzig, 1924).

LGB 1682 Gottfried Vopelius, *Neu Leipzig Gesangbuch, von den schönsten und besten Liedern verfasset* (Leipzig, 1682); see also J. Grimm, *Das Neu Leipziger Gesangbuch des Gottfried Vopelius (Leipzig 1682): Untersuchung zur Klärung seiner geschichtlichen Stellung* (*Berliner Studien zur Musikwissenschaft 14*; Berlin, 1969).

LGB 1717 *Geistreicher Lieder-Schatz; oder Leipziger Gesang-Buch, Worinnen der Kern aller Evangelischen Lieder, sonderlich aber diejenigen enthalten, welche in Leipzig und andern Chur-Sächsischen Kirchen beym öffentlichen Gottesdienste pflegen gesungen zu werden* (Leipzig, 1717).

Lh F. G. Leonhardi, *Geschichte und Beschreibung der Kreis- und Handelsstadt Leipzig nebst der umliegenden Gegend* (Leipzig, 1799).

LKA *Leipziger Kirchen-Andachten: Darinnen der Erste Theil, Das Gebetbuch oder die Ordnung des gantzen öffentlichen Gottes-Dienstes durchs gantze Jahr...Der Ander Theil, Das Gesangbuch...ed. J. F. Leibniz (Leipzig, 1694).*

LKS *Leipziger Kirchen-Staat: Das ist, Deutlicher Unterricht vom Gottes-Dienst in Leipzig* (Leipzig, 1710).

MGG *Die Musik in Geschichte und Gegenwart: Allgemeine Enzyklopädie der Musik* (Kassel, 1949—).

ML Christhard Mahrenholz, *Musicologica et Liturgica: Gesammelte Aufsätze*, ed. K. F. Müller (Kassel, 1960).

MuK *Musik und Kirche* (Kassel, 1928—).

NBA *Johann Sebastian Bach: Neue Ausgabe sämtlicher Werke* [Neue Bach-Ausgabe], jointly issued by the Johann-Sebastian-Bach-Institut, Göttingen, and the Bach-Archiv, Leipzig (Leipzig and Kassel, 1954—).

N*VT* Werner Neumann, *Sämtliche von Johann Sebastian Bach vertonte Texte* (Leipzig, 1974).

Rm Johann Georg Rosenmüller, *Pastoralanweisung: Zum Gebrauch akademischer Vorlesungen* (Leipzig, 1788).

Ro *Nachricht, Wie es, in der Kirchen zu St. Thom. alhier, mit dem Gottesdienst, Jährlich sowohl an Hohen Feste, als andern Tagen, pfleget*

8

	gehalten zu werden, auffgezeichnet von Johann Christoph Rosten, Custode ad D. Thomae, anno 1716 (Manuscript; continued by later hands).
Sc*AL*	Christoph Ernst Sicul, *Annalium Lipsiensium* (Leipzig, 1723).
Sch*BLKM*	Arnold Schering, *Johann Sebastian Bachs Leipziger Kirchenmusik* (Leipzig, 1936).
Sch*ML*	Arnold Schering, *J. S. Bach und das Musikleben Leipzigs im 18. Jahrhundert* (Leipzig, 1941).
Sc*JL*	Christoph Ernst Sicul, *Das wegen der durch Göttliche Gnade über zweyhundert Jahre feststehenden Evangelisch-Lutherischen Religion Jubilirende Leipzig* (Leipzig, 1731).
Sc*LJG*	Christoph Ernst Sicul, *Leipziger Jahr-Geschichte 1721* (Leipzig, 1723).
Sc*NA*	Christoph Ernst Sicul, *Neo annalium Lipsiensium Continuatio II: Oder des mit 1715ten Jahre Neuangegangenen Leipziger Jahrbuchs Dritte Probe* (Leipzig, 1717).
SM	F. Blume, *Syntagma Musicologicum I: Gesammelte Aufsätze* (Kassel, 1963).
Spi	Philipp Spitta, *Johann Sebastian Bach: His Work and Influence on the Music of Germany, 1685—1750*, trans. C. Bell and J. A. Fuller-Maitland (3 vols.; London, 1899).
WF	*Johann Sebastian Bach*, vol. 170 of *Wege der Forschung*, ed. Walter Blankenburg (Darmstadt, 1970).
WGB	*Andächtiger Seelen geistliches Brand- und Gantz-Opfer: Das ist, vollständiges Gesangbuch* (8 vols.; Leipzig, 1697). The work is also referred to as the "*Wagnersches Gesangbuch*" since it was compiled by the Leipzig Bürgermeister, Dr. Paul Wagner,
Wz	Anton Weiz, *Verbessertes Leipzig; oder vornehmsten Dinge, so von Anno 1698 an biß hieher bey der Stadt Leipzig verbessert worden, mit Inscriptionibus erleutert* (Leipzig, 1728).

Editor's Introduction

The problem the historian always faces is that of seeing his area of study through the filter of his own philosophy and presuppositions. What he most readily sees are those things that support and demonstrate his own convictions. This is clearly demonstrated in the field of Bach studies. The early biographer Forkel painted a picture of the composer in terms of the ideals of the Enlightenment. Bach was therefore first and foremost an artist and hero of the German nation. In the later 19th century, under the influence of Romanticism, biographers such as Bitter and Spitta drew an enlarged picture of Bach as the deeply religious composer of church music. This understanding of Bach, which persisted well into the 20th century, led to the somewhat extravagant claim that the Leipzig cantor was the "Fifth Evangelist."[1] This well-established image was called into question by Friedrich Blume in the early 1960s. Reflecting the secular climate of our contemporary age, he suggested that Bach was not particularly religious at all; he simply looked for positions that would enable him to use and extend his enormous talent.

It is not that these interpretations were necessarily wrong. Forkel was trying to come to terms with the incredible music of this prodigious composer; Bitter and Spitta were attempting to explain the motivation that produced such sublime music for the worship of the church; and Blume was trying to do justice to the recently discovered "new chronology," which suggested that Bach gave up composing church music after his early years in Leipzig. However, all these interpretations were, to a greater or lesser degree, one-sided in the sense that not all the evidence regarding the contemporary context of Bach's life and work was brought into view.

The book by Günther Stiller that is presented here in translation attempts to investigate the church life in Leipzig at the time of Bach in order to determine the content and function of Bach's cantatas and also the composer's motivation and Christian commitment in composing them. By an examination of documentary sources, both manuscript and printed, Stiller demonstrates to what extent the Bach pictures of Forkel, Bitter/Spitta, and Blume are on the right lines and where they are misleading and overdrawn.

Stiller's book originated as a doctoral dissertation presented to Leipzig University in 1966,[2] and was published jointly in Berlin and Kassel in 1970. It is therefore silent on matters that have come to light subsequently—such as the Calov Bible commentary once owned by Bach (see below)—or that have been discussed in studies published in the meantime. This later Bach literature can be discovered in the bibliographies of Rosemarie Nestle and the survey of Walter Blankenburg.[3] Biographies that take into account recent Bach research appear in standard reference works such as *The New Grove Dictionary of Music and Musicians*, and *Theologische Realenzyklopädie*.[4] Numerous symposia and collections of essays have also appeared, two of the most recent and important being *Bachforschung und Bachinterpretation heute: Wissenschaftler und Praktiker im Dialog. Bericht über das Bachfest-Symposium 1978 der Philipps-Universität Marburg*, edited by R. Brinkmann (Leipzig, 1981), and *Bachiana et alia Musicologica: Festschrift Alfred Dürr zum 65. Geburtstag am 3. März 1983* (Kassel and New York, 1982).

Numerous studies that deal with the specific theological and liturgical issues considered in this book have been published subsequently. W. E. Buszin has investigated the background of the chorale, J. Tolonen the significance of chorale melodies for Bach's clavier works, and M. Petzoldt and R. Ganzhorn-Burkhardt the theological importance of the chorales in the Passions.[5] Paul Brainard has explored Bach's use of parodies in the St. Matthew Passion, and Robert L. Marshall the whole question of Bach's approach to composition.[6] On the issue of the influence, negative or positive, of the Enlightenment on Bach, J. Birke has described the background and K. Geiringer, M. Petzoldt, and the contributors to the symposium edited by R. Szeskus, have made various statements and investigations.[7] The conflict between Bach and J. A. Ernesti, the rector of the *Thomasschule*, has been presented by Paul S. Minear as a debate between protagonists of the old orthodoxy and the new Enlightenment.[8] The controversy between orthodoxy and Pietism in connection with Bach has been considered by W. Blankenburg, W. Zeller, and H. L. Holborn, and particular theological and liturgical questions have been studied by U. Siegele, U. Meyer, L. Prautzsch, R. A. Leaver, and Günther Stiller himself.[9]

Gerhard Herz reviewed the fruits of recent Bach research but came to different conclusions than those of Blume.[10] The reason is to be found in the discovery of a three-volume Bible commentary, edited by Abraham Calov, which was once owned by Bach.[11] The find was not made public until the Heidelberg Bachfest of 1969, and therefore these volumes did not figure in the studies of either Stiller or Blume. The marginal comments in Bach's hand in these volumes confirm Stiller's thesis and contradict Blume's.[12]

12

However, Blume's earlier conclusions have lost little of their significance. In 1947 he wrote:

> With great courage Schering attempted a completely new interpretation of Bach's music and with his discovery of symbolism he opened a new approach to Bach's innermost conception of religion and dogma. Schering was able to show that Bach in his vocal works was...symbolizing the hidden relationships, the ultimate ideas...which elude the untutored reader and listener, since to understand them, a whole training in the subtleties and sophistications of the old Lutheran scholasticism is required. This interpretation seems to open a door on the whole world of Bach's innermost conceptions and ideas. To open still further must now be one of the most urgent concerns of Bach research.[13]

Stiller agrees, and in response to Blume's 1947 essay he charts the important theological Bach studies that preceded his own substantial contribution. Nevertheless he has to conclude that "all published treatises and essays of a scientific-theological nature still represent only a very small part, only a beginning in view of the great mass of problems that have yet to be tackled."[14]

Bach wrote his music from a strongly Lutheran perspective, and therefore to fully understand his approach to his art it is necessary not only to study his music but also the theological climate and church conditions within which he lived and worked. This involves above all a study of orthodox Lutheran theology and the various deviations from it that occurred during Bach's lifetime, such as Pietism on the one hand and the Enlightenment on the other. In order to further such research that Blume saw as necessary in 1947 and Stiller saw as largely unfulfilled in 1966, a small group of theologians and musicologists met at the Berlin Bachfest of 1976 to see whether some kind of group ought to be set up to foster such work. The Internationale Arbeitsgemeinschaft für theologische Bachforschung was founded that winter with Walter Blankenburg as its (very active) president, and the new society held its first working conference in February 1977 in Schlüchtern. All the members of this somewhat select group are working in various areas connected with Bach's faith and theology; most have published substantial books and articles or have such projects in preparation. The members to date are

Dr. Elke Axmacher (Berlin)
Dr. Walter Blankenburg (Schlüchtern)
Prof. Dr. Johan Bouman (Marburg)
Dr. Alfred Dürr (Bovenden)
Prof. Dr. A. Casper Honders (Groningen)
Pfarrer Harro Hoyer (Lausanne)
Prof. Erich Hübner (Heidelberg)
Rev. Robin A. Leaver (Oxford)
Ludwig Prautzsch (Kassel)

Prof. Dr. Ulrich Siegele (Tübingen)
Prof. Dr. Lothan Steiger (Heidelberg)
Dr. Renate Steiger (Heidelberg)
Dr. Günther Stiller (Stralsund)
Dr. Helene Werthemann (Basel)
Prof. Dr. Winfried Zeller (Marburg)

Since the first conference of 1977 six further meetings have been held at which papers have been given. Many have subsequently appeared in print, among them:

U. Meyer, "Johann Sebastian Bachs theologische Äusserungen," *MuK* 47 (1977): 112—18.

U. Meyer, "Zum Problem der Zahlen in J. S. Bachs Werk," *MuK* 49 (1979): 58—71.

U. Meyer, "Überlegungen zu Bachs Spätwerk," *MuK* 50 (1980): 239—48.

U. Meyer, "Zahlenalphabet bei J. S. Bach? Zur antikabbalistischen Tradition im Luthertum," *MuK* 51 (1981): 15—19.

R. Steiger, "Methode und Ziel einer musikalischen Hermeneutik im Werke Bachs," *MuK* 47 (1977): 209—24.

R. Steiger, "Bach und Israel," *MuK* 50 (1980): 15—22.

R. Steiger, "Die Einheit des Wehinachtsoratoriums von J. S. Bach," *MuK* 51 (1981): 273—88; ibid. 52 (1982): 9—15.

E. Axmacher, "Ein Quellenfund zum Text der Matthäus-Passion," *BJ*, 1978, 181—91.

W. Blankenburg, "Eine neue Textquelle zu sieben Kantaten Johann Sebastian Bachs und achtzehn Kantaten Johann Ludwig Bachs," *BJ*, 1977, 7—25.

U. Siegele, "Schöpfungs- und Gesellschaftsordnung in Bachs Musik," *Im Gespräch: Der Mensch. Ein interdisziplinärer Dialog. Joseph Möller zum 65. Geburtstag* (Duesseldorf, 1981), pp. 276—85.

T. Wilhelmi, "Bachs Bibliothek: Eine Weiterfürung der Arbeit von Hans Preuss," *BJ*, 1979, 107—29.

In 1983 the Internationale Arbeitsgemeinschaft für theologische Bachforschung began a series of monographs that explore theological themes connected with the life and work of J. S. Bach. The first three in the series are

1. R. A. Leaver, *Bachs theologische Bibliothek* (English and German text; Stuttgart, 1983).

2. E. Axmacher, *"Aus Liebe will mein Heyland sterben": Unter-suchungen zum Wandel des Passionsverständnisses im frühen 18. Jahrhundert* (Stuttgart, 1984).

3. L. and R. Steiger, *Bachs Kantaten zum Sonntag Estomihi: Eine theologische-musikalische Auslegung* (Stuttgart, 1984).

A further volume by various authors on Bach's cantatas for the Reformation festival is in preparation.

All this activity puts Stiller's book on the liturgical life of Leipzig at the time of Bach into perspective. It was in a sense the forerunner of the many essays and studies that have come from the Internationale Arbeitsge-meinschaft für theologische Bachforschung, of which he has been a member from its beginning. His is a masterly piece of work based on con-temporary documentary evidence, and although some of the research of re-cent years calls into question some of his minor details about Bach's life and work, the substance of it remains a most valuable assessment and presentation of the richness of liturgical life in Leipzig in which Bach played an important part.

Stiller was not the first to investigate this liturgical life. The Englishman Charles Sanford Terry, as early as 1926, reconstructed, as far as he was able, the main services of worship on Sundays and festival days.[15] Terry's work has its faults, as Stiller points out,[16] but this English historian was more right than wrong. Stiller had access to all the sources, whereas Terry could only work with handwritten transcripts.[17] The most important document that both Stiller and Terry used is the sexton's manuscript (Ro), which details the liturgical practices of the Leipzig churches. Terry wrote that this source "is so valuable and minute a record of the ritual observed at St. Thomas' in the eighteenth century that it is surprising to find it as yet unpublished."[18] The document has still to be published, and a critical, an-notated edition would be a great assistance to the next phase of research in this area.

However, for all its faults, Terry's attempt at reconstructing the Leip-zig liturgy was earthed in a fundamental understanding that is shared by Stiller. Terry's basic thesis was correct: "As church music Bach's cantatas are fully intelligible only when their texts are viewed in relation to the liturgy they served. . . . The essential fact regarding Bach's cantatas is that they were part of a closely coordinated religious service."[19] Here Stiller in-vestigates more fully than Terry was able to do this rich liturgical context within which Bach's cantatas were performed. But he does so within the larger context of the theological framework of Lutheran orthodoxy. In Lutheran orthodoxy it was impossible to consider liturgy as a separate field of study without theology; the study of theology included all its practical outworking as well as its theoretical formulations. For example, Abraham

Calov, who edited the Bible commentary Bach once owned, wrote in his *Systema locorum theologicorum* (Wittenberg, 1655):

> Theology propounds the mysteries of our faith not that we might acquiesce to them with bare cognition but that we should embrace them with a true and living faith. . . . The intention of theologians, and therefore of theology, is not the mere acquaintance with our faith, but it is to turn men to faith and salvation. . . .
>
> [The practical nature of theology is seen] from its usual function or activity. Since all activities [*functiones*] of theologians . . . are by their very nature practical, the theology from which they get their name has to be practical. And this is certainly the case with all the activities of theologians as theologians, whether they are teaching or exhorting or warning or consoling, whether they absolve penitent sinners or administer the sacraments, whether they initiate examinations or exercise church discipline—all these activities are in the nature of the case practical.[20]

Since Bach's liturgical music was so closely related to this practical working out of theology in the preaching and teaching of the Word and the administration of the Lord's Supper, it cannot be fully understood outside this theological setting. For Bach himself his cantatas were expressions of doxological theology, as is witnessed by the letters "S. D. G." (*Soli Deo gloria*) at the end of many of his manuscript scores.

Robert Preus, in summarizing the understanding of theology held in common by the theologians of 17th- and 18th-century orthodoxy, states:

> The first characteristic that marks the discussions of theological prolegomena and all the theology . . . is a commitment, a devotion to the principle of *soli Deo gloria*. Belief in the divine monergism of grace . . . becomes apparent at every step in the discussions of prolegomena. There was among the theologians of the Orthodox period a deep awareness of man's—and this means also the theologian's—waywardness and sinfulness and congenital blindness, which pervaded also the realm of the intellect. This view of man's spiritual condition was not merely dogma to which these theologians gave their assent, but it was also a principle that underlay and affected all their theological activity. Correlative to this view of man was a recognition among the theologians of that period that the theologian in particular was in constant need of God's grace and of the Spirit's enlightenment, that the theologian to carry out his calling must depend in faith on Christ and His Word and must be a man of prayer.[21]

In composing cantatas for the worship of the church Bach stood alongside the theologian, and it is Stiller's thesis that, like the theologian, in order to carry out his particular calling the composer had to depend in faith on Christ and His Word and be a man of prayer.

It has been a great pleasure to have worked with three such distinguished translators, a pleasure that is tinged with the sadness that two did not live to complete the project: Herbert Boumann, who also translated Hans-Werner Gensichen's *We Condemn: How Luther and 16th-Century Lutheranism Condemned False Doctrine* (St. Louis: Concordia Publishing House, 1967) and Edmund Schlink's *The Doctrine of Baptism* (St. Louis: Concordia Publishing House, 1972); and Daniel E. Poellot, who was involved in translating and editing six volumes of the American Edition of *Luther's Works*.[22] Together they were responsible for the basic translation of about a quarter of the book. The remainder is the work of Hilton C. Oswald, editor, in whole or in part, of 11 volumes of *Luther's Works*,[23] as well as translator of the important Trautmann article on the Calov volumes from Bach's library.[24] The editorial work has been concentrated mainly in the footnotes and in the bibliography. The attempt has been made to quote from more accessible sources that were not available to Stiller when he wrote, to relate the text to existing English translations of other works, to take account in some measure of subsequent scholarship, and to make the author's meaning as clear as possible in English.

Oxford, October 1983

Robin A. Leaver

Author's Preface

Although the Evangelical Church is able to cite a number of renowned theologians who have in a creditable manner exerted themselves in word and deed on behalf of the work of Johann Sebastian Bach and its dessemination—Hans Besch, Walter Blankenburg, Martin Dibelius, Karl Greulich, Friedrich Hashagen, Friedrich Haufe, Wolfgang Herbst, Max Herold, Theodor Knolle, Adolf Köberle, Christhard Mahrenholz, Hans Preuß, Georg Rietschel, Albert Schweitzer, Julius and Friedrich Smend, Friedrich Spitta, and others—scientific-theological cooperation in Bach research has remained extremely meager. Even Albert Schweitzer wrote his well-known book on Bach, first published in 1908, primarily as a writer on musical esthetics. In the first sizeable scientific-theological work, *Johann Sebastian Bach: Frömmigkeit und Glaube*, published in 1938, the author, Pastor Hans Besch of Hamburg, could only make the embarrassing statements: "In Bach research theological endeavors occupy comparatively a very small space," and "Nearly everything said on the important problem of Bach in church history was contributed by nontheologians who strove, in part arduously, to do justice to this question but also, in part, were unconcerned about its true significance and irreparably damaged Bach's picture in this regard" (2d ed. [Kassel and Basel, 1950], p. 159). Similarly the noted musicologist and Bach authority, Friedrich Blume, in his essay, *Two Centuries of Bach: An Account of Changing Taste*, translated by S. Godman (London, 1950), severely criticized the failure of evangelical theology in Bach research: "No attempt was made even to undertake a thorough scientific study of Bach from the theological point of view, and the Evangelical Church has still to pay a debt of honor in this respect" (p. 70). It is true that Blume came to this conclusion in connection with the way the situation was presented at the beginning of the 20th century. However, the second half of the citation shows unmistakably that even when he published his essay in 1947, he felt that the situation remained unchanged.

To be sure, this state of affairs cannot remain unchallenged, for in 1947 the quite extensive work of Besch was already in print. In addition, two quite important theological contributions to scientific Bach research had appeared, namely the two essays by Hans Preuß, *Johann Sebastian Bachs Bibliothek* (Leipzig, 1928) and *Johann Sebastian Bach, der Lutheraner* (Erlangen, 1935). Furthermore, the various issues of the *Bach Jahrbuch* and the books of the Bach festivals had already featured contributions by Friedrich Smend, whose research should be considered to be "of very special significance, since it combines theological reflection with the most thorough analyses of compositions."[1] Hence there was on the part of theology at least "the attempt of scientific Bach research" already since World War I, an attempt that inaugurated a completely new epoch for the whole evangelical theology and church and above all led to a radically new consideration of the Reformation heritage. Since World War II this scientific-theological work has been continued, now in a far more intensive way. In 1947 Friedrich Smend in Berlin published his *Luther und Bach*, as well as his six-volume *Johann Sebastian Bach: Kirchen-Kantaten* (2d ed., Berlin, 1950). In 1951 the same author produced the highly significant *Bach in Köthen* (Berlin, 1951). In 1948 Martin Dibelius published an important contribution to the interpretation of Bach's Passions and therefore of his church music in general.[2] In addition to a number of informative studies, among which those by Christhard Mahrenholz,[3] Walter Blankenburg,[4] and Hans-Rudolf Müller-Schwefe[5] are especially noteworthy, two scientific—theological treatises in recent years stand out. These were dissertations presented to the theological faculties of Erlangen and Basel universities. Wolfgang Herbst subjected Bach's relationship to Lutheran mysticism to a searching analysis,[6] and Helene Werthemann delved into the role played by Old Testament narratives in Bach's cantatas.[7]

The beginnings of theological cooperation in scientific Bach research are, therefore, undeniably and clearly discernible.[8] At the same time we must not fail to see that all published treatises and essays of a scientific-theological nature still represent only a very small part, only a beginning in view of the great mass of problems that have yet to be tackled. What Walter Blankenburg said as early as 1950 still applies in full measure: "If today Bach shines in a different light, if in fact his picture is at present not clear—surprisingly—this fact reveals not least some neglect on the part of theological research" ("Bach—geistlich und weltlich," pp. 36—37). Evangelical theology should, therefore, feel compelled to make up this neglect, for there is in fact no excuse for it. Already Philip Spitta, in his essay *Die Passionsmusiken von Johann Sebastian Bach und Heinrich Schütz* (Hamburg, 1893), had appealed unmistakably, though indirectly, to theologians for cooperation in scientific Bach research. He said: "No one can properly appreciate Bach's music unless he is in more vital contact with the church and is thoroughly familiar with its liturgy, with the Bible, and with the melodies and texts of the chorales" (p. 21).

Thus this present endeavor, too, desires to be a small contribution towards achieving a goal that cannot be surrendered, namely, to make up for the "neglect of theological Bach research" as quickly as possible.

The Problem

The real starting point for the problems dealt with in this book is the discussion revolving around the unanswered questions of Bach research, whether and in what manner the Bach cantata has a genuinely *liturgical* right to exist in contemporary evangelical worship. When the Neue Bach-Gesellschaft was organized on 27 January 1900, paragraph 2 of its constitution established the special goal "of creating an invigorating force among the German people and in lands open to serious German music for the work of the great German composer Johann Sebastian Bach, and especially to make his works composed for the church serviceable for the worship service."[1] This objective aimed particularly at recapturing Bach's church cantatas for Evangelical worship. Thus, for example, the *Bach-Jahrbuch* of 1917 opened with the complete order of worship for the festival service at the third small Bach festival in Eisenach. This was supported by the unequivocal explanation: "The Neue Bach-Gesellschaft regards it as one of its chief objectives to make the resources inherent in Sebastian Bach's creations increasingly usable for the Evangelical Church, and especially to reintroduce his cantatas into the main services" (p. 1). When a revision of the Neue Bach-Gesellschaft's constitution was undertaken in 1935 and ratified by the membership in connection with the Leipzig Bach festival, 22 June 1935, this second paragraph dealing with the "purpose of the Neue Bach-Gesellschaft" was taken over unchanged. Thus the special objective of the society to recapture Bach's cantatas for evangelical worship services was reemphasized. At its Bach festivals the Neue Bach-Gesellschaft attempted to achieve this goal in practice by combining all the festival worship services with the performance of a Bach cantata. Beyond this, however, in spite of many even notable attempts and experiments, the society nowhere came decisively nearer the goal of recovering Bach's cantatas for evangelical worship. There are, of course, specific reasons for this state of affairs, among which the failure of theological research in the solution of this problem is undoubtedly the decisive cause of all lack of clarification. It is surely significant that the last controversy concerning the question whether the Bach cantata has a liturgical right to exist in the evangelical service of today was waged, not among theologians, but between the church musician and musicologist Hermann Keller[2] and the Leipzig St. Thomas cantor Günther Ramin.[3]

As for a long time previously, so also at that time the official Evangelical Church and theology contributed nothing at all to solving this problem. (This situation is not changed by the fact that occasionally, especially at the beginning of the 20th century, some theologians advocated and personally involved themselves in recapturing the Bach cantatas for Evangelical worship; this was done exclusively in an enthusiastic manner, and not on the basis of thorough theological reflection.) The fact that an organization that is consciously completely independent of the church and consists of Christians and non-Christians, as in the case of the Neue Bach-Gesellschaft, should adopt the goal of recapturing Bach's cantatas for evangelical worship—this fact gives us cause for reflection.

However, it cannot be the business of extraecclesiastical societies and clubs, nor primarily the business of musicologists and church musicians, to decide what should be done in evangelical services of worship. To that extent the Neue Bach-Gesellschaft acted very properly at the Bach festival in Leipzig (June 1962) when it decided in a revision of its constitution to alter paragraph 2 and eliminate the objective of previous decades, namely to recapture Bach's works for evangelical worship services. It is up to the Evangelical Church, after thorough theological reflection, to decide what is to be justified or to be rejected in liturgical practice. Hence also the question whether Bach's cantatas have a legitimate liturgical place in contemporary Evangelical worship must be subjected, first of all, like every other problem of church practice, to a strictly theological reflection. Only after the problems connected with a liturgical use of Bach's cantatas have been somewhat clarified theologically can the practical-liturgical complex of questions be answered in a meaningful way.

But theological reflection on Bach's cantatas as a liturgical problem is confronted by a host of questions that cannot be satisfactorily solved within a single scientific work, unless one determines in advance to forego a generally comprehensive clarification of the problems under discussion. Günther Ramin briefly indicated the mass of questions that need to be thoroughly considered here when he wrote: "Again and again serious questions arise. Do Bach's cantatas still have a vital meaning for the church? Are not his texts so time-bound that only a revision of the texts can preserve the work of art? Is this music truly religious, or is it not rather a concert-type form of expressing a spiritual musical content? Yes, is it not more appropriate to provide an entirely different secular textual basis for the cantata? Can Bach's cantatas be included at all in the current efforts at renewal in the church and in worship? Do they not represent only a disturbing hindrance for the efforts at liturgical reform? And many more such questions'' (Ramin, p. 1159). It is, indeed, a whole complex of questions that comes into view in connection with the problem whether Bach's cantatas can serve a liturgical purpose in today's Evangelical service, and these questions await theological clarification.

First of all, the most important question, still largely unclarified, is without doubt the question of the theological evaluation of Bach's cantatas. This question at once gives rise to a second, namely, how the whole worship life at the time of Johann Sebastian Bach, especially in Leipzig, should be theologically evaluated; for the real native soil for the rise of Bach's cantatas was the Lutheran principal worship service [*Hauptgottesdienst*] in the first half of the 18th century. A proper solution of this problem could be of basic significance for all further discussion regarding the function of Bach's cantatas in the service. Hermann Keller rejects Bach's church cantatas as liturgical music in the modern worship service for the reason, among others, that with respect to both their musical and textual forms these cantatas clearly manifest the advanced secularization of the Lutheran Church at the time of Bach. Keller sees the development of the Lutheran Church in the 17th and especially the 18th century as an increasingly obvious apostasy from the Reformation and therefore as a time of decay. He regards music as ''the great guardian'' of the church that has ''resisted this decay.'' In fact, it is music *alone* ''that effectively checks the Lutheran Church's decline and prevents it for two hundred years—from Luther to Bach. But then its strength is exhausted and spent, and Protestantism enters . . . the stage of its greatest decay'' (Keller, p. 1426). Thus, although Keller regards music as belonging ''to the most potent preservative forces of the church,'' which has prevented ''most effectively the gradual drying up of religion into moralism and dogma'' (ibid., p. 1425), and although ''evangelical church music by means of the new baroque style . . . has experienced a powerful stimulus and an immense dissemination'' (ibid.), all these works of church music, including Bach's church cantatas, can no longer be called church music in the proper sense, precisely because they have sprung up in the soil of an already heavily secularized church. They are taken as products of secularization; they are in no wise the ''Alpha and Omega of evangelical church music,'' but they stand very ''close to the edge.'' Consequently, all ''well-meant attempts'' to revitalize these works as music for the worship service must ''be opposed for fundamental reasons'' (ibid., p. 1430). ''In spite of their extraordinary variety in structure and quality these works preserve their unity, not because they are music for the worship service, but because they have their place in the powerful and domineering style of the baroque'' (ibid., p. 1427).

Hermann Keller is not alone in these opinions. The evangelical pastor Rene Wallau presents quite similar theses in an essay delivered at the second congress of the Gesellschaft für Musikforschung, Lüneburg, 1950.[4]

He, too, sees in Lutheran worship during the baroque period, "in spite of the liturgical profusion that characterizes it," basically a "deteriorating form" and "a manifestation of the dissolution of worship" (Wallau, p. 107). After the Thiry Years' War the "prophetic, living character" of Lutheran worship is said to have been lost, and thus it "forfeited its living heart" and became "frozen" and "extravagant in its external form" (ibid., p. 108). Like Keller, Wallau also interprets the musical product of the baroque, the cantata, as a "welcome relaxation" of the worship service, which "permitted people to forget the one-sidedness and theological rigidity of the sermon" (ibid.). Nevertheless, the cantata—as in Keller's judgment—is regarded as a phase of secularization that has "overgrown" the worship service (ibid.). Although the cantata was undoubtedly a "liturgical work," its "baroque exuberance" has "introduced incompatible elements into the worship service," and "the music has forsaken its servant role and become a dominating factor" (ibid., pp. 107, 108).

These are harsh judgments on the worship and church music of Lutheran orthodoxy, judgments that need to be examined carefully. It is clear at the outset that if Bach's cantatas are in fact products of an unmistakable secularization, we need no longer concern ourselves and be involved with their liturgical use in present-day evangelical worship services. Indeed, all attempts at recapturing the Bach cantatas for the Evangelical service must be "opposed for fundamental reasons" (Keller). But the situation appears completely different when an evaluation of the worship service together with the practice of church music in the days of Lutheran orthodoxy arrives at a predominantly positive conclusion. Then the question must somehow be raised as to what evangelical theology and church intends to do with this heritage and how it plans to preserve it in a fitting manner.

Hence we must, first of all, subject to a thorough examination the liturgical life in Leipzig during the first half of the 18th century. This is the city of Bach's creative activity, which in a special way shares in the great mass of the cantatas of Johann Sebastian Bach. This book, then, desires to be essentially a contribution to the worship practices of Lutheran orthodoxy. The activity of Johann Sebastian Bach in connection with the worship services, above all the creation of his cantatas, can be evaluated theologically only against the background of worship practices in Leipzig. We must also investigate the problem of Bach's inner relationship to the worship services of his time, for this inner relationship of the heart, on the one hand, permits certain inferences about the vitality of worship practices and, on the other hand, helps to place the works created for the worship services into the proper light with regard to their theological significance. This involves the question, which is not unimportant for a theological evaluation of the Bach cantatas, whether Johann Sebastian Bach with his uncommonly great talents was, first of all, simply a musician who ultimately did not care whether he created his works for the church and evangelical worship or for other institutions and purposes, or whether precisely behind his cantatas his unconditional will to proclaim becomes visible, and thus behind his creative activity for worship services in general stands his specific calling to a ministry of worship.

Church music in the St. Thomas Church under the direction of Johann Kuhnau, Bach's predecessor. (Engraving from *Unfehlbare Engel-Freude oder Geistliches Gesangbuch* [Leipzig 1710], appendix to *LKS*, p. 125. Source: Bernhard Knick, ed. *St. Thomas zu Leipzig: Schule und Chor*, with an introduction by Manfred Mezger [Wiesbaden, 1963].)

A.
Liturgical Life
in Leipzig
in the First Half
of the 18th Century

In the history of the church and of thought the 18th century is quite generally regarded as the century of the Enlightenment, with which a secularization particularly of liturgical life is most intimately associated. To be sure, the beginning of the age of secularization must be placed at a much earlier date. Although the Enlightenment is also customarily called the "end of the culture of religious unity,"[1] it must not be overlooked that the way to this end was already prepared in the late Middle Ages and that it reached its first climax during the Italian Renaissance. It was only the Reformation that stopped this whole development toward secularization in a decisive way, at least in Germany. But the Enlightenment was blooming in Holland already in the middle of the 17th century—after all, Descartes died as early as 1650, and Spinoza in 1677! And shortly thereafter, near the end of the 17th century, this was also the case in England. In Germany the Enlightenment set in at a relatively later time, in substance only in the 18th century, although Gottfried Wilhelm Leibnitz, regarded as the actual inaugurator of the German Enlightenment, died as early as 1716. In Leipzig Christian Thomasius, who had caused tremendous excitement by his lectures at the university as one of the most influential pioneers of the Enlightenment, was forced to vacate his position and leave the city as early as 1600. Also the philosopher Christian Wolff, very influential in Halle since 1706, had qualified for teaching in Leipzig in 1703 and taught here for three years. In 1724, one year after Bach's coming to Leipzig, Johann Christoph Gottsched, a decided supporter of Wolff's philosophy, entered Leipzig and quickly advanced to the highest offices at the university. He even became the most influential personality in the city's intellectual life, so that henceforth the views and principles of the Enlightenment asserted themselves in Leipzig, slowly at first, but still irresistibly, with the university as the real focus of this new movement.[2] The Enlightenment was promoted by Johann Abraham Birnbaum, from 1721 lecturer in rhetoric; Lorenz Christoph Mizler, qualified for professorship since 1736; Johann August Ernesti, from 1742 professor at the university; and Christian Fürchtegott Gellert, in 1743 master and from 1744 tutor at the university. These men quickly gained great influence over the student body, so that there can be no doubt about the progress of the Enlightenment and the change in the academic spirit in Leipzig during Bach's official tenure.

It is all the more astonishing that the church life and specifically the liturgical life in the city of Leipzig appeared for some time to be totally unaffected by this new spirit of the Enlightenment. In view of developments in Germany generally we may indeed assert that in the liturgical life of the parishes "rationalism began to prevail already around 1700"[3] and that thus at "the time of J. S. Bach's death it was no longer a glorious age in the history of worship in the Lutheran Church."[4] However, this verdict is purely a generalization and it does not apply in every case. At any rate, the church life and the liturgical life in Leipzig appears to have remained completely inaccessible to the spirit of the Enlightenment far into the 18th century. In fact, that life seems to have experienced a very impressive late flowering. Even the theological faculty at the university appears to have been guided to a large extent by the spirit of Lutheran orthodoxy beyond the middle of the 18th century. There had, indeed, been tensions as early as 1714 between the strictly orthodox Lutheran theological faculty of Wittenberg University and the theological faculty of Leipzig, when the Wittenbergers felt compelled to attack the "innovators" in Leipzig. But Professor Rechenberg of Leipzig had emphatically protested against the Wittenberg theologians, sitting in "Luther's chair" and therefore claiming a "monopoly of orthodoxy" for themselves.[5] Furthermore, in 1715 and 1720 in connection with filling vacancies in theological professorships there had been considerable tension between the Oberkonsistorium in Dresden and the theological faculty at Leipzig. The Dresden Oberkonsistorium was not convinced that the position of the candidates was completely orthodox Lutheran.[6] However, all this in no way signifies entry of the Enlightenment into the theological faculty. For example, Christian Börner, for more than 40 years theological professor in Leipzig (1713—1753), protested against "the daring hypothesis of the human origin of the Hebrew vowel points," as Humphrey Prideaux had presented it; he "abhorred...the rationalistic Wertheim Bible" and "was responsible for...its confiscation in Leipzig." He even instituted "proceedings against those who had favorably reviewed it, certainly with the concurrence of his colleagues."[7] Still largely committed to the Lutheran tradition, Börner also radically rejected Wolff's philosophy as one that "created nothing but confusion and disaster in the church."[8] Beside Börner there were soon two other notable theologians who had studied in Wittenberg and then for some decades, up to and beyond the middle of the 18th century, taught theology in Leipzig in the strictly orthodox Lutheran sense. They were Heinrich Klausing (1720—1745) and Salomon Deyling (1721—1755). The fact that until far into the 18th century Leipzig could maintain its reputation as one of the "stoutest strongholds of Lutheran orthodoxy" is primarily due to them.[9]

The last-named Salomon Deyling, beside his scholarly activity at the university—he was later Professor primarius in the theological faculty—was simultaneously and primarily the chief pastor at St. Nicholas and superintendent minister of the city, as well as member of the Leipzig Consistory, and thus stood for some 35 years at the summit of the church's life in the city and was in a position to exert a decisive influence on the whole of church life and worship. In view of these facts the invasion of the Enlightenment into the church life, and specifically worship life, of the Leipzig parishes must be regarded from the outset as highly unlikely. To gain clarity in this area we shall now attempt to sketch as comprehensive and unequivocal a picture as possible of liturgical life in this city during the first half of the 18th century.

1.
Description of Liturgical Life in Leipzig

Philipp Spitta reported quite extensively on liturgical life in Leipzig at the time of Johann Sebastian Bach.[10] However, the great defect of this presentation lies in the fact that although based on reliable source materials, the sources themselves are actually cited far too little, and the reader is often left in the dark as to the specific source used. The same defect attaches to the relatively shorter description offered in an incidental way by Arnold Schering in his *Musikgeschichte Leipzigs*.[11] On the other hand, Charles Sanford Terry cited the sources more extensively and labeled them accurately in his *Joh. Seb. Bach: Cantata Texts*. This description, which, moreover, offers only a listing of the most important liturgical elements and details of the Sunday services, is deficient in that it takes only a part of the sources into account and occasionally cites even these in an unreliable manner; indeed, it employs sources that are completely beyond verification.[12] Hence a fresh examination of existing sources is long overdue. The Bach scholar Friedrich Blume, in a personal letter to the author, 9 February 1962, stated what the music historian expects of a scholarly work on "The Bach Cantata as Liturgical Problem"[13] "What matters, in my opinion, is to establish clearly, once and for all, which liturgical elements and trains of thought were demonstrably parts of the regular forms of worship in Bach's time, somewhat like the attempt made by Terry many years ago in his heavy tome, long out of print, *Bach's Cantata Texts*." To be sure, in contrast to the studies of Spitta, Schering, and Terry, a new investigation of the sources must not be interested solely in exhibiting purely historical facts, but be combined at the same time with a theological evaluation and interpretation (see the second chapter!). Naturally, our first concern must be to let the sources speak for themselves, and that will be done chiefly in this first chapter.

a) The Sources

In spite of some quite serious losses from Leipzig archives and libraries caused by the destruction and dislocations in the last world war, a sizable store of first-class sources continues to be available on liturgical life in Leipzig during the first half of the 18th century. For the most important of these see the abbreviations of frequently cited sources and the bibliography and check the detailed publication data. One of the most valuable sources, the *Leipziger Kirchen-Staat* of 1710, is not accessible in Leipzig itself but in Halle University Library. A further valuable source long considered lost, the *Leipziger Kirchen-Andachten* of 1694, I was able to rediscover in the Stadtgeschichtliches Museum, Leipzig.

The *Leipziger Kirchen-Andachten* of 1694 is a comparatively early source presenting a graphic picture of the worship life of the two principal churches, St. Nicholas and St. Thomas, together with many details concerning the orders of worship for all Sundays and festivals at the turn of the 17th to the 18th century. However, the other sources of the 18th century used here leave no room for doubt that the Lutheran orthodoxy prevailing in Leipzig far into the 18th century provided for a very faithful transmission of Lutheran worship at every point from generation to generation. Consequently, Terry, who in the twenties of our century researched the various Leipzig archives and unearthed valuable material, was not at all on the wrong track when in his *Joh. Seb. Bach: Cantata Texts* he also sought to reconstruct the individual liturgical components of every service in the church year when Bach was in Leipzig and did so on the basis of the *Leipziger Kirchen-Andachten.*

Yet the two chief sources for a description of worship life in Leipzig during the first half of the 18th century are the *Leipziger Kirchen-Staat* of 1710, mentioned above, and Christoph Ernst Sicul's *Neo annalium Lipsiensium Continuatio II* of 1717. In the latter source the Leipzig chronicler offers a thorough description (pp. 565—89) of the rich liturgical life of Leipzig in the second decade of the 18th century. In its first part the *Leipziger Kirchen-Staat* proposes to offer guidance on the proper conduct of worship and devotions, especially (as stated in the preface) for the "many strangers and foreigners who either pass through our worthy city of Leipzig, or visit our fair, or otherwise sojourn here for a while."

The handwritten notes by Johann Christoph Rost, sexton (*Custos*) at St. Thomas, must be rated a particularly valuable source. He had studied theology, and he informs us that he functioned as sexton at St. Thomas church from 1716 to 1739, that is, during the greater part of Johann Sebastian Bach's official tenure in Leipzig. To have an accurate grasp at all times of the individual services and devotions for the Sundays and festivals with their many liturgical particulars, Rost laid out a detailed memorandum book to which he kept adding throughout his term of service and which was continued down to the twenties of the 19th century by his successors, especially by Gottlob Friedrich Rothe, pupil at St. Thomas school, 1744—1752, and sexton at St. Thomas from 26 September 1772 to the day of his death, 23 December 1813.[14] This source gives us highly gratifying information about the individual services of the year and all special liturgical arrangements, and it confirms the already mentioned fact that the description of liturgical life with its rich liturgical forms, as presented by the *Leipziger Kirchen-Andachten*, the *Leipziger Kirchen-Staat*, and Ernst Christoph Sicul, maintained itself almost intact as a firm tradition far beyond the middle of the 18th century.

The same state of affairs is clearly set forth also in the report of Ernst Christoph Sicul in his *Jubilierendes Leipzig* and the simultaneous Leipzig annals of 1731 regarding the worship events connected with the three-day celebration of the Reformation anniversary in June 1730. This report gives us precise information on the individual worship arrangements in the city of Leipzig, especially on the liturgical form of these services and devotions.

Of basic significance for the liturgical structuring of the various services and devotions in detail was also the *Agenda* of Duke Henry, first published for Electoral Saxony in 1540 and still appearing in the 18th century in ever new editions. The new edition of this Agenda in 1712 is the one used in Leipzig services during Bach's tenure. The copy used for this book, now preserved in the archives of St. Nicholas Church, received— according to the gold-engraved stamp on the binding—a new leather binding in 1723, because the old and original binding had been damaged by constant use. Also the *Vollständiges Kirchenbuch* of 1743, likewise preserved in the St. Nicholas archives, cited here only for comparison, was used in St. Nicholas Church in Leipzig, as expressly noted on the binding, and for this purpose was rebound in leather in 1763. What is prescribed and recommended in the Agenda of 1712 with regard to the liturgical structure of the different services on Sundays and festivals as well as weekdays, including the tones to be chanted by the liturgist and reader, is contained verbatim already in the Agenda of 1647—without deletions and additions—and still recurs unchanged in the Agenda of 1771.

The specifics of the Leipzig worship tradition become evident especially also in the various Leipzig hymnbook publications of that time, just as, in general, the *Leipziger Kirchen-Andachten* of 1694 and the *Leipziger Kirchen-Staat* of 1710, in addition to their detailed instructions for the proper conduct of the various services and devotions, and in addition to their aim to supply a general prayer book, also sought to be a hymnbook especially for the Leipzig worshipers. The basis for all subsequent Leipzig hymnbook publications at the time of Johann Sebastian Bach was the *Neu Leipziger Gesangbuch*, published in 1682 by Gottfried Vopelius, cantor at St. Nicholas Church. With its 415 hymns and numerous four- and six-part choral settings on 1100 pages, this book was designed first of all for the choir in its presentation of church music. Later editions, all of them without music and considerably less unwieldy than the 1682 edition, were substantially enlarged, especially the much altered edition of 1729 and the greatly augmented edition of 1734. Nevertheless, the churches clung to the old core collection of Reformation and post-Reformation hymns, to the extent that they had become a firm hymn tradition in Leipzig.

The Dresden hymnbooks also deserve our consideration, for from the celebrated jurisdictional dispute about church hymns between Johann Sebastian Bach and Magister Gaudlitz we know that in the year 1728 the hymns for the services were announced also according to the Dresden hymnbook. In his petition to the city council on 20 September 1728, Bach speaks of "the ordering of the hymns...in accordance with the Gospels and the *Dresdener Gesangbuch* based on the same."[15] Likewise, from Gesner's handwritten "Anmerkungen über die Ordnung der Schule zu St. Thomas," 1732, we learn that the Dresden hymnbook was used in that school. Gesner says, "It will be quite necessary to include in the regulations that every pupil must bring with him a Bible and the Dresden hymnbook and be ready to produce them at all times, and that the corector and cantor, who are in charge of inspection in the church, see to it that it is done."[16] With regard to the Dresden hymnbooks used in Leipzig during those years, the edition involved can only be *Das Privilegirte Ordentliche und Vermehrte Dreßdnische Gesang-Buch* that was published simultaneously in Leipzig and Dresden, whose content remained almost entirely unchanged throughout Bach's stay in Leipzig. A second Dresden hymnbook publication, also appearing in those decades, was the *Auserlesenes und vollständiges Gesang-Buch, worinnen 755 der besten und geistreichsten Lieder, welche in denen Chur-Sächß. Kirchen pflegen gesungen zu werden, enthalten* (Select and complete hymnbook, containing 755 of the best and most ingenious hymns that are accustomed to be sung in the churches of Electoral Saxony). This book was designed not so much for use in Dresden and Leipzig as rather for general use throughout Saxony. We must be careful, however, not to attach too much importance to the fact that Dresden hymnbooks were used in Leipzig services in the 18th century, for quite obviously two reasons were decisive for this practice. In the first place, the production of hymnbooks in Leipzig during the first three decades of the 18th century, down to 1729, had remained quite meager, so that the Dresden hymnbooks, which in those days appeared frequently, often in annual editions, helped to close the gap in Leipzig at a time when there was so great a demand for hymnbooks. Furthermore, the various Dresden hymnbook editions were richer in content and more up to date, as well as substantially more modern and easier to use in their whole makeup than the Leipzig hymnbook publications, which appeared antiquated. For example, the Dresden hymnbook of 1725 already contained all 17 of Paul Gerhardt's hymns utilized by Johann Sebastian Bach, while the Leipzig

37

hymnbooks of the time contain appreciably fewer of Gerhardt's hymns.

Yet the entrance of the Dresden hymnbook into the liturgical life of the city of Leipzig by no means signifies a surrender of the specific Leipzig tradition of church hymns.[17] On the contrary, the publication of the old *Vopelisches Gesangbuch*,[18] so strongly promoted since 1729 but now in a thoroughly revised and considerably enlarged edition, demonstrates unmistakably how closely the people of Leipzig were determined to cling to the old hymnic tradition. In all subsequent editions of this hymnbook until far beyond the middle of the 18th century, the title page contains the express information "formerly by Vopelius." These Leipzig hymnbooks, appearing in ever new editions, must gradually have stemmed the spread of the Dresden hymnbooks in the Leipzig services. In any case, in our description and evaluation of the worship life in Leipzig we will have to refer especially to these hymnbook publications as sources of the first rank. As to the extent that the Dresden hymnbook was used in the Leipzig services, it would only have been employed within the framework of the Leipzig hymn tradition. Already Terry established that the Leipzig hymnbook of 1729 contains nearly all the hymns used by Bach (with the exception of eight).[19]

The *Verbessertes Leipzig* of Anton Weiz offers many details on the development and condition of liturgical life in the first three decades of the 18th century. On the beginning and progress of liturgical life in the so-called "New Church," later known as St. Matthew's, we are given extensive reports in the handwritten *Allerhand Geschichte, die Neue Kirche betreffend*, which was compiled during Bach's tenure in Leipzig. It contains entries, and especially many personal references, down to the year 1739. For this project we were able also to make use of the annual editions of the Leipzig Directory,[20] appearing since the beginning of the 18th century. Besides accurate personal data concerning the clergymen responsible for the individual worship services and devotions in all Leipzig churches, this publication presents an exact overview of all regularly conducted services and devotions in the city. For an evaluation of the eucharistic piety there were at our disposal from the archives of St. Nicholas and St. Thomas the Registers of Communicants, complete for St. Thomas since 1691, but with some gaps for St. Nicholas. In addition, the Stadtgeschichtliches Museum contains a Register of Communicants for the New Church for the years 1729—1740. Valuable details for our study are also contained in the *Historie der Kirchen Ceremonien in Sachsen*, published in 1732 by Christian Gerber, a pietistically inclined Saxon pastor. It pictures the various liturgical customs and usages in the Saxony of that day and critically evaluates them, occasionally featuring liturgical peculiarities in the two cities of Dresden (cf. pp. 355, 398, 504, 650, 657) and Leipzig (cf. pp. 355—56, 398, 456, 650, 681).

Thus all the writings referred to here constitute excellent source materials that enable us to offer an exact description of liturgical life in the city of Leipzig at the time of Johann Sebastian Bach. To complete the picture and make comparisons with a later time, we shall also have to refer to some noteworthy sources from the period after 1750.

b) Intensification of Liturgical Life
at the Beginning of the Century

In the discussion of the history of liturgy during the 18th century there is scarcely any mention of an intensification of liturgical life. Paul Graff deserves much credit for having shown emphatically that in many places in Germany "already around 1700 rationalism...had carried off the victory,"[21] that is, that attitude of mind that in a decisive way contributed ultimately to the collapse of worship life in the Lutheran Church, a life that until then had been exceedingly rich. If we bear in mind, furthermore, that "where the Enlightenment has been achieved, worship services really serve no further purpose,"[22] it must occasion considerable surprise to have anyone report on a rich and living worship tradition anywhere in Germany, to say nothing of an intensification of liturgical life during the first half of the 18th century, a time that in general was no longer a glorious age for the worship of the Lutheran Church. However, in view of the conditions in Leipzig during the first half of the 18th century, we cannot deny the fact that here many clear indications point to an actual intensification of liturgical life. In what follows the most important phenomena will be considered.

First of all, in order to be kept from a false evaluation of this unmistakable intensification of liturgical life by means of the statistics offered here, we must briefly look at the population growth of the city of Leipzig between 1679 and 1779. In this 100-year span the number of inhabitants is reported as having increased from 19,936 in 1679 to 26,656 in 1779, hardly a noteworthy process of growth. During this period the number of inhabitants—although generally on a slight increase—went up and then down again. The population of 19,936 reported for 1679 was reduced to 17,440 already in the following year, 1680, because of a raging pestilence. The count of 23,203 reached in 1697 decreased in the next years and amounted to only 21,696 in 1700— just a few more than 21 years earlier. In 1709 the city had 24,832 inhabitants and as many as 28,448 in 1719, and for some three decades this figure remained nearly constant—1729: 29,552; 1739: 28,508; and 1748: 29,760. The number reached 32,384 in 1753, but this level was not maintained. Already in 1756 the figure had sunk to 29,792 and to 28,352 in 1763, while in 1779 there were only 26,656. Until the end of the 18th century this situation remained much the same, namely, that in the course of years and decades the population generally increased only very gradually.[23]

Under these circumstances the practice up to the turn of the century of having only two churches, St. Nicholas and St. Thomas, available for the total worship life of the city would seem adequate, especially since around 1700 rationalism was generally pushing forward, a phenomenon equivalent to a gradual but steady decrease in the number of people attending services and the Lord's Supper. As a result, arranging for new services and devotions in churches especially erected for this purpose was not at all a timely undertaking. This very state of affairs, however—that buildings intended for worship purposes but in part no longer used for worship services and devotions since the days of the Reformation were again being opened, and thus the number of services and devotions in the city was significantly increased—is characteristic of church life in Leipzig at the beginning of the 18th century. The entire vital force of orthodox Lutheranism may not least be measured by this constant increase of worship services and the reopening of churches for this purpose. To avoid misunderstanding, it should be remembered that all these measures were not the result of endeavors definitely originating with the church authorities or the municipal government but almost exclusively the result of what the church members wished and longed for.

The first innovation in the city's worship life came already in 1694 when the two main churches, St. Nicholas and St. Thomas, were given an additional Communion service during the week in connection with the customary morning worship, on Wednesdays at St. Nicholas and Thursdays at St. Thomas. To be sure, such midweek Communion services had been held occasionally before in times of pestilence and war—for example, in 1575, 1598, 1631, and 1680. However, they did not become a regular practice until 1694 (Ro, p. 152). The first midweek Communions were celebrated on Wednesday, 7 March 1694, and on Thursday, 8 March 1694. For the rest of the 18th century these services were conducted nearly always during weeks that had no other festival day apart from Sunday. This measure had become necessary in order to reduce the steadily growing crowds attending Communion at the main service on Sundays and festivals.

A far more incisive event in the city's worship life was the restoration of the old Franciscan Church that had not been used for worship purposes since the Reformation (Wz, p. 13). We are told explicitly that the restoration of the church, begun in July 1698, was being undertaken at the request and cost of the merchants and guilds. "Several honorable citizens had repeatedly and urgently requested in writing that the Franciscan Church, so long dilapidated, be repaired and reopened for worship services" (AG, p. 1; cf. Wz, p. 13). These requests, in turn, sprang from the fact that the strong church attendance of the Leipzig members brought about an increasingly obvious overcrowding in the two chief churches, St. Nicholas and St. Thomas. On the basis of these petitions from the population the city council approved completion of the work of renovation. After the church was "lifted out of its ruins and the process of rebuilding was excellently begun, it was furnished not only with a splendid altar, a neat pulpit, graceful chapels, and lovely and well-lighted galleries, but also a fine spire...and an excellent organ" (Wz, p. 13). The work, carried on with great zeal and actively supported by "men and women, academicians and merchants" in an equal measure,[24] could be substantially completed in one year. The house of God, known since then as "New Church," was dedicated on 24 September 1699. The church was assigned "two priests, as well as a deacon and subdeacon, of whom one preached on all Sundays and festival days in the early services and the other preached at Vespers" (Wz, p. 14). Although this church was restored only to relieve congestion in the rich worship life and church attendance at the two chief churches, St. Nicholas and St. Thomas, and thus did not become an independent parish church—not until 1876 did it become a parish church and since 1880 was called St. Matthew's—it quickly reached great significance for the city's worship life. In this church Georg Philipp Telemann, in Leipzig as a student, contributed so much to church music from 1702 to 1704 that even in 1722 the city council had not forgotten him, but would have liked to have him succeed Johann Kuhnau as choirmaster at St. Thomas. Also in this church on Good Friday 1717 there was presented a Passion oratorio for the first time (Wz, p. 15), a practice that did not become established at St. Thomas until 1721. The importance of this New Church for the city's worship life is evident also from the fact that the church music offered here soon competed seriously with that offered by Cantor Kuhnau at St. Thomas. For this reason Kuhnau felt compelled to petition the city council for help, since these church music offerings lured some valuable musicians away from him.[25]

Shortly after the restoration of the New Church in 1701, the rebuilding of the hospital at St. George was begun, together with "the house of correction and the orphanage incorporated with it" in the marsh. The hospital and the Church of St. George connected with it had originally stood at the Ranstadt Gate until 1631, when it was completely destroyed by fire. Thereafter it "was situated at the Grimma Gate near the cemetery" (Wz, p. 68), hence for a considerable time in the immediate vicinity of the old St. John Cemetery (cf. also *Bn*, p. 44; *ChV*, p. 78). In this new building a place for worship was provided "by including an uncommonly neat church hall in the whole building. On the lower level are the prisoners, who can hear the preacher but can be seen by no one in the church. On the next floor, a flight of stairs above, is the place for the women and the orphans, another floor up the place for the men, and a floor beyond that a place for more prisoners" (Wz, pp. —21). When the building was finished, the room set aside for worship was dedicated on 2 February 1705 and since then was known as the "Orphanage Church" [*Waysenhauß-Kirche*].

At first this church meant little to the average worshiper in the city, since the hospital was a self-contained complex of buildings that served at the same time as orphanage, school, prison, penitentiary, and insane asylum.[26] Nevertheless, the erection of this place of worship and the intensification of the worship life connected with it were featured and appreciated by various contemporaries as a substantial component of the church life of Leipzig. When Johann Friedrich Braun published the *Leipziger Gesangbuch* in 1717, he included an introductory overview of the most important endeavors in the city at the beginning of the century toward an even greater revitalization of the worship life, and he makes explicit mention of the fact that the Orphanage Church was "completely renovated" for use as a place of worship (*LGB* 1717, Dedication). The Leipzig chronicler Sicul offers a detailed description of the worship life and includes reference to the practice at St. George (Sc*NA*, pp. 567ff.). In fact, at one place he emphasizes that in a previously mentioned regularly observed devotion at St. George the reference is to a "public hour of prayer and edification" (Sc*NA*, p. 581), to which, therefore, the city people had access. The significance attached to this new Orphanage Church in Leipzig is evident also from the state of affairs that after a 70-year vacancy this church was again assigned its own pastor in January 1705, just before the dedication of the church. After the church's destruction in 1631 the "pastorate at St. George's" had not been filled since 1636, and the church had been served "since 1671 by the pastor of St. John, and since 1701 by the pastor of St. James and six members of the Thursday staff of preachers and the teacher at the orphanage" (*ChV*, p. 78). At the time of Johann Sebastian Bach this church was called "the sixth church in the city," which, like the other churches, "also had its custodian [*Vorsteher*], to whom is entrusted at the same time the inspection of the entire institution" (Wz, p. 20).

Shortly thereafter another place of worship became important in the city's church life. In July 1710 the reopening of St. Peter was begun. It had also not been used for worship since the Reformation and "for some time before its renovation was known simply as the limekiln" (Wz, p. 17). Earlier this place of worship "had resembled a den of murderers more than a church, because during the Thirty Years' War barracks had been built in it, and all kinds of people lived there with each other," but now it was "cleansed of its filth and transformed into an attractive house of God" (Wz, p. 17). "At the request of very many inhabitants of the St. Peter quarter and Magister Teller, current deacon at St. Nicholas," the city council resolved to reopen also this fully secularized church for the purposes of worship. Not only did the council have this church "completely rebuilt, but also had it enlarged by the addition of small dwellings" (*Bn*, p. 46). The citizens "took a lively interest in the new house of God"[27] in furnishing the church, so that it could be solemnly dedicated already on 29 May 1712. Already in December 1711 a pastor had been called to the new St. Peter. Although he was an "ordained priest," he did not "perform any parochial functions" (Wz, p. 18), since St. Peter did not become an independent parish church until 1876, but he was to make provision for the total worship life on Sundays and festivals, as well as during the week.

Among the newly opened and renovated places of worship we must list also the complete renovation of the "Lazareth Church at the Ranstadt Gate," situated outside the city wall (Wz, p. 2). In 1713 it was "rebuilt entirely from the ground up" and then, "on the first Easter day, 21 April 1714, the first sermon was...delivered" (Wz, p. 29). So at the beginning of the 18th century another church was made accessible to Leipzig church people, a place of worship on the ground floor of the hospital known as "Victory House." Here worship was conducted in the forenoon on Sundays and festival days, as well as special devotions on two forenoons during the week.

Also St. Paul, the university church, hitherto used only for academic purposes, was reopened in 1710 for worship and for this purpose was "improved in a most attractive way and adorned with many lovely chapels, pews for women, and galleries" (Wz, p. 10). They "removed the old organ from the south side and put it at the west end" and "recast the pipes" (Wz, p. 11). At the beginning of the '20s the university church also received "a special director of music, Johann Gottlieb Gerner, for the usual music offerings on Sundays and festivals" (Wz, p. 12). After the first service in the university church on 31 August 1710, the 11th Sunday After Trinity, a morning service every Sunday and festival day continued thereafter; a vesper service began to be conducted from 1712 on the afternoons of all Sundays and festival days (Wz, p. 10; cf. *Bn*, pp. 46—47).

The increased building activity to open places for worship at the beginning of the 18th century manifested itself finally in the enlargement of the churches already used for worship purposes. Thus in 1705, "a piece was added" on the north side of St. Thomas Church, "and on both sides of the prince's pew various chapels, as well as above them new galleries adorned with many pews for men" (Wz, p. 5). In 1715 the little hospital church of St. George was enlarged for a better conduct of the worship services and devotions (*LGB* 1717, Dedication).

The renovation of the chancel of St. Thomas Church in 1721, when an entirely new altar of "costly red, white, and black marble" was installed

(Wz, p. 6),* as well as the renovation of the interior of St. John near the city gates, "totally ruined" in the Thirty Years' War and then "completely rebuilt," equipped with an organ in 1695 (Wz, p. 21), and then also made accessible for services and devotions to members of city churches at the beginning of the 18th century—formerly to be used only by the inmates of the hospital closely associated with the church—these too are of a piece with this manifest display of interest in Leipzig at the beginning of the century. In 1728 this situation, completely changed in so short a time, is briefly described as follows:

> While after the salutary Reformation and until A.D. 1699 the praise of God was heard in only two churches within the city walls, namely, the two chief churches, St. Nicholas and St. Thomas, the orthodox believers are now taught every Sunday and festival day from six pulpits, in six separate houses of God, namely, in the just-mentioned two chief churches, together with St. Paul, New, St. Peter, and Orphanage or the Church of St. George, and are instructed faithfully in the Lord's commandments. In addition, there are the two outside the gates, St. John at the Grimma Gate and the Lazareth Church at the Ranstadt Gate, in part newly built from the ground up, but in part only renovated and made ready for the worship of the true God. (Wz, pp. 2—3)

We have already emphasized that this interest in a purely external increase, enlargement, and beautification of the houses of God must be traced back also to a profoundly inward participation of the church members in the intensification of liturgical life. We now call attention to a long line of further measures designed to elevate the worship life. Without an echo coming from the congregation, such measures would appear incomprehensible.

Arranging for weekly Communion services in 1694 at the same time involved an intensification of the practice of confession, for Communion services were never held without prior opportunity for confession. But in Leipzig throughout the 18th century only the form of private confession was used, and for this purpose opportunity was given before the Communion services themselves as well as on the previous day from noon onward. With the addition of Communion services during the week, the practice of "hearing confession also during the week" (Ro, p. 99) was inaugurated, beginning 8 March 1694, on Tuesdays at St. Nicholas and on Wednesdays at St. Thomas. In 1713 a further measure was adopted to increase the time for making confessions. "Early Sunday morning confession," once

---

*The contemporary engraving by Johann Christoph Weigel is reproduced in W. Blankenburg, *Einführung in Bachs b-moll-Messe, BWV 232*, 3d. ed. (Kassel, 1974), p. 65.—Ed.

discontinued in 1670 but to a large extent reintroduced because of the large number of communicants, had been banned once again on 29 October 1713 and was to be reserved only for "the old and infirm" and "pregnant women." Now, since Saturday, 11 November, "confessions were heard" not only from 12 noon, but already from 8:00 a.m. and the bells were "especially tolled" (Ro, p. 99; cf. *Bn*, p. 48). However, since 1713 opportunity for confession was given not only on all Saturdays but also on the eves of all festival days during the week, always from eight in the morning until late in the afternoon—except during Vespers (Ro, p. 99). In the days of Superintendent Stemler (1755—1773) opportunity for confession was extended for the whole day also on Tuesdays at St. Nicholas and on Wednesdays at St. Thomas (*Bn*, p. 48). Occasionally an increase of opportunities for confession is reported also for the other churches in the city. Thus in New Church at its restoration only one confessional booth had been provided, and "at first only Magister Steinbach as head deacon was permitted to hear confessions. Soon thereafter, however, a confessional booth was provided also for Magister Werner, and he was authorized to hear confessions" (*AG*, p. 25). The rapid growth in Communion attendance at this church and the steadily growing number of confessors was responsible for this measure. Furthermore, the arrangement made during the Easter season of 1713 at St. John to combine the chief service with the celebration of Holy Communion every two weeks—instead of doing this only once a month, as previously—led also to having confession at this church every 14 days (*Bn*, p. 48). This practice remained still unchanged at the end of the century (Lh, p. 421).

Many new measures were enacted particularly for the catechizations during the worship services designed primarily for children and young people. After the restoration of St. Peter the newly called pastor was obliged from the beginning to be in charge of this practice that had been decreed by the city council and later labeled *Catecheticum*. On the basis of an electoral edict of 10 February 1710, this feature was intended to move the office of catechist and catechetical instruction of both young and adult more strongly than ever into the area of worship life and at the same time serve as training ground for the city's clergy.[28] Just before a pastor was called to St. Peter, an ordinance of 1 September 1711 specified that the catechetical instruction was "ordered to be conducted every Sunday and then to be introduced also at New Church, St. John, and St. George for the school boys, hospital inmates, and orphans." This catechization was first held on 15 July 1688—during the time Spener was *Oberhofprediger* at Dresden—and since then "every 14 days, alternately in both chief churches after Vespers."[29] In January 1712, only a month after the new pastor was called to St. Peter, the practice of conducting catechetical instruction was begun not only on Sundays but also regularly on specified weekdays, now directed also to adults (cf. *Bn*, p. 47). The rapid impact of these catechism services for the city's worship life is evident from the fact that already in February 1713 the city council "assigned an additional eight learned Masters [*Magistri*] as catechists" (Wz, p. 18) to the pastor of St. Peter, who was primarily responsible for these services and designated as "preacher at St. Peter's and Leipzig Catechist" (Sc*NA*, p. 580), because this catechetical work had become too extensive. By 1723 the number of weekly sessions of catechetical instruction in the city had grown to 11 (cf. LA 1723, pp. 78ff.). They were distributed among the individual churches as follows: At St. Nicholas on Sundays in connection with Vespers and Wednesdays at 2:00 p.m.; at St. Thomas on Sundays in connection with Vespers and on Tuesdays at 2:00 p.m.; at New Church on Sundays after Vespers; at St. Peter on Mondays and Thursdays always at 2:00 p.m.; at St. George on Sundays at 2:00 p.m.; at St. John on Sundays at 2:00 p.m.; and at St. James on Wednesdays and Fridays following the prayer service at 9:00 a.m. Weiz informs us that at St. John Church in 1728, in addition to the Sunday catechetical instruction, two further sessions had become established during the week, namely on Tuesdays and Thursdays in the early afternoon (Wz, p. 22). Nearly all of these catechism sessions were conducted regularly throughout the century as they had been arranged during the second and third decade of the 18th century.[30]

In other respects the people of Leipzig at the beginning of the 18th century were concerned in every way about further intensifying liturgical life. In New Church, since 3 April 1711, a special Good Friday Vesper sermon was given annually, a practice hitherto restricted to St. Thomas. Furthermore, it became customary in this church from 24 July 1711 to have a Vesper sermon regularly every Friday, and from 28 July of the same year a regular prayer service every week on Tuesday afternoon at 3:00 p.m. (Wz, p. 15; Ro, p. 147). We are told also that the scheduling of this "weekday sermon," as well as the weekly prayer service, was arranged at the request of "the local citizenry, especially those who live in that area" and who had often made this request (*AG*, p. 46). Shortly thereafter in March 1712 regular Vespers on all Sundays and festival days were introduced in St. Paul's Church. These services were initially conducted by members of the "Monday and Thursday College of Preachers," and since Michaelmas 1712 by especially chosen "Vesper preachers" (usually seven to nine unordained theologians, who had earned the master's degree). Further, in this church it became customary since 26 March 1728 to have an annual Vesper service on Good Friday, a practice observed at St. Nicholas since 26 March 1723 and finally introduced at St. Peter in 1744. Regular Vespers on the Festival of the Reformation were begun on 31 October 1733 at St. Nicholas and St. Thomas and were established also at New Church in 1736. A significant innovation was introduced in 1715 to the main services on Reformation Day at St. Nicholas, St. Thomas, and New Church. The festival service, hitherto conducted without the Communion liturgy, was now always combined with the celebration of Communion and thus placed on the same level with the other chief services on Sundays and festival days (Ro, p. 36). A further innovation was the introduction of the "confessional sermon," also called "exhortation to penitence" (ScNA, pp. 581ff.), in certain prayer services during the week. Finally, attention is called to the inauguration of Passion oratorios, first performed in New Church on Good Friday, 26 March 1717 (Wz, p. 15), but not until 11 April 1721 in St. Thomas Church and even 1724 in St. Nicholas (Ro, p. 24).

All of these measures, adopted at the beginning and in the first half of the 18th century, are a clear indication of an ever growing intensification of liturgical life in a way that was scarcely evident elsewhere in Germany at the same time. Many contemporary sources attest that also the citizens of Leipzig themselves were fully aware of their faithful nurture of the Reformation heritage and all the liturgical details, as well the revival of the entire worship life, that was everywhere clearly in evidence in their city. The dedication in the Leipzig hymnbook of 1717, addressed to the "most noble patrons" of the city and written by Friedrich Braun, self-designated citizen and book dealer, says:

Leipzig is indeed a famous city, famous for its many learned people, famous for its wise and praiseworthy government, famous for its flourishing business establishments. In particular, also the well-ordered worship has a special reputation everywhere, whether reference is to the excellent men who address the people in public or to other practices, including the divinely hallowed singing. In all these matters the praise and the truth compels us to look to Your Magnificence and Noble Excellencies as to those whom God has set as pillars of this glorious city. For, just as the fortunate conduct of the city government is done with wise counsel and intelligent action, so also a later posterity will have a record of how faithfully these men always provided for the care of the church of Christ and the arrangement of the beautiful worship services. Permit me to cite only what became obvious to all during the last 18 years either because of renovated or newly erected houses of God. In 1699 New Church and in 1712 St. Peter Church, both of which had long been in ruins, were restored for worship. Likewise, in 1705 the Orphanage Church was completely renovated, and in 1715 the little chapel in St. George's Hospital was considerably enlarged. The indescribable attendance at all these churches, those that were there before as well as the newly remodeled and erected churches, is truly astonishing. In view of this state of affairs, we must have a general and comprehensive record of this highly praiseworthy care for the churches ....(LGB 1717, Dedication)

The Leipzig chronicler Sicul writes in the annals of the city:

The infinite mercy of God cannot be praised sufficiently and thus also publicly that it not only kept special watch over the good city of Leipzig by preserving the light of the saving Gospel for 200 years, but also and especially because in the last few years...has permitted the pure Word of God to dwell among us in such rich measure, that only very recently there were only half as many worship services as there are now, praise God! Consequently, there are certainly few cities that can boast of such fine order and so many public church affairs as Leipzig....(Sc*NA*, p. 566)

There can be no doubt that the worship life in the city of Leipzig during the first half of the 18th century enjoyed a steady revival. Nothing would be farther from the truth than to characterize this world of orthodox Lutheranism, as manifested in Leipzig at that time, as merely a frozen and petrified world. We will have to look a little more closely at this worship life, so that we may then correctly judge and evaluate the entrance of Johann Sebastian Bach into this world of orthodox Lutheran piety.

c) Sunday Services

The entire public life of Leipzig throughout the first half of the 18th century and far beyond was characterized already by a purely numerical frequency of worship services and devotions. To a large extent this was no longer the case in other communities. In his description of the manifold liturgical customs and usages in the Saxon parishes, Christian Gerber has emphasized the unimaginably important role that worship played particularly in the life of the Leipzig parishes around 1730. After briefly describing the richness of Sunday services and devotions in Leipzig, he characterizes in the following word what is distinctive of this city: "We may surely call this the riches of divine goodness! Great is the host of those who bore the tiding" (Gb, p. 399 [Ps. 68:12. Luther translated: The Lord offers the Word through a large number of evangelists—Trans.]). If we take the entire context into consideration, it seems that Gerber was especially concerned to show that worship in Leipzig was even richer and more varied than in Dresden. In any case, in both main churches of Leipzig, St. Thomas and St. Nicholas, it happened not infrequently, especially on festival days, that one service followed hard upon another, so that the citizens of this city could attend services and devotions from early morning until the afternoon. The number of those who on a Sunday or festival day attended two services cannot have been small. We are even told that "there are also devout Christians who wait for and hear all three sermons in the city" (*LKA*, p. 543).

The cycle of Sunday services began already at five o'clock with the ringing of the "Matins bell" at St. Nicholas, followed soon thereafter by the prayer for the time of day in Latin according to the old liturgical order of Matins, conducted by 10 specially appointed "choralists." To be sure, they conducted this devotion for themselves alone, for "except for them no one else is in church" (*LKS*, p. 4). These "choralists" were students who had taken over the regular conduct of Matins under the direction of the St. Nicholas cantor and therefore received special stipends from the city council. While the regular observance of these canonical hours in St. Nicholas Church at different times of the day had become customary since Jubilate Sunday 1494, the hours had been observed only once since the Reformation (*Bn*, pp. 67—68). The various office books repeatedly gave these instructions with regard to the Sunday Matins: "Early at Matins let them have the students chant one, two, or three psalms with the antiphon proper to the Sunday or festival, then a reading from the Old Testament, followed by the Benedictus with an antiphon proper to the Sunday or festival, and closed with a collect. If it is desired, the people may be asked to sing the German Te Deum Laudamus" (*Ag*, p. 78). In the days of Johann Sebastian Bach Matins were conducted on all festival days at five o'clock, on ordinary Sundays not until 5:30. As late as the end of the century we are told that "every Sunday and festival day the canonical hours taken over from the Roman Catholic Church are still being chanted beforehand at 6:30 a.m." (Lh, p. 416).[31]

The first public worship of the city was conducted in St. John at six o'clock, at which the "regular pastor" as a rule preached on the Gospel of the respective Sunday or festival and "after the sermon...every other Sunday, that is, every two weeks, the office was performed" (Sc*NA*, pp. 567—68). Although "in fact only the brothers and sisters of St. John's Hospital were members" of this church, it had long become customary for "a large number of the inhabitants of suburban Grimma and the neighboring cabbage gardens to attend this church" (Lh, p. 422).

At seven o'clock the "early service" (so designated in the *Leipziger Kirchen-Staat*) began. This was the main Sunday service. In addition to the sermon this service always included celebration of the Holy Communion and, if there was a large Communion attendance, lasted "at times until eleven o'clock" (Sc*NA*, p. 572), that is, a service that regularly lasted three to four hours.[32] Also in New Church and in St. James the main Sunday service began at seven o'clock, while the respective services at St. Peter and St. George did not begin until eight o'clock (Sc*NA*, p. 586). In fact, in St. Paul the service did not begin until nine o'clock (Sc*NA*, pp. 574—75). Occasionally the scheduled starting times at St. George and St. James were changed. We are told that in the year 1723 the services at St. George began already at 7:30, but not until eight at St. James, while also at St. John the service began at six only in summer and at 6:30 in winter (LA 1723, pp. 83—84).

At 11:30 the bells were rung for the "Noonday Service," also known as "Noonday Preaching" (*LKS*, pp. 11—12; cf. also Sc*NA*, p. 575), and the service began at 11:45. Sundays this service was held in only one of the two main churches, St. Nicholas and St. Thomas alternating. On the first days of the three great festivals, Christmas, Easter, and Pentecost, the noonday service was held in both St. Nicholas and St. Thomas (Ro, p. 21), but on the second day of these festivals it was conducted only "in the church where the main music was performed in the early service." As a general rule for all special festivals of the church year throughout the 18th century the noonday service was always conducted in the church where earlier in the main worship the cantata had been presented by the cantor of St. Thomas (*LKS*, p. 20; Ro, p. 41). In the course of the 18th century this noonday service became constantly more important. In 1710 it was still expressly stated that there was no noonday service on Maundy Thursday and Good Friday, as well as the third day of the three great festivals of the church year (*LKS*, pp. 20—21, 24, 26). But then we learn from Rost that a noonday service had become customary on Maundy Thursday at St. Thomas (Ro, p. 21), and Sicul tells us that at the great three-day Reformation anniversary in June 1730 noonday services were held on all three feast days (Sc*JL*, pp. 118ff., 169ff., 195, 215—16). These noonday services were still observed on the third days of the great festivals at the end of the 18th century. They were now conducted as a rule by the "Lazareth preacher" and always at St. Nicholas. In the days of Johann Sebastian Bach the noonday service always lasted one and one half hours and was ended at 1:15 (*LKS*, p. 12).

Throughout the 18th century there was ample provision for services and devotions also for the afternoons of all Sundays and festivals. At St. Nicholas, St. Thomas, and New Church the "Vesper sermon," which already at the time of the Reformation had been set back to early afternoon, began as early as 1:15 (Sc*NA*, p. 576; cf. also *LKS*, pp. 12ff.), which regularly included *Catechismus-Examen* (Sc*NA*, p. 576; Ro, p. 17—18), except on high feasts and festival days of the church year.[33] Also in the other city churches special services and devotions were conducted in the afternoon. At St. Peter at two o'clock "a chapter of Holy Scripture was expounded from the pulpit" (Sc*NA*, p. 578). In this afternoon service, conducted regularly since the dedication of the new St. Peter Church, a chapter of the Bible, in continuous sequence, was expounded verse by verse, without regard to festival days and the course of the church year. In this way until the end of the 18th century the entire Bible was "preached through" four times, the first time between the First Sunday After Trinity 1712 and the Fourth Sunday in Advent 1732; the second time between Christmas Day 1732 and the Fourth Sunday After Trinity 1753; the third time between the Fifth Sunday After Trinity 1753 and Quasimodogeniti

1781; and the fourth time between Misericordias Domini 1781 and the 16th Sunday After Trinity 1799.[34] Likewise, at two o'clock "an edifying *Catechismus-Examen*" was conducted both at St. John and St. George, while at St. Paul Vespers did not begin until 3:15 (Sc*NA*, pp. 577—78).

Following his detailed presentation of liturgical life in Leipzig, Christoph Ernst Sicul offers a concluding overview of the customary services on Sundays and feast days. He is, however, interested only in the preaching services, and he finds that the "sum of evangelical Sunday sermons" in Leipzig on individual Sundays and feast days always totals 14. With a touch of pride in this abundance of services, he concludes: "If the Papist and Reformed preaching is included, there are 16 sermons here in Leipzig every Sunday; in addition, there are occasionally one or two funeral sermons, so that the total number of sermons on a single Sunday comes to 17 or 18" (Sc*NA*, pp. 586ff.). As a comparison with Leonardi's description of the worship life clearly shows (Lh, pp. 412ff.), this numerical wealth of services remained unchanged throughout the 18th century.[35]

d) Weekday Services

Not only were the individual Sundays and festival days amply provided with services and devotions from an early hour onward, but also on individual weekdays there were many opportunities in Leipzig to attend worship and devotions. This arrangement continued beyond the middle of the 18th century. Following a strict schedule for all city churches, the people could attend forenoon and afternoon services and devotions in various churches every day. The schedule of worship for every week, strictly observed in the days of Johann Sebastian Bach, was as follows:

Monday:
> 6:30 a.m. Early service with preaching at St. Nicholas[36]
> 2:00 p.m. Short prayer service and exhortation to penitence at St. Thomas
> 2:00 p.m. Instruction in the Cathechism and the Bible at St. Peter

Tuesday:
> 6:30 a.m. Early service with preaching at St. Thomas
> 2:00 p.m. Major prayer service and confession at St. Nicholas
> 2:00 p.m. Instruction in Catechism and Bible at St. Thomas
> 3:00 p.m. Prayer service and exhortation to penitence at New Church
> 3:00 p.m. Prayer service and Bible exposition at St. John[37]
> 5:00 p.m. Instruction in Catechism and Bible at St. George[38]

Wednesday:

6:30 a.m. Early service with sermon and Holy Communion at St. Nicholas

9:00 a.m. Prayer service and instruction in the Catechism at St. James

2:00 p.m. Minor prayer service and confession at St. Thomas

2:00 p.m. Instruction in Catechism and Bible at St. Nicholas

Thursday:

6:30 a.m. Early service with sermon and Holy Communion at St. Thomas

2:00 p.m. Minor prayer service and exhortation to penitence at St. Nicholas

2:00 p.m. Instruction in Catechism and Bible at St. Peter

3:00 p.m. Prayer service or exhortation to penitence at St. John[39]

Friday:

6:30 a.m. Penitential service with sermon at St. Nicholas

9:00 a.m. Prayer service and Catechism instruction at St. James

2:00 p.m. Major prayer service at St. Thomas

3:00 p.m. Weekday sermon at New Church[40]

5:00 p.m. Bible instruction at St. George[41]

Saturday

1:30 p.m. Weekday sermon at St. Nicholas

1:30 p.m. Weekday sermon at St. Thomas

It is noted that for a complete picture of the worship life we should really add "the large number of practice sermons delivered by students of theology in their homiletics classes" (Sc*NA*, p. 587). Such sermons, delivered by students of theology, were given regularly on Tuesday at St. John before the beginning of the afternoon devotions. The Leipzig chronicler reports in connection with the "Bible Instruction" beginning at three o'clock that "shortly before the service a student of theology from the homiletics class under the direction of the local pastor delivers a sermon. To be sure, this sermon is held only for the sake of practice, but nobody is kept from listening in, and those coming for the exposition generally turn up for it" (Sc*NA*, p. 581). In addition, also "in other homiletics classes certain sermons are delivered, but only for practice," at St. Paul on Mondays and Thursdays (LA 1723, p. 32). Even without counting these student sermons, the numerical wealth of the worship forms in Leipzig during the week is obvious.

The large number of weekday services, as shown by the schedule, must be divided into three groups: We must distinguish between what Sicul calls "weekday sermons," "prayer services," and the "examinations in Catechism and Bible" (Sc*NA*, p. 587—88).

The weekday sermons were full services, often lasting up to two hours. While in these the liturgical elements were kept at a minimum, they always featured a full-length sermon, in distinction from the other devotions. Of the sermon we are told that "the sermon lasts no longer than one hour" (*LKS*, p. 40). With regard to the Sunday sermons we are told explicitly that they usually lasted one hour: "The proper time of the sermon is one hour" (*LKS*, p. 7). Except for Saturdays, these weekday sermons were held daily at 6:30 a.m., either at St. Nicholas or at St. Thomas, and on Fridays at three o'clock in New Church and Saturdays at 1:30 p.m. in both St. Nicholas and St. Thomas. In addition, the early services on Wednesdays at St. Nicholas and on Thursdays at St. Thomas were combined with the celebration of Holy Communion, where the full Communion liturgy as used on Sundays was observed. Among the early services special significance attached to the "Friday sermon at St. Nicholas," for we are told: "This service is more solemn than the other weekday sermons, and the doors of the merchants' places of business and the shops of craftsmen are closed during the service" (*LKS*, p. 41; cf. also *LKA*, p. 72). This service was usually begun "with the hymn 'A nobis Domine' or some other penitential hymn...followed by the chanting of the Litany," and, in line with old tradition, "there was always a penitential sermon" (*LKS*, p. 41). In the afternoon service on Friday in New Church "a sermon on the articles of the Christian Creed was held and...in addition to other hymns, the Litany was chanted" (Sc*NA*, p. 584; cf. also Ro, p. 147; *AG*, p. 50).

Following a listing of these eight weekday sermons in Leipzig, Sicul summarizes his findings: "In sum, the evangelical sermons delivered from Sunday to Sunday and thus available to be heard throughout the week in Leipzig total 22" (Sc*NA*, p. 587).

Sicul combines the second and third forms of weekday services in the designation "services without preaching" (Sc*NA*, p. 587). Here, however, we must distinguish between the "prayer services" and the "Bible and Catechism instruction." The prayer services are again divided into "major," or "long," and "minor," or "short," ones—terms used interchangeably in various sources, and in one source they are used side by side (Sc*NA*, pp. 580, 582, 584, 588). The minor prayer services were always held at two o'clock on Mondays and Wednesdays at St. Thomas and Thursdays at St. Nicholas. Since 1714 these services had been augmented on Mondays at St. Thomas and on Thursdays at St. Nicholas by an "exhortation to penitence," also called "confessional sermon" (so Sc*NA*, pp. 581, 583) or "penitential sermon" (so Sc*NA*, pp. 579, 588). This involved a brief address, but one that in the course of the 18th century became increasingly important, for at the end of the century this devotion on Mondays at St. Thomas is referred to only with the words: "At two o'clock in the afternoon there is a sermon which is generally known by the name of exhortation to penitence, and which began on Monday after New Year's Day in 1714" (Lh, p. 413). It is not clear whether this short sermon was delivered within the prayer service itself or in immediate connection with it. The Leipzig directory of 1723 refers to "a short prayer service, followed by the exhortation to penitence" (LA 1723, pp. 79, 81). Sicul, on the other hand, reports that the exhortation to penitence was given "after the prayers and a chapter of the Bible were read" (ScNA, p. 582). This exhortation to penitence was primarily intended to prepare the communicants for confession and was omitted only when a special festival of the church year was celebrated the next day (Ro, p. 2). The major prayer services were always held at two o'clock on Tuesdays at St. Nicholas and on Fridays at St. Thomas. In addition to the cited prayer services at St. Nicholas and St. Thomas a special weekly prayer service "together with a confessional sermon" was conducted in New Church on Fridays at three o'clock (ScNA, p. 581).

The latest arrangements in the worship life of the city were the various "Bible and Catechism instruction sessions," occasionally also known as "prayer services," and at times actually expanded into a prayer service. Of the weekly devotions at St. James we are told: "Wednesdays and Fridays: Prayer service and Catechism instruction at nine o'clock in the forenoon" (LA 1723, p. 84). The service at St. John on Tuesdays at three o'clock, is called "prayer service and Bible exposition" in the Leipzig directory of 1723 (LA 1723, p. 83), while Sicul lists it among "Catechism and Bible instruction sessions" (ScNA, p. 588). At another place Sicul offers more detail: "...a Biblical examination which is conducted officially by the pastor and which is to be attended alternately by the schools of those residing at the Grimma Gate and those under the supervision of the pastor of St. John, as well as their teacher" (ScNA, pp. 580—81). Also the "prayer service and exhortation to penitence" at St. John on Thursdays (so named in LA 1723, p. 84) is labeled *Catechismus-Examen* by Sicul (ScNA, p. 582). The so-called "prayer services" (in Wz, p. 20; LA 1723, p. 83) conducted at St. George Tuesdays and Fridays at five o'clock are also listed by Sicul among the "Catechism and Bible instruction sessions" (ScNA, p. 588) and are described as "...a public hour of prayer and edification on the Bible, during Lent however, based on the Passion history according to a different evangelist each year" (ScNA, p. 581). Occasionally an additional special devotion was held at St. George Thursday at three o'clock, a service not included in the weekly schedule of services listed above. It is described as follows: "At St. George on this day the regular preacher at times conducts an hour of penitence and edification, not open to the public, exclusively for the prisoners and inmates, who are examined and instructed on the essential elements of Christianity" (ScNA, p. 583). The different names given to these devotions might be accounted for by the fact that they contained important liturgical elements of the prayer services, on the one hand, but, on the other hand, also gave due consideration to catechetical instruction. Catechism and Bible instruction conducted in the two main churches separate from the real prayer services bore a distinctly liturgical character in that they were always held in church in the presence of children and young people as well as older members, and were always begun and concluded with the singing of a hymn, as well as collect and benediction at the altar, following the instruction period.

The liturgical life of Leipzig, so uncommonly rich in a purely numerical sense, was regarded as a great peculiarity in the Saxony of that day, as Christian Gerber states expressly: "Happy is he who can live in a city where worship is conducted publicly every day. In this respect the inhabitants of Dresden and Leipzig are fortunate, because in these two cities preaching and prayer services are held every day, so that they are enriched with all speech and knowledge and are not lacking in any spiritual gift [1 Cor. 1:5-7]"(Gb, p. 355). In this connection Gerber emphasizes that over against Leipzig the city of Dresden even lagged behind, since it had no Saturday Vesper preaching, a fact he deeply regrets.

Thus already at this point we may establish as a fact that the worship life of Leipzig, shaped by Lutheran orthodoxy, was still full of vital force and that it is therefore totally inappropriate to characterize this late orthodox Lutheranism as a world already paralyzed or even dead.

e) The Church Year

The number of weekly services and devotions was considerably higher in weeks where extra festival days fell on weekdays, a not uncommon occurrence at that time. The whole wealth of worship life in Leipzig was manifested also in the rich liturgical formation of the church year in a way that the Lutheran Church cannot otherwise demonstrate in the course of its history.

For example, the three-day observance of the three high festivals of Christmas, Easter, and Pentecost was still taken for granted in Leipzig throughout the 18th century. The first two days of the three festivals were treated alike with regard to liturgical structuring, while the third day was always treated like an ordinary Sunday. In accordance with ancient tradition the second and third Christmas days were observed year by year as the

Day of the Protomartyr St. Stephen (26 December) and as the Day of St. John, Apostle and Evangelist (27 December). To be sure, the sources have almost nothing to say on this matter. Only the *Leipziger Kirchen-Andachten* remarks briefly that the third Christmas day was observed year by year as St. John's Day (*LKA*, p. 54), and the *Leipziger Kirchen-Staat* says of third Christmas days "that on those days in alternate years there was preaching on John 1:1-14 and John 20:1-24" (*LKS*, pp. 20-21). But also on on second Christmas days an alternate use of the liturgy for the second festival day and St. Stephen's Day occurred. This is clear from Bach's cantatas, BWV 40 and BWV 57, which were performed on the second Christmas day in 1723 and 1725 and which are fully intelligible in their textual settings only in the context of the liturgy for St. Stephen's Day.[42]

Treated as almost on the same level with the three chief festivals were the following in the course of the church year: New Year's Day, Epiphany—also called "the great New Year or Feast Day of the Three Kings or of the Revelation of Christ" (*LKS*, p. 21), the Purification of Mary (2 February), the Annunciation (25 March), Ascension, Trinity, St. John the Baptist (24 June), Visitation of Mary (2 July), and Michaelmas (29 September). On all of these festival days the main service used the Latin Preface, which was a special mark of festival days already in Bugenhagen's church orders. On these days the customary Catechism instruction conducted on ordinary Sundays was omitted altogether, as also on the three high festivals (Ro, pp. 3, 15, 32, 35). Furthermore, on the eves of all these festivals there was a festive ringing of all the bells, and the festivals were inaugurated with a solemn Vespers immediately afterward. Rost reports: "When a festival falls on a weekday and not on Sunday, all the bells are tolled on the eve at two o'clock," but "when a festival falls on a Sunday, all the bells are tolled on the preceding Saturday at 1:30" (Ro, p. 2). This was because in this Vesper service the usual Saturday Vesper sermon was delivered, while in the Vespers on the eves of those festivals there was no preaching. These Vespers on the eves of special festivals of the church year were conducted even if they fell on the afternoon of Sunday, where the usual Vesper service would have been conducted in any case. For example, when the Feast of the Annunciation fell on Monday after Palm Sunday in 1720, the Vespers of Palm Sunday afternoon did not follow the usual liturgy, but in its place the Vespers for the eve of the Annunciation (Ro, p. 15). These circumstances in any case demonstrate the prominence still given to the three Marian festivals, which since the Reformation were celebrated as festivals of Christ. This may also be clearly seen from Johann Sebastian Bach's rather significant cantatas for these festivals, e.g., BWV 1 and BWV 147. At any rate, the Feast of the Annunciation was so highly regarded that it was always observed on Palm Sunday if it fell on Maundy Thursday, Good Friday, or Easter (*LKS*, p. 22; Ro, p. 14). When this festival was celebrated on Palm Sunday or another Sunday, the customary "instruction" connected with Vespers on Palm Sunday and all ordinary Sundays was omitted (Ro, p. 14). Also in cases when a festival day fell on a Monday, the Catechism instruction of the previous Sunday was omitted, since the Vespers on that Sunday was celebrated as a prelude to the festival to be observed the next day (cf. Ro, pp. 3, 7, 14, 15, 16, 34, 35, 46).

In time, especially in the 18th century, the Reformation Festival, observed annually on 31 October, had become a special festival day, known also as "Luther Festival" (*LKA*, p. 103), "Lutheran Reformation Festival" (*LKS*, p. 29), and *Festum Reformationis Lutheri* (Ro, p. 36). In electoral Saxony the territorial government "had arranged for its celebration the first time in 1667" (*LKA*, p. 103), in other words, not until the 150th anniversary of the day on which Luther posted the Ninety-five Theses. On this day it soon became customary for all Leipzig churches to have "music and preaching as on a high festival" in the forenoon (*LKA*, p. 103). This festival day, like all special days, was begun at 6:00 a.m. with the ringing of all bells in two rhythms for a quarter hour (*LKA*, p. 104).[43] In 1715 the festival service on Reformation Day was given the same rank as the main services of other festivals by combining the celebration of the "Communion" with it.[44]

In 18th-century Leipzig also apostles' days were given special recognition. Although regarded only as "half holidays" (*LKA*, p. 85; *LKS*, p. 44), and introduced by the ringing of bells only at 6:30, like ordinary Sundays (Ro, p. 49), they nevertheless constituted a peculiarity in the city's worship life after they had been abolished in Saxony generally already in 1681.[45] Strangers who were familiar with these apostles' days in their homeland often missed them in Saxony (cf. Gb, pp. 115, 178ff.). Although these apostles' days were frequently relegated to the following Sunday or other suitable days already in the 16th century, this kind of practice was unknown in Leipzig. In his notes Rost affirms that these apostles' days were observed on all weekdays, even on Saturday (Ro, pp. 49—50). We cannot tell precisely which of the many apostles' days were observed in Leipzig, but it is very probable that most of them were celebrated there. As late as 1714 there is reference to the observance of nine apostles' days in neighboring Weißenfels.[46] Hence it is quite unlikely that in Leipzig, with its uncommonly rich liturgical tradition, there were fewer such celebrations. From Rost we learn incidentally that the day of the apostle Andrew (30 November) was observed in Leipzig (Ro, p. 50). Although there is no record of its observance in Weissenfels. In 1724 also the day of the apostle James (25 July) was observed in Leipzig (Ro, p. 50). From the 1723 communicant roster of St. Thomas we learn that on a Thursday the usual weekly Communion service was celebrated as on "the festival of the apostles Simon and Jude" (28 October). Also the festival of the apostle Matthias

(24 or 25 February) must have been observed in Leipzig, for Rost specifies that when an apostle's day falls during Lent, the "blue pulpit parament was used," and also the organ was played, contrary to ordinary Lenten custom (Ro, p. 50)—but only when the day of Matthias fell during Lent. All of these apostles' days were observed in regular forenoon worship services. Rost's remark that these services were "celebrated like a festival" (Ro, p. 49) refers to the liturgy of the main service but is only conditionally correct, for beside the usual absence of the sacramental section, there was no cantata either. The Lord's Supper was celebrated only when it would have been celebrated on the respective day in any case, even without the observance of an apostle's day. Rost notes: "When the apostle's day falls on a Thursday, there will be early confession as usual on Thursday," and "when Holy Communion is celebrated on an apostle's day (as on Thursday), the full clerical robes will not be put on until after the sermon. Before the sermon only the white surplice is worn" (Ro, p. 49).

Furthermore, the church year, at least in its first half, was richly arranged into various long and important cycles, and within these it was often full of a living tradition, especially during Advent and Lent.

The season of Advent in Leipzig continued to be regarded as a closed season, observed entirely under the sign of expectation and preparation for Christmas. It was explicitly ordered "that throughout Advent...no wedding and social affair (or banquet) be planned...but that it be transferred to another time" (*LKA*, p. 52). In the chief Sunday services during this period of the church year the Litany was always chanted immediately after the reading of the Epistle "and no other music was offered in the church," yet the organ—in distinction from Lent—"was used on all four Sundays" (*LKS*, p. 32; cf. also *LKA*, p. 52). Rost notes a little more exactly: "Throughout Advent the organ is played. But on the Second, Third, and Fourth Sundays in Advent there is no [further] music" (Ro, p. 44), for the First Sunday in Advent, which begins the new church year, was often emphasized as a special festival day over against the rest of the season, which was usually observed as a time of penitence. Rost, too, affirms—quite apart from the fact that Johann Sebastian Bach's cantatas do the same—that the First Sunday in Advent was observed as a "festival," for he took note of the custom that *no* Preface (a special characteristic of the festival liturgy) was chanted on the First Sunday in Advent, "even though it is a festival" (Ro, p. 44). It must, however, be called an inconsistency that the whole Litany for penitential days and seasons was chanted in the church in which the cantata was presented on the First Sunday in Advent. That this actually happened is confirmed by Rost and even by Johann Sebastian Bach's record of the liturgy for the First Sunday in Advent in his own handwriting.[47] Rost appears to have sensed the contradiction when he noted: "The Litany, too, is always chanted on the First Sunday in Advent, whether other music is offered in the same church or not'' (Ro, p. 44). In the noonday and vesper sermons on Sundays and weekdays during Advent "the Catechism hymns were sung, because in these four weeks the Catechism was usually explained as a proper preparation for the holy Christmas time'' (*LKA*, p. 52). The remark made in the *Leipziger Kirchen-Staat* that "during the whole Advent season the Catechism was preached in the noonday and vesper services instead of the Gospel'' is inexact to the extent that the words "instead of the Gospel'' can refer only to the noonday services, since in the Sunday Vespers the sermon was always based on the proper Epistle. Rost, however, confirms that at the time of Bach the "Catechism was explained'' also in the Vespers (Ro, p. 44).

The Christmas season was initiated with Vespers on the eve of the first Christmas Day. In this service there was a sermon only if the day fell on a Saturday, when the usual Vesper sermon would have been delivered in any case (Ro, p. 46). The Christmas season lasted until the Feast of the Purification of Mary, for on this festival day Christmas hymns were sung for the last time (*LKA*, p. 56; *LKS*, pp. 22—23). Concerning the liturgy for New Year's Day it is stated that "it remains in all respects like that of the first Christmas Day, except that in addition to Christmas hymns also New Year's Day hymns are sung,'' and concerning Epiphany "...everything is done as on the first Christmas Day'' (*LKS*, p. 21). These remarks clearly show that New Year's Day and Epiphany were celebrated altogether in the light of Christmas. At both festivals, as also on the three festival days of Christmas, the Latin hymn "Puer natus in Bethlehem'' was sung at the beginning of the forenoon and afternoon services and the German version, "Ein Kind geborn zu Bethlehem,'' at the end (*LKA*, p. 55; *LKS*, p. 21). The close connection of New Year's Day with Christmas also finds expression in the fact that "the Preface, chanted on Christmas Day, was again chanted today'' (Ro, p. 3). Furthermore, the *Leipziger Kirchen-Staat* has no separate Preface for New Year's Day, as it does for Epiphany. When New Year's Day fell on a Monday, the Vespers on New Year's Eve were observed as was usually done, not with a view to the next day's festival, but in very close connection with Christmas, namely as the Vespers for the Sunday After Christmas, for a liturgical observance of New Year's Eve as we now have it was still unknown at Bach's time (Ro, p. 3).

The season of Lent in Leipzig began with Invocavit Sunday (we hear nothing of Ash Wednesday). Lent was observed as a strict "time of fasting'' in the proper sense. During this season of the church year—similar to Advent—all music in churches and homes was forbidden by the government and "it was also ordered that no wedding and social affair (or banquet) be scheduled for this time'' (*LKA*, p. 58). Consequently, on the Sundays in Lent "no banns were published after the sermon,'' because "all weddings throughout this season were forbidden'' (*LKS*, 34). The people were also instructed to beware of "all excess especially in costly food and drink...and, all in all, of everything that may lead to voluptuousness and luxury and hinder or lessen our devotion" (*LKA*, p. 58). In the main Sunday services—as in Advent—the Litany was always chanted following the Epistle, but now—in distinction from Advent—there was no organ playing (*LKA*, p. 58; *LKS,* p. 34). In the Vespers "throughout Lent the Passion history instead of the Epistle was expounded in sermons" (*LKS*, p. 34; cf. also *LKS*, p. 58; Ro, p. 10). The last three Sundays and festival days of Lent, namely, Palm Sunday, Maundy Thursday, and Good Friday, had an especially rich liturgical structure. On Palm Sunday the main service at St. Nicholas began at 6:30 a.m. and was distinguished by the fact that on this day in place of the Gospel the whole "Passion according to the evangelist Matthew was chanted" (*LKS*, p. 59; cf. also *LKS*, pp. 35—36; Ro, p. 17). This was done in front of the lectern in the chancel "by an alumnus as evangelist,...yet in a way that every subordinate character with a speaking part was represented by a fellow pupil. A deacon had the role of Christ, and the choir that of the people" (*Bn*, p. 54). The performance of this almost entirely unison recital of the Passion used a composition that tradition assigned to Johann Walter and dated around 1530, as reprinted in the Leipzig Hymnbook of 1682 (*LGB* 1682, pp. 179—227). Only small parts of the Passion history, spoken by several disciples and the people, were arranged for several voices. The words of Judas, Peter, Caiaphas, Pilate, and the maid were assigned to various pupils and set for one voice. With regard to the performers, it is attested already in the *Leipziger Kirchen-Andachten* that "one of the deacons...represents the person of the Lord Christ" (*LKA*, p. 60), whereas Rost noted that "the priest and the pupils" usually chanted the Passion history (Ro, p. 17). In connection with this presentation, "which the congregation devoutly hears while standing," was the singing of the motet *Ecce quomodo moritur justus* by Jacob Gallus in a four-part setting printed in teh Leipzig Hymnbook of 1682 (*LGB* 1682, pp. 263ff.). In addition, "after the sermon this or that motet" was sung (*LKA*, p. 60; *LKS*, p. 36). Also the service of the "choralists" was more extensive on this Sunday than ordinarily. The service was begun with the Gregorian antiphon "Pueri Hebraeorum," followed by the customary Palm Sunday Introit, "Humiliavit semet ipsum," with which the service at St. Thomas and New Church usually began at seven o'clock (*LKS,* p. 35). After the reading of the Epistle "the choralists in St. Nicholas Church sang the hymn of Theodulph, 'Gloria laus et honor.' This was answered by the choir in parts [*figuraliter*] in alternation with the organ" (*LKS*, pp. 35—36). This Gregorian hymn is the only unison setting assigned to the Passion season in the Leipzig Hymnbook of 1682 (*LGB* 1682, p. 158). All other hymns and chorales with music in the section of Passion hymns are set for several voices. The playing of the organ on Palm Sunday applies only to the main

St. Nicolai Church. Source: W. Neumann, *Auf den Lebenswegen Johann Sebastian Bachs* (Berlin, 1953), p. 158.

service. In the Vespers on Palm Sunday eve as well as in all other services on Palm Sunday the organ was not played, not even during the Communion in the main service (cf. Ro, p. 17). Similarly, Maundy Thursday was observed as a festival day jutting out from Lent, with a full main service in the forenoon at the usual hour. In this service the customary Lenten Litany was omitted, the Communion liturgy was embellished in an unusual way, and the sermon was based "on the Words of Institution," that is, the Epistle for Maundy Thursday (*LKS*, p. 24; *LKA*, p. 60). This emphasis was necessary, because otherwise the sermon in the main service was always based on the Gospel for the day. In the Vespers, conducted on this day only at St. Nicholas (Ro, p. 22), the sermon was on the Gospel for the day. Maundy Thursday was also introduced by a Vesper service on Wednesday evening, but the organ was not played, as it was on Maundy Thursday itself (Ro, p. 20). But in the Maundy Thursday Vespers the organ was no longer played, since this service was conducted liturgically as the Vespers of Good Friday eve. In the main service on Good Friday "instead of the Gospel . . . the Passion according to St. John was sung"—as the St. Matthew Passion was sung on Palm Sunday (*LKS*, p. 25). It was sung in the musical setting printed in the Leipzig Hymnbook of 1682 (*LGB* 1682, pp. 227—263). The text of the "chanted" St. Matthew and St. John Passions was printed in the second part of the *Leipziger Kirchen-Staat* (pp. 74ff.; 85ff.) so that the congregation could follow the words. With regard to the musical performance, the same thing applies as to the rendering of the St. Matthew Passion on Palm Sunday; however, the role of Christ was customarily sung by a subdeacon, whereas on Palm Sunday this role was sung by the archdeacon (Ro, pp. 17, 23).

On Good Friday the organ was not played, and the sermon in the main service "was in alternate years either on Isaiah 53 or on Psalm 22" (*LKS*, p. 25; *LKA*, pp. 61—62). The Vesper sermon had long been given "only in St. Thomas Church" (thus *LKS*, p. 26), but from 1723 onward a Vesper service was conducted regularly also at St. Nicholas on Good Friday, Superintendent Deyling himself preaching the first sermon. A special high point of this service, at St. Thomas since 1721 and at St. Nicholas since 1724, and thereafter alternately in both main churches, was the performance of a Passion oratorio (Ro, p. 24). This *Music* was omitted only in 1733 because of a nationwide court mourning, so that the sequence could not be continued at St. Thomas until 1734. Rost even mentions that in 1736 this *Music* was presented at "St. Thomas with both organs" (Ro, p. 24). Also the communicant registers of St. Thomas occasionally refer to this Passion music; e.g., on Maundy Thursday 1726 "there was *Music* at St. Nicholas," on Good Friday 1729 "Passion: *Music* at St. Thomas," and on Maundy Thursday 1730 "Passion *Music* at St. Nicholas."

The degree to which the observance of these special festival days and seasons of the church year with all their services and devotions influenced the entire public life of the city is clearly discernible from the fact that on all Sundays and festival days the city gates remained closed throughout the day, and thus all public traffic came to a halt. As late as 1799 we are told: "During the service iron chains in the streets and alleys close the approaches to the churches in order to prevent all disturbance. Furthermore, the inner city gates are open only to pedestrians, for the large gates may be opened during the service only by previously obtained permission from the municipal council" (Lh, pp. 424—25). In this connection there is reference to the following noteworthy tradition on Maundy Thursday: "Here we must not forget an old custom engaged in by the butchers on Maundy Thursday. As you know, on this half holiday all trade must stop during the service. So also the Leipzig butchers must close their shops. Since they cannot go far away from their places of business, they conduct a devotion from eight to nine with prayer and song behind closed doors." All public traffic, including all business, was also shut down at least once a week on an ordinary workday, namely on Friday, by old tradition observed regularly as a day of penitence, early in the morning at the time of the service (cf. sources cited above, p. 53). In the course of time special importance was given to the "general days of fasting, prayer, and penitence" prescribed by the Elector, always observed on Fridays as "high festival days" (*LKA*, pp. 91ff.). About these "great days of fasting, penitence, and prayer" the *Leipziger Kirchen-Staat* reports: "These days are announced on the previous Sunday, and the royal and electoral charter issued for this purpose is read" (*LKS*, p. 45). To these days of penitence and prayer applied in a special way the order: "All commerce and trade, all weekday work, all excesses, whatever their name, must be omitted throughout this day" (*LKA*, p. 92). To "promote devotion" it was even urged that people should "voluntarily abstain from all eating and drinking until after the service, and those who can do so abstain until evening as they did in the ancient church, so that also the body may experience its chastening, and the spirit may deal all the more freely with God the Lord in prayer and song" (*LKA*, p. 92). These great days of penitence and prayer were always inaugurated in this way, that "every week on the previous Thursday there is a preparatory sermon early in the morning, conducted like other weekday services" (*LKS*, p. 45; *LKA,* p. 94). In addition, on Thursday afternoon "at two o'clock a prayer service was conducted in all three churches, announced by the ringing of the bells as on high festivals" (*LKS*, pp. 45—46). The days of penitence and prayer themselves [on Friday] were begun at six o'clock with the ringing of "all the bells" (*LKS*, p. 46; cf. also *LKA*, p. 94). The main services, called "early sermon" but held without the Sacrament of the Altar, began at seven o'clock as on Sundays and holidays, as well as the noonday preaching services and Vespers at the usual hour (*LKS*, pp. 46—47). Besides this, a special prayer service was conducted following the Vespers (*LKS*, p. 48; cf. also *LKA,* p. 95).

These great days of penitence and prayer were conducted throughout Saxony twice a year until 1710, and even three times a year thereafter (Gb, p. 568). However, in 1730, when a three-day Reformation jubilee was observed in the month of June, only two great days of penitence and prayer were prescribed in view of this anniversary. Gerber, who supplies this information, at the same time notes that evangelical "days of thanksgiving"—that was the chief accent in the three festival days of the Reformation jubilee—"are and are called true and serious days of penitence at the same time." In his opinion, therefore there can be no talk of abridging the days of penitence and prayer with regard to their frequency even in the year 1730, in view of the fact that all main services of the three festival days of that jubilee were combined with the celebration of the Sacrament of the Altar, which is equivalent "to genuine antecedent penitence and turning to God" (Gb, pp. 568—69). Such great anniversaries were observed in Leipzig also at other times for three days, as in the case of the three high festivals of the church year. In 1709 the 400th anniversary of the university and in 1717 the 200th anniversary of Luther's Ninety-five Theses were observed as three-day festivals (Wz, pp. 117— 18). This was also done in 1739 to observe the 200th anniversary of the introduction of the Reformation in Leipzig in 1539.

In addition to these special festivals there were many worship traditions that were annually observed on a specific Sunday. Thus we are told that on the Second Sunday After Epiphany and the Second Sunday After Trinity (but only on the First Sunday After Trinity according to the *Leipziger Kirchen-Staat*) in the noonday service "the order of marriage was read together with an exhortation to the congregation" (*LKS*, p. 37; Ro, p. 33). Doing this especially in the noonday service was probably due to the fact that then "mostly the servants and workmen usually attended, since they were prevented from attending the early service either because of lack of sitting or standing room or because of necessary and permissible work" (*LKA*, p. 42). On the Tenth Sunday After Trinity "in the Vesper service the history of the destruction of Jerusalem was read . . . and the preacher also admonished to penitence and improvement" (*LKS*, pp. 37—38). On the Sunday preceding the day of the apostle Bartholomew (24 August) the "council election" was announced (*LKS*, pp. 37—38). The election was then held on the first Monday after this apostle's day and observed with a festival service—think of Bach's thoroughly festive cantatas for these festival days: BWV 29, BWV 69, and BWV 119.

Throughout the 18th century the living structure of the church year in Leipzig included observing the liturgical colors for the different seasons of the church year and the wearing of the liturgical vestments by the clergy and the acolytes serving at the altar.* From the notes made by the sexton at St. Thomas we learn many details. On the eve of Reformation "the blue pulpit parament was hung," or on the Purification of Mary "the green pulpit parament was hung, and likewise the green paraments for altar and lectern" (Ro, pp. 7, 36). Although "black paraments" were used throughout Lent, the "bright hangings" were put up on the eve of Palm Sunday, and "this decoration remained the whole day, even though the Passion is preached at Vespers" (Ro, pp. 14, 17—18). Also on the eve of Maundy Thursday "bright colors were used," but after the noonday service on Maundy Thursday "the bright colors were removed and replaced by the black." Also regarding Easter Eve it is reported that "bright colors were used," and the remark concerning the First Sunday in Advent is interesting: "No black paraments are used, but the red and the green colors remain" (Ro, pp. 20—21, 26, 43). We are also told that the eucharistic vestments corresponding to the seasons of the church year were worn. On Maundy Thursday "the liturgist [*Administrator*] is robed in the green chasuble" (Ro, p. 21). For Good Friday: "On this day the liturgist wears the black chasuble" (Ro, p. 23). For Epiphany: "On this festival the dark chasuble [*das Meßgewand mit dem Mohr*] is customarily used" (Ro, p. 5). Also on Palm Sunday "the liturgist donned the green chasuble" (Ro, p. 17). This chasuble was worn only by the liturgist functioning at the altar, while the other clergy wore the white surplice over the black cassock. In connection with the dedication of New Church in 1699 we are told explicitly that before the end of the musical rendering of the Kyrie "both clergymen, namely the head deacon in the chasuble, but Magister Werner in the surplice, came out of the sacristy" (*AG*, p. 29). This report also informs us that in Leipzig the eucharistic vestments were worn not only during the celebration of the Communion but throughout the service. Rost confirms this state of affairs. In his record of the liturgy for the main service on Maundy Thursday, after the statement that the candles are lit at seven o'clock, followed by the organ prelude, he immediately adds the words, "the liturgist is vested in the green chasuble," and then he continues with the rest of the liturgical materials (Ro, p. 21). The sexton at St. Thomas indirectly supports this in his note regarding the exceptional regulation applying to the Communion services on apostles' days, that then "the priest is not vested until after the sermon, wearing only the surplice before the sermon" (Ro, p. 49). Also the acolytes were accustomed to wearing liturgical robes proper to the seasons of the church year, as is clear from the notice

---

*For the general background of the use of vestments, see Arthur Carl Piepkorn, *The Survival of the Historic Vestments in the Lutheran Church After 1555*, Graduate Study Number 1 (St. Louis: School for Graduate Studies, Concordia Seminary, 1956).—Ed.

for Invocavit Sunday: "Beginning with this Sunday and throughout Lent the boys wear the black and white robes at the Communion" (Ro, p. 10).

The rich liturgical structuring of the church year with its many festivals and special traditions thus constitutes an unmistakable characteristic of liturgical life in Leipzig during the first half of the 18th century. This we must certainly take into consideration if we wish to understand correctly and to appreciate the entrance of Johann Sebastian Bach into this world of Lutheran orthodoxy and his activity in the worship of this city.

f) The Clergy

For all services and devotions on the individual Sundays and festivals as well as on the various weekdays there were always on duty specific clergymen, following a minutely detailed regulation. Until 1876 the city of Leipzig was divided into only two parishes, centering in two parish churches called "main churches," St. Nicholas and St. Thomas. Each church had five clergymen, namely, "four priests, to wit, one pastor, one archdeacon, two deacons, plus a Saturday preacher, who faithfully and tirelessly performed the work of the Lord in teaching, preaching, and administration of the holy sacraments according to Christ's command and institution" (Wz, p. 7). The "Saturday preachers," as distinguished from the "four priests," were unordained clergymen, who had been additionally appointed since 1569 in St. Thomas and 1606 in St. Nicholas, and whose duty it was to conduct Vespers on Saturdays.[48] All other worship and parish duties were minutely distributed among the ordained clergymen.

At the head of each congregation was the actual "pastor," sometimes also called "pastor and official preacher" (LA 1729, p. 15; LA 1735, p. 25). His chief task, besides that of spiritual leadership of the congregation, was to preach the "official sermon" in the main services on Sundays and festivals and an additional sermon in one of the weekly early services. Since "the superintendent of the local diocese" was always one of those pastors "before whom the country priests had to offer the circuit sermons on the day when the superintendent ordinarily had to preach in the church" (Wz, p. 7), the pastor who held the office of superintendent was often relieved of the second sermon of the week.* To be sure, this applied only to the time between Trinity and Advent, for only during that time did the "country priests" preach the "circulating sermons" (ScNA, p. 581). At the time of

---

*Clergy from the villages and small towns around Leipzig were called to preach, according to a set rota, in the Leipzig churches. Thus when one of these pastors was preaching in St. Nicholas, the superintendent was relieved from the duty.—Ed.

Johann Sebastian Bach, Wednesday was the day for "the weekday sermon of the superintendent or pastor of St. Nicholas," and occasionally he would let "a student preach...when other official duties prevented him" (ScNA, p. 581). At St. Thomas the weekly preaching day of the pastor was Thursday. Thus the weekly sermons of the two chief pastors were preached in those early services that always included the celebration of the Holy Supper.

Now during the entire ministry of Bach at Leipzig the office of chief clergyman at St. Nicholas remained in the hands of one and the same person. The officiating superintendent there was Dr. Salomon Deyling, called by the magistracy of Leipzig to St. Nicholas Church in 1720. He had preached his "initial sermon" on Misericordias Domini Sunday, 27 April 1721,[49] and then served more than 34 years at this church. He died on 5 August 1755, thus surviving Bach by five years. In contrast, five successive pastors were active in the office of chief clergyman at St. Thomas during Bach's time. Dr. Christian Weiß, who had been subdeacon since 1699, deacon since 1708, and archdeacon at St. Nicholas since 1710, served as pastor at St. Thomas for 23 years, from 1714 to his death, 10 December 1736. But after that four clergymen followed each other in the office of pastor at St. Thomas in quick succession. Friedrich Wilhelm Schütz, who had been subdeacon at St. Thomas since 1709 and then subdeacon since 1710, deacon since 1714, and archdeacon at St. Nicholas since 1721, served as pastor at St. Nicholas barely two years, 1737—1739. He died on 27 January 1739. His successor, Urban Gottfried Sieber, likewise served as pastor at St. Thomas for only two years, after having served this church since 1710, first as subdeacon, then as deacon since 1714 and archdeacon since 1730. He had also been professor of theology since 1715. He died on 15 June 1741. He was followed by Gottlieb Gaudlitz, a substitute subdeacon at St. Nicholas since 1726, deacon since 1731, and archdeacon at St. Thomas since 1739. He, too, served as pastor at St. Thomas for only three and one-half years, 1741—1745. Likewise Romanus Teller, pastor at St. Thomas 1745—1750, died already on 5 April 1750. He had been subdeacon since 1737 and deacon since 1739 at St. Thomas, had been transferred to St. Peter in 1740, and had been regular professor of theology since that time, as well as junior judge in the consistory since 1748.

The three clergymen who functioned alongside the two chief clergymen at each main church had to preach only one sermon a week. The archdeacon, next in rank to the pastor, preached his weekly sermon at St. Nicholas on Mondays and at St. Thomas on Tuesdays, always in the customary early service. For that reason these two clergymen of the main churches were listed in the directories of Leipzig also as "archdeacon and Monday preacher" (at St. Nicholas) and "archdeacon and Tuesday preacher" (at St. Thomas) (LA 1723, pp. 78—79; LA 1735, pp. 24—25). At the end of the 18th century the archdeacon of St. Nicholas is designated as "Friday preacher," indicating that in the course of the century a change in the weekly preaching days of the clergy at St. Nicholas took place. At the time of Sicul's report on the worship life in Leipzig, the "Monday preacher" always preached "on the letters to the Corinthians," and regarding the "penitential sermons" on Friday of each week it is reported that "Licentiate Teller delivered them on the prophet Isaiah." Thus one notes that, in contrast to the Sunday and festival services, the respective preacher in the weekday services had free choice to preach "on a book of his preference of the Old or New Testament" (Sc*NA*, pp. 579, 583—84).

The third and fourth clergymen of the two main churches were officially called "deacon" (Wz, p. 7; LA 1723, pp. 78—79), but there was a distinction between the "highest" and the "lowest" deacon (Ro, p. 2). The "highest" deacon at St. Nicholas was also designated as "Friday preacher" (LA 1723, p. 78; LA 1735, p. 24), because he was always to offer the sermon in the early services on Fridays. At the end of the 18th century the third clergyman at St. Nicholas was called "deacon and Monday preacher" (Lh, p. 416). Thus the aforementioned change in the case of the archdeacon at St. Nicholas was an exchange between the second and third clergymen of this church. The "highest" deacon at St. Thomas was called "deacon and Vespers preacher" or "deacon and Sunday Vespers preacher" (LA 1723, p. 79; LA 1735, p. 25), since his chief duty was to preach the sermon in the Vesper services on Sundays and festivals. At St. Nicholas the presentation of the Sunday and festival Vesper sermons was the duty of the subdeacon, whose official title was "deacon and Vespers preacher" or "deacon and Sunday Vespers preacher" (LA 1735, p. 24; LA 1723, p. 78). The subdeacon at St. Thomas was called "deacon and noonday preacher," since he was to conduct the Sunday noon services, which regularly alternated between the two main churches (LA 1723, p. 79; LA 1735, p. 25).

This distribution of sermons among the pastors of the two main churches remained unchanged for generations (cf. *LKA*, pp. 70—71).

To be sure, there was a special preaching order on festivals. Thus in the case of the three high festivals the pastors of the main churches customarily preached in the chief service only on the first two holidays, while on the third holiday of these festivals the archdeacon was given the preaching assignment. That order applied likewise to all extraordinary three-day festivals, as the distribution of sermons for the Reformation anniversary of 1730 indicates (Sc*JL*, pp. 141ff.). The Vesper sermons on the first day of the three-day festivals and also on the thrice-yearly days of penitence and prayer were always preached by the archdeacon, while the noonday sermons at St. Nicholas were preached by the subdeacon of St. Nicholas Church (although on the days of penitence and prayer by the "highest" deacon) and at St. Thomas by the "highest" deacon of St. Thomas Church (cf. Lh, pp. 415—16). The noonday sermons on the third holiday were normally preached by the "Lazareth preacher," and in the Vesper service on third holidays at St. Thomas the preacher was always the subdeacon of that church, who at St. Thomas also preached the "preparatory sermon" customary on the eve of days of penitence and prayer. With respect to the preaching assignment in all other services of the high festivals and also of special festivals of the church year the same order was observed as on ordinary Sundays. The only exceptions were the apostles' days, observed as "half holidays," for in the distribution of sermons in the services on those days precisely the same order was followed as otherwise on the respective weekdays.

Likewise, the various liturgical functions in the services, to the extent these were to be done by the clergy, were distributed among the clergy according to a consistently and precisely observed schedule for all Sunday and festival services as well as for the individual weekdays. All main and Vesper services on Sundays and festivals, as well as all weekday services that included a sermon, were during all of the 18th century in Leipzig always conducted by several clergymen. In the main services of the two main churches two clergymen always officiated in addition to the pastor of the church, who only preached the sermon and made the announcements. One of these served as liturgist at the altar, and the other as lector and as assistant in the distribution of the Lord's Supper. Of course, in keeping with an old tradition, the reading of the Gospel was often done by the priest serving at the altar. Thus we hear in 1694 that the Epistle "was chanted by the deacon at the lectern," but the Gospel "by the priest at the lectern" (*LKA*, pp. 14ff.). For the sake of clarification, the pertinent description in the *Leipziger Kirchen-Staat* may be quoted: "After the collect has been chanted, another priest steps to the lectern and chants the Epistle.... After the hymn the priest at the altar chants the Gospel" (*LKS*, p. 6). Occasionally the readings were offered by the same priest, as is casually reported by Rost (Ro, p. 50), from whom, in fact, we learn a great many details about the services of the liturgist and the distribution of liturgical functions in St. Thomas Church. Thus the liturgist serving at the altar was also called *Administrator* (Ro, pp. 17, 21, 23), because his chief duty was the "supervision" of the Sacrament of the Altar. Furthermore, we learn that on Sundays, after "the candles had been lighted at seven o'clock" and the service had been "opened with the organ," the priests were vested and customarily came out of the sacristy after the singing of the Introit-motet, at the last verse of the Kyrie-eleison, and approached the altar for prayer (Ro, p. 36). This rubric applied to the Reformation anniversary but was very similar for the other Sundays and festivals. The version "after the Kyrie has been sung, at the last verse, the priests go out to the altar to pray" (or a similar one) often recurs (Ro, pp. 26, 36, 44, and elsewhere).

Regarding the division of liturgical functions, it is reported that on the first holiday of the three high festivals of the church year it was customary that "the archdeacon always performed the office," and "the highest deacon, as Vespers preacher, normally presented the chalice" at Communion (Ro, p. 2). In the main services of the second holidays the sequence was then reversed: The "highest" deacon presided as liturgist at the altar, and the archdeacon presented the chalice at Communion (Ro, p. 2). On the third holidays the "noonday preachers always officiated" (Ro, p. 2). Even at the weekday early services it was customary for a number of clergymen to officiate according to a precisely determined order, as the following memorandum shows:

> In the year 1724 the Day of St. James fell on Tuesday, when the one who had officiated on the previous Sunday would go to the altar and intone the Gloria, the Dominus vobiscum, etc. Now since on this day Dr. Carpzow, as archdeacon, was to preach, Licentiate Sieber must chant both Epistle and Gospel. As a rule, however, the clergyman of the week must intone the Gloria, but if the apostle's day falls on Thursday, the one who had officiated on the previous Sunday must intone the Gloria (Ro, p. 50).

Likewise, in the Vesper services that included a sermon several—as a rule two—clergymen officiated. Thus we are told concerning the three Vesper services on the three high festivals of the church year, that on the first holidays besides the preaching archdeacon also the "highest" deacon, on the second holidays besides the preaching "highest" deacon also the subdeacon, and on the third holidays besides the preaching subdeacon also the archdeacon would officiate as liturgists at the altar (cf. Ro, pp. 2, 26—27). Preaching the sermon and officiating at the altar was done by two different clergymen as a matter of principle. This is confirmed by the following description of the Vesper service customary on Good Friday: "After the sermon a motet is sung, such as *Ecce quomodo moritur justus*...and then the hymn 'O Traurigkeit,' during the last verse of which the clergyman of the week, provided he has not preached the sermon, goes to the altar and speaks the Lenten collect and the benediction" (Ro, p. 24). Also elsewhere Rost emphasizes the fact that the rule concerning liturgical functions applied to the respective liturgist only "if he does not preach" (Ro, pp. 26—27).

In this connection we should briefly focus our attention on the official duties of the "clergyman of the week." That title was given to the "deacon who was to supply and maintain the duties of the week, such as baptisms, marriages, blessings, confessional exhortations, and services of prayer" (Lh, p. 413). This week-long tour of duty always began on Sunday, thus including besides the mandatory official acts also the altar duty in all ordinary services and devotions of the week. Likewise, "that deacon who on the previous Sunday began the week's duties" would always conduct the prayer services and penitential exhortations that were liturgically presented, for the most part, from the pulpit (cf. Lh, pp. 413—14, 416—17). The extent of this week-long duty of the clergyman is made clear especially by the fact that "the marriage and baptismal ceremonies were performed only in the two main churches" (LA 1723, p. 80).

When New Church was reopened for worship, it is expressly stated: "It was moreover deliberately determined that, in order to prevent any anticipated disorder in the parishes, baptisms should never be performed in this church and that therefore no baptismal font was installed" (*AG*, p. 25). In both main churches it had become customary to conduct baptismal services not only on Saturdays but also every Sunday and weekday. On weekdays this was always done after the afternoon devotions, at about 3:00, but on Sundays only after conclusion of the Catechism class that would last until about 4:00 (cf. Lh, pp. 413—14, 417). When the number of those "born" in the city in the years 1723—1730 is successively listed as 966, 913, 940, 887, 877, 785, 861, and 798 (Lh, p. 262), and when one considers that the Sacrament of Baptism in those days was often administered immediately after birth or only a few days later, the number of children born would be about the same as that of children baptized. In effect, this means than on the average between 15 and 20 children were to be baptized in the two main churches each week. To be sure, one must remember that these statistics include also the members of the Evangelical-Reformed and the Roman Catholic congregations. However, in those days these congregations were numerically very small, so that the instances possibly to be subtracted would be minimal. Again, it had become customary as time went on "that also in instances occurring in the Lazareth Church and the church of the house of correction, the children born to inmates of both institutions were baptized" (Lh, pp. 411-12). But these cases must have remained quite rare, for only in August 1799 "the pastor of St. James, by agreement with the pastors of St. Thomas, was authorized to baptize all children born in St. James Hospital, while up to this time this was permitted him only in the case of emergency baptisms" (*Bn*, p. 46), and, of course, this applied similarly to the pastor of St. George.

Also the number of weddings to be performed was considerable at that time. Between 1723 and 1730 the number of couples married in successive years was 306, 276, 260, 264, 245, 276, 270, and 341 (Lh, p. 262). Rost distinguishes three different types of weddings, namely, "quarter weddings" as well as "half" and "full bridal masses," and lists also the respective fees for them (Ro, p. 81). However, "full bridal masses," at which there would also be festival *Music* with participation by the St. Thomas choir, town musicians, and professional violinists, were relatively rare. During the whole career of Bach in Leipzig only 31 "full bridal masses" were held at St. Thomas, and a similar number could be estimated also for St. Nicholas.[50] Wedding days were the first days of the week, chiefly Tuesday besides Sunday and Monday. On Sundays the weddings could take place only in late afternoon, after the Catechism classes and baptisms, and then only as "full" or "half bridal masses." It is still reported at the end of the century that "every form of wedding" was held on Mondays, and that on Sundays "every form of wedding" was permissible only when the special festivals of the church were observed the following Mondays and Tuesdays (Lh, p. 417).

Thus while nearly all official acts in the city came into the official purview of the clergy of the two main churches,[51] the clergy of the other churches were entrusted almost exclusively with only the functions of the regular services and devotions in their churches and the pastoral duties related to them. New Church had "two priests, to wit, a head deacon and a subdeacon," of whom "the former preaches early on Sundays and festivals, but the other at Vespers" (Wz, p. 14). For that reason the Leipzig directories call them "head deacon and early preacher" and "deacon and Vespers preacher" (LA 1735, p. 25). The "penitential exhortations on Tuesdays and Vesper sermons on Fridays" were "always offered alternately by the one who had the responsibility for the week" (Wz, p. 14; cf. AG, p. 50). In the main services on Sundays and festivals both of the clergy always officiated, so that the head deacon had the whole liturgy at the altar as well as the sermon, while the subdeacon read the two Scripture lessons and assisted at the distribution of the Lord's Supper (cf. AG, pp. 26ff., especially 29ff.). When the subdeacon was once incapacitated for some time because of illness, the superintendent assigned to the head deacon another clergyman to assist at Communion. In fact, it was called an emergency measure when on two Sundays in 1720 the head deacon had to "administer the most holy Supper alone, from beginning to end" (AG, pp. 70, 73).

The other four churches of the city—St. Peter, St. George, St. John, and St. James—always had only one ordained clergymen. The pastor at St. Peter, later also called "head catechist," who had to preach in this church "each Sunday and festival day at 8:00 in the forenoon on the regular Gospel" (Wz, p. 18), had as his primary duty the conduct of the Catechism instruction on Tuesdays at St. Thomas and on Wednesdays at St. Nicholas, as well as on Mondays and Thursdays at St. Peter, which he had to "attend to himself or through someone from the seminary" (ScNA, p. 580). Most often he attended to the instruction at the two main churches himself and was therefore commonly called "early preacher and catechist at St. Nicholas and St. Thomas Church" (LA 1723, p. 82). But in both, Sunday Vespers and the weekly Catechism classes at St. Peter, he would have a substitute who would be one of the eight unordained theologians assigned to him as assistants by resolution of the city council of 22 February 1713. In return for this, these theologians, called "Vesper preachers, catechists, and candidates for the ministry" in the Leipzig directories (LA 1723, p. 82), received an annual stipend from the city council and were also called on for other substitute services in the city. In one respect, however, St. Peter was at a disadvantage over against the three other secondary churches of the city, for in this church confession and the Sacrament of the Altar were not allowed to be offered. At St. George, St. John, and St. James regular opportunity for confession and the reception of the Sacrament of the Altar was necessary because of the clientele in attendance there, to whom access to the main churches was closed because of sickness, infirmity, and the like. The arrangement made at St. John in 1713, to have the Sunday main services in connection with the Sacrament of the Altar every two weeks, was still in force at the end of the 18th century: "Communion is celebrated on alternate Sundays" (Lh, p. 421). The Communion services that at the beginning of this century took place at "Lazareth Church only every four weeks" (ScNA, p. 572) were later in the course of the 18th century increased in frequency to a two-week cycle—exactly as in the new schedule at St. John. Here, too, the report of 1799 is that "Communion is celebrated every second Sunday" (Lh, p. 422). In contrast, it seems that at St. George "the Holy Supper was adminsistered only every quarter-year" (ScNA, p. 572).

Besides the conduct of these Communion services and minor devotions, the clergy of those three secondary churches had to preach only once a week, in the main services on Sundays. Beyond this, the clergy of these churches needed to perform mostly pastoral duties. Thus Weiz calls the clergyman at St. James an "ordained priest who richly comforts the poor sick people with the only-saving Word" and the clergyman at St. George an "ordained priest who strives to edify richly the poor prisoners and orphans and diligently instructs" them (Wz, pp. 20, 30). Likewise the clergyman at St. John was entrusted especially with the pastoral care of the residents of St. Johns' Hospital.

At St. Paul, the university church that since 1710 was restored for worship services but held a separate status, "an ordained university preacher was appointed" only from Pentecost 1834, and since then he held "a celebration of the Lord's Supper for the students twice a year" (Bn, p. 47). Before this, there were no Communion services in this church. In the main services on Sundays "the professors who could preach and were theologians would by turns" preach their "sermons," and for the function of the Vesper services "several learned tutors were appointed" (Wz, p. 10), as a rule seven to nine clergymen not yet ordained.

The rigid system of the distribution of offices and duties among the clergymen of the city of Leipzig, continued during all of the 18th century, is therefore an obvious fact that by all means must be considered in the description of liturgical life in Leipzig at the time of Johann Sebastian Bach.

g) The Church Music

In this extensive liturgical life of the town, church music, highly regarded in the Lutheran Church since the beginning of its existence, occupied a solid place. Likewise the liturgical office of cantor, for about three centuries almost equal to the office of clergyman, was still of central importance. To be sure, the cantor could not, as had long been the case in the towns of Pomerania, also be the early or Vespers preacher. Nor was a complete university training any longer an indispensable requisite for the administration of the post of town cantor, as in the time of the Reformation, but in many instances the office was still held by academically educated persons. For that matter, many theologians aspiring to the parish ministry in the 16th and 17th centuries had for some time been active as cantors.[52] Georg Philipp Telemann and Christoph Graupner, Bach's two competitors for the office of cantor at St. Thomas in Leipzig, had pursued studies in law at the university. We also know that Johann Kuhnau, Johann Sebastian Bach's predecessor in office at Leipzig, had even, while organist at St. Thomas in Leipzig, continued the study of law he had been pursuing long before and in 1688 had attained the right to be a practicing attorney by presenting his published dissertation, *De Juribus circa musicos Ecclesiasticos*.[53] The broad range of Kuhnau's erudition was well known. When in his annals of 1723 Sicul took note of the deceased Cantor Kuhnau of St. Thomas, he characterized him as "oriented in theology, skilled in oratory, trained in poetry, and more expert in both Eastern and Western languages than one would suppose or expect of him." He also says of him: "In the matter of languages, this is certain, that he daily read the Scriptures, both Old and New Testament, in their original languages, and that he translated and edited various things from French and Italian" (Sc*AL*, pp. 60ff.).

The longstanding custom of presenting proof of a university education for the administration of the post of town cantor is related chiefly to the fact that the cantor was always required to teach a foreign language as a scholarly instructor at the Gymnasium or at least at the Latin School. Thus Johann Sebastian Bach accepted the responsibility of teaching Latin when he began his work at Leipzig. His position was first of all an educational one, for he was cantor of the school of St. Thomas, and the St. Thomas choir was simply a school choir, the choir of St. Thomas School at Leipzig. Since the time of the Reformation the school choir had become responsible for contrapuntal music in worship. Thus also in Leipzig in the 18th century the chief exponent of the performance of church music was still the choir of St. Thomas School. The St. Thomas cantor had full responsibility for the regular programing of church music in the various services in the city churches, which since the beginning of the 18th century included not only the two main churches of St. Nicholas and St. Thomas, but the New Church and St. Peter Church as well. Thus he was responsible for the entire church music life of the city, with exception of the university church, which had a special status. The St. Thomas choir, during the tenure of Johann Sebastian Bach numbering about 55 pupils, had to be divided into four *Kantoreien* on Sundays and festivals, in order to offer liturgical services at the aforementioned four city churches.

Now, of course, the musical competence of these 55 pupils differed widely. Bach himself, in his *Kurtzer, iedoch höchstnöthiger Entwurff einer wohlbestallten Kirchen Music* (Short but most necessary draft for a well-appointed church music) of 23 August 1730, describes as most wretched the singing of the fourth Kantorei which would always perform under the direction of the fourth prefect at St. Peter and on festival days also at St. John and would sing only German hymns. He calls this Kantorei the "remainder, namely those who do not understand music and can only just barely sing a chorale" (cf. *BD* 1:60; *BR*, p. 121). The musical ability of the third Kantorei was somewhat better. Their Sunday role was at the New Church, where besides sharing in the congregational singing they were also to sing motets. The best singers were assembled in the first and in the second Kantoreien. Their regular Sunday role always included the two main churches, where each Kantorei alternated its services from Sunday to Sunday between St. Nicholas and St. Thomas. Numerically, the composition of each of the first three choruses included at most 14 singers.[54]

The best singers of the choir, assembled in the first Kantorei under the leadership of the cantor, were to provide for the musical content of the main services on Sundays and festivals, either at St. Nicholas or at St. Thomas. Here the most important duty of the St. Thomas cantor was to supply the two main churches alternately with the *Music,* that is, the Sunday and festival cantata, for *Music* and *musiciren* in worship services were in those days always understood as the presentation of contrapuntal music accompanied by obligato instruments. Bach confirms this fact in his petition to the city council of Leipzig on 15 August 1736, where concerning the role of the third Kantorei at the New Church he declares that "the students have nothing to sing but motets and chorales, and have nothing to do with other *Concert Musique*" (cf. *BD* 1:87—88; *BR*, p. 140). The cantata, as the most important music in worship, was usually Bach's own original work, specifically composed for the particular Sunday or festival. In the aforementioned writing of 1736 Bach himself describes the assignment to be done by the first Kantorei as follows: "...especially since the concerted church pieces that are performed by the Kantorei, which are mostly of my composition, are incomparably harder and more intricate than those that are sung by the second Kantorei (and this only on feast days), so that I must be chiefly guided, in the choice of the same, by the competence of those who are to perform them" (cf. *BD* 1:88; *BR*, pp. 140-41).

Accordingly, the first Kantorei was to master the musical tasks that were by far the most difficult. The second Kantorei would be charged with more difficult tasks only on special festivals, for we are frequently told in sources other than Bach that then also the second Kantorei would perform [*musizieren*]. In 1717 the function of the first two Kantoreien was described as follows:

> As for high festivals, concerted music is presented by the said cantor in both main churches as follows: The principal music in the forenoon at the church where the superintendent preaches—let us say, St. Nicholas—is supplied by the cantor himself, but in the other church—that is, St. Thomas—by the pupils of St. Thomas; in the afternoon, however, the principal music at St. Thomas is directed by the cantor, while in turn the less important music at St. Nicholas is directed by the prefect of St. Thomas. Then on the second day of the festival the principal music in the early service at St. Thomas and in the afternoon at St. Nicholas are reversed from the previous day (Sc*NA*, pp. 568—69).

The notes of the sexton at St. Thomas indicate unmistakably that such *Music* was heard in both main churches not only on the first two days of the three high festivals of the church year, but besides that also on the following festivals: New Year, the Annunciation of Mary, Ascension, Trinity, St. John's Day, the Visitation of Mary, St. Michael's Day, and the Reformation anniversary. Rost clearly declares that on these special festivals the liturgical order of the main service was observed exactly as that affirmed for high festivals (Ro, pp. 28, 32, 34—35). However, Rost reports also the presentation of the *Music* on the first and second days of the high festivals at St. Thomas in the main service as well as at Vespers, and since this *Music* was omitted on the third day, he systematically notes: "On the third day there is no *Music* in the early service at St. Thomas, thus only at St. Nicholas" (Ro, p. 27). Furthermore, Epiphany and the Purification of Mary are to be added to the special festivals, for from the extant libretto of the cantatas offered in the Christmas season of 1734—1735 we learn that the sixth cantata of the *Christmas Oratorio* was probably offered on Epiphany 1735 at St. Thomas in the morning as well as at St. Nicholas in the afternoon.[55]

That there was *Music* in the Vesper services of these special festivals, something which never happened on ordinary Sundays, is distinctly noted by Rost in his listing of the liturgical peculiarities of Trinity, St. John's Day, the Visitation of Mary, and St. Michael's Day (Ro, pp. 32, 34—35). Also the comment concerning New Year's Day: "At Vespers: There is no prayer service at the lectern," as well as a very similar note made for the Visitation of Mary: "Since this is a festival, there is no prayer service at the lectern at Vespers in the afternoon" (Ro, pp. 3, 15), unmistakably refer to the *Music* usual in the Vesper service on these days, since the "prayer service" at the beginning of the Vesper service was always omitted only when the *Music* took place. This is clearly formulated in the *Leipziger Kirchen-Andachten*: "On high festivals no prayer services are held, but *Music* is presented" (*LKA*, p. 45; cf. also *LKS*, p. 18).

At the same time, however, with regard to the presentation of the *Music*, the cycle of special festivals of the church year seems not to have been rigidly limited. Concerning the First Sunday in Advent 1730 we are told—Rost notes this, since it was evidently exceptional—that the second Kantorei also presented the *Music* in connection with the reading of the Gospel: "In 1730, First Advent, the second Kantorei was here at St. Thomas. The 'Credo' was intoned, but the 'Patrem' was not sung, but there was *Music* such as the second Kantorei sings, and then the creed" (Ro, p. 45).* The same thing had happened during Kuhnau's cantorate in 1720, and then, too, Rost noted it as unusual (Ro, p. 44). How often such *Music* on the First Sunday in Advent was offered by the second Kantorei in the following years, and whether the second Kantorei appeared for the *Music* also on certain other Sundays, cannot be determined. Most likely the appearance of the second Kantorei for the *Music* would apply only on the festival days mentioned, and even that *Music* on the First Sunday in Advent 1730 would have been an exception at the time of Bach, otherwise Rost would surely have made further comments. In any case, it is noteworthy that the following later entry in the notebooks of the sexton at St. Thomas assumes the presentation of a cantata in only one of the two main churches: "In 1784 it was decided by the superintendent that on the First Sunday in Advent the Litany should be omitted in the church where the *Music* is presented, and this happened for the first time at St. Thomas in this year" (Ro, p. 43).

When one considers that the supply of good instrumentalists was not available to a satisfactory extent even for the first Kantorei, as Bach's *Kurt-*

---

* The liturgist intoned the Latin "Credo in unum Deum"—which is employed by Bach at the beginning of the *Symbolum Nicenum* of the *Mass in B Minor* (BWV 232)—but the continuation, "Patrem omnipotentem" (*LGB* 1682, No. 173), was not sung. Instead the Kantorei performed a cantata, which was followed by the singing of the *Glaube*, that is, Luther's creedal hymn "Wir glauben all an einen Gott" (*LGB* 1682, No. 174).

zer, iedoch höchstnöthiger Entwurff einer wohlbestallten Kirchen Music
clearly states, it would not have been within the range of possibility for the
second Kantorei to present the *Music* frequently already because of the lack
of qualified instrumentalists. In 1730 Bach describes the situation: "The
number of persons engaged for church music is eight, namely, four town
pipers [*Stadt Pfeifer*], three professional violinists [Kunst Geiger], and one
apprentice. Modesty forbids me to speak at all truthfully of their qualities
and musical knowledge. Nevertheless it must be remembered that they are
partly *emeriti* and partly not at all in such *exercitio* as they should be."
Then, after listing these musicians by name, Bach continues: "Thus there
are lacking the following most necessary players, partly to reinforce certain
voices, and partly to supply indispensable ones, namely: two violinists for
first violin, two violinists for second violin, two to play viola, two
violoncellists, one violonist, two for the flutes (cf. *BD* 1:61—62; *BR*, pp.
121—22). However, despite this shortage of instrumentalists, which "has
had to be supplied hitherto partly by the *studiosi* [of the university] but
mostly by the *alumni* [of the St. Thomas School]," Bach was evidently
obligated to distribute all available instrumentalists in such a way that on
festival days it was possible to perform concerted music in both main
churches in the forenoon as well as in the afternoon, for he continues his
report: "Thus far only the Sunday music has been touched upon. But if I
should mention the music of the holy days (on which days I must supply
both the principal churches with music), the deficiency of indispensable
players will show even more clearly, particularly since I must give up to the
other Kantorei all those pupils who play one instrument or another and
must get along altogether without their support" (cf. *BD* 1:62; *BR*, p. 122).
For decades the procurement of competent instrumentalists for the performance of church music remained a difficult problem for the cantor at St.
Thomas, as is attested by the change in the practice of church music introduced by Doles, Bach's second successor in the office, according to
which the second Kantorei was relieved of its responsibility to perform
regularly on festival days. In the notebook of the sexton at St. Thomas we
read: "In the year 17[   ] the duplicate church music hitherto customary
on high festivals and other feasts at St. Thomas and St. Nicholas was
abolished. Before this there was music in both churches on the first and second days of Easter, Pentecost, and Christmas, and likewise on every other
festival day. However, upon a presentation of Cantor Doles...the wor-
shipful consistory resolved to abolish the music of the second Kantorei."
This was done because of a lack of instrumentalists (Ro, p. 154; the exact
year was evidently not available to the writer of those lines, and he left a little space for an intended but never supplied later entry.)

We do not know which compositions the second Kantorei in Bach's
time would sing and play on festivals and also on the individual ordinary

Sundays. In 1710 it is said of the service of the first two Kantoreien inserted after the reading of the Gospel: "Then there either follows concerted music, or a hymn in keeping with the Gospel...is sung" (*LKS*, p. 6). The report of 1717 is more explicit: "...in the two main churches, where both concerted and chorale music depend on direction of the cantor of St. Thomas, there is on ordinary Sundays alternately counterpoint music in the one church, while in the other only German hymns are sung and the organ is played" (Sc*NA*, p. 568). Thus the ordinary Sunday function of the second chorus seems to have involved simple part-singing of those hymns that were appointed for each Sunday in addition to the hymn of the day and for which one could find four- to six-voice arrangements in the *Neu Leipziger Gesangbuch* of 1682, so that the second Kantorei had a broad selection at its disposal for its services. The directions for worship we have for the Reformation anniversary of 1730 support the fact that at Bach's time the second Kantorei usually did sing such hymns. According to these directions, either "the *Music* or 'Wo Gott der Herr nicht bei uns hält' " was offered after the reading of the Gospel at the place ordinarily held by *Music* in both main churches on the third day of the anniversary, which like all third days of the high festivals conformed in its liturgical and musical structure to the ordinary Sunday worship services (Sc*JL*, p. 121). Here *Music* must be understood to mean the cantata *Wünschet Jerusalem Glück* that was presented by the first Kantorei in St. Nicholas (cf. Sc*JL*, pp. 133ff.), for which we have only the text [cf. N*VT*, p. 334], and the additional reference to "Wo Gott der Herr nicht bei uns hält" means the part-singing of that familiar hymn by the second Kantorei, which functioned at St. Thomas on that day. But even the contrapuntal music with instrumental accompaniment performed by the second Kantorei on festival days was in Bach's own words substantially simpler and easier in its whole musical composition and construction than the cantata presented by the first Kantorei, so that it can be firmly concluded that the second Kantorei did not present any cantatas by Johann Sebastian Bach. This conclusion is supported also by the fact that the librettos we have for the Sunday and festival cantatas in the two main churches always include only the text of cantatas presented by the first Kantorei, and that these were always compositions by Johann Sebastian Bach.[56]

In these librettos, which always offered in booklet form the cantata texts for several Sundays and festivals, the custom of combining a sizable number of Sunday cantata texts in a booklet for the congregation to follow was maintained after Kuhnau's cantorate throughout the 18th century, and the place of performance, either St. Nicholas or St. Thomas, is always indicated. These printed texts also show that on festivals the cantata presented in one of the two churches was then sung in the other church at Vespers on the same day. The fact that we have no printed texts of the compositions presented by the second Kantorei on festivals and that evidently none were prepared—otherwise each of the main churches would doubtless have issued its own printed texts—leads to the conclusion that the text of these compositions must have been comprehensible by itself and that they were substantially shorter in performance time than the works presented by the first Kantorei.

Without a doubt, then, only the first Kantorei, under the direction of the St. Thomas cantor, executed the cantata of major dimension that it was Johann Sebastian Bach's task to compose and present. In his outline of the liturgy for the main service on the First Sunday in Advent Bach himself called the presentation of the cantata the "Chief Music" [Hauptmusic] of the Sunday.[57] Except for the time between the Second and Fourth Sundays in Advent, the Sundays in Lent, the special days of penitence and prayer, and general seasons of mourning, as well as the apostles' days falling on a weekday, the cantata had its established liturgical place between the reading of the Gospel and the creedal hymn ("Wir glauben all an einen Gott") in all the main services on Sundays and festivals, where the provision of music was the responsibility of the first Kantorei. The organist introduced the presentation of the cantata with a free improvisation on the organ. According to the time schedules in Lorenz Mizler's Musikalische Bibliothek (IV, 5, 108) the cantata was to last no longer than 35 minutes in summer and 25 minutes in winter. For the introductory improvisation, Bach wrote himself a memo: "Prelude to the main music."

Not infrequently the cantata was constructed in two parts, of which the second was presented after the "pulpit service" [Kanzeldienst] of the preacher and was often simply marked "after the Sermon." To be sure, only a little more than 10 percent of the church cantatas of Bach are officially known as works in two sections, but there is urgent need to investigate whether a substantially larger number of the cantatas not considered to be works in two sections were not actually presented in two parts. From the point of view of content, a large number of the cantatas can surely be divided into two, occasionally even more, sections. In this connection it must be considered highly important that on all three festival days of the Reformation anniversary of 1730 Bach presented cantatas in two sections, of which the second section was always presented "after the Sermon" (cf. ScJL, pp. 130ff.). This fact deserves special attention also because the original versions of these reworked cantatas—namely BWV 190, BWV 120, and BWV Appendix 4— do not outwardly appear as works in two sections (cf. NVT, pp. 39—40, 172.). Furthermore, it is really remarkable that in the first weeks of his work at Leipzig Bach presented almost exclusively cantatas in two sections, and this on ordinary Sundays, too. Indeed, even the presentation of two cantatas in the same service is probably demonstrable.[58] Again, the planned division of the cantatas offered on the Reformation anniversary of 1730 shows that not infrequently only two or three movements would be offered in the first part of the cantata and that this first section could often be concluded with an aria and thus not necessarily with a chorale or a movement by a participating choir. Similar standards for a break in the ordinary Sunday cantatas for which we have no authorized division could therefore very well have existed and been applied. And since Werner Neumann in his reprint of the librettos for those three festival cantatas does not identify them as works in two sections, this authorized division is herewith offered (cf. Sc*JL*, pp. 130ff.): The first part of the cantata *Singet dem Herrn ein neues Lied*, presented at St. Nicholas on the first festival day, included movements 1—3 (chorus, recitative, aria), the second part, movements 4—7 (recitative, aria, recitative, chorale); the first part of the cantata *Gott, man lobet dich in der Stille,* sung at St. Thomas on the second festival day, included only two movements (chorus, aria), but the second part four movements (recitative, aria, recitative, chorale); and likewise in the cantata designated for the third festival day at St. Nicholas, *Wünschet Jerusalem Glück*, the first part included only two movements (chorus, aria), but again the second part four movements (recitative, aria, recitative, chorale).

The music "after the Sermon" did not follow immediately upon the Sermon, but after the close of the whole pulpit service. This is evident from the outline for the liturgy of the main service in the *Leipziger Kirchen-Staat*. There item 14 lists details about the Sermon (*LKS*, p. 7), then follows item 15 with many instructions about the official announcements immediately after the Sermon (*LKS*, pp. 7ff.), and only then item 16 says, shortly after a reference to the prayer "when the priest leaves the pulpit": "After the Sermon a hymn is sung, or several stanzas of a hymn appropriate to the Gospel; one may also, when there is *Music*, meditate on the prayers found on page 103" (*LKS*, p. 10), whereupon items 17—20 list details for the Communion liturgy and the close of the worship (*LKS*, pp. 10—11). This *Music* after the conclusion of the pulpit service and before the beginning of the Communion liturgy was therefore customary in Leipzig long before Bach began his work there. We are also told about Johann Kuhnau, perhaps regarding the main service on the first day of Christmas 1721, in connection with the dedication of the newly built altar in St. Thomas Church: "After the Sermon...(he) presented beautiful music" (Sc*LJG*, p. 176). It was an old tradition that on apostles' days "after the Sermon one of the motets" always be sung (*LKA*, p. 86; cf. also *LKS*, pp. 44; Ro, p. 49). The same custom is reported also for Palm Sunday (*LKA*, p. 60). It is furthermore known that on special occasions the Te Deum laudamus was presented "with special music" at this point in the main service, and thus, perhaps, on every Reformation Day (*LKA*, p. 105; *LKS*, p. 30; Ro, p. 37). The same custom is still reported for St. Michael's Day in

1752, although then "there was thanksgiving for the happy confinement of the electoral princess" and "the Te Deum was sung with trumpet and drums" (Ro, p. 111). *Leipziger Kirchen-Andachten* even speaks of additional *Music* at this point in the service on the anniversary of the Reformation: "The Te Deum laudamus was sung, together with organ and trumpets. This concluded, there is more music, and after the music the singing of 'Nun danket alle Gott' " (*LKA*, p. 105).

However, we must take into account that selected parts of cantatas were also used as music for the Sacrament on certain Sundays and festivals. While it cannot be shown to what extent the first and second Kantoreien would sing motets and even present contrapuntal instrumental music during the Distribution, there was always special music for the Sacrament at Communion on Sundays in both churches. On ordinary Sundays this would mean only certain motets, but on festival days there would also be *Music*, and on certain festivals this meant the same composition each year, as for example on Maundy Thursday, when at the beginning of the Communion "the Latin motet *Jesus Christus Dominus noster*" was always sung (*LKS*, p. 24). Twice *Leipziger Kirchen-Andachten* emphasizes with regard to the musical structure of the sacramental office: "At Communion there is, first *Music* or a motet, then hymns are sung" (*LKA*, Index) and "At Communion (before the German hymns begin) a cantata [*ein Stück musiciret*] or a motet is sung" (*LKA*, p. 36). Also Sicul refers to the custom that on festivals "a concerto or motet is performed" during Communion (ScNA, p. 571). Bach himself indicates by his outline of the liturgy on the First Sunday in Advent, that on this Sunday, not really a festival, there was concerted music with instruments during Communion. Following the words *Verba Institutionis* at item 13, he notes at item 14: "Prelude to the *Music*, and after that alternately prelude and the singing of chorales until the Communion is ended, and so forth."[59]

It cannot be established that this *Music* referred to part two of the cantata, as Wilibald Gurlitt suggests in his study *Johann Sebastian Bach—The Master and His Work* (St. Louis, 1957, p. 111). Cantata BWV 61, which was composed in Weimar and performed again at Leipzig in 1723[60] and on the cover of which Bach wrote the order of service, is considered a one-part cantata and because of its performance time of only 17—18 minutes is remarkably brief, so that purely for reasons of time its presentation in two sections does not seem to be required but even rather unlikely. At the same time it cannot be denied that the cantata permits an easy division into two sections, and that especially the second section of the cantata, including movements 4—6, indicates clearly a relationship to the Sacrament of the Altar. This relationship is indicated already at the end of the third movement in the words "Preserve sound doctrine and bless pulpit and altar." Then the following recitative (movement 4) expressly mentions the Holy

Supper as it sets to music the Bible passage: "Behold, I stand at the door and knock. If any man hear my voice and open the door, I will come in to him, and will sup with him, and he with me" (Rev. 3:20). Likewise the fifth movement of the cantata, "Open full and wide, my heart, Jesus comes to enter in," contains a clear reference to the Sacrament of the Altar, for the entrance of Christ into the human heart can in the light of the preceding passage be understood only sacramentally. Also the return of Christ, proclaimed and anticipated in the closing passage, is most meaningfully related to the preceding text of the cantata, since also in the time of Lutheran orthodoxy, as in the early church, the Holy Supper was thought to be a foretaste of eternal salvation.[61] Besides, the last stanza of Philipp Nicolai's hymn "Wie schön leuchtet der Morgenstern," used in this closing movement, is taken from a piece of hymnody that in several stanzas clearly alludes to the Holy Supper and therefore—as in *Leipziger Kirchen-Andachten* of 1694 and in *Hoch-Fürstliches Sachsen-Weißenfelsisches Vollständiges Gesang- und Kirchenbuch* of 1714—served as hymn of the day for the 20th Sunday After Trinity, which annually took note of the Sacrament of the Altar in a special manner through the Gospel reading with its parable of the royal wedding feast (Matt. 22:1-14) and the sermon on that text. This hymn had its established place in the service on the 20th Sunday After Trinity also in the hymnbooks published in Leipzig and Dresden in the 18th century, and Bach, too, used it relatively often in his cantatas. Stanzas of this hymn appear not only in Cantata BWV 61, but also in Cantatas BWV 36, 37, 49, and 172. Besides, Cantata BWV 1 is entirely based on this hymn.

In this connection we must note also the truly striking fact that in his cantatas Bach not infrequently used stanzas of hymns that at that time were regarded as Communion hymns. Cantatas BWV 64, 70, 81, 124, 147, 154, 157, and 180 contain such stanzas from Communion hymns. Cantata BWV 180 is in some old listings, e.g., already by Breitkopf in 1761,[62] even "called simply Communion Cantata." The only reasonable explanation for this is that this cantata, originally composed as music for the Sermon and first heard on the 20th Sunday After Trinity, 22 October 1724,[63] was heard during the Distribution of the Holy Supper again and again in subsequent years, so that its accepted name, Communion Cantata, had not disappeared even after Bach's death. Besides, one must take seriously the possibility that also apart from this, Bach used certain parts of cantatas or individual movements from cantatas as music for Communion, even when these were originally intended as music for the Sermon and were thus performed after the Gospel or "after the Sermon." In any case, it is remarkable that besides the cantatas mentioned, which in their choice of hymn give attention to Communion hymns, a great number of other cantatas refer to the Holy Supper in their textual layout. The following Bach cantatas contain such distinct references and allusions to the Sacrament of the Altar:[64] BWV 1 (3, 4), 3 (2), 4 (5—7), 5 (2—6), 6 (3), 7 (1, 4, 8), 12 (3), 21 (8), 27 (1), 32 (6), 46 (6), 49 (entire cantata), 58 (5), 74 (7), 75 (3), 76 (2, 10), 78 (4, 5), 80 (2— 4, 6), 84 (4, 5), 89 (4—6), 92 (2), 101 (6), 105 (4), 112 (4), 113 (4—8), 120 (6), 123 (2), 129 (2), 131 (2—4), 132 (5), 134 (3—6), 136 (4—6), 140 (entire cantata), 145 (4), 147 (4—10), 149 (2), 151 (3), 154 (3—8), 158 (1), 162 (2—6), 165 (2—6), 166 (6), 168 (4—6), 172 (2—6), 174 (4), 180 (entire cantata), 182 (3—6), 190 (5), and 199 (6—8). One could substantially increase the list of movements of Bach cantatas appropriate as music for the Sacrament if one recalls that it was customary during Communion in Leipzig to supplement explicit Communion hymns especially with hymns of penitence (*LKA*, p. 4), and that Bach loved to use hymns of penitence in his cantatas. The established core of hymns sung in Leipzig during Communion included, besides the intrinsically penitential and Communion hymns, also selections such as "Es wolle Gott uns gnädig sein," "Nun lob, mein Seel, den Herren," and "Der Herr ist mein getreuer Hirt." These were frequently listed as Communion hymns (cf. *LKA*, p. 38; *LKS*, p. 10) and also occur frequently in Bach's cantatas.

Even if these sections of cantatas that either related to the Sacrament of the Altar or directly referred to it were originally not performed during Communion, this does not preclude that such cantatas or movements of cantatas appropriate as music for the Sacrament were occasionally offered during Communion at a later time, especially on festivals. Already Arnold Schering seriously considered the possibility that Bach reutilized certain movements of his cantatas as music for the Sacrament.[65] Likewise Philipp Spitta thinks that the individual movements of Bach's *Mass in B Minor* were surely performed "during Communion,"[66] and Friedrich Smend is inclined to agree, at least for the movements from "Osanna" to "Dona nobis pacem."[67] One must also consider a comment of Spitta to the effect that a supportive notation of Bach's at the second section of a continuo score for Cantata BWV 194 indicates the presentation of this second section during Communion.[68]

At any rate, music for the Sacrament still was of no mean importance in the Leipzig worship services during all of the 18th century, even though there are only very meager authentic directions and indications for such use in individual cases. From the notes of the sexton at St. Thomas we learn in passing that, perhaps on Palm Sunday, a motet was sung and the organ was played (Ro, p. 17), and that was unusual in liturgical practice and needed to be mentioned, because organ music and the performance of contrapuntal music was otherwise not customary during Lent. A later entry in the notes of the sexton at St. Thomas, dating from the second half of the 18th century, distinctly emphasizes concerning the liturgy for Holy Communion on the Reformation anniversary: "At Communion there is no *Music*, but the hymns selected by the officiating preacher are sung" (Ro, p. 37). That calls attention to an unusual feature of just this festival, since music for the Sacrament was otherwise self-evident on all special festivals of the church year. The omission of music for the Sacrament on the Reformation anniversary, however, is evidently to be traced to the fact that in the main service of that festival there was not only the usual cantata, but after the pulpit service of the preacher "the Te Deum laudamus was performed with trumpets and drums" and already at the beginning of the service "the Kyrie was performed" in addition to the usual Introit motet" (LKS, pp. 29—30; cf. also LKA, pp. 104—05; Ro, p. 37). Besides, the Reformation anniversary was never considered fully equal to the other festivals of the church year despite its increasing significance in the 18th century.

Also in the second half of the 18th century music during Communion remained customary in the main services in Leipzig on specified festivals. In 1766 the practice was begun to perform oratorio Passion music, heard only at Vespers on Good Friday up to that time, in the main services of Palm Sunday at the one main church and on Good Friday at the other, and then the second section was always presented during Communion (cf. Ro, pp. 18— 22). Even during the tenure of Hiller as cantor at St. Thomas (1789—1800), during which the advance of the Enlightenment into the worship life at Leipzig took place most decisively, there was still music during Communion. Schering referred to an original libretto of the works presented in the services on the festival of the Presentation of Mary, 2 July 1789, among which were two compositions performed "during Communion." In fact, he reports concerning Hiller: "He especially loved the music for the Communion. It took on a new significance since at this place he called for the singing of arias and duets by the best German and Italian masters of the *bel canto*."[69] Such music for the Sacrament was then still possible because Hiller, too, could relate to a living tradition.

There can be no doubt, therefore, that it was one of Johann Sebastian Bach's regular responsibilities that, besides the Sunday and festival cantata as the "chief music" for the respective day, he was also to select and prepare the music for the Sacrament, presented at the beginning of Communion. This circumstance is not altered by the fact that Bach himself, like his predecessors in office, occasionally left the church and turned the direction of the motet over to the prefect.[70] It seems one can safely assume that in the selection of this music Bach not infrequently gave consideration not only to the well-known motets but also to movements of his own taken from his cantatas. Noteworthy in this connection is the "Cantata at Communion" included in the third section of poems by Picander of 1732, where the text, composed of three arias and two interspersed recitatives, clearly shows that with regard to the whole formal arrangement of the textual and musical structure of the music for the Sacrament there was no basic difference from the cantatas created for the expository part of the service.

On festivals it was furthermore customary that in the especially festive Communion liturgy designed for such days the choir should perform the Sanctus. The sexton of St. Thomas affirms this for the first day of Easter (Ro, p. 26). His notes also show that that practice was observed on all first and second holidays of the three great festivals of the church year as well as on all special festivals of the church year that were placed on the same level with these high festivals. We have also this directive for exceptions: "If on a festival the Te Deum laudamus is sung, the Preface is omitted" (Ro, p. 2). Because this directive for exceptions was once waived for a special reason, the notation was made: "In the year 1752, the 29th of September, on the festival of St. Michael, there was thanksgiving for the happy confinement of the electoral princess, the Te Deum was sung with trumpets and drums, immediately followed by high mass, and the Sanctus was performed [*musiciret*]" (Ro, p. 111). The term "high mass" means the parts of the Latin Preface sung antiphonally only on festival days by the liturgist and the choir, ending in the Sanctus. The revision of the church music done under Doles, Bach's second successor in office, according to which the *Music* to be presented by the second Kantorei on festival days was dropped, still maintains the "Sanctus in counterpoint" by the second Kantorei on festivals (cf. Ro, p. 154). From Johann Sebastian Bach we have not only the great Sanctus of the *Mass in B Minor*, but five others as well, substantially smaller Sanctus compositions for performance on festivals that were either composed or at least arranged by Bach (cf. BWV 237—241).

In addition to the music in the sacramental part of the service and the cantatas and motets offered in connection with the Gospel reading and the Sermon, the function of the choir always included the singing of the Introit following the organ prelude at the beginning of the service. This Introit was usually executed "in counterpoint" [*figuraliter*], in the form of a polyphonic motet. We know that these motets were "taken mostly from the *Florilegium* of Bodenschatz" (*LKA*, p. 9), referring to the *Florilegium Portense*, a motet collection of Cantor Erhard Bodenschatz at Schulpforta, used chiefly in northern and central Germany until well into the 18th century. This rather extensive collection included motets for four or more voices by numerous German and Italian masters and "in its principal contents had a hundred years' tradition in the choir of St. Thomas."[71] The fact that Bach ordered a new copy as late as 1729 confirms the use of this collection of motets in the worship services at Leipzig until well into the 18th century.[72] The Introit motets customary for all the Sundays and festivals are listed in part two of the *Leipziger Kirchen-Andachten* (*LKA*, pp. 235ff.). Only "during Lent and at times of public mourning, when there was no contrapuntal music," one "began with the Benedictus, or 'Canticum Zachariae,' and 'Vivo Ego,' etc., whereupon an Introit, etc., was sung"

(*LKA*, p. 9; cf. also pp. 58—59). Also these canticles and Introit psalms, sung in Gregorian style, were fixed for all the Sundays of Lent. Thus, for example, we are told that the main services on Palm Sunday as well as on Maundy Thursday and Good Friday always began "with the antiphon 'Pueri Hebraeorum' " and the Introit psalm "Humiliavit semet ipsum" (cf. *LKS*, pp. 23, 25, 35; *LKA*, pp. 59ff.). On the three high festivals and several other festival days of the church year the main service "began with a Hymn" (*LKA*, p. 9) instead of the Introit motet. These "Hymns"* referred to the Latin hymns taken over from the medieval church. In most hymnbook publications in Leipzig in the 18th century they appear under "festival hymns" [*Fest-Lieder*], and the Latin text for them was for the most part printed in such a way that the German translation would appear alongside or beneath the individual stanzas or even following the entire hymn. Each year the following Hymns were sung at the beginning of the main morning service as also of the Vesper service: "Puer natus in Bethlehem" on the third day of Christmas and on New Year's Day and Epiphany, "Ex legis observantia" on the Day of the Purification of Mary, "Heut triumphieret Gottes Sohn" on the third day of Easter and on Ascension Day, "Spiritus Sancti gratia" on the third day of Pentecost and on the Trinity festival (cf. *LKA*, pp. 53ff., 63ff.; *LKS*, pp. 16, 18, 20ff., 26—27; Ro, pp. 28, 30, 32, 47). Concerning the festivals of St. John, the Visitation of Mary, and St. Michael it is specified that always on these days "as on Sundays the beginning was made with a prelude on the organ and then a motet was sung" (*LKA*, p. 67). It is distinctly stated that on festival days the Hymns were sung in place of the motets (not in addition to them!): "Instead of the Introit a Hymn is sung..." (*LKA*, pp. 281, 293). Also Rost supports this, for the outline of the liturgy on the first day of Christmas says that immediately following the Hymn sung at the beginning of the service the organ played the prelude to the Kyrie (Ro, p. 47). It was one of the functions of the choir to sing these Hymns in four-part settings as contained in the *Neu Leipziger Gesangbuch* of 1682 and the *Florilegium Hymnorum* of Erhard Bodenschatz. The fact that this so-called little *Florilegium* of Erhard Bodenschatz, containing the Hymns of the ancient church in the arrangement by Calvisius, was newly ordered in multiple copies for St. Nicholas and St. Thomas in 1736 and 1737[73] indicates that the Kantoreien of Bach's time would sing the Hymns according to this choir edition. That this rendition was done exclusively by the choir is to be concluded from the fact that the Hymns were sung in place of the otherwise customary motet. Evidently the congregation never joined in the singing of

---

*To distinguish these Latin hymns from those in the vernacular, the term "Hymn" is given with capitalization.—Ed.

any Latin hymns and liturgical songs. Rost likewise confirms the singing of the Hymn by the choir when, for example, he writes concerning the services on the holidays of Pentecost: "...at seven o'clock the beginning is made with the Hymn 'Spiritus S. gratia' by the choir" (Ro, p. 30). Besides, we know that in all those festival services the German version of the Latin Hymn was once again sung by the congregation at the end of the service. Thus we read concerning the Hymn at Christmas: "On this festival the service on all three days (as also on New Year's Day and that of the Holy Three Kings), in both forenoon and afternoon, is begun with the Latin Hymn 'Puer natus in Bethlehem' and closed with the German 'Ein Kind geborn zu Bethlehem' " (*LKA*, p. 53). The singing of these Hymns was maintained in Leipzig into the second half of the 18th century. We are told that the Hymn "Puer natus in Bethlehem" was sung for the last time in the services on the first and second Christmas days of 1774 and on New Year's Day and Epiphany of 1775 and then was dropped "because of some offensive remarks" and "upon expressed wishes" (Ro, p. 138), after the singing of the Hymn was no longer customary on the third day of the high festivals.

Furthermore, it was an old tradition that the Kyrie and the Gloria in the opening part of the main service were "performed in concerted settings" on certain Sundays and festivals (cf. *LKA*, Index and pp. 11—12; *LKS*, pp. 5—6; Sc*NA*, p. 569). Spitta's conjecture, that such performance of these liturgical pieces took place "during the church's seasons of mourning" (Advent, Passiontide, days of penitence)[74] is totally unfounded and most improbable. The presentation of contrapuntal music contradicted the serious nature of such days in the church year and therefore was on principle not done, at least not in the worship services in Leipzig at that time. What has been said concerning the musical form of the Introit during Lent, namely, that it was sung in simple Gregorian form, applies likewise to all other choral offerings in the seasons to be observed under the sign of penitence (cf. comments on pp. 58—63, 86). Of informative value is also the observation that the *Neu Leipziger Gesangbuch* of 1682 offers only the monophonic Gregorian setting for the well-known penitential Hymn "Aufer a nobis Domine" (cf. *LGB* 1682, pp. 511—12). It should rather be considered quite probable that above all on the festivals of the church year and also on special festive occasions that kind of performance of the Kyrie and Gloria would take place besides any other church music already customary. Thus we are told that in the festival service held in the New Church on the 16th Sunday After Trinity, 24 September 1699, on the occasion of that church's rededication for worship purposes, the St. Thomas cantor, Schelle, ordered the Kyrie and Gloria to be performed in addition to the Introit motet and special *Music* after the Gospel reading (*AG*, pp. 29—30). We know of the time of Bach's tenure in Leipzig that in the main services on the first two holidays of the Reformation anniversary in 1730 the "Kyrie was performed [*musicirt*] in Latin" (Sc*JL*, pp. 117, 119), and this custom is affirmed in general for the annual Reformation anniversary (cf. remarks on p. 84). The note in Bach's own hand for the liturgy in the main service on the First Sunday in Advent, "Play the prelude to the Kyrie, which is performed in its entirety," clearly shows that such performance of the Kyrie and Gloria extended beyond the actual festivals of the church year. The expression "performed in its entirety" evidently refers to the following Gloria, for there was no partial performance of that liturgical piece, but since the time of the Reformation the Kyrie and Gloria were so closely connected that in the Lutheran orders of service one often finds the complete text of the Gloria printed under the heading "Kyrie."[75]

To be sure, the practice still in regular use at the turn of the century, that immediately following the intonation "Gloria in excelsis Deo," "alternately in the one church the choir continued in Latin but in the other church the German 'Allein Gott in der Höh' was sung" (LKA, Index), had greatly declined since the beginning of the 18th century. The *Leipziger Kirchen Staat* still reports concerning the form of the Gloria that after the usual intonation by the liturgist at the altar "the choir continues either in German with the hymn 'Allein Gott in der Höh sei Ehr' ... or in Latin with musical accompaniment 'Et in terra pax' " (*LKS*, pp. 5—6). However, already this report fails to show clearly whether or not the polyphonic performance of this liturgical piece was the practice for the first Kantorei every Sunday. The German would naturally be sung by the second Kantorei. At that time such performance of the Gloria was declining, as is evident from the report of Sicul in 1717: After the liturgist "intoned the 'Gloria in excelsis Deo,' the hymn 'Allein Gott in der Höh sei Ehr,' etc., is sung, and sometimes the choir responds with the Latin 'Et in terra pax' " (Sc*NA*, p. 569). This "sometimes" clearly indicates that meanwhile it had become common practice to perform the Gloria with concerted music only on festival and special occasions. The notes of the sexton at St. Thomas lead one to conclude that on the first two days of the three high festivals, as well as on all other festivals of the church year, the Gloria was performed polyphonically. Rost says nothing about the musical execution of the Kyrie and Gloria. However, in his notes for the liturgy on the first day of Easter—as for the second Easter day, Rost explicitly refers to the practice he describes on the first day of Easter—he mentions only the singing of "Et in terra pax," but not that of the Gloria hymn. Furthermore, on the Sundays in Lent, including Maundy Thursday and Good Friday, as well as on the apostle's days, the "Et in terra pax" as well as the Gloria hymn "Allein Gott in der Höh sei Ehr" would be sung. Both of these facts demand the conclusion that in the light of the curtailment of all contrapuntal music during Lent the "Et in terra pax" was offered only "in monophonic form" [*choraliter*] and thus made possible the additional singing of the Gloria hymn, while on festival days the concerted form of the "Et in terra pax" in "counterpoint" [*figuraliter*] made the singing of the Gloria hymn groundless and unnecessary (cf. Ro, pp. 10, 15, —23, 26ff., 30, 34—35, 43—44, 47, 49). Confirmation of the situation here described is found in a two-fold notation in Rost for the liturgy in the main service on the First Sunday in Advent. The first applies to instances where the second Kantorei supplied the choral service at St. Thomas. Then only the Gloria hymn would follow the intonation of the Gloria. However, when the first Kantorei ministered in St. Thomas, then "Et in terra pax" was sung after the Gloria intonation, but not the Gloria hymn (Ro, p. 44). Here, too, only the concerted form of the Gloria can be meant. Compare this with Bach's own notes on the liturgy for that Sunday. Of informative value is also the note for the festival of the Annunciation of Mary, which always falls in Lent, to the effect that upon the intonation of the Gloria only the "Et in terra pax" followed (Ro, p. 15), but not the Gloria hymn, which was otherwise customary in Lent. Here, too, as on all festivals, only the polyphonic concerted form can be meant, for it is unthinkable that on festivals the structure of the Gloria should be less colorful than on ordinary Sundays in Lent.

Thus at the time of Johann Sebastian Bach the practical feasibility for presenting contrapuntal music in the Lutheran main service was still quite extensive. Precisely because Bach himself not only composed and presented his own works but also copied and arranged many works of the older masters—and that applies above all to the compositions for the Kyrie and the Gloria[76]—the available church music was marked by great versatility. In this the work of the choir was still a truly liturgical service. The choir was responsible not only for all the required contrapuntal music but also primarily for the whole responsive liturgy in almost all services. We are told that after the intonation of the Gloria "the choir continues in the name of the church," or, with reference to the salutation "Dominus vobiscum," "the choir responds in the name of the church: 'Et cum Spiritu tuo,' that is, 'And with your spirit' " (*LKA*, p. 11—12). The choir also had to lead the congregational singing of the hymns, for organ accompaniment for these hymns was not yet customary in Leipzig in the first half of the 18th century. In those services and devotions where no choir was available, specific persons were to lead the hymns. We are told concerning the practice in the two main churches: "In the prayer services the *Baccalaureus Funerum* of St. Thomas does the singing, and in the noonday services as well as in half bridal masses the German hymns are intoned by a student or by the sexton" (Wz, p. 8). At St. George "the German hymns . . . were begun by an instructor of the orphan children" (Wz, p. 20), and of St. James we are told: "The housefather begins the German hymns" (Wz, p. 30). Concerning St. John there is this report: "The sexton (who formerly began the German hymns) is to ring the bells, besides his other duties, and the hymns are from now on sung by a teacher'' (Wz, pp. 22—23). The role of the fourth Kantorei, which Bach was to supply for St. Peter but which was not in the usual sense a Kantorei, extended only to the leadership of congregational singing in this church: "The German hymns are sung by a pupil of St. Thomas who is assisted by a few others" (Wz, p. 18). Also Sicul had referred to the fact that in St. Peter "there was no organ music, much less any counterpoint" (ScNA, p. 574). Apart from the main churches there was contrapuntal music only in the New Church and in St. Paul. But even in the New Church there was "very fine *Music* only now and then, especially on high festivals" (ScNA, 568). However, this *Music* was presented not by the third Kantorei usually functioning in this church, but by the organist of the church and by singers and instrumentalists available to him for that purpose. Weiz reports the following on musical functions in the New Church: "Because the cantor of St. Thomas could not do everything, a director of music was appointed, who on every festival presents fine *Music* together with the Collegium Musicum, consisting mostly of students, but otherwise plays the organ for the German hymns intoned by a prefect from St. Thomas School" (Wz, p. 14).

The organ still had its independent function in Leipzig, as also Luther valued "the organ, not as accompanying or substitute instrument, but as a liturgical factor competent to perform independent worship assignments," because of which the organist was considered to be "an independent servant of the Word."[77] In Leipzig, too, the office of organist and that of cantor were on principle held by two separate church musicians. In 1723 the following organists officiated in the city: Johann Gottlieb Görner at St. Nicholas, Christian Gräbner at St. Thomas, Georg Balthasar Schott at the New Church, Johann Michael Steinert at St. John, and Georg Irmler at St. Paul (cf. LA 1723, pp. 32, 78, 80—81, 83). It was the duty of the organist in the main service on Sunday to open the service with a prelude, to provide the intonation for the liturgical singing of the clergy, the choir, and the congregation, to enrich the hymn singing of the congregation through interludes, to introduce the cantata with a prelude, and to assist in the *Music*, as well as to furnish a part of the music during Holy Communion in the form of appropriate organ selections.[78]

Only during Lent was the use of the organ not customary, with the exception of the festivals of the Annunciation of Mary, Palm Sunday, and Maundy Thursday, but even on these three festival days it was severely restricted (cf. remarks on pp. 59—62). Also at Vespers on Sundays and festivals, with the exception of Lent, independent liturgical organ music was customary, as is affirmed by the *Leipziger Kirchen-Staat* (*LKS*, pp. 12, 14), by the orders of Vespers for the three days of the Reformation anniversary of 1730 (ScJL, pp. 118—24), and by numerous notes of the sexton at St. Thomas (cf. Ro, pp. 9, 14ff., et al.). The organ was played even at

Vespers on Saturdays and on the eve of a festival (cf. Ro, pp. 14ff., 26, 28, 43). Strangely enough, the organ was silent at Vespers on the eve of the Reformation anniversary, and there were special directives for organ music at Vespers on festivals observed during Lent (cf., Ro, pp. 14ff., ff., 36). Thus the organ was allowed to be played at Vespers on Palm Sunday only in instances when the festival of the Annunciation of Mary was observed the next day, since this Vesper service was liturgically governed by the coming festival. However, if the festival of the Annunciation of Mary fell on Palm Sunday itself or needed to be moved to that Sunday, the use of the organ at Vespers on the Saturday before was not permitted (Ro, pp. 14ff.). Incidentally, the remarks in the notebook of the sexton at St. Thomas clearly show that this tradition affirmed for the liturgical use of the organ existed until the end of the 18th century.

On Sundays and festivals contrapuntal music was heard not only in the main service but also at Vespers—with the exception of Advent and Lent and in established seasons of public mourning. On ordinary Sundays this began with the singing of a motet following the organ prelude (*LKA*, p. 43; *LKS*, p. 12). It is emphasized that this practice applied to the main churches and the New Church (Sc*NA*, p. 576). The fact that there was no contrapuntal music at Vespers in Advent and Lent and seasons of public mourning is stressed in the sources with the additional remark that then the service always began "with Psalm 3 chanted in Latin" (*LKA*, p. 43). In 1710 it is noted that in Advent "a psalm was sung at the beginning of Vespers," or concerning Lent: "The beginning of Vespers is made with the Third Psalm: 'Confitebor tibi Domine' " (*LKS*, pp. 32, 34). The distinction between the singing of the motet and that of the psalm, which is definitely supported by the sources, clearly shows that psalm singing can mean only the monophonic Gregorian chant in general use in Leipzig in these seasons of the church year. The rubric for festivals, "After the motet there is more music" (*LKS*, p. 18), refers to the presentation of the cantata customary on these days (cf. remarks on pp. 75—79). Apart from this, "the Magnificat was sung in German on ordinary Sundays, but on high festivals it was performed in Latin and in a concerted setting" (Sc*NA*, p. 576). The notes of the sexton at St. Thomas show that the Magnificat was performed in a concerted setting not only on the first two days of the three high festivals, but on all festivals of the church year (Ro, p. 60). As also Johann Sebastian Bach's "Magnificat" demonstrates, the performance of this liturgical piece almost always involved settings of the Latin text. Thus the *Leipziger Kirchen-Staat* first says about the Vesper services in general: "When the priest leaves the pulpit, the Magnificat or Mary's song of praise is sung in German after an organ prelude...or it is performed [*musicirt*] in Latin," but regarding the three high festivals: "After the sermon the Magnificat is performed [*musiciret*] in Latin" (*LKS*, pp. 14, 19). That this does not apply to the third day of the high festivals Rost affirms in his note for the third day of Easter: "Vespers are observed like a Sunday, and 'Meine Seele erhebt den Herrn' is sung" (Ro, p. 27). In 1714 the formerly customary Latin setting of the Magnificat was replaced by the German one in the Vesper services on Saturdays (Ro, p. 123). Whether or not the German setting was always sung in parts, perhaps according to the arrangement by Johann Herman Schein contained in the *Neu Leipziger Gesangbuch* of 1682 (*LGB* 1682, pp. 440ff.), is problematical. It is true that the order of Vespers for the second day of the Reformation anniversary of 1730 says: "The Magnificat may be performed in German," but the order of Vespers for the third day of this anniversary—and third holidays were always most closely related to the practice for Sundays— clearly states: "In monophonic form [*choraliter*]: 'Meine Seele erhebet den Herren' " (Sc*JL*, pp. 120—21). It is noteworthy that Johann Sebastian Bach's arrangements of Magnificat compositions by older masters deal only with the Latin version.[79]

The presentation of contrapuntal music in weekday services is affirmed only for Saturday Vesper services at St. Thomas. The references in the *Leipziger Kirchen-Andachten*, to the effect that "in St. Thomas Church several motets, but in St. Nicholas Church, as well as in both churches during Advent and Lent, the appropriate ancient *responsorium* and *antiphona* for the following Sunday are sung, and then a German hymn" (*LKA*, p. 84), recur almost verbatim in the *Leipziger Kirchen-Staat* (*LKS*, p. 42). The expression "several motets" [*ein paar Moteten*] is to be understood literally, for also Rost affirms that in certain Vesper services two motets were sung. Thus on the eve of festivals of the church year falling on a Monday it was customary to sing not only one motet, as would otherwise have been done in the respective Sunday Vespers, but two motets (Ro, pp. 1, 7, 34—35). Apart from this, no motets were sung in Vesper services on the eve of festivals of the church year during the week. At the same time, there was a motet on the eve of the Reformation anniversary (Ro, p. 36) and likewise when the eve of the first Christmas day fell on the Fourth Sunday in Advent (Ro, p. 46). The singing of two motets at the beginning of the Vesper service was customary also on the third day of Easter (Ro, p. 27), probably also on the third day of Pentecost, for Rost declares that the three days of this festival were observed exactly like the three days of Easter (Ro, p. 30). On the third day of Christmas, however, two motets were sung only when that day fell on a Saturday (Ro, p. 47).

A description of the extent of church music in the Leipzig worship services is not complete without a brief reference to the concerted music offered in connection with official acts. No public weddings or funerals were held without the participation of a choir, already because the choir was indispensable for leading congregational singing. A small choir would take part even in weddings at home. Thus we are told of a house wedding at which eight pupils were appointed to sing the usual wedding hymns. At the beginning they sang "Was Gott tut, das ist wohlgetan" and "In allen meinen Taten," then "after the vows" the hymn "Sei Lob und Ehr dem höchsten Gut" and after the benediction "Nun danket alle Gott" (Ro, p. 80). These are the same hymns about which Johann Sebastian Bach composed cantatas that significantly lack application to a worship service and in the new chronology of Bach's cantata offerings (cf. Dürr, *Chronologie*) cannot be assigned to a specific Sunday of the year. These are cantatas BWV 97, 100, 117, 192. Now since Rost mentions only those four hymns as customary at weddings, and since we also have three more chorale arrangements with instrumental accompaniment for three of these hymns intended for the wedding service (cf. BWV 250—252), it must be concluded that Bach composed those cantatas for weddings, although that does not preclude a later use of these works in Sunday services. Motets and cantatas, however, were offered only at "full bridal masses" (cf. remarks on p. 71). Schering's opinion that motets were not sung at weddings[80] is incorrect. There is express evidence that festive bridal masses began with a motet and that there was *Music* twice more during the wedding (Ro, p. 79). This implies the presentation of a cantata in two sections or even two distinct cantatas. Also the five cantatas of Bach definitely composed especially for weddings during his Leipzig tenure are organized in two sections.[81] Rost also affirms that there was no *Music* at "half bridal masses" (Ro, p. 81).

The choir's role at funerals was especially time-consuming and often dangerous to health, for funerals began at the house of mourning, and already there, and then along the whole way to the cemetery and at the grave, the choir had to sing funeral hymns. If the obsequies for prominent persons took place in the church, the organ music would be supplemented by the singing of special funeral motets and burial music that the bereaved would request and suitably remunerate. Not infrequently since the beginning of the 18th century special "memorial sermons," dedicated to the memory of deserving men and women, were held in churches, and this was often done in the place of the Sunday Vesper service. According to Rost, the first "memorial sermon" took place in St. Thomas on Palm Sunday, 9 April 1713, when it replaced the Vesper service (Ro, p. 96). And the sexton at St. Thomas records a number of such memorial services in subsequent years (Ro, pp. 94ff.). We know that Bach composed his motets largely for such services of mourning and that in such services and celebrations of mourning also the use of instruments and even of complete cantatas was not unusual.[82]

Thus one can say without reservation that at the time of Johann Sebastian Bach church music still had fundamental significance for the total worship life of Leipzig. And when one then considers the singing at New Year and the caroling [*Kurrendesingen*] in the streets and squares of the city and the frequent service of the first Kantorei of St. Thomas at the sickbeds and deathbeds of prominent citizens, men and women—Schering suspects that "many of the death cantatas" were completely or in part "offered at sickbeds and deathbeds of prominent citizens"[83]—the result is a truly live appreciation of the service of church music that at that time was still a focus of general public interest.

2.
An Evaluation of Liturgical Life
in Leipzig

How are all these individual phenomena to be evaluated theologically? What about the opinion frequently heard that the worship of orthodoxy is marked by baroque exuberance or baroque wordiness burdened with foreign ballast and unhealthy growth, indeed, that this worship has lost the prophetic and vital character and has regained a certain vitality only through its music? Was there actually an infiltration of the worship and particularly of the church music of orthodoxy by essentially foreign elements? In the age of orthodoxy how are we to evaluate piety in worship, or more generally, the piety of the average citizen and that of the clergy, so often referred to as fossilized? How does orthodoxy value the heritage of the Reformation, and what is its attitude over against the new trends initiated by Pietism and the Enlightenment? What about the constant references to tendencies toward disintregation in the liturgical practice of that time?

These are the questions we must now address and answer. We must penetrate to the heart of these problems and more clearly perceive the pulse of that liturgical life.

But this chapter is not to be a mere look backwards to achieve a practical application of our presentation so far. Its object rather is to point out particularly characteristic features for an evaluation of the liturgical practice and to subject these to a theological evaluation.

a) Worship and Piety

At the beginning of the 18th century new buildings were constantly being opened in Leipzig for worship and devotion, and also those places of worship already in existence were redecorated and enlarged. This fact alone ought to help guard against a negative appraisal of Lutheran orthodoxy in its late period.

But all these measures to intensify liturgical practice would hardly have been imaginable in their true extent without the favorable reaction of the people who attended church in Leipzig.

Participation in worship in Leipzig must be considered very lively. This is proved by the fact that a man like the Pietist pastor Christian Gerber[1] felt that he had to acknowledge and point out the special profusion in the Leipzig liturgical life as something exceptional for all of Saxony in his time (cf. the documentation on pp. 48, 55). This favorable evaluation by an outsider who had much opportunity for comparisons is all the more valuable because Gerber otherwise was definitely very critical and reserved over against the manifold liturgical traditions of the Lutheran Church. Likewise, the special praise of the almost unexampled worship situation in Leipzig as intoned by Sicul (cf. the documentation on p. 48) can hardly be a matter of grossly exaggerated self-glorification.

The open-mindedness of orthodoxy toward the various demands of the time becomes apparent in Leipzig especially in the manner of these services and devotions. In their form and implementation great care was exercised to have regard for the reform movements within the church. For example, the Catechism and Bible classes for young and old within the framework of worship, as they had gained great prominence in Leipzig since 1688 and especially since 1711, had been promoted diligently particularly through Pietism, which had gained influence in Leipzig toward the end of the 17th century but had then been decisively rejected. In addition, another favorite purpose of Pietism had been the dissemination of the Bible and the intensification of Bible study, promoted in Leipzig especially since the reopening of St. Peter Church in 1712. Yet it would be a complete mistake to give credit to Pietism alone for this stimulation of Catechism and Bible instruction in Leipzig, for the Lutheran Church had always had a strong appreciation of the fundamental importance of instruction for youth and of Bible study, and the Lutheran reform theologians of the 17th century had again and again made efforts in this direction.[2] In Leipzig, too, the most diverse ideas and plans for reform had again and again been expressed in the age of Lutheran orthodoxy and come to the attention of the citizens, for here the theological faculty of the university had throughout the 17th century kept in the closest contact with the decidedly reform-minded theologians of Wittenberg University and in all theological controversies had formed a united front with the Wittenbergers.[3] The two Johann Benedikt Carpzovs, father and son, among many others, had developed extensive reform activity in Leipzig, and especially the latter had at the end of the 17th century agitated for better training of the young people in the basic truths of the Lutheran Confessions. This Carpzov II

St. Peter Church. Source: W. Neumann, *Auf den Lebenswegen Johann Sebastian Bachs* (Berlin, 1953), p. 172.

(1639—1699), who was pastor of St. Thomas and at the same time professor of theology, had become the leading figure in church life at the end of the 17th century through his active pulpit ministry. In his extensive activity in reform, he was able to experiment in depth with the suggestions for reform made by his school friend Philipp Jakob Spener. Both had been permanently influenced by the reform theologians Dorscheus and Dannhauer during their student days in Straßburg. In fact, Carpzov believed to have found in Spener an ardent ally for his own reform activity and accorded him the highest praise.[4] For Carpzov, Lutheran theology and a lively piety were in no way contradictory. An anecdote from the life of the radical Pietist Christoph Tostleben of Böhlitz, the most noteworthy separatist in the Leipzig area, bears witness to the profound effects of Carpzov's sermons. Because the sermons of the pastor in Gundorf did not satisfy him, Tostleben set out for Leipzig very early in the morning, even in the worst winter weather, "and then waited at the Leipzig city gate until he could be admitted, only to be able to hear the sermons of Joh. Ben. Carpzov."[5]

Even as late as the time of Johann Sebastian Bach's activity in Leipzig, later orthodoxy—molded as it was after the heritage of the fathers—developed a piety of life of considerable proportions alongside all of its purity of doctrine. This becomes evident in the large number of cantata texts set to music by Bach, texts that Bach research has repeatedly judged to be typically pietistic and that have also been designated so officially. We have only to recall Hermann Kretzschmar's estimate: "Bach used a heavy preponderance of pietistic texts in his compositions."[6] In reality, however, all these texts are to be attributed to the mysticism that gained a foothold at just this time of later Lutheran orthodoxy. Such is the conclusion of Wolfgang Herbst's research in his dissertation *Johann Sebastian Bach und die lutherische Mystik* (Erlangen, 1958, p. 160): "The late orthodox doctrine of the mystic union [*unio mystica*] is the point where Pietism and orthodoxy converge." In his use of this doctrine, which is expressed so prominently in the cantata texts, "Bach definitely stood on the firm ground of his orthodox position and still had the inner piety, the love of Jesus, and the ability to overcome the rigid dogmatism characteristic of orthodoxy" (ibid.). Like Spitta, Herbst comes to the conclusion that "among the Bach cantata texts there is not a single pietistic one" (ibid.). This situation also calls for a revision of the view repeatedly advanced that Bach's supervising pastor at St. Thomas, Christian Weiß, was a representative of "mellowed Pietism."[7] The theologians who preached from the pulpits in Leipzig in those days were by and large pious personalities, but that does not mean that they immediately have to be called representatives of Pietism. This, too, becomes clear in an extremely remarkable report of Christian Gerber, who graces with extravagant praise those preachers in Leipzig who impressed him with their lively proclamation of the Word:

"Surely this must be called an abundance of divine goodness! Here 'The Lord gives the command; great is the host of those who bore the tidings' " (Gb, p. 399 [Ps. 68:11]). Expanded type for the second sentence provided added emphasis for the praise of the fortunate circumstances in Leipzig already sufficiently evident in the words themselves. Thus only unfamiliarity with the true situation could have led to the view that all evidences of a life of piety had to be credited to Pietism and therefore had to be labeled as pietistic. At the time of Johann Sebastian Bach and even before, theologians definitely inclined toward Pietism could not be ordained and appointed in Leipzig in the first place. We know, for instance, that Magister Friedrich Gottlieb Krantz, who had been called as "Saturday preacher at St. Thomas" in 1723, "achieved the diaconate at Taucha" in 1727 but "because of his quarrels with Pastor Hoffmann there and because of his leaning toward Pietism was suspended in 1734 and toward the end of the year 1735 was removed from his office altogether."[8] Also Magister Adam Bernd, active as Matins preacher and first catechist at St. Peter since 1711, was removed from office in 1728, among other things because of his leanings toward Pietism. As a movement, Pietism had had its beginning in Leipzig in the second-last decade of the 17th century, but by 1690 it was already banned officially there, and then it lost its influence and importance rapidly. The end of the movement among students, where it had found especially fertile ground before, can be assumed at the year 1692. In Leipzig, as in all of Saxony, the movement eventually ended in Separatism.[9]

It is true, Bach's cantata texts, originating largely with Leipzig authors and without doubt Leipzig theologians, represent a reflection of genuine Lutheran piety, but they also give clear evidence of another characteristic, namely their firm orientation in Holy Scripture. Precisely in the so-called free verse of the recitatives and arias the cantata texts are to an astonishing degree modeled after the images and even the language of the Bible, for in these texts a single sentence frequently uses and quotes several images and passages of Holy Scripture. These texts faithfully reflect the unusually close acquaintance and familiarity with the Bible common among Christians of that time. But it was simply characteristic of the worship practice in Leipzig at Bach's time that not only an uncommonly large number of sermons were preached every week, but that these sermons distinguished themselves in extraordinary versatility in their choice of texts and themes. In addition to the regular sermons on the traditional Gospels and Epistles in morning and afternoon services on Sundays and festival days, there were sermons on Luther's Catechism in the Sunday Vespers of Advent, on the Passion of Jesus in the Sunday Vespers of Lent, and on entire books or connected chapters of the Old and New Testaments in the various weekday services. The practice of expounding the entire Bible from beginning to end in the afternoon services held on Sundays and festival days, a practice begun in St. Peter in 1712, became a firm tradition in the course of the 18th century (Lh, p. 421; cf. also the discussion on p. 50). Even in the weekday services sermons were occasionally preached on Luther's Catechism or on other prescribed themes, as in the case of the sermons with set themes in New Church (cf. p. 53). But in addition to these, the sermons in Matins on Fridays in St. Nicholas as well as in Vespers on Saturdays in both main churches were always on penitential texts. If we consider further that since the beginning of 1714 also special "penitential admonitions or confessional sermons for the prospective communicants" (Bn, p. 48) were preached once a week in St. Nicholas, St. Thomas, and New Church, as well as every two weeks in St. John, and this in connection with the usual weekly prayer service (cf. the discussion on p. 53), we may say about the Leipzig situation in later orthodoxy that "many evangelical clergymen in the age of orthodoxy were indeed aware of their duty to rouse the consciences of their parishioners,"[10] for obviously in Leipzig, too, an intensification of confessional practices is recorded about the same time (cf. pp. 44—45). Penitential sermons on the prophet Isaiah were presumably preached on Fridays in St. Nicholas in 1717, and in the same year, on Mondays, the epistles to the Corinthians, which particularly invited penitential sermons again and again, were expounded in the same church (ScNA, pp. 579, 583—84). With such penitential sermons the Leipzig preachers followed a firm tradition, for the use of penitential texts, especially of the Old Testament, was customary in the Lutheran Church from the beginning and had now "reached its climax in the age of orthodoxy."[11]

This tradition was obviously alive and well to a marked degree in Leipzig in the time of Johann Sebastian Bach. Bach's cantata texts are a reliable documentary witness for this fact, for they have a way of letting the call to repentance dominate the scene, and above all, in their choice of church hymns they emphasize the hymns of penitence in large numbers. But it would be a complete mistake to conclude from this emphatic announcement of a call to repentance that a growing alienation from church and morality was active. Following faithfully in the footsteps of Luther, the theologians in the age of orthodoxy could choose no other way but to preach this call to repentance constantly, because it simply belonged to the essence of the Christian message. And because Pietism, too, very definitely called for repentance and faith, that movement was at first able to enjoy almost unlimited approval in Leipzig and also in Dresden, for the ideals of Spener, who "liked to link his own efforts to the thought of reform held by the Lutheran theologians of the 17th century," lay very close to the efforts at reform put forth by the Leipzig theologians.[12] Not only Carpzov II but also the other Leipzig professors had accepted Spener's proposals and initiatives for reform with approval, and in part even with enthusiasm.

Among these we may possibly also list August Pfeiffer, who at one and the same time was active as archdeacon at St. Thomas and enjoyed a good reputation as "a productive writer of devotional literature" far into the 18th century.[13] Even the estate catalog of Johann Sebastian Bach's library lists nine titles of Pfeiffer's books, so that he could even be called Bach's favorite author.[14]

On account of these inclinations of the leading Leipzig theologians toward the pietistic movement, it becomes very clearly apparent that they showed a very lively interest in a genuine life of piety among their fellow citizens and congregations and therefore also put their efforts toward reform into practice in a similar way. Indeed, they were themselves pious Christians. Under the influence of both professors, Carpzov II and Olearius, Bible study was presumably pursued more actively again at the university, and August Hermann Francke and Paul Anton had, for instance, been moved by a sermon for a day of repentance by Carpzov in 1686 to establish their *Collegium philobiblicum* (Circle of friends of the Bible) in Leipzig.[15] In this connection we should also call attention to the descendants of the widely ramified Leipzig theological family Carpzov, which throughout the 18th century played a not insignificant role in the church life of Leipzig and was of course also in direct contact with Bach. A contemporary of Carpzov I (1607—1657) said of him: "Whoever knows this man intimately will bear witness that he had a true piety in his heart that showed itself in many ways."[16] This applies also to his son, Johann Benedikt Carpzov II (cf. p. 99), and the latter's brother, Samuel Benedikt Carpzov, since 1681 superintendent in Dresden, who likewise was a pious personality and at first stood in agreement with the pietistic efforts of Spener.[17] Not only they, but all the descendants of this family in one way or another followed this pattern. In the first years of Bach's tenure in Leipzig a Johann Benedikt Carpzov served as pastor of St. James and a Johann Gottlob Carpzov as archdeacon at St. Thomas, and one of the daughters of the latter stood as sponsor at the baptism of one of Johann Sebastian Bach's children.[18] Much later another Johann Benedikt Carpzov (d. 1803) still defended Lutheran orthodoxy against the Enlightenment.[19]

After all the observations we have now made, we should give due notice to the fact that almost immediately after Pietism had been repudiated in Leipzig, the first measures toward an intensification of public liturgical life were taken, for the amplification of the liturgical life that developed so spectacularly in the 18th century lies in closest continuity with the efforts at reform made in the 17th century. In the midst of such a pronounced inclination toward a genuine life of piety, as we seem to perceive it definitely among the Leipzig theologians of the 17th century,[20] the dangers of Pietism's tendency toward Separatism were still recognized, and Pietism was then definitely repudiated. In its place independent measures toward a permanent improvement of piety were taken. Only the entire lively surge of strength of Lutheran orthodoxy in its late period is able to shed the proper light on this phenomenon. We cannot emphasize it strongly enough that by itself neither Pietism nor rationalism was able to contribute anything decisive to the intensification of public worship life, for both the ideal promoted by Pietism, conventicle Christianity, and rationalism's view of worship as an arrangement for educational purposes could not contribute to the upbuilding of Lutheran worship practices but had to work destructively. It is significant that immediately after Pietism's inroads on the citizens of Leipzig there were noticeable effects in the slackening of church discipline. In fact, Pietism's rejection of the church and all of its institutions, as it dangerously exercised its influence on church life for some time in the area surrounding Leipzig, decisively helped to win the victory there for rationalism.[21] In Leipzig itself, however, after the rift between Pietism and orthodoxy, which "led to a division that spread from Leipzig across all of Protestant Germany,"[22] a surprising late flowering of Lutheran orthodoxy followed.

Thus a beautiful witness to inner piety, a definite proof that a living faith is active in love, is furnished by the charitable activity of Leipzig, which was known far beyond its own borders. After a special "relief project" had been instituted to provide assistance when begging flourished here in 1704, "when poverty increased daily," even Weiz in his *Verbessertes Leipzig* felt he had to provide a detailed account of the organization of charitable endeavors in the city (Wz, pp. 108—14). About this work of love, from which many hundreds of people benefited at that time, he wrote: "This relief project is so well organized that few places in Germany are able to boast of anything comparable" (Wz, p. 110). With these words he in no way intended to support a feeling of self-satisfaction and complacency, but he was completely aware that the real credit for this generous charitable endeavor belonged not to people, but to God. He emphasizes it this way: "Now no one ought to be surprised why Leipzig is daily growing, increasing, and improving. This comes from the Lord of heaven and earth, who richly rewards this city for all it does for His poor members" (Wz, p. 111; cf. also Leu*Ref*, p. 33). An especially precious testimony concerning a charitable endeavor carried out in a very loving way is furnished by the reception in Leipzig in 1732 of the Salzburgers, who were exiled on account of their faith. At their arrival "the people of Leipzig literally competed with one another for these emigrants"[23] in order to have the privilege of welcoming them as their guests and to present them with a variety of gifts. In this testimony of the chronicler (quoted in our Appendix of Sources, No. 1) not only the mention of many deeds of love in the interest of like-minded fellow believers impresses us, but especially also the definite evidences of an ample care of the emigrants by means of preaching of the Word, providing for the sacraments, and speaking pastoral words of comfort. Unless we are completely mistaken, the chronicler, in addition to his interest in the historical account, was at the same time intent on memorializing the faith of the Leipzigers as it was active in practical works of love. He obviously identifies himself with the stance of faith of the Salzburgers, who were so attractive to him and the other citizens of Leipzig, for even under the worst blows of fate these people considered gathering about Word and Sacrament to be the prime commandment and therefore, in spite of all the hardships of the flight already endured and all the toil still to come, would not rest but insisted on strengthening their faith in these few days of their stay in Leipzig by coming together about God's Word and Sacrament. For the Salzburgers, as also for the Leipzigers, a reality that was still a lively experience and therefore definitely a determining factor in their faith life lay in the central concept of the fathers of the Reformation that "through the Word and the sacraments, as through instruments, the Holy Spirit is given, and the Holy Spirit produces faith, where and when it pleases God, in those who hear the Gospel" (AC V 2, German).

Further witnesses for a truly pious life in the city of Leipzig are seen especially in the large number of literary works published and disseminated here, among which, beside the basic dogmatic, exegetical, and apologetic writings of Lutheran orthodoxy, a mass of devotional works are found. Johann Sebastian Bach's library, too, with its large number of theological works, of which a considerable number were devotional books,[24] is a tangible witness to show how high the interest to possess and read that type of literature was even among nontheologians. In these works used by Bach in addition to those of Luther we see primarily "the phalanx of orthodox literary production deployed."[25]

In addition, clear witnesses for judging the piety are the Leipzig hymnbook publications, which throughout the 18th century carry on the hymn tradition of 16th and 17th centuries in a most conservative way and only halfheartedly open their pages for the reception of the newer hymnic materials but everywhere present evidence of a genuine life of faith and solid piety. Thus the *Leipziger Kirchen-Staat* contains extensive instructions and directions how "a devout Christian" might begin "his personal devotions" already at the time when the choir members conduct the Matins not open to the public. In this connection, for instance, mention is made of Scriver's devotional works (*LKS*, p. 4). Also, before the beginning of the seven o'clock service one is to "use the following prayers...to pray earnestly for the grace of the Holy Spirit...for keeping the Sabbath holy...for a proper attitude with heart and soul for the Word of God, so that nothing shall keep us from giving attention to it...for the time when we are about to go to church...for the time of the ringing of the bells, etc."

(*LKS*, pp. 4—5). To enliven the liturgy used, the compiler provides a large number of prayers for the individual parts of the liturgy that are to promote a worthy participation of the worshiper in the service, such as "a prayer during the playing of the organ or while the Latin motet is being sung...while special music is performed...prayers before the Sermon...a prayer before the Creed is chanted, etc." (*LKS*, pp. 5ff.). The entire hymnbook represents an impressive reflection of a genuine life of piety at public worship and in the home. In every respect the compiler leaves the impression that he is concerned about a genuine life of prayer in church and home. With this hymnbook arrangement the compiler in Leipzig follows a solid tradition, for the *Leipziger Kirchen-Andachten*, published at the time of Carpzov II, is very similar in its layout; indeed, it contains as Part III a "Direction for Devotions of Home and Heart" and then as Part IV the "Devotions of Home and Heart" themselves, which contain "a preparation for a useful Sabbath and festival celebration for the whole year based on the regular Gospels."

If we look on all the indicated phenomena of a genuine life of piety and the efforts toward continuous improvement of a vigorous liturgical practice as forming a genuine unit, each part having a proper regard for the other, we shall be protected against the false judgment that the endeavors toward intensification of liturgical practice should perhaps be understood as purely external hustle and bustle. All of this liturgical practice in the first half of the 18th century in Leipzig was completely under the influence of genuine faith life and profound piety. In view of this liturgical practice Gerber is able to call the people of Leipzig "blissful," because they are "enriched in all doctrine and in all knowledge and are lacking in no gift" (Gb, p. 355 [1 Cor. 1:5-7]). But precisely this judgment of this pietistically oriented pastor is a strong witness to the fact that this liturgical practice of late orthodoxy in Leipzig represented a most impressive world of piety.

Under these circumstances we must now also subject to a special consideration and evaluation Leipzig's rich liturgical traditions as we encounter them in practically undiminished number still in the 18th century. Here, too, we are in no way dealing with institutions that are already mere fossils and have degenerated to meaninglessness. The Lutheranism of late orthodoxy in Leipzig always possessed so much vitality that the process of disintegration definitely observable otherwise in the liturgical practice of the Lutheran Church in Germany as early as 1700 (cf. p. 39) remained wholly inoperative at least in this city. Paul Graff calls attention to the fact that it is the attitude toward the church year that always reveals very definitely how far any disintegration of liturgical forms has progressed. But the wealth of liturgical arrangements for the church year reported for Leipzig throughout the first half of the 18th century and far beyond unmistakably shows with what fidelity the tradition received from the fathers

105

was thought of as something to be preserved and in individual instances even to be amplified (cf. the discussion on pp. 57 and 64). Thus up to the end of the 18th century not a single festival of the church year was dropped or diminished in importance. Also the three-day duration of the chief festivals of the church year was faithfully adhered to throughout the 18th century, even though this had not been the custom any longer anywhere else in Germany and in many places had experienced a reduction already in the 17th century.[26] The third festival days of these chief festivals were not dropped until 1831. In that same year the three great days of penitence and prayer usual for the year were reduced to two, and a reduction of the festivals occurring in weekdays was undertaken (*Bn*, pp. 70—71).

This faithfulness over against liturgical traditions instituted or retained by the Reformation could go so far as always to include the sounding of the little "consecration or Mass bell" (*Bn*, p. 61) during the chanting of the Words of Institution in the services of both of the main churches in Leipzig up to the year 1787. This was done regularly by the sexton as he knelt at the altar during the consecration of the bread and wine. Rost, too, mentions the use of this little bell (Ro, pp. 21, 23, 26, 37). And that this was a custom of a special nature, a tradition long gone everywhere else in Saxony, is attested by Gerber as follows: "When I heard this bell the first time in Leipzig as I was joining in the Communion, I was startled by this ringing, for the sexton rang the bell very loud and very close to the altar. I did not know what it was to signify. In fact, my thoughts were diverted, and I thought more about this ringing and clanging than about the principal business, namely the showing forth of the death of Christ and the reception of His body and blood" (Gb, p. 456).

The vibrant organization of the church year, which left its imprint on every part of church and city life, effectively embodied a strict observance of Sunday and faithful attendance at services, by which the Lutherans impressed particularly foreign visitors deeply;[27] a halting of public traffic even during the services of repentance every Friday morning; a strict observance of Advent and Lent as periods of penitence, in which not even the presentation of polyphonic and instrumental music was allowed in Leipzig; and a particularly strict observance of the three great days of penitence and prayer every year. The strictness with which the rule about polyphonic and instrumental music during penitential seasons was applied particularly in Leipzig can be seen in a comparison with the practice in this matter in Lutheran Weimar. In Weimar it was permissible to perform cantatas both in Advent and in Lent. Johann Sebastian Bach composed cantatas in Weimar for Advent and Lent, but later in Leipzig he was able to use these cantatas only after reworking them for other purposes (cf. cantatas BWV 70, 80, 147, 182, 186).

The fact that Lutheran orthodoxy so actively identified itself with this lively organization of the church year must be valued the more highly since it was not rationalism but Pietism long ago that had decisively contributed to the disparagement and the decline of the church year. In this connection we should refer to the monumental lack of understanding that a man like Gerber has expressed over against this liturgical tradition. He knows "that the common people are still closely attached to externals and are captivated by beautiful altars, clerical garb, candles, altar and pulpit cloths, the sign of the cross, and the like," in fact, "that not only the common people but also among people of rank" individuals are found "who have a very high regard for externals and imagine that God is especially honored in them." He simply cannot understand that "there still are always people who have such things crafted and then present them to the church," even though "many churches, especially in large cities, have plenty of clerical vestments and altar linens." In spite of all of this, he wants people "to get rid of those wax lights that burn in broad daylight, those chasubles, and that wide variety of altar and pulpit hangings," for all of these things are "superfluous and completely useless," and so "not only could much money be saved and be used for more necessary things, but also the common people could be kept from esteeming external things too highly" (Gb, pp. 115—16). Only the apostolic age, not the Reformation, served as the great ideal for Gerber's proposals for liturgical reform. The Reformation had only made the very first beginning for reform. "When Luther got rid of many abuses, he still had to retain this and that ceremony, because not everything could be altered and done at the same time" (Gb, pp. 110ff.). Because Christ Himself had instituted "no new ceremonies" and because in the apostolic age "the church and especially the service had been burdened and overloaded with so many customs and ceremonies that the true inner devotion of the heart was almost erased thereby," Gerber wants to see the Christian service "reduced again in accordance with apostolic simplicity" (Gb, pp. 111—12, 116). For that reason he also carried on a strong campaign against the large number of festivals, especially those that occurred on weekdays, because they were so much abused by the people as "days of drinking, dancing, and gaming" (Gb, p. 155). Although many of the festivals still retained by Luther, such as the Finding of the Cross, the Raising of the Cross, the Nativity of Mary, and the Assumption of Mary, were no longer celebrated in Gerber's day, he wondered "why the Festival of the Wise Men from the East, the Purification of Mary, St. John's Day, the Visitation of Mary, and St. Michael's Day have not been eliminated as well" (Gb, p. 160). According to Gerber's opinion, there was presumably no justification at all for the existence of the apostles' days, because they had originated "from purely human fancy and invention." And about St. Thomas Day he is bold to say: "Therefore we have every reason to thank God that He gave our forefathers the good sense to abolish this festival"

(Gb, p. 185). Gerber fights a particularly fierce battle against "the so-called St. Michael's Festival, of whose dissolute, wretched, and idolatrous origin the Roman Church should have been ashamed long ago" (Gb, pp. 156—57). Gerber contends that there is a lot of superstition associated with this festival, for he was very serious in his worry that St. Michael's might be "celebrated in honor of the angels." For that reason he demands the abolition of this festival, just as he does also for St. John's Day and the Visitation of Mary (cf. Gb, pp. 155ff.).

A comparison of these tendencies, which had their origin in Pietism and finally dissolved the Lutheran service and its liturgical traditions, with, let us say, the efforts of Johann Georg Rosenmüller, whose orientation was rationalistic and who served as superintendent in Leipzig from 1785, yields results that are in many ways remarkably identical. Thus we read in the latter's *Pastoralanweisung* (Pastoral guide) of 1788: "Whether the Words of Institution are chanted or spoken is basically immaterial. But the money spent on wax candles, chasubles, and other vestments for the Mass could be spent more profitably. I hope that in our day a person will not easily find a clergyman for whom such things would be so important that he would rather leave the ministry than exchange his cope and chasuble for a gown, as happened in Prussia, Pomerania, Magdeburg, and Halberstadt about 50 years ago."[28]

Thus we could not easily overstate our high regard for late orthodoxy as it obtained in Leipzig. In its fruitful insistence on a lively organization of the church year and in its continuance in the liturgical tradition that had been maintained in the Lutheran Church and had become familiar there, orthodoxy was able to endure in waging a war on two fronts, on the one hand against Pietism and on the other against rationalism, and thus to meet head on, and in a decisive and impressive manner, the entire process of dissolution of the liturgical life of the congregations. Also, we must emphasize in relation to the conditions in Leipzig that "the tendencies that really were destructive to liturgy and finally made complete havoc of our divine services never emanated from orthodoxy itself," but that, in fact, "Lutheran orthodoxy displayed great faithfulness in understanding, retaining, and celebrating the divine service as 'the real spiritual occurrence.' "[29]

b) Worship and Liturgical Order

An unmistakable characteristic of late orthodoxy as it prevailed in Leipzig is the consistency with which it advocated the retention of the existing order of service almost throughout the 18th century. Our section dealing with the Leipzig clergy and their offices and duties that remained virtually unchanged for generations (cf. pp. 66—74), as well as the fact that the large number of services and devotions and their distribution to the individual churches remained almost constant throughout the entire century, provides graphic illustrational material to point out the order, strictly organized and then strictly implemented, according to which all of the liturgical practice of Lutheran orthodoxy developed.

The same applies also to the orders of service always used in Leipzig. To be sure, already at the beginning of the 18th century the phenomenon could be observed everywhere that wherever rationalism became influential in church life, and especially in liturgical practice, a relaxation and finally a complete disintegration of existing worship orders followed quickly. Of this process of disintegration, generally well attested for the entire first half of the 18th century, there was in Leipzig hardly a trace. On the contrary, here people were apparently very keenly aware of these tendencies that brought about a disintegration of the liturgy. At the beginning of the *Leipziger Kirchen-Staat* there is a "Dedication to a lady of high rank in Leipzig who loves God and virtue," in which the author in an extended discourse professed his loyalty to a good, constant order of service. In praise he points out that this lady "in performing her devotions always considered the order of the service the priceless jewel," and at the same time he emphasizes "the experience" made again and again "that all rites that are not governed by a desirable order as their moving force must expect nothing but instability and transience rather than performance." Although the author saw the danger "of writing an oration of praise for the order," still, at the wish "of many strangers and foreigners, who either pass through our esteemed city of Leipzig or attend our Masses or for some other reason stay here a while," and in the realization "that our devotion often suffers serious impairment in a strange place if the order of service there is not known well enough," he was "intent on nothing else" in the first place in the compilation of his book of hymns and prayers "than to delineate in a brief concept the glorious order of service which our esteemed Leipzig possesses in its public services and thus to provide many people with a better opportunity to support their devotion with increased attention in the chapels." A conspicuous characteristic of the orders of service presented after this introduction, however, is that Leipzig clung to the old 16th-century Lutheran orders of service and considered this completely self-evident. The generations that followed were always surprised at this, and Philipp Spitta's evaluation of the rich treasury of liturgical forms of the Leipzig services at the time of Bach resulted partly in amazement and partly in a lack of understanding. Thus he was misled to speak of a "continued cultivation of the original forms of certain parts of the Catholic rite" and to describe the entire Lutheran order of service as "a recast of the Catholic rite of the Mass."[30]

Actually, the entire history of the worship service of Lutheran orthodoxy remains unintelligible unless it is viewed in close continuity with the reorganization of the Lutheran service at the time of the Reformation. On its part this reorganization generally maintained a close connection with the Western worship tradition in an extremely conservative way and eliminated only what was unmistakably contrary to Scripture. Wherever developments in the history of the liturgy of Lutheran orthodoxy miscarried, these failures do not represent a particular characteristic of orthodoxy but were clearly established by the Reformation itself. This applies especially to the large number of weekday services that still appeared, in Leipzig at least, in the 18th century as Matins and Vespers, usually amplified by means of a comprehensive sermon, or at least revealed their provenance as from those old canonical hours and were still conducted in closest connection with them. After all, in his *Formula missae et communionis* (1523) Luther had expressly recommended the institution of certain hours of prayer in place of the daily workday Masses that were abolished, and he thought primarily of Matins and Vespers. Also, the Reformation and post-Reformation orders of service contain detailed directions for the conduct of the hours of prayer, and in them there was always an effort "to suit the daily worship to the powers of comprehension of the hearing and praying congregation."[31] The Matins that then became customary in the Lutheran Church, however, combined liturgical elements both of the *Matutinae* and the *Laudes* and at times also of still other hours of prayer. But this combination had obviously been present already in Luther's mind.

For conducting the weekday Matins (for those of Sunday, cf. p. 49), the agendas used in Leipzig also contain the direction: "Where boys are available, they may be allowed to sing before the Sermon on workdays (on which preaching is done throughout the week) before reading in school is begun, as is prescribed for Matins on Sunday, so that the people gather for the Sermon and, when the boys have finished their singing, that the preaching begin. After the Sermon, however, the people should be permitted to sing a German psalm or another spiritual song, much or little, as convenient" (*Ag*, pp. 81—82). But this practice was followed only at St. Thomas. About the early service Mondays and Wednesdays at St. Nicholas we read: "In this St. Nicholas Church 10 special choirboys are provided, who in the early hour, at six o'clock, alone, without the presence of any audience, conduct the early Matins according to the following order: (1) A Latin psalm and responsory is chanted. (2) Two of the choirboys are appointed to read at the lectern, one a German psalm, the other a Latin one. (3) The choirboys sing the Latin Benedictus, and they close these Matins with the 'Benedicamus Domino, Deo dicamus gratias.' After this the bells are rung at seven o'clock, and then at 7:45 the service is begun with the singing of a morning hymn. In addition, another hymn suitable for the season or the Gospel, but on Wednesdays the Creed, is sung. Then the priest ascends the pulpit, and the Sermon is preached on a specified text from the Old or New Testament. The Sermon is not longer than an hour (until about eight o'clock). The prayers, intercessions, and thanksgivings and announcements are handled as on Sundays.... After the Sermon a hymn is sung, the Collect is read at the altar, the Benediction is pronounced, and with a hymn the service is concluded. But because Holy Communion is celebrated on Wednesdays, the priest soon after the conclusion of the first hymn chants the Lord's Prayer and the Words of Institution, and as on Sundays, there is singing of hymns during the distribution. Only then is the Collect read and the Benediction pronounced" (*LKS*, pp. 39—40). About the early services on Tuesdays and Thursdays at St. Thomas we read that they begin with the ringing of the bells at 6:30 and "at 6:45 the boys at St. Thomas begin the early Matins (which at St. Nicholas is sung by the choirboys at six o'clock)," but otherwise the same order of service as at St. Nicholas is in effect (*LKS*, p. 41). In other words, the difference between St. Nicholas and St. Thomas lay in this, that at St. Thomas Matins was connected immediately with the early service, but in St. Nicholas it was completely separate from it. Appropriately Sicul therefore characterizes the early service on Tuesdays at St. Thomas with the words: "A Sermon, exactly as on Mondays at St. Nicholas, except that the St. Thomas boys sing and read several Latin psalms and the Benedictus, as well as a German psalm and at the end the Benedicamus Domino" (Sc*NA*, p. 580). Also the *Leipziger Kirchen-Andachten* testifies to this variant practice in the main churches and reports the order of service used in almost the same words (*LKA*, pp. 71—72). In the Vespers on Saturdays at both main churches the Sermon was incorporated in the middle of the old order of Vespers (cf. Appendix of Sources, No. 2).

A comparison of the individual proposals of the reformers regarding the order of these daily secondary services with the liturgical practice in the first half of the 18th century in Leipzig reveals a surprisingly extensive agreement between the requirements of the reformers and the liturgical practice in late orthodoxy. In addition to the essential liturgical elements of these hours of prayer, the Reformation requirement that reading, Sermon, and prayer be in the language of the people also found the highest favor in Leipzig, and this was to let these hours of prayer, which in the Middle Ages had already been held exclusively in monasteries and by priests, again become what they originally were, namely a worship event of the whole congregation. The fact that in the process the Sermon became the dominant core and center of these prayer hours, through which the basic character of the prayer hour was definitely changed to a real congregational prayer, is traceable to a requirement of Luther's. Luther wanted to see the reading of Scripture expanded to a least half an hour,[32] as in general the right presentation of Scripture was Luther's main concern in the reorganization of the services. The Sermon then gradually began to occupy an increasingly larger role in these daily services, and this eventually led to pure preaching services instead of Matins and Vespers. This development, too, was initiated in no accidental way but fostered by Luther's pedagogical and pastoral concern to use these weekday services primarily for instructing the congregation, and especially the youth, in Holy Scripture.

Added to this instructional purpose, which was itself far removed from the original hours of prayer, was a further completely foreign aspect. This was the ideal that these services should also have the humanistic purpose "of keeping the young people in touch with the Latin language of the Bible and of training them in it," because "training in reading and hearing the psalms and the Scripture readings" was presumably "good and necessary."[33] The Leipzig agendas of Bach's time still read: "Vespers should be conducted every day so that the boys may be exercised in the Psalter and Holy Scripture. From time to time also they should be given opportunity to sing all the good, pure responsories and hymns. From these the young people may learn what the holy church has always confessed and kept as the true faith" (*Ag*, p. 82). For this reason the choirs of the Latin schools were the real leaders in the hours of prayer conducted in Latin in the city parish churches. In addition to taking part in the regular services already mentioned, the Leipzig St. Thomas students always had to serve also in the services of prayer according to the old order of Vespers the evening before special festivals in the church year, that is, if these evening services did not occur on Saturday or Sunday, for in that case Vesper services with Sermon and polyphonic music took place. The St. Thomas sexton called these public prayer services, for which the "weekday preacher" conducted the opening and closing, "festival Vespers," and he wrote down a large number of notes that let us recognize the employment of the following order: *Ingressus* (in Latin, in alternation between liturgist and choir), Psalm singing, Gospel readings for the following festival day chanted (and that in Latin and German successively by two different students), Magnificat (German version), Versicle, Prayer, and Benediction (cf. Ro, pp. 3, 7, 15, 17, 20, 22, 24, 28, 35—36, 46, etc.). In St. Nicholas, too, these Vespers on evenings before festivals were held, and this with the "choralists," who also customarily served in prayer services Tuesdays and Thursdays at 1:30 p.m., before the beginning of the usual hour of prayer in this church (cf. Sc*NA*, pp. 580ff.; Lh, pp. 417—18).

Thus in Leipzig during the 18th century the custom was, in keeping with the tradition received from the Middle Ages, to provide Matins and Vespers, largely in Latin, as a chanted service by the St. Thomas students and the "choralists" with the cooperation of a liturgist in the altar area of the church, and this also corresponded to the wishes and the practice of the reformers. Many other details in the implementation of the weekday services in Leipzig at the time of Bach are likewise traceable to the time of the Reformation, for example, prescheduling the Vesper services at early afternoon, or providing for a special sermon in the Saturday evening Vespers, or in general the richer elaboration of the Saturday and Sunday Vespers.[34] These Vespers were distinguished especially by greater consideration for the hymns sung by the congregation and by the singing of polyphonic choral music in place of Gregorian psalm singing (The Order of Vespers, cf. Appendix of Sources, No. 3). The Vesper services on special festivals were also distinguished by the fact that additionally at the beginning a festival hymn was sung and that immediately after the singing of the motet the cantata was heard (cf. the discussion on pp. 76, 86, 92). To compensate for this, the "hour of prayer" was omitted (cf. p. 77), and here we are to understand the reference to be to the reading of the psalms at the lectern and to the prayers spoken there at the beginning of the Vespers services (cf. *LKA*, pp. 43ff.; *LKS*, pp. 18ff.; Sc*NA*, p. 576).

Also the "Catechism prayer services" [*Katechismusbeten*] held in Leipzig in connection with the great prayer services on Tuesdays in St. Nicholas and Fridays in St. Thomas were customary in certain prayer services already at the time of the Reformation.[35] The great prayer service at St. Nicholas, which was preceded by the Vespers of the "choralists," followed this order: "(1) A hymn is sung; (2) the entire Catechism without the explanation is read from the lectern; (3) in an unoccupied area, one boy, upon interrogation of another, prays one chief part of the Catechism with the explanation; (4) the Litany is chanted; (5) from the pulpit a chapter of the Bible and also the prayers of the prayer service are read; (6) with a hymn and Collect and Benediction the service is closed" (Sc*NA*, p. 580). The *Leipziger Kirchen-Andachten* and the *Leipziger Kirchen-Staat*, which attest the same liturgical order for these long hours of prayer, characterize the section of the devotion spoken responsively by the two boys and reported by Sicul under point (3) as an act of prayer, too.

Even the Bible and Catechism instruction periods that came into their own in Leipzig from 1688 and 1711 hark back to a practice attested already in Reformation times. At the time of the Reformation "the liturgical employment of the Catechism" had taken up "considerable room" already for the reason that "the instruction of youth in the Christian faith" was "one of the most important concerns of the church for the reformers."[36] For this reason the church orders of the 16th century contain "detailed regulations conerning the catechetical instruction of youth."[37] We must leave unanswered the question to what extent such liturgical Catechism instruction had been customary in Leipzig even before 1688. According to Gerber, there are many kinds of references to Catechism services present in Saxony before the Thirty Years' War.[38] (Order of Catechism Instruction at the Time of Bach, cf. Appendix of Sources, No. 4.)

113

It is safe to say that in the liturgical practice in Leipzig at the time of Johann Sebastian Bach there was still a definite dependence, even to the smallest details, on the worship practice of Reformation times and specifically also on the directives of Luther. Thus one may say almost without reservation that "on the whole the period of orthodoxy faithfully preserved the heritage of the Reformation."[39] But in spite of this statement, we should in no way fail to recognize the weaknesses and the unsatisfactory solutions of the Reformation orders of worship and directives, which are, however, not a part of our discussion. Still it is not proper to describe this liturgical practice [in Leipzig] as dead and thereby to characterize the whole period as one of decay just because orthodoxy contributed virtually nothing to the solution of the problems left unsolved by the reformers. The very liveliness and versatility of the weekly program of services in Leipzig can be discerned from the fact that all of these weekday services were not conducted according to a single, definite order that took into consideration all Reformation directives but that precisely the whole range of orders implemented created an extremely great variety that could only prove stimulating and helpful in the life of piety of the individual. In spite of all the faithful ties to Reformation directives, there was no legalistic rigidity. This is apparent in the relatively late implementation of the lesser and greater prayer services as well as the penitential services on Fridays every week. The lesser prayer services, on record since 1619 in Leipzig, began with a hymn, and then "a chapter from the Bible together with the Lord's Prayer and the prayers usual for prayer services and one against war were read from the pulpit," whereupon "another hymn was sung, and Collect, Benediction, and a further hymn brought the service to its close" (*LKS*, pp. 42— 43; *LKA*, p. 74). The penitential services on Fridays followed the pattern of the preaching services on Mondays in St. Nicholas; the only exception was that at the beginning of the former services the Gregorian hymn "Aufer a nobis Domine" was sung, followed by the Litany, and during the services there was always a series of penitential hymns (*LKA*, pp. 72—73; *LKS*, p. 41; Sc*NA*, p. 583). Also on the year's greater days of penitence and prayer only preaching services were held in the forenoon, but these were amplified with the following additions: "At the beginning of the service two hymns are sung: 'Nimm von uns Herr du treuer Gott' and 'Ach Gott thu dich erbarmen.' Then the Collect is chanted at the altar, followed by the hymn 'Allein zu dir Herr Jesu Christ.' Now the priest goes to the lectern and reads, instead of the usual Epistle, a chapter from the Bible assigned for this purpose. Then follows the hymn 'Du Friedefürst Herr Jesu Christ.' Instead of the Gospel another chapter from the Bible is read, and then the Litany is chanted." Here the Sermon follows, and all the rest follows the pattern of the customary preaching services (*LKS*, pp. 46—47).

1. Die St Thomas Kirche. 2. Die Thomas Schule.
3. Der Steinerne Waßer=Kasten.

St. Thomas Church. Source: W. Neumann, *Auf den Lebenswegen Johann Sebastian Bachs* (Berlin, 1953), p. 164.

In spite of all their multiplicity and diversity, the weekday services conducted in Leipzig may be summarized, liturgically, in the following basic forms: (1) The independent Matins of the "choralists" in St. Nicholas; (2) the pure Vespers in both main churches the evenings before festivals; (3) the greater prayer services with the "praying of the Catechism," also in connection with the Vespers of the "choralists" (Tuesdays at St. Nicholas); (4) the lesser prayer services, also in connection with a special penitential exhortation, Thursdays except when in connection with the Vespers of the "choralists"; (5) the Bible and Catechism instruction periods; (6) pure preaching services both on Bible texts (Mondays in St. Nicholas) and on certain articles of faith (Fridays in New Church); (7) preaching services in immediate connection with Matins (Tuesdays in St. Thomas); (8) early services with Sermon and complete Communion liturgy (Wednesdays in St. Nicholas); (9) early services with Matins, Sermon, and complete Communion liturgy (Thursdays in St. Thomas); (10) special services on Fridays; (11) preaching services on the basis of the complete order of Vespers (Saturdays in both main churches), with polyphonic choral music (in St. Thomas).

In spite of the implementation of such a variety of orders of worship, Lutheran orthodoxy did not tolerate arbitrariness in setting up orders of service but with unswerving fidelity upheld the existing tradition from generation to generation and with a consistent observance of these orders mounted a determined resistance to all tendencies destructive of the liturgy.

This becomes most clearly evident when the order of the main service as practiced in Leipzig in the 18th century is subjected to a critical evaluation. This order shows clearly and without gaps the entire form of the Mass for every Sunday and festival. Its liturgical structure was so rich in its parts that even the sexton of St. Thomas, Rost, kept a special notebook for the various peculiarities of the services of the individual Sundays and festivals in order not to forget anything in the customary discharge of his duties. Johann Sebastian Bach, too, even after he had already served in his office in Leipzig for half a year, noted down on the inside front cover of his cantata BWV 61 the complete outline of the liturgy for the main service of the First Sunday in Advent, which on this particular day took a course somewhat different from the usual one. He obviously did this to avoid making a mistake in the elaborate liturgy of the services of that time.[40]

The Leipzig order of the main service had in no respect become a fossilized and rigid form but still represented a live fabric. This is discernible at the very outset in the diverse shaping of the three liturgical pieces of the entrance section—Introit, Kyrie, and Gloria, in which the choir, the congregation, and the liturgist took part exactly according to the Reformation directives. "The reduction of the liturgist's burden in favor of the participation of the congregation, the choir, and other liturgical functionaries," as carried out in the Reformation orders of service, in which especially the congregation and the choir "were again included with complete awareness in the liturgical action and were made an independent liturgical factor,"[41] was still consistently observed and realized also in the liturgical practice of the first half of the 18th century in Leipzig. After the early and final "ringing of the bells at seven o'clock" (*LKS*, p. 5), the choir's first duty was to sing the Introit after the organ prelude had been concluded (cf. the discussion on pp. 86—87). After another, shorter organ piece, the Kyrie eleison followed. The presentation of this unit in both main churches always varied according as the first or, respectively, the second Kantorei was performing its Sunday tour of duty. The first Kantorei, to which the more difficult assignments were always given, regularly "chanted" the Kyrie in Latin or "performed it polyphonically" [*musiciret*], but "in the church where the other choir is, as well as in other towns, the Kyrie is sung in German," that is, in the chorale form, "Kyrie, Gott Vater in Ewigkeit" (*LKA*, p. 11). The *Leipziger Kirchen-Staat*, too, confirms this, that the Kyrie "was now sung in German, now performed polyphonically [*musiciret*] in Latin" (*LKS*, p. 5). So does Sicul, according to whom the "Kyrie! Gott Vater in Ewigkeit" was "alternately sung in German in one church and in Latin in the other" (Sc*NA*, p. 569). This German Kyrie hymn was "especially popular already in Reformation times";[42] in its German and Latin version ("Kyrie Fons bonitatis") it was always printed in a monophonic version in the *Neu Leipziger Gesangbuch*, 1682 (pp. 423ff.). In the 18th century in Leipzig, therefore, the church still favored an organization of the liturgy considered ideal and practiced by the reformers and particularly by Luther, an arrangement tending essentially toward two different forms of worship—one primarily related to the medieval tradition, extremely conservative and controlled by the Latin language, and alongside this the other, of fully equal rights, one that elevated the German song form to the liturgical congregational hymn. It may safely be assumed that in both main churches every other week the congregation sang along when the German Kyrie hymn was sung. Friedrich Smend's emphasis on the fact that the congregation first sang customarily in the "main hymn" [*Hauptlied*], sung between Epistle and Gospel,[43] needs to be modified by the consideration that this refers only to one of the two main churches. That the congregation in one of the two main churches customarily sang along in the German Kyrie hymn every Sunday is already confirmed in the *Leipziger Kirchen-Staat*, which immediately at the beginning of Part Two, representing the actual hymnbook, lists the four hymns sung by the congregation in the main service every Sunday: "Kyrie, Gott Vater in Ewigkeit," "Allein Gott in der Höh sei Ehr," "Wir glauben all an einen Gott," and "Herr Jesu Christ, dich zu uns wend." After all, these German songlike arrangements of liturgical pieces had been created specifically for the sake of the congregation in Reformation times, and the congregation was accustomed to singing them as everywhere else in Germany.[44] Consider the emphatic statement that Leipzig stayed with the singing of the Kyrie hymn "just as in other cities" (*LKA*, p. 11). It would have been strange indeed for Leipzig to assign the singing of those hymns to the choir alone, contrary to the directive of the reformers. The choir usually merely intoned these hymns and then led the singing of the congregation, and this is the real reason why our sources hardly make mention of the singing of the congregation, for it was considered self-evident.

The Kyrie eleison was therefore sung either by the choir alone or in the form of the German Kyrie hymn with the congregation, but in the arrangement of the "Gloria in excelsis Deo" the liturgist for the first time in the service took the lead as he intoned this piece at the altar. The Leipzig agendas contain four different Latin Gloria intonations "together with the 'Et in terra,' as it has at all times up to the present been sung" (*Ag*, p. 99). The *Neu Leipziger Gesangbuch*, 1682, adds to this possibility also the other, that the Gloria was intoned in German; for after the printed text of the German Kyrie hymn we read: "Here the priest intones at the altar 'Ehre sey Gott in der Höhe,' and then 'Allein Gott in der Höh' is sung" (*LGB* 1682, pp. 423ff.). About 1700, in analogy to the Kyrie arrangement, a regular alternation between a Latin and a German Gloria arrangement is still reported. At the beginning of the 18th century, however, the German arrangement obviously came into always greater prominence. This may possibly have happened at exactly the same time as the Latin Magnificat was supplanted more and more by the German version (1714). In the same process also the polyphonic setting of "Et in terra pax" by the choir was heard less frequently. At the time of Bach the Gloria was probably presented polyphonically [*musiciret*] as a rule only on festival days, and then in both main churches simultaneously. Very significantly the note of Rost for the first festival day of Easter states: "The Gloria is intoned . . . 'Et in terra pax' . . . then Dominus vobiscum," and for the third festival day of Easter: "The Gloria is intoned. 'Allein Gott in der Höhe sey Ehr' . . . Dominus vobiscum" (Ro, pp. 26—27). On both days, however, the second Kantorei functioned in St. Thomas.[45] Besides, Sicul's contrast, that "the hymn 'Allein Gott in der Höh sey Ehr' was sung and sometimes also the Latin 'Et in terra pax' came as a response from the choir" (Sc*NA*, p. 569), lets us know definitely that the congregation really was in the habit of singing along in the Gloria hymn—exactly as in the Kyrie hymn. Otherwise the emphatic use of the words "came as a response from the choir" would seem completely pointless in this sentence. Sometimes all the stanzas of the Gloria hymn were sung; during the last stanza the priest again approached the altar (Ro, p. 10) to chant the Salutation, which was always given in Latin, "Dominus vobiscum," to which the choir, substituting for the congregation, responded "Et cum spiritu tuo." Then the priest brought the entrance section of the service to a close with the Collect. All sources emphasize unanimously that until far into the second half of the 18th century the Salutation and the Collect were given only in Latin (*LKA*, p. 12; *LKS*, p. 6; Sc*NA*, p. 570; Ro, pp. 15, 17, 19, 23, 26—27, 43—44, 49, 154, etc.). The *Leipziger Kirchen-Andachten*, which in the appendix contains all the Latin Collects current in Leipzig, notes in connection with this Collect: "Instead of this, a layman (who does not understand Latin) can read a German Collect," as they "are used in other places and churches" (*LKA*, pp. 12—13). Not until the second half of the 18th century was a beginning made to use the Salutation and the Collect in German, too (Ro, pp. 20, 22, 48), although it was not the agenda of 1748, as Terry maintains,[46] that first contained Collects in German, but earlier agendas as well (cf. *Ag*, pp. 145ff.).

In spite of many a criticism that is perhaps justified, it may still be emphasized that the manifold and rich practice reported for Leipzig, as it becomes evident already in the liturgical arrangement of the entrance section of the main service of Sundays and festival days, and as it was faithfully preserved in principle until the end of the 18th century, was entirely in keeping with the thought of Luther. For to have side by side the Latin and German languages, participation by choir and congregation, Gregorian song and polyphonic choir music finds its foundation in Luther's own wish and thought: "For in no wise would I want to discontinue the service in the Latin language...if I could bring it to pass, and Greek and Hebrew were as familiar to us as the Latin and had as many fine melodies and songs, we would hold Mass, sing, and read on successive Sundays in all four languages, German, Latin, Greek, and Hebrew. I do not at all agree with those who cling to one language and despise all others."[47] Because Luther desired great variety in the service, he was able on the one hand to cling to the musical treasure of the pre-Reformation Mass with complete self-evidence and enthusiastic acceptance,[48] but on the other hand he could create and recommend suitable German songs for the liturgy to let the congregation have an active part in the liturgical singing. But the uninterrupted sequence of a number of German congregational hymns (Entrance hymn, Kyrie hymn, Gloria hymn) very early led to this, that Kyrie and Gloria were entirely lost sight of,[49] and the understanding for this section of the service disappeared entirely. This is confirmed in many places, but it did not happen in Leipzig. The notebook of the sexton at St. Thomas everywhere gives evidence that all the essential elements of the liturgy held their own almost to the end of the 18th century. Even the "Et in terra pax" is still maintained in the *Neue Liturgie seit anno 1779* for the First Sunday in Advent, while the German Gloria is not (Ro, p. 43). In elevating the principle of variety with an accompanying emphasis on the best organization possible to be the main thrust of the organization of the worship service, late orthodoxy as it flourished in Leipzig represented a latitude and an openness over against the whole stream of Reformation tradition that was always bent on shutting the door on legalistic narrowness and rigidity. The entrance section of the main service still had the character of a real prayer section, of an actual offering of praise and thanksgiving. Many details indicate this, above all also the prayers given in various hymnbooks for the individual liturgical pieces. These the congregation was to use all the time, but especially during the singing of the choir. Even the shortest liturgical pieces were furnished with such prayers, for example, the Salutation or the moment when "the priest mounts the pulpit" and "when the priest leaves the pulpit" (*LKS*, pp. 7, 10). The Dresden *Auserlesenes und vollständiges Gesang-Buch* of 1750 still contains an abundance of prayers of that kind, as, for instance, "For the Gloria in excelsis Deo," "For the Kyrie eleison," "For the Dominus vobiscum" (cf. also the discussion on p. 105). The long tradition of the Latin Collect can be explained only on the basis of this fact, that the members of the congregation had been trained to read along and to pray along from the hymnbooks and prayer books.

After this entrance section of the service, entirely dominated by prayer and thanksgiving, had been concluded with the Collect as the summary of the prayer section, the reading of the Epistle ushered in the second section of the service, a section primarily governed by the idea of proclamation. This "Service of the Word"[50] had in Reformation times become the most important section of the whole service so far as the organization of the Lutheran main service was concerned, for Luther "never tired of extolling the fundamental significance of the proclaimed Word and of emphasizing preaching above all other ingredients as the preeminent item in the Christian service."[51] Thus it is not at all strange that in the worship of late orthodoxy in Leipzig in the 18th century this Service of the Word (including the announcements-and-prayer section appended to it) still appears as the most important of the whole service. But in spite of the great importance of this section of the service, we cannot speak of a development in the Leipzig service of that time that was entirely partial to this Service of the Word, as the development of the entrance section of the service already definitely revealed.

A detailed comparison between the liturgical ingredients of this Service of the Word as practiced in Leipzig in the first half of the 18th century and those of the Reformation orders of worship reveals a surprising and extensive concurrence of practice of Reformation and late orthodox worship also in this section of the service. In spite of a good deal of criticism, the Reformation had kept the double reading from Scripture, Epistle and Gospel, and this was also continued as self-evident in the Leipzig main services at the time of Bach. In addition, this was done in complete conformity with the suggestion of the reformers, at least so far as this relates to the selection of the pericopes made for each Sunday and festival day or taken over from the medieval church together with their performance according to the lesson tone.[52] Also still known in Leipzig was the practice followed by the reformers according to the use of the ancient church according to which two of the three clergymen involved in the service took the part of lectors of the Epistle and the Gospel and also of assistants during the Distribution in the Sacrament of the Altar (cf. the discussion on pp. 69—70). Together with the faithful retention of both readings, also the congregational hymn still had its established place between the two readings and in this position in the liturgy maintained an almost unchallenged place throughout the 18th century. This hymn had been created by the Reformation and then, as chief hymn [*Hauptlied*] of the service, had turned into the theme hymn for any given Sunday or festival day (Cf. Ro, pp. 3, 10, 15, 18, 19, 21, 23, 26, 44, 48—49, etc.).

The order of the service in use in Leipzig at the time of Bach was a very lively affair and in no sense a proposition solidified to a mere formality. The truth of this statement can best be realized by considering the increasing importance of the cantata, presented every two weeks or oftener—when the frequency of festival days called for it—in both churches in connection with the Gospel and so representing the most modern element in the liturgy of the main service. In a time when the church music in the Lutheran service had already been subjected to many a criticism and had therefore quite commonly been restricted, this music in Leipzig, particularly in Bach's cantata compositions, experienced an impressive late flowering that can be accounted for satisfactorily only in this way, that in Leipzig, with its unusually strong emphasis on a continuation of the Reformation practice in worship, people were still conscious of the high valuation accorded to church music by the Lutheran reformers and especially by Luther himself. Add to this the obvious fact that throughout the age of orthodoxy we have generally the record of an intense theological reflection concerning the nature of church music in the Lutheran Church.[53] But finally we must apply also to the Leipzig situation what is true for the Lutheran Church generally, namely "the observation that the richness of church music" always "grows with the richness of the liturgy."[54] Accordingly, the rich church music tradition of this city must be understood to be a necessary result of its rich liturgical practice. The worshipers at church received special librettos of the texts presented in music so that a proper hearing of the cantata might result. Concerning this recent arrangement in worship practice in the city, Sicul reports: "So that this polyphonic music, especially on high festivals, may be heard with the greater devotion, it has become custom for some time for the honorable cantor to have the texts of the music printed beforehand...under the title *Kirchen-Music*, so that everyone can provide himself with these and read along" (Sc*NA*, p. 570). Otherwise, during the presentation of the cantata, as in general during the whole Service of the Word in the main service, the congregation was to follow the progress of the liturgy with its prayers. That is why the hymnbooks contain prayers "after the Epistle" and "after the Gospel." Concerning the cantatas we read: "If there is a musical presentation and a person wants to promote his devotion in another way, the following prayers may be found serviceable: (1) During the Musical Presentation, (2) The Prayers Before the Sermon, (3) For Fruitful Hearing of the Word of God, (4) The Prayer Before the Creed Is Sung" (*LKS*, p. 7; see also the Appendix of Sources, No. 5).

But above all, the Leipzig liturgical practice was able to demonstrate its faithfulness to the Lutheran worship tradition in respect to its retention and various use of the Creed, for already in the 17th century the Creed had often been "severely relegated to the background or replaced by other hymns," a process "which of course had no small connection with the disintegration and the perversion of the contents of the Creed caused by rationalism."[55] In Leipzig the Creed maintained a secure and inviolable position between the Gospel and the Sermon all the way to the end of the 18th century, not only in the Sunday and festival day main services but also in the early weekday services held at times on Wednesdays and Thursdays. As the Reformation had clung to the singing of the Creed, so the liturgical tradition of late orthodoxy in Leipzig still carried on. In keeping with Luther's suggestion in the *Deutsche Messe* (1526), the congregation regularly followed the custom of singing the Creed in the hymn form of Luther's German *Credo* hymn "Wir glauben all an einen Gott" (*LKS*, p. 6). But also Luther's suggestion in the *Formula missae et communionis* (1523) to let the Nicene Creed be sung—and most of the Lutheran orders of service of Reformation times followed this suggestion—was observed far into the 18th century in Leipzig. For beside the creedal hymn sung by the congregation, the choir additionally and preceding the creedal hymn of the congregation was accustomed to singing the Nicene Creed throughout Advent and Lent and on apostles' days and days of public mourning. Only in the church where the cantata was presented on the First Sunday in Advent was the Nicene Creed dropped. For this Sunday Rost jotted down the following note: "The Creed is intoned, that is, the choir's 'Patrem omnipotentem' [Nicene Creed]. . . . Whenever there is concerted music on the First Sunday in Advent, the Creed is not intoned. The order of the early service is: (1) Kyrie is sung; (2) Gloria; (3) 'Et in terra pax'; (4) Dominus vobiscum; (5) Epistle; (6) Litany; (7) Hymn; (8) Gospel; (9) Then the concerted music..." (Ro, p. 44). Conspicuously, this double form of the Creed, already registered in various service orders of Reformation times for one and the same service, that is, the Nicene Creed chanted by the choir and Luther's creedal hymn sung by the congregation, was always used in

122

those times of the church year in which the cantata or motet, otherwise performed by the Kantoreien after the Gospel, was dropped; although also the Leipzig agendas contain the prescription: "After the Gospel the Latin Creed is to be sung all the way through, according to the usual notes; likewise the German 'Wir glauben' " (*Ag*, p. 114). But this double form of the Creed was customary in Leipzig already in the 17th century, but only in the services in which no "polyphonic composition or concerted piece" was presented (cf. *LKA*, Index and p. 17). It is true, in Leipzig the custom prevailed for a long time to intone at the altar "Credo in unum Deum" immediately after the Gospel, even when neither choir nor congregation took up a continuation of the Creed so intoned and when the cantata followed immediately. This certainly points to an earlier customary use of the Nicene Creed. Not until the tenure of Rost as St. Thomas sexton was this absurd custom presumably dropped, for Rost, in his catchword notes concerning the order of service for the individual Sundays and festival days, points out again and again: "The Creed is not intoned" (Ro, pp. 3, 14—15, 17, 23, 26—27, 32, 35, 44, 47). Already at the beginning of his notebook he reminds himself: "In general, note that...on the festivals of Easter, Pentecost, Christmas, Candlemas, the festivals of Mary, Ascension, St. John, and St. Michael...the Creed is not intoned" (Ro, p. 1). In addition to the festivals mentioned, this custom was followed also on New Year's Day, Good Friday, and on the First Sunday in Advent—at any rate in the church in which the cantata was presented (Ro, pp. 3, 23, 44). Sicul still reports that the intonation of the Creed took place regularly, even when immediately after it the cantata was presented: After the Gospel " 'Credo in unum Deum' is intoned, and then, in Advent and Lent, as well as on apostles' days, the entire Nicene Creed is sung in Latin by the choir, and beside this a concerted piece is presented [*eine Concerta musiciret wird*].... Once the polyphonic music is concluded, the Creed is sung in German" (Sc*NA*, p. 570; cf. also *LKA*, index and p. 16). The *Leipziger Kirchen-Staat* does not mention the intonation at all. Obviously it thought of it as completely incidental. Only in connection with the presentation of the peculiarities of the Maundy Thursday liturgy does it specify: "After the reading of the Gospel the priest at the altar intones the Nicene Creed: 'Credo in unum Deum,' which the choir continues. After its conclusion the *Glaube* is sung" (*LKS*, p. 23). The same direction is then given again for Advent and Lent and for the apostles' days (*LKS*, pp. 32, 44—45). The St. Thomas sexton also confirms this usage only for Advent and Lent and the apostles' days (Ro, pp. 10, 21, 44, 49). Not until Maundy Thursday, 1787, "was the Creed and its response omitted" (Ro, p. 20). After all, even Bach himself, in his outline of the service for the First Sunday in Advent, crossed out the words already noted down: "Creed is intoned."[56] Even if the Nicene Creed, frequently retained in the service orders of Reformation times only in the Latin language, was sung in Leipzig in Bach's time, it was always done in Latin and in the monophonic Gregorian form, as is expressly indicated already in the *Leipziger Kirchen-Andachten* after mention of the intonation "Credo in unum Deum" and in respect to the continuation of the Creed: "In Advent, in Lent, and in times of public mourning the rest of the words are sung in unison [*choraliter*] as follows. This Latin confession, in the Appendix of Part II, runs as follows in our German language:..." (Here follows the German Nicene Creed. Cf. *LKA*, p. 16). The *Leipziger Kirchen-Staat* contains the Nicene Creed only in Latin, because it was sung only in this language in the services, and then, parallel to it and as a kind of German translation, it presents the three stanzas of Luther's creedal hymn. We have no evidence, at least not for Leipzig in the 18th century, that the Creed was presented on certain Sundays and festival days by the choir also in polyphonic settings.

The principal item in the Service of the Word was and always remained (except on Maundy Thursday, Good Friday, and the Reformation Festival) the Sermon on the Gospel of the Sunday or festival day in question. After the pastor had ascended the pulpit during the last stanza of the creedal hymn, the pulpit service of the preacher always began with the *Präambulum*, also called *Praeloquium* or *Antritt* (*LKS*, pp. 7, 18). These terms signified the pulpit greeting and the admonition to prayer attached to it. The congregation's response was in the form of a short prayer hymn for proper hearing of the Word of God or, in festival times, a seasonal hymn. These were hymns prescribed once and for all time: for ordinary Sundays "Herr Jesu Christ, dich zu uns wend," in the Christmas season up to the Purification of Mary "Ein Kindelein so löbelich," at Easter up to Rogate Sunday [Sixth Sunday of Easter] "Christ ist erstanden," for Ascension Day and Exaudi Sunday [Seventh Sunday of Easter] "Christ fuhr gen Himmel," for Pentecost "Nun bitten wir den heiligen Geist," and for the Reformation Festival "Erhalt uns, Herr, bei deinem Wort" (Ro, pp. 29, 139; cf. also *LKA*, pp. 7, 17, 26, 30; *LKA*, pp. 48, 53, 63, 65, 105). Immediately after this hymn the Lord's Prayer was prayed silently, and then the Gospel was read once more and the Sermon was preached. This Sermon section[57] of the service, usually so organized in its individual elements already since the Reformation, always began "about eight o'clock" in Leipzig and always continued for an hour, for the rule was: "The normal time for the Sermon is one hour, and the priest usually closes the Sermon at nine o'clock or shortly after" (*LKS*, p. 7). The Sermon section of the service was followed by a prayer section elaborately filled with prayers, thanksgivings, intercessions, and announcements of all kinds (cf. Appendix of Sources, No. 6).

About the regular close of the pulpit section of the service we read: "Finally the congregation is admonished to be generous over against poverty, for which purpose every church door has its 'poor boxes.' Then comes the close with a silent Lord's Prayer, and the priest leaves the pulpit with the Pauline words 'The peace of God, which surpasses all understanding, etc.' " (*LKS*, p. 9—10). Only now did the congregation sing the hymn "after the Sermon or several stanzas of a hymn suitable for the Gospel" (*LKS*, p. 10), or not infrequently was the second section of the cantata performed.[58] That such polyphonic music at this point in the service was possible beyond the actual festival days we can plainly see from the two-section cantatas Bach composed for ordinary Sundays. Consider, for example, cantatas BWV 17, 20, 35, 39, and 45.

The question whether the General Prayer of the Church belongs to the Service of the Word or the Service of the Sacrament was not clearly answered by the Reformation, and Luther himself left the question completely open.[59] For that reason we also have no right to see a degeneration of the Lutheran service in orthodoxy, no, not even a one-sided emphasis on the Service of the Word, when we behold the fact that in the Leipzig liturgy of the 18th century a rather long prayer section followed the Sermon immediately and was therefore considered a part of the Service of the Word. The extensive prayer-and-announcement section is generally given word for word already in the *Leipziger Kirchen Andachten* (*LKA*, pp. 18ff.), and thus a firm tradition is indicated. Since the main service at that time lasted three and one-half hours on average, there was in any case a good full hour left for the organization and observance of the third large main section of the main service, the Service of the Sacrament. Therefore this section of the service also in Bach's time was without doubt thought of as the concluding climax of the main service.

For the liturgical organization of the Service of the Sacrament there were two different orders, one for the main services on ordinary Sundays and one for the main services on festival days. The order used on ordinary Sundays consisted of this, that after the conclusion of the "pulpit hymn," so called by Rost (Ro, p. 18), or after the presentation of the concerted music immediately "the liturgy of the Holy Communion was celebrated at the altar," that is, "with the chanting of the Lord's Prayer and the Words of Institution" (*LKS*, p. 10). This form of Communion liturgy is without doubt a grave impoverization of the richness originally present. But this curtailment of the Communion liturgy, which has been called a "torso,"[60] must not be imputed to Lutheran orthodoxy. It was present in this form already in Luther's *Deutsche Messe* (1526). On festival days, however, the Communion liturgy was essentially richer in its organization. In the *Leipziger Kirchen-Staat* we read: "When the priest leaves the pulpit, the deacon who will be the celebrant goes to the altar and intones the Latin Preface, or Antiphon, 'Dominus vobiscum.' This is then continued antiphonally by him and the choir" (*LKS*, pp. 17—18). The climax of the Preface was the

125

polyphonic presentation of the Sanctus (cf. the discussion on p. 86). In addition to the Prefaces for the various festivals in a unison setting, the *Neu Leipziger Gesangbuch* (1682) also offers the Sanctus separately in three additional forms, of which one is in six voices and the other two are in unison (*LGB* 1682, pp. 1084ff.). Here we also find the sections of the Preface sung by the choir (but without the Sanctus), variously in four and six voices. In the second Communion liturgy, however, the one for festival days, the Lord's Prayer was omitted (cf. *LKS,* p. 18; Ro, p. 26), so that the Preface was immediately followed by the Words of Institution and then the distribution.

The second form of the Communion liturgy used in Leipzig also represents an old Lutheran tradition, for already Bugenhagen had made provision for a chanted Latin Preface on festival days, and Luther himself in his *Formula missae et communionis* (1523) indicated that he wanted the Preface kept by all means.[61] Throughout Bach's tenure in Leipzig the Latin Preface always maintained its place on the following festivals: First and Second Christmas Days, New Year's Day, Epiphany, Purification of Mary, Annunciation, First and Second Easter Days, Ascension Day, First and Second Pentecost Festivals, Trinity, St. John's Day, Visitation of Mary, and St. Michael's. The *Leipziger Kirchen-Staat*, Part II, contains the complete text for all the customary Prefaces in order for the apostles' days, St. John's, and St. Michael's, for Christmas and New Year's Day, for the Day of the Holy Three Kings, for Easter, Ascension Day, and Pentecost, for the Festival of the Holy Trinity, and for the three festivals, the Purification of Mary, the Annunciation of Mary, and the Visitation of Mary. Rost, too, confirms that on the festival days mentioned the Preface was chanted (Ro, pp. 3, 5, 14—15, 19, 26ff., 32, 34—35). He also mentions the fact that on Reformation Day no Preface was heard but the Communion liturgy of the order commonly used on ordinary Sundays was used (Ro, p. 37). On the third festival days of the three great festivals of the church year "the Latin Preface was not chanted before the Communion, but in place of it a hymn was sung, or only several stanzas of it" (*LKS*, p. 20).

Also on Maundy Thursday it was still customary for some time in Leipzig "to chant the Latin Preface after the Sermon as on high festivals," and the Preface used was the one customary for the Marian festivals (*LKS*, p. 24). But the Communion liturgy for Maundy Thursdays represented a unique specialty in the church year, for on this day, in addition to the Latin Preface and immediately attached to it, "the paraphrase, or explanation, of the Lord's Prayer, together with an exhortation to prayer for the people" was usually read, and beside that the Lord's Prayer was also chanted before the Words of Institution (*LKS*, p. 24). According to the notes of the sexton of St. Thomas, however, the chanting of the Latin Preface must have been dispensed with on Maundy Thursday in the first half of the 18th century, for he reports: "After the Sermon only a hymn is sung, as on Sundays, at the last stanza of which the priest goes to the altar, and the preface to the Lord's Prayer is read, as on Oculi [Third Sunday in Lent].... When this preface is concluded, the sexton rings the bell," that is, for the Words of Institution that follow (Ro, p. 21). For a better understanding of this note we must compare the one for Palm Sunday regarding this point: "After the Sermon, even though this is like a festival, nevertheless no Preface before the Words of Institution is chanted, but a preface to the Lord's Prayer is read, as usually in Lent, and then the Words of Institution follow" (Ro, p. 17). This comparison makes it clear that the term "preface to the Lord's Prayer" refers to the Communion exhortation that was customary in Leipzig only in the Communion services during Lent, at least from Oculi on. For Good Friday Rost set down this note for himself: "The preface to the Lord's Prayer is read as on Oculi; also the same custom for the ringing of the bell" (Ro, p. 23). This Communion exhortation also is not an arrangement of Lutheran orthodoxy, but it was already Luther's creation, and it found a place in various church orders of Reformation times.[62]

If we add this unique liturgical tradition in Lent, and specifically that of Maundy Thursday, as a separate item, we arrive at the conclusion that in the course of the church year in Leipzig four different orders of the Communion liturgy were in use, but all of them in the last analysis must be traced to the two basic types already present with Luther in his *Formula missae et communionis* and in his *Deutsche Messe*.[63] The *Leipziger Kirchen-Andachten* describes the Communion tradition for this city as follows: "At high festivals...a Latin Preface is chanted before Communion.... Then the service of the holy Mass, or Communion, is celebrated at the altar, and this is done according to the church order and the same agendas.... Thus the priest reads to the people the paraphrase, or explanation, of the Lord's Prayer, together with the exhortation to prayer before Communion as follows." (Here follow the precise words of the Communion exhortation.) "But this explanation and exhortation is read in our churches only in Lent. Otherwise and on other Sundays only the Lord's Prayer and then the Words of Institution...are chanted" (*LKA*, pp. 33ff.). It is true, the reference to the Leipzig agendas is something of a problem in that they present a picture of colorful variety, and moreover their directions hardly seem obligatory. Thus we read at first: "After the Sermon, read the paraphrase of the Lord's Prayer to the people at the altar, together with the exhortation for the Sacrament. Then chant the Words of Institution in German.... When these words have been chanted, let the people sing 'JEsus Christus unser Heyland'...or 'GOtt sey gelobet.'...Also at certain times, especially on festival days, the reading of the paraphrase and the exhortation to the people may be dispensed with, and the Latin Preface may be chanted instead, and then the Latin Sanctus may follow. After that, chant the Lord's Prayer and the Words of Institution in German . . . and then during the distribution the Agnus Dei in Latin, including the German hymn 'JEsus Christus.' Also Psalm 111 ('Ich dancke dem HErrn von gantzem Hertzen') may be sung, according as there are many or few communicants'' (*Ag*, pp. 79—80). Later we read: "After the Sermon a Latin Preface may be chanted on festival days and at certain times on Sundays, as the season dictates, according to the same tune." (Here the Prefaces respectively for Christmas, Epiphany, Easter, Ascension, Pentecost, Trinity, and the "daily one" are given.) "Then the priest should read the paraphrase of the Lord's Prayer as follows: Exhortation to prayer before Communion." (Here follows the text of the exhortation and then two musical settings of the Words of Institution.) "If desired, instead of the paraphrase or exhortation to prayer, the priest may chant the Lord's Prayer on these notes and then the Words of Institution also on the same tone, as follows." (Here follow the Lord's Prayer and the Words of Institution.) "On festival days and when there are many communicants, the Latin Agnus Dei may be chanted, . . . or if one or more German hymns have been sung (such as 'JEsus CHristus unser Heyland,' . . . the German Sanctus 'Esaia dem Propheten das geschah,' or the Psalm 'Ich dancke dem HErrn von gantzem . . .'), the conclusion may be made with the German Agnus Dei'' (*Ag*, pp. 114ff.).

During the distribution in Leipzig, in addition to the special music for the Sacrament, a whole series of church hymns were sung, and of these especially seven came to belong to the standing set sung for generations during the distribution, namely "Jesus Christus, unser Heiland," "Gott sei gelobet und gebenedeiet," "Nun freut euch, lieben Christengmein," "Wo soll ich fliehen hin," and the three already mentioned on p. 84 ["Es wolle Gott uns gnädig sein," "Nun lob, mein Seel, den Herren," and "Der Herr ist mein getreuer Hirt"].

After the distribution the Service of Communion, and with it the main service as a whole, was concluded with a closing Collect chanted by the liturgist at the altar and the pronounced Benediction, plus the closing hymn sung by the congregation, "Gott sei uns gnädig und barmherzig," and on festival days special hymns (cf. p. 88; *LKS*, p. 11). According to the *Leipziger Kirchen-Staat*, the closing Collect, even in Vespers and prayer services, was always chanted, whereas the Benediction was spoken (cf. *LKS*, pp. 14, 20, 31), but Rost notes throughout that both the Collect and the Benediction were spoken, and that in all services (Ro, pp. 2—3, 9, 14—15, 20, 22, 24, 26—27, 35ff., 46). But Rost apparently does not distinguish between what is spoken and what is chanted, as the following note for the Sunday Estomihi [Quinquagesima, or Sunday before Lent] clearly indicates: "Both on this Sunday and throughout this whole week no Lenten

128

Versicle and Collect are spoken" (Ro, p. 9). "Lenten Versicle" refers to the versicle preceding the closing Collect, which was never "spoken" at that time but always chanted by the choir, and then only in Vespers and in the prayer services (cf. *LKS*, pp. 14, 19, 21ff., 26ff., 31; also Ro, pp. 15—16, 22, 24, 28, 34—35, 46, etc.). In the main services the Versicle preceding the closing Collect was chanted only at the Reformation Festival and on apostles' days (*LKS*, pp. 30, 45; Ro, p. 37). Significantly, these were main services that frequently were held without the Communion section. Not until 1715 was the main service at the Reformation Festival combined with Holy Communion (cf. Ro, p. 36). The Leipzig agendas also contain German Collects to be used "during the celebration of the Mass (before the Epistle) and elsewhere" without exhibiting a preceding Versicle (*Ag*, pp. 145ff.), and then again they show a second group of German Collects for all festival days that are in each case connected to a Versicle (*Ag*, pp. 163ff.).

The order for the Sunday main service basically remained the same for all Sundays and festivals. At the beginning of the enumeration of all the peculiarities of festival days, the *Leipziger Kirchen-Staat* expressly emphasizes that the main service on the three main festival days, so far as the arrangement of the Kyrie, Gloria, Salutation, Collect, and Epistle is concerned, proceeded in principle exactly as on ordinary Sundays (*LKS*, p. 16). At the end of the description of services on Sundays and festivals the emphasis is repeated: "Otherwise nothing is altered in the order that the first division above contains, and one can safely be guided by it every Sunday" (*LKS*, pp. 37—38). This order of service in effect for ordinary Sundays could on occasion be expanded a little—perhaps in Advent and Lent by the insertion of the Litany between the Epistle and the main hymn [*Hauptlied*] of the Sunday. But on Palm Sunday, Maundy Thursday, Good Friday, and the Annunciation this Litany was not used (cf. Ro, pp. 10ff.). Still this order of service was in its basic structure unalterable in the entire first half of the 18th century. Not only in the two main churches, but in the subordinate churches of the city as well, the best possible uniformity was aimed at. In describing the services, Sicul emphatically states that although his description pertains only to the two main churches, the situation is not much different in New Church, where also "the liturgy is always celebrated," and similarly in St. John, St. George, and St. James the same liturgical order is observed as in the main churches (with the Service of the Sacrament of course only on Communion days; Sc*NA*, p. 572). The Reformation Festival of the year 1734, which fell on the 19th Sunday After Trinity, shows us to what lengths people went in their effort, even on special occasions, to cling to the propers of a given Sunday. The Sermon in the main service on that day was not based on a special text commissioned by the consistory, as was the regular custom otherwise, but on the traditional

New Church. Source: W. Neumann, *Auf den Lebenswegen Johann Sebastian Bachs* (Berlin, 1953), p. 171.

Gospel for the 19th Sunday After Trinity. When New Church was again rededicated with much festivity on 24 September 1699, the whole festival service was organized very carefully on the basis of the liturgy for the 16th Sunday After Trinity, a liturgy completely unsuitable for such a festival. Not only were the traditional readings used and the Gradual hymn "Mitten wir im Leben sind" sung, but even the Sermon was based on the Gospel for that Sunday (the raising of the young man at Nain), and then the hymn "Ich hab mein Sach Gott heimgestellt" was sung (*AG*, pp. 29ff.). The same source stresses the fact that the plan of the Vespers followed "exactly the same ceremonies as were introduced in other parish churches here," indeed, that the Catechism instruction, held for the first time on 7 May 1702 in New Church, was arranged exactly like the order customary for the other churches of the city (*AG*, pp. 34ff., 37—38). There is further emphasis on the fact that it never became custom to drop a service or devotion, once it was firmly established, not even in the case of sicknesses among the clergy (*AG*, p. 74).

Only the University Church with its special status had its own orders for the services of the forenoon and afternoon. But these do not merit further attention here because all of them were purely preaching services, in which the professors only preached the Sermon from the pulpit and added a section containing prayers and announcements. In the Vespers they also used an additional reading. This pulpit service was framed by the singing of church hymns, each with an introductory organ prelude, and in individual cases special concerted music after the prayers-and-announcements section (cf. Sc*NA*, pp. 574—75; Sc*JL*, pp. 122ff.).

There can therefore be no doubt that Lutheran orthodoxy, with its faithful stand for a consistent use of the traditional orders of worship, rendered a distinguished service toward the preservation of the Lutheran worship tradition, and it did this in an age in which heavily destructive forces on the part of rationalism and Pietism were aimed precisely at the liturgical practice of the congregations and were successful everywhere. We therefore agree fully with Friedrich Kalb, who at the end of his treatise comes to the conclusion: "We have every reason to acknowledge gratefully the zeal of the orthodox fathers for 'the beautiful services of the Lord.' "[64]

c) *Worship and Holy Communion*

In our effort to evaluate the quality of worship life we shall always be obliged to consider the rate of attendance at Holy Communion a very important and revealing indicator. Although even in the earliest Christian times as well as in the Reformation era we occasionally find something we might call "neglect of Holy Communion,"[65] yet it cannot even remotely be compared with the neglect of Holy Communion that appeared so obviously when rationalism invaded the liturgical life of the Lutheran Church, a neglect that has not been overcome decisively down to our own time. Still one can safely say that in the worship life at the time of Johann Sebastian Bach—at least in Leipzig—we can in no way speak of a neglect of Holy Communion. On the contrary, as we study the sources, we get the impression that in Leipzig at the beginning of the 18th century the joy in Holy Communion experienced an even greater revitalization, which is completely in agreement with the intensification of worship life observable there otherwise. And the celebration of Holy Communion, except in the case of Communion for the sick, occurred on principle only in the *public* worship of the congregation. Especially after the inroads of rationalism on the worship life everywhere, there was evidence of a tendency to separate the celebration of Holy Communion from the actual main service of the congregation and to conduct it in an attached separate service for communicants only. But in Leipzig this did not make its appearance until the beginning of the 19th century. Throughout the 18th century, however, the regular main service in Leipzig, in agreement with the old Lutheran order of service with its two high points, the Sermon and the celebration of Holy Communion, was incontestably the center of worship life on all Sundays and festival days, and this fact applies not only to the two main churches of the city but also to New Church. It is expressly reported that the first two clergymen of this church after its restoration, Head Deacon Steinbach and Vespers Preacher Werner, were from the very beginning "permitted to administer the Holy Supper every Sunday and festival day as in the other parish churches here" (*AG*, p. 25). Already the dedicatory service held on 24 September 1699 was as a matter of course patterned after the order of the main service customary for both of the main churches, and in it "at the hands of both honorable clergymen...the blessed Holy Supper was administered" (*AG*, p. 33). It is true, in this first service in New Church only 31 communicants received the Holy Supper (*AG*, p. 31), but this does not allow us to draw conclusions concerning Communion attendance otherwise. After all, the particularly rich musical makeup (cf. p. 88) of this service already required an unusually long time, and therefore a prolonged celebration of the Holy Supper would not seem particularly suitable, at least not in the view of those who attended this service. But much more important for understanding the small number of guests at the Communion would be the fact that a real congregation for worship and for the celebration of the Holy Supper would have to develop little by little, because the reestablishment of worship in New Church was undertaken only to relieve the congestion in the other two churches. The parish boundaries remained unchanged. In fact, a constantly growing congregation gathered here for worship very quickly, with the result that already on 1 January 1712 the grateful observation could be made "that up to the present very many have come to hear the sermons" and "the number of the communicants has increased remarkably" (*AG*, p. 54). Only a single Communion register, the one covering the years 1729—1740, remains after the total destruction of New Church in World War II, and this provides us with a good insight into the rich participation in Communion by the worshipers during the tenure of Bach in Leipzig.

Thus we learn that in each of 37 services of the total of 68 main services on Sundays and festival days in 1729 more than 100 communicants received Holy Communion. The largest numbers of communicants in that year were registered for the services of the Seventh Sunday After Trinity with 226, the 20th Sunday After Trinity with 206, the Third Sunday in Advent with 205, and the Fourth Sunday in Advent with 235. The total number of participants for the year was 7,221. In the following years the annual total number of communicants even showed a tendency toward increase. Thus there were a total of 7,404 guests at the Holy Supper in 1730, 7,420 in 1731, 7,337 in 1732, 7,736 in 1733, 7,399 in 1734, and 7,419 in 1735.

But it is true that the participation in Holy Communion in the two main churches as compared with that registered for New Church was still considerably greater. In St. Thomas Church "figures of almost 20,000 Communion guests per year were not unusual,"[66] and in St. Nicholas, too, Communion registration figures of the same size for the entire first half of the 18th century are recorded. For Bach's time of service in Leipzig the following annual Communion guest figures of the two main churches for the two decades between Bach's inauguration in 1723 and 1743 are a matter of record:[67]

Year	St. Nicholas	St. Thomas	Year	St. Nicholas	St. Thomas
1723		19,088	1734	15,382	18,040
1724		17,689	1735	17,112	18,836
1725	17,393	16,645	1736		18,312
1726	16,864	16,645	1737		17,861
1727	14,758	13,037	1738		17,043
1728	17,154	14,014	1739		16,463
1729	16,766	16,458	1740		16,203
1730	16,069	15,906	1741		17,026
1731	14,594	17,869	1742	18,618	16,875
1732	15,024	18,038	1743	16,302	17,414
1733	15,955	18,753			

These uncommonly high figures for Communion attendance make it undeniably clear that the Sacrament section of the Sunday main service still represented the second climax of the service. To prevent this main service from becoming altogether too long on account of the Communion, special Communion services during the week had since 1694 also become customary. These weekly early services were, however, at first not as large as those of Sundays and festival days, and yet, not infrequently they exceeded the count of 100 and occasionally even 200. In the course of time the weekday Communion services grew in importance, so that at Bach's time we can hardly speak of an appreciable difference in the Communion attendance figures between the Sunday and the weekday Communion services (cf. the table for the years 1728/29 and 1742/43 in the Appendix of Sources, No. 7).

The figures for these years side by side clearly show that we can in no way speak of a tendency toward decline in Communion participation in the two main churches at the time of Bach; in fact, many services of 1742/43 show even larger numbers of Communion participants than those of 1728/29. But the comparison of these years also reveals how the weekday Communion services approximate those of Sunday and festival days more and more closely in numbers of participants among the members of congregations. Already in the church year 1718/19 in St. Nicholas only three weekday Communion services registered more than 200 Communion guests, namely on the Wednesday after the Third Sunday in Advent (208), after Judica [Fifth Sunday in Lent] (255), and after the 23d Sunday After Trinity (248). Similarly, 10 years later in St. Nicholas there were only three weekday Communion services that registered more than 200 Communion guests. In 1742/43, however, there were already nine such weekday Communion services. In St. Thomas there were six in 1728/29 and already 12 in 1742/43. Until the thirties of the 18th century the preponderance of Communion participation was definitely in the Sunday and festival day services, in which attendance figures not uncommonly exceeded 300, occasionally even 400.

For seven years we are able to give the total Communion attendance figures for the two main churches and for New Church, namely for 1729, 40,445; for 1730, 39,379; for 1731, 39,883; for 1732, 40,399; for 1733, 42,444; for 1734, 40,821; and for 1735, 43,367. From this it becomes clear that the decline in the services with the uncommonly high Communion registrations in the thirties, especially in St. Nicholas, represents no basic decline in Communion participation but rather only a different distribution of the communicants to the various services. In any case, in Bach's time we cannot in any sense speak of Holy Communion as becoming separated from the Sunday main service in favor of a special Communion celebration already detached from the service of the whole congregation. In spite of the growing importance of the weekday Communion services, the largest figures for Communion attendance are still registered for the Sunday main services in the thirties and forties. In St. Nicholas not a single weekday service up to 1744 registered more than 300 communicants.

Accordingly, for Leipzig at the time of Johann Sebastian Bach we cannot speak of a decline in Communion participation but must rather think of a certain increase when we consider that beside the establishment of the weekday Communion services in both of the main churches and of the regular Sunday and festival day Communion services in New Church, also in St. John and in St. James the number of Communion services had been doubled in number in the first half of the 18th century.

Because we lack the sources for St. John, St. James, and St. George, the figures for the number of communicants there can only be estimated. A total annual figure of between 5,000 and 6,000 communicants for these three churches could hardly be thought of as too high an estimate. Since the communicants at St. John and St. James were primarily sick and old people, who might possibly even be inclined to claim the comfort and strength of Holy Communion for themselves rather often, this total figure could perhaps be thought of as even larger. The Communion registration of the sick at St. John, formerly available and recorded at least since 1739, in any case reported "2,000—3,000 communicants annually."[68]

For Communion services for the sick we have records only in the registrations of St. Thomas, and these contain an annual figure of between 300 and 400 almost throughout the first half of the 18th century.

Overall, therefore, at the time of Johann Sebastian Bach in Leipzig we have to think of an annual number of 45,000-50,000 communicants, while the population of 29,000 remained fairly constant between 1720 and 1750. But this represents a Communion participation of over 150 percent for that time.

These uncommonly high numbers of Communion guests, which over the decades remained quite constant, infallibly prove that the liturgical life even in late orthodoxy was still full of lively strength. To preclude misapprehensions, we must emphasize that this intensely active participation in Holy Communion was on a voluntary basis; there was no prescription for anyone "how often he is to receive the Holy Supper, but this is left to the freedom of every member of the church" (Gb, p. 465). Those who did not participate in Holy Communion were not forced to do so (Gb, p. 466). This needs to be emphasized here because the service of orthodoxy has again and again been criticized as an undertaking definitely based on government and police procedures.[69] At the time of Johann Sebastian Bach there were still reports for Saxony in general about congregation members "who of their own free will and their own desire come to the Table of the Lord four, six, or more times a year and feel heartily strengthened through the reception of the Sacrament" (Gb, p. 466). Frequent participation in Holy Communion was desirable and was considered a genuine sign of piety: "Thus anyone among us may come to the Table of the Lord as often as he wishes. . . . Therefore pious hearts must consider this a great benefit if they may partake of the Holy Supper frequently" (Gb, p. 466). Gerber knows of "fellow believers" in the Diaspora who have to travel a long way to a Lutheran church, and he reports how they "sigh with desire for the Holy Supper and often have to go without it for a long time. By contrast, a congregation in which Holy Communion is celebrated publicly every Sunday is indeed blessed. . . . We should also thank God that among us the Supper of the Lord is recognized as a great benefaction of God by most of the people and therefore some people turn up every Sunday who desire it and partake of it. Among the Papists many people are content with frequent confession and rarely go to Communion. And many a person would put it off altogether if he were not forced to go at Easter time" (Gb, p. 466—67). According to Gerber's view, it was the Lutheran Church of his time that definitely took the leading role in holding Holy Communion in high regard. Gerber reports even about county life in Saxony that "many a preacher in rural areas is obliged to serve a hundred or more communicants every Sunday" and to do this "alone and without colleagues or assistants" (Gb, p. 489).

This active participation in Holy Communion was in the final analysis a palpable fruit of that genuine Lutheran realization still alive and effective in late orthodoxy that knows that the sacraments in a peculiar way transmit the presence of Christ.[70] We may even say that this vigorous use of Holy Communion is a clear indication that there was still a close connection between theological reflection and practical application, for the Lutheran dogmaticians were in the habit of treating especially the theology of Holy Communion very thoroughly in their dogmatical systems, and this was completely in accord with their high regard for the sacraments. Thus Leonhard Hutter, for instance, with whose well-known *Compendium locorum theologicorum* Johann Sebastian Bach became intimately acquainted already in his school days in Lüneburg, "wrote only 17 pages about the sacraments in general and about Baptism, but by contrast 45 pages about the Holy Supper," and so "this ranks immediately after Christology in importance."[71] When the theologians of Lutheran orthodoxy over against other theological movements persistently clung to "the merciful mystery of the sacraments, that God is pleased to be found also physically" and tried "to encompass this miracle of the physical presence in the concept *materia coelestis* of the Sacrament,"[72] they created the foundation for the Communion piety that has become so remarkably vigorous in the Lutheran Church. We are indebted to Hans Preuß for bringing it to our attention that "the prattle about 'dead orthodoxy' that is constantly being revived . . . must also be shattered by the warm Communion piety of these orthodox theologians" that "blazes up in the so-called *usus*, that is, the practical applications of dogmatics, especially in the

Locus de coena Domini (The doctrine concerning the Supper of our Lord)." "As the *coronis*, that is, the crowning conclusion," Johann Gerhard "even adds to his treatise on Holy Communion," which bears the characteristic title *Meditationes sacrae ad veram pietatem excitandam* (Sacred meditations for arousing true piety), "prayers of the fathers, of Ambrose, Basil, Chrysostom, John of Damascus, and even Thomas Aquinas."[73]

Already this reference to the old church fathers and even to medieval theologians clearly shows that the Lutheran theologians in the age of orthodoxy were in the habit of orienting themselves in many directions when engaged in research. It simply is not true that Lutheran orthodoxy in its Communion piety knew and cultivated a very narrow and completely one-sided view of Holy Communion, one that was related entirely to the gift of the forgiveness of sins. Preuß rightly emphasizes: "As in the primeval church, Holy Communion is again thought of as the anticipation of eternal salvation, for only then will what is here begun be completed." Because this is true, "the lovely tones of Lutheran Communion joy sound forth," and here especially "in the abundance of the church hymns, whose number no one can disregard, a fragrant garden of this kind is in full bloom." About these hymns in general it is true: "With an intimacy, yes, an ardor that sometimes reminds one of that of the Dominican nuns, they echo through the halls of the Lutheran Church and the walls of its chambers. Here Lutheran Communion piety achieves its highest beauty. We still feed on it today. What our fathers in those days managed to sing about the body and blood of our Lord and about the blessedness they bring is simply indispensable for us today."[74]

Also in the Leipzig hymnbook publications Communion hymns occupy considerable space among the church hymns. The eight-volume *Wagnersches Gesangbuch* (*WGB*) of 1697 contained a special volume entitled *Buss- und Catechismus—Lieder/wie auch vom H. Abendmahl* (vol. 5), even though the first volume already had contained Catechism hymns (pp. 352—84) as well as hymns under the headings "Concerning Confession and Penitence" (pp. 384— 409) and "Concerning Holy Communion" (pp. 409—40). The *Vollständiges und vermehrtes Leipziger Gesang-Buch* of 1730 contains 51 Communion hymns among its 856 church hymns, and the *Privilegirtes Vollständiges und verbessertes Leipziger Gesangbuch*, enlarged anew in the middle of the fourth decade and remaining in use in that form almost unchanged until the end of the 18th century, retained a large number of Communion hymns.

Beside the actual Communion hymns there is a whole series of church hymns that definitely contain references to the Sacrament of the Altar, especially Philipp Nicolai's "Wie schön leuchtet der Morgenstern," which in the Leipzig hymnbooks is to be found among the hymns "Concerning the Word of God and the Christian Church" and belonged among "the acknowledged favorites of Bach."[75]

Bach used this hymn in six different cantatas, and this frequency of use of a single hymn in the cantatas was surpassed only by the hymn "Was Gott tut, das ist wohlgetan." If we consider to what a strong degree "the Sacrament expressly or in substance takes its place ... in the old stock and store of hymns, especially in the hymns concerning the church,"[76] and that Johann Sebastian Bach, in addition to the large number of cantata compositions referring to the Sacrament of the Altar, specifically chose most of the hymns for his cantatas from the hymn section "Concerning the Word of God and the Christian Church," then we can rightly appreciate the fundamental importance the Sacrament had in the life and thought of the evangelical Christians in the age of orthodoxy. The Lutheran Church was then still the church of Word *and* Sacrament. Beside the proclaimed Word stood the Sacrament of the Altar at the very *center* of the Sunday and festival day main service as "the most sacred mystery of the body and blood of Christ" and the "true source of grace and inexhaustible fountain of mercy."[77] Considering this high regard for the Sacrament, we can also understand a custom taken over from the medieval church, according to which special napkins were held up to the communicants during the distribution of the Holy Supper to prevent spilling. This service, administered in Leipzig by the "four altar boys or schoolboys," was not abolished there until 1830 in St. Thomas and 1832 in St. Nicholas and New Church (*Bn*, p. 70).

The custom of singing Communion hymns during the distribution, a custom instituted by Luther that became tradition in the Lutheran churches, was considered the best device for focusing the devotion on the mystery of the Holy Supper. Already the hymn "after the Sermon" was to serve this purpose, that "heart, mind, and emotion be encouraged and awakened toward a devotion for and a consideration of the great mystery of the reception of the body and blood of Jesus Christ" (Gb, p. 451). During the music accompanying the Sacrament those members of the congregation who were not communing were to present prayers of thanksgiving and intercessions for the communicants (Gb, p. 471). The *Leipziger Kirchen-Staat* contains many prayers for the Communion section of the service, such as "Prayer When One Sees People Going to the Table of the Lord" or "Prayer When One Witnesses the Distribution" (cf. *LKS*, pp. 108ff.). The nuisance reported in many places that worshipers immediately after the preacher's pulpit service leave the church and so are no longer present for the Communion section—an abuse already present in Luther's time in Wittenberg[78]—does not seem to have appeared to a disturbing degree in Leipzig. The thought of separating the Communion section from the main service[79] was never expressed publicly in Leipzig throughout the age of orthodoxy. The solid union of the Communion section and the Sunday main service is strikingly portrayed in the engraving found in the *Leipziger Kirchen-Staat* [Reproduced in *BD* 4:185.—Ed.], which gives us a view of the interior of St. Thomas Church during a service. The two focal points of the main service, Sermon and Holy Communion, are here depicted: In a church filled to capacity the pastor is preaching from the pulpit, and simultaneously two other clergymen at the altar are distributing the Holy Supper to a crowd of people thronging toward them. Gerber, too, emphasizes the solid union of Communion and the Sunday main service in Leipzig in contrast to the obviously lax practice in Dresden when he writes that in Holy Cross Church in Dresden "from five to six in the morning the so-called early sermon is held, and after that the large Communion for from 400 to 600 people is held.... In the world-famous city of Leipzig also very many sermons are preached: In St. Thomas and St. Nicholas two Communion sermons [*Amts- Predigten*] are held in the morning. These derive their name from the fact that Holy Communion, which is customarily called *Amt*, is celebrated in conjunction with them" (Gb, p. 398).

Only if we keep in mind this high regard for the Holy Supper can we fully understand certain other procedures. Before their first reception of Communion the young people were to be "examined," and these "examinations" respecting the Sacrament of the Altar were to be repeated annually among the young people up to their 20th year (cf. Gb, pp. 650—51). Also the regulation of the year 1713, effective for all of Saxony, can be understood only from the viewpoint of this high regard for the Sacrament of the Altar. According to this regulation, "all those who want to come to confession and thereafter to Communion should come to see the preacher the week before," and that means for the Catechism examination (Gb, p. 502). In any case, Gerber emphasizes that only those should receive Communion who know how to value it and that this examination, based on that "most laudable and useful regulation," is only to serve the purpose of ascertaining whether the Holy Supper is being received worthily, for in the confessional booth a conversation regarding this matter could not take place because of the crowd of people (Gb, pp. 449—50, 502). This Communion registration was then practiced in a variety of ways in Saxony. Especially in the larger cities it seems generally to have become a mere formality, so that the people coming to confession often were also registered [for Communion] through others (cf. Gb, pp. 449—50, 502—03). In the last analysis, this Communion announcement was to meet a concern of Luther's, that the father confessor was to assure himself primarily in confession that his communicant was "correctly instructed concerning the Sacrament."[80]

Whether certain church members also were in the habit of partaking of Holy Communion without confession and absolution is a question we cannot answer. The Reformation as well as Luther knew of a participation in Holy Communion without preceding confession and also of confession without subsequent reception of Holy Communion, but in the 17th and 18th centuries the idea that going to Communion was to be preceded by confession and absolution had "gained complete supremacy."[81] The Leipzig communicant lists regularly report the names of those coming to confession [*Konfitenten*] and the total number of communicants for the individual services, and we observe that the number of communicants is always appreciably, frequently five or ten times, greater than the number of those who have come to confession. If we additionally consider that in Leipzig, beside the private confession, there was in every main service at the beginning of the announcement section also "the general public confession in church" and that "the public confession" sufficed[82] for those who had the reputation of being advanced [*geförderte*] Christians, the participation in Holy Communion without preceding private confession in Leipzig could certainly not have been impossible, especially since we know of people in the age of orthodoxy who very frequently, even daily, had a desire for Holy Communion,[83] and that can hardly have been preceded by private confession each time.

Amid all this high regard for the Holy Supper observable in Leipzig, it is therefore not a matter of chance that Bach's cantatas, which textually belong to the area of the Sermon, point to the Sacrament of the Altar to so great an extent. These cantatas are in their way models in answer to a demand made in the present time, that "in sermon, prayer, and hymn of the Service of the Word the regard for the Sacrament of the Altar must not be forgotten," for "Word and Sacrament in Luther's church form a liturgical unit," as even already "Luther's sermons often at their close exhibit a pastoral exhortation concerning the Sacrament."[84] Bach, who in his library also had collections of Luther's sermons, may have known about this thrust [cf. Leaver, Nos. 7 and 28—Ed.]. This well-known growing regard of Bach's for the Sacrament of the Altar is further underlined by the fact that Bach also pointed to Holy Communion by means of his large selection of hymns that speak of sin and repentance, for "the justification of the sinner, on which the Sacrament sets its seal," always "presupposes knowledge and acknowledgement of sin," so that "the warning and searching of conscience ... is an indispensable prerequisite of the offer of the Sacrament."[85]

But this emphasis on sin and repentance in no way represses or even overlooks the eschatological regard and the joyful nature of Holy Communion. Bach's cantatas, with their rich strains of genuine Communion joy and exulting thanksgiving, make this clear in a most impressive manner. Consider the cantatas BWV 1, 49, 140, and 180. Above all, the two cantatas composed for the 20th Sunday After Trinity, BWV 49 and 180, strike the brightest and at the same time most delicate tones of true Communion joy.

At the beginning of Cantata BWV 49 there is a festal symphony for obbligato organ and orchestra in E Major. The cantata closes with a duet on the well-known text "Wie bin ich doch so herzlich froh, daß mein Schatz ist das A und O, der Anfang und das Ende" (What joy to know, when life is past, The Lord we love is first and last, The end and the beginning!—the closing stanza of "Wie schön leuchtet der Morgenstern"). In the middle of the cantata there is an aria for soprano with oboe d'amore and violoncello piccolo accompaniment. This violoncello piccolo with its particularly tender timbre Bach uses only in nine arias in his entire cantata output. Conspicuously, among the few instances beside the aria mentioned in Cantata BWV 49, this violoncello piccolo has been used also in the middle of Cantata BWV 180, intended for the same Sunday, as well as in two additional cantatas that in a special way clearly show the high regard for the Sacrament of the Altar (BWV 6 and 85). Cantata BWV 180 is also a splendid example of exulting Communion joy. The opening chorus conveys the impression of a festive dance (consider the twelve-eighths rhythm and the instrumentation consisting of three flutes, two oboes, and strings!). About the tenor aria that follows in the trio form, "Ermuntre dich; dein Heiland klopft" (Awake, my heart; your Savior knocks), Albert Schweitzer said that "the flute represents the joyous hastening by means of an extremely animated version of the 'joy' motif."[86] Another gem in the cantata is the soprano aria "Lebens Sonne, Licht der Sinnen, Herr, der du mein Alles bist" (Sun of living, Light of senses, Lord, you are my one and all), couched in dance form and in the brilliant key of B Major, which "is accompanied by the orchestra in majestic, flowing, wavelike lines."[87] About the arioso for soprano in the middle, with its violoncello piccolo part playing about the cantus firmus of the voice in an accompaniment in sixteenths, Friedrich Smend says: "Here the gentleness and goodness of the Prince of Life, who approaches us in the Sacrament, is expressed."[88]

We can therefore hardly overestimate the Communion piety of Lutheran orthodoxy, and that is even more true because Pietism has contributed practically nothing to enliven sacramental piety. Preuß makes the point that "in looking for samples of pietistic Communion piety he was impressed" to learn "how relatively unimportant a role this sacrament actually ly plays in Pietism," and "what a genuine exception the Moravians with their glowing love for Jesus represent."[89] Gottfried Arnold "went so far as to say that the more perfect a Christian is, the less he is in need of Holy Communion, and that it is only an aid to the weak."[90] In Leipzig, too, "immediately after the inroads of Pietism on the people, the Leipzig clergy complained that attendance at worship and participation in the sacred acts was no longer as regular as before among the adherents to Pietism."[91] And since rationalism, too, had only a destructive effect on Communion piety,[92] the great honor for having taken up the cause for a vital Communion piety in a time of general weakening of faith belongs to Lutheran orthodoxy alone (see also Appendix of Sources, No. 8).[93] Whoever considers the service of that time a one-sided act, characterized by altogether too much indoctrination, or looks on orthodoxy as an epoch that in its zeal for Lutheran orthodoxy finally shows an interest only in dogmatic formulas and in controversies but has almost entirely lost contact with practical life, simply ignores reality. We cannot repeat too often what Simon Schöffel in his studies of Lutheran orthodoxy in Hamburg has stated with great emphasis: "Nothing is more foolish and more ridiculous than to speak of 'dead' orthodoxy, which has only brought forth letters but has not promoted life. Only monumental ignorance gives a person the right to reject it as 'dead.' "[94]

d) Worship and Music

Polyphonic singing and music making, as it was practiced in Lutheran services at the time of the Reformation on such a large scale, would not have been thinkable without the high valuation of music for the evangelical service on the part of Luther and his co-workers. The principles concerning the liturgical incorporation of polyphonic music in the Lutheran service, inaugurated and implemented by the reformers, remained effective for more than 200 years in the areas accessible to the Lutheran Reformation and led to an amazing flowering of evangelical church music, which reached its final climax in the work of Johann Sebastian Bach. Neither was this period of bloom in evangelical church music materially impaired by the circumstance that since the 17th century an entirely new style originating in Italy found its way into the music of Germany, which until then had been dominated totally by polyphony. This new style definitely emphasized the importance of the performance element and therefore led to the steadily growing development of independent instrumental music as well as the vocal solo, a style that unmistakably "reflects the subjectivism and individualism of the Renaissance."[95]

In other words, this new style doubtlessly brought along elements of "secularization." Already this observation is revealing, that subsequent to medieval music and musical thought, which appeared to be a single large unit, a definite schism in style had now come about, distinguishing on the one hand a *stilus ecclesiasticus* (church style) and on the other hand a *stilus theatralis et cameralis* (theatrical and chamber music style), and that it was in Italy especially that this development was definitely begun and made effective.[96] (As a distinction in style the differentiation between sacred and secular music was used for the first time by Pietro Pontio in 1588.) Even if we leave out of account the fact that this change of style (from polyphony to homophony) did not achieve the same significance in Germany as in Italy, the new style was in no way understood to be a phenomenon of secularization in the areas of Germany that were under the control of Lutheranism. It is worth noting that the musicians and the musical theorists of the 17th and 18th centuries who lived within the range of the evangelical Lutheran Kantorei tradition did not know the distinction between *stilus ecclesiasticus* and *stilus theatralis*, so that in Germany we can speak of a "monism of style" as one of the "main characteristics of the Lutheran music tradition" as opposed to the development in Italy, which was definitely dominated by a "dualism of style." And so "the age of aesthetics" in Italy began already with the great change of style around 1600, but "in Protestant Germany the dominance of musical aesthetics did not commence until the collapse of the Lutheran Kantorei tradition in the 18th century."[97]

"For the Reformer himself and for the Reformation and its worship that followed him one of the most significant characteristics was an openness toward the world."[98] For this reason Lutheranism, following faithfully in his footsteps, could hardly adopt any other stance than a basic openness over against the tendencies in music and musical thought that were coming from Italy. Therefore the acceptance and use of the new musical forms such as recitative and aria in German Lutheran church music in no way represent a secularization of church music to begin with, for according to Lutheran thinking everything finally depended on the answer to a much more fundamental question, namely whether or not these new musical forms presenting themselves could become "vessels and bearers of ecclesiastical proclamation" and "ecclesiastical confession."[99] This question almost always received a positive answer in Lutheran orthodoxy. It is not a matter of chance that the later Hamburg chief pastor, Erdmann Neumeister (1671—1756), a theologian standing firmly on the foundation of strict Lutheran orthodoxy, was considered the real founder of the newer art of writing librettos for cantatas that had become prevalent since the beginning of the 18th century, for he "was generally looked upon as the founder of the new style already while he was still living," even though "he did not provide anything new at all," but "merely took the last step on a pathway already walked before him."[100] In general, "the cantata librettists were as a rule clergymen, who took the substance of their poetry from their sermons for Sundays and festival days."[101]

Accordingly, Lutheran theology and the Lutheran Church, also in the phase of late orthodoxy, played an important role in upholding and continuously developing the rich tradition of church music. Without the vigorous Lutheranism of that time even Johann Sebastian Bach's entire work for the service of worship would not have been possible in its fullness and richness. We have only to think of Bach's request for his release at

Mühlhausen, in which (as a consequence of theological controversies there!) he expressed his heavy uneasiness about the future practice of church music, about the "regulated church music to the glory of God," for "only much-maligned orthodoxy" at that time "clung to such a conception of the regulated church music, that is, a church music that is duly installed [*wohlbestallt*], based on a firm ecclesiastical and governmental order and acknowledged and supported as such by all."[102] And the breakdown of the evangelical Kantorei tradition accordingly began at the end of the age of Lutheran orthodoxy.

But of course we cannot overlook the fact that Lutheran orthodoxy failed to produce a thorough theological study regarding the nature of the music of its time, saturated as it was with completely new tendencies. "When at the beginning of the 17th century the *stile nuovo* forced its way in from Italy, the revolutionary nature of this music...was not at all dealt with properly by contemporary theology. The position of orthodox theology over against music remained, as in the case of Luther, too, almost entirely oriented to the style of the epoch of the Netherlands school," with the result that "people tried to do justice to the new music with old standards."[103] But this approach consequently led to great uncertainty in the theological evaluation of music in the evangelical service, specifically also for a number of Lutheran theologians of reform in the 17th century,[104] such as Johann Konrad Dannhauer (1603—1666), who otherwise held church music in high esteem.[105] For this reason Pietism, with its fundamental antipathy and in many ways harshest hostility to the church music of that time, not infrequently had an easy time combining its attitude with the efforts at reform that had arisen within the Lutheran Church. But of course in the open disregard and hostility for church music shown already in the middle of the 17th century in the Lutheran Church, as in the case of Theophil Großgebauer, who was again and again listed among Lutheran theologians of reform, we are definitely dealing with the dissemination of Reformed [i.e., Calvinistic] thinking.[106] We cannot here determine to what extent in general Calvin's decision against polyphonic singing and the use of instruments in worship had an effective influence on the attitude of the Pietists, who again and again preferred to appeal to Großgebauer. It is interesting to note that Calvin already "consciously rejected the musical unity of sacred and secular song" and "instead demanded a *separate ecclesiastical and sacred style*."[107] Wherever Reformed and Pietistic activities became effective in the Lutheran Church, there were disastrous consequences for the practice of church music, as Bach's leaving his Mühlhausen position after barely 10 months alarmingly illustrates.[108]

In Saxony, too, there were in Bach's Leipzig days such tendencies that strongly contributed toward a disintegration of the life of church music, of which Christian Gerber is the best example, for in his *Historie der Kirchen-*

Ceremonien in Sachsen (Dresden and Leipzig, 1732) he also took a stand over against the questions of church music in his time. Gerber emphasizes, it is true, that he is not an enemy of church music, but that he is for it by all means "when it is organized in a moderate and devotional manner"; indeed, he manages to come up with the confession that "vocal and instrumental music in its proper use should of course be considered a gift of God and may be used to magnify the praise of God and to excite devotion" (Gb, pp. 280, 284). In spite of this, everywhere "his words reveal the ideals of Pietism, the endeavor to revert to the simple piety and the simple forms of worship of the first Christians"[109] (cf. the discussion on pp. 107—08). Although Gerber has to admit that even the Old and New Testaments bear witness to the use of instrumental music in worship (Gb, Preface), this observation is not by a long way a justification for instrumental music in the public service: "To be sure, the apostle says 'Make melody to the Lord' [Eph. 5:19]. But he also immediately adds how this 'making melody' is to be done, namely 'in your hearts.' In other words, he is speaking as in a parable, not of physical playing but of spiritual playing. Whoever wants to apply the words of the apostle to physical instruments does violence to these words and allows himself a great deal of liberty. Also, we certainly know very well how the first Christians, in Paul's own time, amid nothing but persecution, affliction, and fear had to conduct their worship, as secretly as possible; how could they have used instruments and *Figural Music*?" (Gb, Preface). Because Gerber is thinking only of "the true religion of the heart" and the "inner worship of the heart," he is in the last analysis indifferent to all "external ceremonies," indeed, he again and again displays a total lack of understanding for the external nature of worship (Gb, pp. 112, 289), and all church music belongs to this area.

But Gerber's special battle is against organ and instrumental music of his time in worship (cf. Appendix of Sources, No. 9). Organs, he admits, are "up to a point very useful in a church," namely for accompanying the hymn singing of the congregation and above all for giving the pitch, otherwise "the congregation sings along below pitch" (Gb, p. 279; in this connection warning examples are cited, such as that of a cantor who repeatedly could not find the correct pitch and had to start the singing anew several times because there was no organ). But for independent liturgical organ playing Gerber displays very little understanding, and as a result he wants to see the use of the organ severely restricted (cf. Appendix of Sources, No. 10). Concerning the use of other instruments in the service, Gerber above all refers to the "famous" Dannhauer, whose Latin thesis he quotes word for word and then translates as follows: "The best we can say for instrumental music is that it is a decorative element in our church, but in no way does it belong to the essence of worship" (Gb, p. 282). To this Gerber adds the following statement: "This same great theologian also rejects the current custom that voices and instruments are combined in performance, and he does so because the words sung in this way can obviously not be understood by anyone while the instruments rumble and bluster. Therefore he is of the opinion that vocal music should be performed alone, without instruments, and instrumental music alone too, each in turn'' (Gb, p. 282).

Gerber's statements thus far sometimes give the impression that he is attacking only certain abuses in the church music practice of his time but otherwise basically has a positive attitude toward church music if it is kept within modest bounds (even if there is instrumental participation). But other statements make it undeniably clear that he considers all of the church music of his time completely secularized, and it is in his view completely superfluous. It is interesting to note in the quotation given in our Appendix of Sources, No. 11, that at the beginning Gerber repeats his reference to Dannhauer and then adds to Dannhauer's thesis that church music is ''a decorative element of the service'' the critical remark that ''it is not endorsed by all theologians.'' Friedrich Smend (after pointing out that Gerber was a student of Spener's, and that Spener in turn was Dannhauer's student and called him *beatus Dannhawerus* and *pater meus in Christo*) remarks: ''It must have been painful for students of Spener's to see a man whom their master had valued so highly make estimates of the musical resources of the services with which the Pietists, at least those of the second generation, were no longer in agreement.''[110]

In his conception of church music Gerber was really filled with the ideals of Pietism and desired to see this conception become reality more and more in the Lutheran Church. This is undeniably revealed again and again in many of the characteristic accents with which he has graced his whole presentation of these problems. He never tires of associating his critical statements about church music with a host of long-known laments and adopted cures of distinguished personalities and thus to justify them (Gb, pp. 280—81). Among these witnesses Theophil Großgebauer and Gottfried Arnold also turn up (Gb, pp. 284ff.). Even from other European countries Gerber introduces witnesses who have become well-known through their negative attitude over against church music. Thus he refers to the ''world-renowned'' Englishman, Dr. Burnet, who published a biography of Icelandic Bishop Wilhelm Bedell, and Gerber wishes ''that all our bishops, pastors, and sextons, also all professors, might read this life story and emulate the example of this bishop,'' about whom it is reported ''that he just never had any pleasure from the bishop's pontifical robe, that he never wanted to put it on when he preached, indeed, all his life he did not want to wear silk. Likewise he never took any delight at all . . . in the artistic musical presentations in the church, for they merely fill the ear but hinder the inner singing of the heart, and when someone else defended such musical presentations as an external means for promoting devotion, he answered that this pretense had opened the door for an endless number of ceremonies and was still doing so and was a beginning of the edema of the church" (Gb, pp. 282— 83). With obvious inner satisfaction Gerber further states that in Denmark the king "has forbidden and abolished church music altogether" and "therefore instead of that nothing but good hymns must be sung" (Gb, p. 283).

Together with the considerable reduction of church music, Gerber also wanted to see the cantor's church music position with its manifold duties, an office that had risen to special honor through the Reformation, restricted materially, and so he is not sparing in his harsh judgments on the profession of cantor (cf. Appendix of Sources, No. 12). Gerber laments again and again that "no limit or rule for their music making is prescribed for cantors and schoolmasters," that they behave "as if command and control in the church and in the service belonged to them"; to be sure, "there are still some sensible and modest men among them, people who know how to control themselves," but nevertheless, "they are few in number," and "therefore one hears people complaining everywhere," so that "one could wish that these lordly cantors and choir directors would listen to the memoirs of Christian teachers and curb their musical presentations. For there are certainly many Christian people who lament when they have to listen to so loud and long a musical performance and nevertheless only rarely understand a word, but never achieve a complete understanding of it, much less derive benefit and edification from it" (Gb, pp. 281, 289).

Similarly Gerber also has no appreciation for the fact that those who attend the service quietly pray and meditate during those parts of the liturgy which the choir sings. He criticizes the prayers printed in the hymnbooks for this purpose (cf. Appendix of Sources, No. 13).

From Gerber's statements it becomes unmistakably clear what great danger for church music arose from the rather strong pietistic efforts within the church. In spite of all his criticism, Gerber undoubtedly wanted to be the kind of man within the church who would, for instance, follow with great interest all the reforms emanating from the High Consistory in Dresden. Thus he expressed approval of the regulation issued a few years before, according to which "the village schoolmasters who wanted to make a musical presentation should not employ for church music performances dissolute beer fiddlers, who run from tavern to tavern, but should themselves train boys or otherwise use Christian men for this purpose" (Gb, p. 281). He deplores the fact "that we lack strict inspection by the superindendents," and he is of the opinion "that a church visitation is of the greatest importance, as the members of the Consistory themselves acknowledge and wish" (Gb, p. 282). He thinks "good souls" must "comfort themselves with the hope that soon the time can surely come, when the chief supervisors of our church will find ways and means to provide good order for the church music and prescribe objectives and limits, so that the music in the church may be organized according to Luther's way of thinking" (Gb, p. 289). But all these remarks cannot hide the fact that Gerber's real purposes are nevertheless determined largely by pietistic ideals. Even the reference to Luther is deceptive. All Gerber can say in this connection about Luther's conception of church music is only this statement attached to a quotation from Luther: "Luther desires an altogether different kind of church music than we have today: 'The whole crowd should sing along,' he says. But among us the whole crowd cannot sing along, for a text is being presented musically that is not familiar to the congregation, and also, the congregation cannot understand the words because of the clangor of the instruments; even if an aria is presented, it, too, is completely new and unfamiliar. On the other hand, when a familiar hymn is sung and instruments are used with it, the whole crowd can sing along and praise and glorify God together with the instruments" (Gb, p. 290). But Gerber wanted not only the church music in the new style of his time curbed but all of church music on principle (contrary to Luther!). This is clearly shown by a significant remark about church music during the centennial celebration of the Reformation in 1617, in other words, when the church music could not as yet show any kind of Italian influence: "It may well be that at the centennial festival of 1617 there was a loud noise with instrumental music, drums and trumpets, pipes and viols, but such extravagance is approved and praised by none but vain natures" (Gb, p. 225).

Properly speaking, in all these pietistic endeavors of Gerber's, typical Reformed ideas also surface when in his statements regarding the Lutheran service he emphasizes again and again that the reformers "did not completely cleanse the church when it was full of filth," that they could not do everything at once and "pattern the service and the entire church discipline after the manner of the first apostolic church," that the work of renewal had to make additional and greater advances in post-Reformation times: "Concerning the state of our church, many great theologians as well as other Christian hearts have long had the wish that what was still left of the papacy in Luther's time and thereafter and could not immediately be done away with might little by little have been dropped and abolished" (Gb, p. 115).

In Gerber's *Historie der Kirchen-Ceremonien in Sachsen* we are dealing with a publication that originated in Johann Sebastian Bach's own sphere of life and one that merits special attention also because the thoughts expressed in it are those of a pastor who is solidly established in the life of the Lutheran Church of Saxony and not of a Pietist who tends toward Separatism. For that reason Gerber's stance had to be delineated here. His statements everywhere make it clear how pietistic endeavors, wherever they became effective within the Lutheran Church, necessarily had to lead to the decline of the service and so to the disintegration of the church music tradition.

Amid all these circumstances serious attention should be given to the fact that of all the theologians of reform active in Leipzig in the various generations not a single one took a position against the church music, not even the instrumental music,[111] and "that throughout Bach's 27-year tenure in Leipzig not a single case is on record in which the charge of secularization was brought by the Consistory or the clergy against the cantor's compositions for the church."[112] This state of affairs can be explained intelligently only in this way, that Leipzig, with its very conservative tradition, entirely in the mold of strict Lutheran orthodoxy, still represented a very vigorous world of faith. Indeed, at that time this city, next to Hamburg, was still thought of as "one of the strongest citadels of Lutheran orthodoxy,"[113] in which, after the brief pietistic intermezzo at the end of the 17th century, one could now all the more vigilantly proceed against all the pietistic and rationalistic trends toward the disintegration of the liturgy, and one could also begin to understand that the tradition present in the practice of church music and steadily growing there was a development taking place wholly in the spirit of Luther, for Luther's high regard for music and its use in worship surely applied to the whole field of music, both to the unison and polyphonic singing and to instrumental music making.[114] Here in Leipzig Johann Sebastian Bach could in any case create and work "in an atmosphere not yet split into sacred and secular areas but essentially of one piece and nourished from the core of the faith of the Lutheran Reformation,"[115] so that the problem of "sacred" and "secular" that constantly bothers us today when we look at Bach's works did not not exist at all for Bach, at least not in this antithesis. Since Catholic theology, too, has definitely subscribed to a splitting of styles when in the Council of Trent in the 16th century it canonized the Palestrina style as the model *stilus ecclesiasticus*,[116] Lutheran theology alone deserves to be credited with avoiding this dualism and thus making possible the continuous development of the Lutheran Kantorei tradition culminating in Bach's cantata compositions.

Only from the viewpoint of this basic frame of mind of Lutheranism, which did not as yet know the modern dismemberment of all being into what is "secular" and what is "sacred" and consequently in the field of music did not as yet undertake a distinction between the "secular" and the "sacred," can the much-discussed problem of the parody also be explained sensibly. The musician of that time who composed in this Lutheran frame of mind did not think he was contributing to a secularization of church music when he appropriated for worship purposes works that he had previously composed for occasions not associated with the church and then reworked more or less extensively for this purpose. Precisely in the use of the new musical forms such as recitative and aria Bach's Lutheran frame of mind showed itself masterfully in that he did not simply imitate these forms as he fashioned them, "did not externally transcribe them but internally created then anew,"[117] and in this process of creation he in so completely conservative a way kept in close contact with the Lutheran Kantorei tradition developing ever since Reformation times that we can establish it as fact that "Bach's strictly voiced contrapuntal world of forms, his preference for cantus firmi, ostinati, and canons that nowhere deny their connection with mensural polyphony, for musical proclamation, rhetorical tropes, and figures, also for number symbolism, and last but not least, for the art of his fugues, ancient in its basic principles, gives the effect of an element of the German Middle Ages in modern surroundings."[118]

But this Bach music in the Leipzig service of that time, which in spite of its modern elements was so thoroughly oriented toward the past, becomes fully intelligible only when we bring the texts used by Johann Sebastian Bach and the theology they embrace into our purview, as in general Bach's cantata music, dependent on a text as it is, can be understood only as an organic unit of art. This fact must simply be a fundamental presupposition for every theological consideration concerning the essence of the Bach cantata.[119] For this reason a frequent approach of the past that distinguished between form and content is completely illegitimate, for the distinction between form and content is useful for the music of the 19th century but does not apply to the problems of the older music. Actually, the form of the music itself is always an element of content already! But these texts used by Bach had been designed exclusively for the use of proclamation in the worship of the Lutheran Church, as of course all of evangelical church music from Reformation times until the day of Johann Sebastian Bach was intent on a compositional technique that could do justice to language and interpret the Word successfully.[120] Already its close affinity to rhetoric shows this,[121] so that "it is not surprising that the Sermon and the musical exegesis of Scripture on the evangelical scene come together in the 'sermon music' [*Predigtmusik*]."[122] Even if we should at times be inclined to deplore the biased development culminating in the special emphasis on the sermon music in the history of evangelical church music—a development that eventually reached its high point in the didactic cantata of the 18th century, we cannot overlook the fact that Luther already wanted to see music employed exclusively "in the service of exegesis and of the enlivening of the Word," that he had in mind "a musical exegesis that might intensify the Biblical text through melodic, rhythmic, harmonic, and contrapuntal means and might thus let it strike the hearer in full force,"[123] indeed, that Luther himself—and Melanchthon followed him implicitly in this musical observation—used the expression *klingende Predigt* (musical sermon).[124] Moreover, if Luther "never tired of glorifying the basic importance of the proclaimed Word and of the Sermon as the most important element in the Christian service, surpassing all others,"[125] we certainly may not characterize the similar emphasis on the Sermon of the Lutheran service in the age of orthodoxy and the growing significance of the sermon music as a miscarriage definitely brought about only by a dominating orthodoxy. The sermon music (all the way to Bach's cantatas) was able to appear as a dominating second legitimate form of the Sermon in the Lutheran service because it had the same goal as the Sermon spoken from the pulpit, namely to practice the interpretation of the Word of God. But if the Sermon, in spite of close association with the liturgy, still always "stands in a certain relation of tension to the suprapersonal liturgical order," and this "precisely because it is an interpretation of the Word of God in the personal witness of a preacher and addresses itself to the personal makeup of the individual hearer below the pulpit," it stands to reason that "the same applies to the sermon music; it, too, to the degree that it is the authorized witness of the composer, must represent an element of independence within the liturgy."[126] From this viewpoint we must also approach the theological evaluation of the emotional language of the Bach cantatas, which has again and again mistakenly been described as altogether too subjective and has therefore been thought of as a typically pietistic mode of expression. We must similarly approach the problem of the solo song. Apart from the fact that Bach's cantata texts cannot be described as "pietistic" at all (cf. the statements on p. 99), the insights of Arnold Schmitz merit our closest attention in this connection: "Bach's expression of piety, . . . so long as he still makes use of an oratorical figure of speech at all, . . . never becomes 'subjective,' that is, purely personal and private," for "the *oratio figurata* (diction that uses figures of speech) is essentially never a private but a public device of speech." Indeed, Schmitz even says: "I should venture to say that a great orator cannot be a Pietist unless he first gives up his oratory."[127] Wolfgang Herbst also emphasizes this point: "*Oratio figurata* (also in music) and personal and subjective speech in the sense of Pietism contradict each other."[128] But concerning the solo song we must emphasize the fact that Bach did not yet know about the professional soloist who makes an independent appearance in a service and about the emphasis on his artistic prowess as a performer. Here, too, Bach remained in close contact with the Lutheran Kantorei tradition, and that should remind us "that the older Kantorei music brought with it numerous assignments that were assumed by special [*favorit*] soloists (*Concertisten, Soloisten*), whereas the tutti parts were assigned to the chorus singers (*Ripienisten, Tuttisten*)," indeed, that "the compositions of the Middle Ages, the motets of the Netherlanders and of Reformation times, the *geistlichen Konzerte* in their numerous forms and varieties in the 17th century, the polychoral works, the cantatas of the 18th century, the countless song

151

forms of all times, the histories and passions, and the masses are unthinkable without the soloist who was necessarily a member of the Kantorei."[129]

Accordingly, a variety of corrections need to be made in the judgments criticizing the altogether too subjectivistic character of the Bach cantatas, which are generally to be considered sermon music, for without doubt "in the case of sermonic music the full weight of personal witness ought to be of greater consequence"[130] than in music that is more strictly liturgical. Besides, the whole collection of Bach cantatas is a very good example to show to what a high degree every single cantata, in spite of all individualistic strains,[131] wants to be looked on as a composition that has evolved entirely on the basis of the Sunday and festival day liturgy and as one that cannot be interpreted without this strict liturgical bond. This liturgical bond becomes apparent in two ways, sometimes in the close connection between the text sung and the Gospel (sometimes also the Epistle) of the current Sunday or festival day, then again in the adoption of those hymn stanzas and tunes that had been taken from the hymn of the day [*Hauptlied*] or from other church hymns assigned to the particular Sunday or festival day in question. For the creation of the whole collection of Bach cantatas, therefore, that presupposition was in full and free force that in the present time has again been elevated to be the guiding principle of all genuine church music, that "the liturgy is the law of church music."[132] Even if at times the impression is gained that "the personal, subjective language of the individual" is in force in the cantatas, it is nevertheless always "the suprapersonal, objective language of the congregation"[133] that gives the cantata text its real distinguishing character. Even a text that at first glance strikes tones that are altogether too subjectivistic, such as that of Cantata BWV 49, which presents a single dialogue between Christ and "the soul," does not find its final explanation in a purely individual interpretation. "Soul" frequently does not denote the individual soul, but the church, just as in the Old Testament the relation between God and His people is presented in the simile of marriage. In Bach's age this mode of expression was still current according to which the statement was individual but the intention collective. This may be seen in an alternating hymn in Volume 3 of the *Wagnersches Gesangbuch* (*WGB*). The hymn is simply in an "I-You" form, but the title tells us that this is to be interpreted as a dialog between Jesus and the *church*. In certain expressions this poetry shows some striking similarities to that of Cantata BWV 49. We might, for instance, compare the third stanza of the hymn, "Du bist schön, meine Schwester! Schöne bist du, meine Braut!" with the cantata's fourth movement, "Ich bin herrlich, ich bin schön," or also the fourth stanza in which "the church" addresses Jesus with "mein Freund"; in the seventh stanza Jesus addresses the church with "Komm, mein Schatz! Dir ists gelungen.

152

St. Paul University Church. Source: W. Neumann, *Auf den Lebenswegen Johann Sebastian Bachs* (Berlin, 1953), p. 173.

Meine Freundin! Komm, komm heim..." (Come, my Love, you have succeeded. O my Friend, come home, come home...); in the tenth stanza the church then sings: "Komm, mein Licht, mein Heyl, mein Leben! Komm, mein Hort, mein Schatz, mein Ruhm!Dir, dir bin ich gantz ergeben. Komm, ich bin dein Eigentum. Ich bin durch dein Blut erkaufft. Ich bin auf dein Blut getaufft. Ich heiß auch nach deinen Nahmen. Ja, HErr JEsu! Komm, komm. Amen!" (Come, my Light, my Help, my Lifeblood! Come, my Home, my Treasure, Fame! To Thy troth am I committed. Come, I am Thine own by name. Bought am I by Thine own blood, Sanctified in Baptism's flood; E'en my name is of Thy naming. Yes, Lord Jesus, come, come! Amen.) This waiting for the second coming of Christ and its relation to Holy Communion, which was thought of as an anticipation of eternal salvation, is also expressed in the final movement of the cantata. While the bass soloist sings "Dich hab ich je und je geliebet, und darum zieh ich dich zu mir. Ich komme bald, ich stehe vor der Tür, mach auf, mein Aufenthalt!" (From all eternity I've loved thee, and still I draw thee as before. Behold, I come! I stand before the door; Oh, open up, My home!), the soprano soloist answers with the hymn stanza "Wie bin ich doch so herzlich froh, daß mein Schatz ist das A und O, der Anfang und das Ende. Er wird mich doch zu seinem Preis aufnehmen in das Paradeis; des klopf ich in die Hände. Amen! Amen! Komm du schöne Freudenkrone, bleib nicht lange! Deiner wart ich mit Verlangen" (What joy to know, when life is past, The Lord we love is first and last, The end and the beginning! He will one day, oh, glorious grace, Transport us to that happy place Beyond all tears and sinning! Amen! Amen! Come, Lord Jesus! Crown of gladness! We are yearning For the day of your returning [*Lutheran Worship* 73:5]). Concerning the text of this cantata we should further observe that, in spite of its mystically tinged manner of expression, it cannot be pronounced typically mystic as a whole, for the aria for bass voice following the introductory symphony at the beginning of the cantata, "Ich geh und suche mit Verlangen dich, meine Taube, schönste Braut" (I go and look about with longing for you, my dove, my beauteous bride), is assigned to *Christ*. This device opens the way for a proper evangelical understanding from the very beginning. In the appropriation of salvation not the active doing of man stands at center stage, but Christ alone, on whom salvation depends. Also in the concluding movement of the cantata the real decisive initiative proceeds from Christ. Care has been taken from the beginning in the whole arrangement of the cantata that there should be no possible faulty relation between the mystical thoughts expressed and the message of justification.

But "the suprapersonal, objective language of the congregation" finds its clearest and its most convincing expression especially in the church hymns that are so numerous in their use in the Bach cantatas and in certain stanzas often form a definite framework for the entire cantata text. Now what is valid for the liturgical use of a certain hymn must also basically be applicable to the Bach cantata—namely that we can never make a binding decision in this matter on the basis of that favorite earlier differentiation between the hymn that typically emphasizes the pronoun *I* and that which stresses the pronoun *we*. Only the actual contents, the message, of a hymn can in the final analysis reveal whether we have in it "the personal, subjective language of the individual" or "the suprapersonal, objective language of the congregation." If we consider that 75 percent of the hymn stanzas contained in the Bach cantatas also appear in today's *Evangelisches Kirchen-Gesangbuch*, we may be permitted to conclude that Bach in his selection of church hymns had a sure eye for what was theologically valuable and lasting in hymns.

If we also look at the theological content of the texts presented in concerted music in the Leipzig services at Bach's time, in other words at the actual content of the proclamation as it was expressed in the sermon music, we everywhere meet with the central themes of the Reformation. If "Bach is to be thought of as belonging to the baroque style so far as the history of art is concerned" and "the glorification of man as *homo divinus* belongs to the essential characteristics" of this epoch of art history, if everywhere "an affirmation of life and with it an affirmation of the world at the highest intensity dominates the field" and therefore themes like "suffering and death are not central themes of art works of the baroque," if there stands victorious at center stage "a very definite hero-worshiping attitude toward antiquity, taken up by the pictorial art as well as by music, which is glorified in opera, that absolutely original creation of baroque music," and if in the musical treatment of Biblical materials "those of the Old Testament achieve a strong prominence, being formed after the heroic pattern,"[134] then of course none of these innermost essentials of that time belong to the proclamation to be found in Bach's works. For "if we want to designate a single theme as the central one for Bach's art, it is the cross and the Crucified," and "for him the world is the world of sinners, fallen and lost, but at the same time rescued through Christ."[135] It is worth noting most emphatically that in spite of "the vast amount of mystic material that we can find in Bach's works,"[136] and in spite of the fact that also in the church hymn writing of the 17th and 18th centuries the proclamation of justification by grace alone and by faith alone is declining noticeably (in Reformation times the Lutheran doctrine of justification was the core and center of hymn writing),[137] still in Bach's cantatas "the impressively strong and emphatic valuation of justification in Luther's sense is a characteristic that pervades the entire inventory of texts" and "that again and again work righteousness is contradicted and the *sola gratia* is contrasted to it."[138] We need to consider the results of Wolfgang Herbst's research critically important, "that the doctrine of justification in Bach's works is in no way dislodged or superseded by a union mysticism," but "that in many instances also the doctrine of union must serve the purpose of intensifying the thought of justification without possessing an importance of its own that goes beyond that of justification."[139] This fact sheds very clear light on the sermons preached in the main churches in Leipzig at Bach's time, for it is unthinkable that the theological content of the cantata texts, the proclamation expressed in Bach's sermon music, should have contradicted the sermons preached from the pulpit or should even only have run along parallel to them without any relevance. At this point we perceive very definitely that the Leipzig liturgical practice, which with its liturgical riches still everywhere maintained a close connection with Reformation perceptions and specifically with Luther's intentions, was not a mere coincidence induced by the struggle to maintain an external continuance of this tradition, but that this entire liturgical tradition was still in a decisive way determined by the central message of the Reformation and therefore belonged to its very core and center; "for the reformers, and specifically for Luther, the doctrine of justification had become the main doctrine, from which there was to be no wavering or retreating." Indeed, as Luther saw it, "*this* doctrine alone determines the life of the church, and likewise it is this doctrine that in the last analysis turns a Christian into an 'evangelical' Christian."[140]

Johann Sebastian Bach, too, was called to participate in the proclamation of this central message through his presentations of the sermon music, and he attended to this assignment with the conviction that, beside his commitment to the liturgy for Sundays and festival days and to the church hymn that had achieved success throughout the Lutheran Church, he was bound above all to Holy Scripture as *the* foundation of all liturgical proclamation.[141] For him the interest of the Gospel is always at stake, for that must be proclaimed purely and clearly. This fact explains all that follows. Thus we can explain his setting the clear Word of the Bible to music. Thus Bach's numerous corrections in the text begin to make sense. Thus we can understand Bach's own text provision and especially his choice of cantata texts. Thus the choice of hymn stanzas is determined. Indeed, thus also his cool relation to the greatest Leipzig poet of his time, Johann Christoph Gottsched, can be interpreted, for this has again and again been thought of as very strange.[142] Bach dedicated all of his art and energy to the proclamation of the Word and to the service of the congregation, and here he stood close to Luther, "who not only credited music with the capability of interpreting and concretizing the Word of God but also designated this as its commission."[143] For this reason the responsible clergymen in Leipzig who walked in the footsteps of Luther could not but encourage the ornately organized polyphonic music of their cantor. At any rate, we never hear that there was any kind of tension between Bach and the leading clergymen of the main churches. In fact, there are even definite indications to the effect that he was on good terms with these pastors. Without doubt, any feeling of tension would at least have resulted in causing the duration of the cantata, which usually required 20—25 minutes, to be cut back appreciably. Such curtailments are on record for many places in those days.[144] Only a theological position that was able to say a decided yes to music as an interpreter of the Word of Scripture and therefore also took the liturgical office of the cantor seriously could make possible the creation of Bach's series of cantatas and guarantee their continued cultivation. Even the time length of the cantata in no way represented an oppressive element for the service of that day. Where the average length of the service was three to four hours, a musical presentation that preached the Gospel in the time length of a Bach cantata was perfectly justified.

In our own time the determination has been made that "a text set to music, no matter in what form, can only then perform a liturgical task if the underlying text is taken from the Bible or the hymnal or is in some other way a text based on Scripture."[145] If this is true, then Bach's cantata music to a high degree measured up to the requirement we have set up. Indeed, it may even be said that Bach's cantatas with their great riches "stand out in bold relief from the narrow confines of their own time through their connection to the form and content of the Bible" and that "their statements thus achieve a validity and reality down to our own day."[146] Beside this cantata music of Bach's, which must be characterized as sermon music, also the other church music, primarily under the heading of adoration, praise, and thanksgiving, was cultivated in the Leipzig services,[147] but that can only additionally underline this favorable review of the liturgical music at Bach's time. In consideration of Bach's activity in Leipzig, we have every reason to admit that, "compared with the decline among us today, the worship and liturgical life of the Lutheran Church at this time showed a diversity and a musical intensity that can only fill us with envy."[148]

e) Outcome and Outlook

The outcome of this investigation of the liturgical life in Leipzig at the time of Johann Sebastian Bach can only be fully evaluated if we also take a brief look at the signs of disintegration in the Leipzig liturgical life that gained ground since the second third of the 18th century, at first very slowly but then from 1785 on with increased strength.

Here and there already before 1785 certain reforms in the Leipzig service had been introduced. Thus in 1766 the Passion compositions of the 16th century that were sung on Palm Sunday and Good Friday in place of the reading of the Gospel in the main service (cf. the discussion on pp. 60—62) were "abolished," and this with the remarkable argument that they "were too theatrical" (Ro, p. 18). Substituted for these on Palm Sunday were the Passion music in one of the two main churches, otherwise not customary until Vespers of Good Friday, and in the other church the hymn "Jesu Leiden, Pein und Tod"; on Good Friday then the tables were turned in the two main churches, so that the Passion music of the prayer services (the first part in place of the Gospel, the second part during Communion) was heard every year from 1766 in *both* main churches, always in the main service of Palm Sunday in one church and in the main service of Good Friday in the other (cf. Ro, p. 18). From 1770 also the hymn "Jesu Leiden, Pein und Tod" was dropped and replaced by the Passion hymns "O Haupt voll Blut und Wunden," "Ein Lämmlein geht und trägt die Schuld," and "O Welt, sieh hier dein Leben," which alternated annually one after another (Ro, p. 18). Additional changes, though essentially insignificant ones, are registered in the liturgical practice for the years 1770, 1774, 1779, 1781, and 1784 (cf. Ro, pp. 16, 18, 20, 22, 43). Compared with what happened after 1785, however, all these reforms are of little importance.

The deciding impulse toward the secularization of the liturgical practice came during Superintendent Johann Georg Rosenmüller's term of office (1785—1815). From the very beginning of his term of office in Leipzig, this leading clergyman of the city methodically advocated a radical change in the liturgical practice of the city. Particularly in his sermons he always tried to introduce the worshipers to the ideas of the Enlightenment. On Pentecost Sunday and Monday and on Trinity Sunday 1786 he regularly preached in the main service and respectively on the basis of the customary Gospels (John 14:23-31; 3:16-21; 3:1-15) on the following themes: "Concerning the True Christian Enlightenment," "Concerning the Principal Impediments to True Christian Enlightenment," and "Concerning Sundry Means of True Christian Enlightenment."[149] Although Rosenmüller emphasizes that he wants to mediate between those who glorify the Enlightenment and those who reject it, he is himself, nevertheless, already a typical representative of the Enlightenment, one who perhaps thinks of the purpose of worship entirely from the viewpoint of instruction. The third sermon is in two parts, in which two "means of true Christian Enlightenment" are treated in detail: "Careful and Wise Use of the Bible and Good Devotional Books" and "Better Training of Youth in Religion."

Because the service is looked on almost only from the viewpoint of instruction, Rosenmüller is now of the opinion that he can make changes everywhere in the liturgy and break with the multiplicity of liturgical traditions just as it would seem advisable to him. In the notebook of the St. Thomas sexton after 1785 memoranda repeatedly turn up that have to do with changes in the liturgy. These often refer to the "new" or even the "newest" liturgy. The changes, made primarily in the first years of Rosenmüller's term of office, aimed above all at replacing once and for all certain hymns thus far sung in Latin in Leipzig (though only in the main churches) with German ones, indeed, also many older German church hymns with more modern ones, and beyond that also to replace with German equivalents the parts of the liturgy sung or performed polyphonically by the choir in Latin (cf., for instance, Ro, pp. 11, 18—21, 48; also *Bn*, pp. 60ff.). In connection with these reforms the *de tempore* hymns so far retained fell into disuse more and more, and older hymns received new tunes. The St. Thomas Cantor Hiller (1789—1800) himself composed such new tunes. So, for instance, Luther's creedal hymn "Wir glauben all an einen Gott" was replaced by a new one composed by Hiller. Hiller generally proved to be an enthusiastic fellow in arms for Rosenmüller to help achieve his plans and goals, for immediately on his accession to office in 1789, he saw to it that the Latin motets customary for Sundays and festival days up to that time were replaced by German ones and that the Kyrie, too, was chanted or presented polyphonically in German. After the use of the organ during Lent and on penitential days had been introduced and the organ had become the accompanying instrument for congregational singing, Hiller in 1793 and 1803 published special tune books for church hymns to provide the accompaniment for congregational singing. A high point in this development was the introduction at Christmas 1796 of an entirely new hymnbook containing 871 hymns. Indeed, this hymnbook is to be designated as the real Leipzig hymnbook of the Enlightenment. Up to that time *Das Privilegirte Vollständige und verbesserte Leipziger Gesangbuch*, first published in 1735, was in use; this hymnbook in its third edition of 1738 contained over 1,000 hymns, and it saw over 30 editions. A whole series of essays and studies about the new hymnbook in 1797 clearly indicates that the introduction of this new hymnbook evoked many critical voices and in part even considerable resistance. With the introduction of this hymnbook also the singing of certain Latin festival hymns ceased. This had of course been somewhat restricted already previously on the high festivals of the church year, but it was still considered customary. At the same time the "unison Litany," always chanted in Advent and Lent as well as on penitential days and in the Friday services, was abolished and replaced by "another suitable hymn" (*Bn*, p. 61; cf. also Ro, p. 11).

Only certain definite, intentional, individual decisions that on principle broke with the received liturgical tradition show clearly to what an extent these numerous, clearly well-meant reforms actually released an ominous process of disintegration. On 23 April 1787 Rosenmüller "for the first time at the altar of St. Thomas Church conducted *public confession*, or preparation for Holy Communion, at the request of the commander of the infantry regiment of Reitzenstein garrisoned in the suburbs and also had the unit receive Holy Communion *immediately thereafter*" (*Bn*, pp. 61—62). With this act the beginning had been made in Leipzig to dissolve private confession and to relegate Holy Communion to certain detached Communion services separated from the worship of the congregation. Rosenmüller repeated such a separate confession and Communion service "also on 1 March 1788 for a number of students here" and "on 28 March 1793 the boys and girls of the council free school, and on 31 March 1799 the students of the orphanage had their first confession of this kind" (*Bn*, p. 62). It is reported that Rosenmüller suffered "various pangs of conscience" on account of this innovation and that these finally "induced him to resign from the confessional altogether in his sermon of St. John's Day 1792" (*Bn*, p. 62). But even before this, Rosenmüller had given evidence of a noticeably diminished interest in private confession,[150] for the Communion registration lists of St. Thomas Church from the very beginning of his term of office in Leipzig register only very few people by name who came to confession, and often none in the column of the chief clergyman (Rosenmüller), whereas the columns of the second and third clergymen from that time on are all the more heavily crowded with the names of those who have come to confession, indeed, are crowded to overflowing (cf. also Appendix of Sources, No. 14). In spite of Rosenmüller's strong efforts to introduce public confession, however, until the end of the century it was practiced only in military, student, and school services. Officially, public confession did not become permissible for individuals and families until by the ordinance of 12 September 1799, but this did not abolish private confession, for this "fell away only gradually as its participants died" (*Bn*, p. 62), but it was in any case continued into the 19th century. In Rosenmüller's last years "very gradually the custom arose to conduct public confession on Communion days, and then before the early service" (*Bn*, p. 62).

A further break with tradition followed at the beginning of 1795, when the wearing of chasubles was abolished. The "little consecration or Mass bell, which the bowing sexton rang twice during the consecration of the bread and wine," fell silent in 1787 (*Bn*, p. 61). After 1788 "it was permitted in St. Thomas Church to have children baptized also without exorcism or adjuration of the unclean spirit" (*Bn*, p. 61). Rosenmüller asserted: "That the superstitious exorcism and the old embarrassing prayers in the act of baptizing have so far had to be retained and must still be retained is a matter about which not only every enlightened preacher but also every well-educated Christian who values religion must feel distressed in his innermost soul."[151] The new pratice of baptism that was at first introduced only at St. Thomas Church also spread to the other churches of the city within a decade. With the abolition of the Latin hymns and liturgical songs also the Latin intonations and collects that were until then still retained were replaced by German ones, for Rosenmüller's basic idea was that "it certainly is not in the spirit of Luther if in many evangelical churches Latin singing and praying still goes on in a time when even Catholics are beginning to introduce German songs and prayers into their services."[152] Thus also the Nicene Creed, which was still chanted at stated times and special festivals, eventually fell away entirely, for it was always presented in Latin. The Latin Prefaces, which were chanted on festival days, maintained themselves longest, but after Christmas 1795 they were presented only on the first of the high festivals and were then abolished altogether at Pentecost 1812. The prayer service of the "choralists," with its many Latin component parts, was not abolished until 1824, it is true, but after 1797 it was held only at 6:30 and "no longer in the high choir" but only "behind the pulpit" (*Bn*, pp. 67—68).

After the chanting of the Epistles and Gospels in the main services was replaced by the reading of these pericopes, a wish long cherished by Rosenmüller was fulfilled in 1810 in that "now and then in the entire land either new texts were assigned for the early services or provisions were made for preaching on the customary Epistles and in the afternoon on texts chosen independently from the Psalms, the evangelists, or the apostolic epistles... or also on the customary Gospels" (*Bn*, p. 63). At the same time "the order was given that, if sermons were preached on the Epistles or Gospels in the early service, *passages chosen independently* from prescribed books of the Old and New Testaments should be read at the lectern" (*Bn*, p. 63). The extent to which Rosenmüller is to be considered a zealous partisan for the disintegration of the systems of readings is clearly indicated by his statements in 1788: "It would be reasonable to abolish the custom of reading at the lectern the Gospel to be preached on (which most of the audience almost know by heart anyhow) before the Creed is sung and to institute the reading of a chapter from the Bible instead where this has not been done so far.... Perhaps it would be a good idea to read only the New Testament and to make a kind of division of the text that would make it possible to read through the whole New Testament within a year.... The reading should never take longer than a quarter of an hour.... It is ridiculous to chant the Gospel. Even the reading of it before the Sermon was in the very earliest times of the Reformation necessary because the people at that time did not even know the Gospels. In our time, when every teacher has the next Sunday's Gospel read on Saturday and every Christian almost knows it by heart, the reading is completely unnecessary. On the other hand, reading the Bible aloud with short explanations and applications is so much more important because reading the Bible is much neglected by most Christians.... The objection that the service would be prolonged by the reading of the Bible is easily answered. We would merely have to omit a few ceremonies and chants that are repeated mechanically and thus without profit every Sunday. In that way the matter would be taken care of."[153]

After 1810 the choice of sermon texts and readings generally rested with the pastor in charge, and together with this arrangement the old orderly rotation of preachers among the pastors formerly in effect in Leipzig was gradually relaxed and changed. Thus Rosenmüller "introduced the custom according to which all three deacons, one after another, substituted for the superintendent if the latter did not preach on a certain Sunday or festival day; this had been done only by the archdeacon before this," an arrangement that applied to both main churches, that is, to both pastors of these churches (*Bn*, p. 63).

After 1792 new prayer formulas began to be published, as it was also "only since Rosenmüller's times permissible to undertake changes in the old prayers and formulas, though not really to use new ones" (*Bn*, p. 62). In 1811 a rather large collection of new prayers for use both in public services and in home devotions appeared for the first time. Already in the very next year "the worship book in Dresden, in use since 1707," now appeared "completely revised in two parts," of which the first part, the "Gospel Book," contained the readings for the Sundays and festival days (of course now with "partly changed Gospels and Epistles"), and the second part the Agenda (*Bn*, p. 63). Since that time it also became customary quite generally for "preachers to devise their own formulas for baptisms, weddings, and other purposes, and they produced a really desirable variety" (*Bn*, p. 63).

It should be evident how thoroughly these decisions and measures had to bring the entire *de tempore* order, with its established set of hymns and its pericopes for the Sundays and festivals, faithfully maintained in the Lutheran Church from the beginning, into a hopeless state of confusion, which could only promote the disintegration of the liturgical practice. The real cause for all these evidences of disintegration lies inherent in that theology of Enlightenment that was more and more blatantly espoused by the spirit of rationalism. Because this theology finally was able to think of the entire service merely as an institution for public instruction, the understanding for the liturgy was gradually lost altogether. The meaningful arrangement and use of the church year was lost, so that the reduction of the number of church festivals undertaken later at the beginning of the thirties of the 19th century was a completely necessary sequel to this liturgical disinterest. Together with the abolition of chasubles, the understanding for every external arrangement of the service disappeared, so that such actions as making the sign of the cross at the consecration of the elements of Communion or at the pronouncement of the Benediction and the laying on of hands in absolution, still retained in the public confession, could be spoken of as superstitious acts.[154] Since Rosenmüller also spoke of the laying on of hands in public confession as superstition,[155] he must have pronounced the absolution in Leipzig from the very beginning without laying on of hands. Concerning the distribution, Rosenmüller writes: "The practice of holding a small napkin up to the communicant, so that none of the consecrated bread and wine may fall to earth, a practice still common in very many places, is based on the notion of transubstantiation, from which also many Evangelical-Lutheran Christians are yet not entirely free."[156]

In all these reforms the tendency to shorten the service as much as possible shows through. Of hymns formerly usually sung in their entirety only certain stanzas are now sung. Certain parts of the liturgy can drop out altogether or be shortened considerably. Thus the notebook of the St. Thomas sexton contains the significant note: "On Good Friday in 1793 and 1794, with the compliance of the superintendent, the Creed was omitted on account of the musical presentation..." (some illegible words follow, from which one may conclude that the Preface was also dropped) and "to shorten the service" (Ro, p. 19; cf. also Ro, p. 22). On Maundy Thursday 1787 "the Creed plus the Response was dropped" (Ro, p. 20). In 1806 official permission was given to use drastically shortened prayers in certain services, but ever since Rosenmüller's term of office every clergyman could change, according to his own discretion, prayer formulas that up to that time were considered inviolable, and therefore the portals had long been flung wide open to every whim. All these reductions made it possible to let the main service of 23 August 1789 begin at 7:30 instead of the usual seven o'clock. Also the beginning of the weekday early service was set at seven o'clock (instead of 6:45, as previously). After Christmas 1815 the Sunday and festival day services in winter did not even begin until eight o'clock, and from 1829 on even in the summer months the service did not begin until eight o'clock.

Also the number of services and devotions held within the week, which earlier had remained unchanged and had followed a rule that was strictly kept through generations and could even be increased, decreased noticeably from the beginning of the 19th century. After 1802 the weekday early services were no longer held at certain times (for instance, during the Leipzig Trade Fair or in weeks in which an additional festival day was celebrated beside Sunday—since 1829 also always throughout the month of January). More and more on certain Sundays and festival days the noonday services or also the Vespers were dropped. For Maundy Thursday the notebook of the St. Thomas sexton contains the note: "In 1805 the noonday sermon was suspended permanently with the permission of the superintendent" (Ro, p. 21). The same applies to the noonday service of Palm Sunday from 1803 on, where for the first time on this day a confirmation service was held in St. Thomas Church (cf. the order of service in Ro, p. 145). After the number of prayer services had already been reduced once in September 1813, the services were permanently suspended in 1826, when also "confessional sermons" and "penitential admonitions" were dropped. After 1822 at St. Thomas and after 1833 at St. Nicholas henceforth only prayer services were held on Saturdays in place of the Vespers always conducted there up to that time. In 1813 all Catechism services were also abolished, except at St. George (*Bn*, pp. 42, 47).

All these cutbacks in services and devotions are moreover unmistakable signs to indicate to what a large extent the attendance of congregation members had declined. Also in the worship life of Leipzig at that time the state of affairs generally accepted for the age of rationalism shows itself, namely that under the influence of the conception of the service as an institution for public instruction, "where rationalism has been achieved, the services really have no further purpose."[157] After 11 years of Rosenmüller's activity in office in Leipzig, the statement made by the then subdeacon Enke in a sermon on the Third Sunday in Advent 1796 in St. Nicholas is indeed significant: "Our city churches have in recent years registered smaller attendance than previously."[158] In spite of everything Enke was optimistic enough to think that this decline in attendance was, among other things, due to the use of the old hymnbook until 1796.

Especially alarming are the declining Communion registration figures, in spite of increases in population. Immediately after Rosenmüller's induction into office, Communion attendance figures for the first time in the 18th century dipped below the annual threshold of 10,000 guests. In 1786 only 9,476 communicants were registered at St. Thomas, after the previous years, 1782—1785, still reported 17,047, 16,467, 16,750, 15,608, and 13,207 communicants respectively. From 1786 on the Communion attendance figures of St. Thomas remain below the annual level of 10,000 communicants (with two exceptions, where this threshold is barely exceeded). Also the number of communicants among the sick at St. Thomas, reported as annually between 450 and 550 from 1776 to 1784, drops to 390 in 1785, to 190 in 1786, and then stays at 0 to 250 almost throughout the years to the end of the century, in other words about 50 percent lower than before Rosenmüller's Leipzig term of office. As time went on, Rosenmüller's idea that as a result of the introduction of public confession "many people will more regularly attend" both at confession and at Communion than before proved to be a tragic misapprehension (cf. the statements on p. 159—60). At the very end of Rosenmüller's time in Leipzig the Communion attendance figures reach a low point that is not matched again throughout the 19th century. In 1813 only 3,316 communicants are counted at St. Thomas, and at the end of that year the Communion registration book carries the note: "in other words, 1,989 fewer than the year before." In 1814 only a total of 2,386 communicants are counted, and in 1815 only 3,655. At the same time the participation in Communion also declined to a minimum at

St. Nicholas. At the beginning of 1809 the communicant figures for Sundays and weekdays drop almost to zero: for New Year's Day, 3; for Epiphany, 2, with the remark "taken care of in the sacristy"; for the First Sunday After Epiphany, 1, with the remark "in the sacristy"; for the Second Sunday After Epiphany, 12; Wednesday thereafter, 7; for the Third Sunday After Epiphany, 6; Wednesday thereafter, 7. In the entire first half of the 18th century, for example, the whole Advent season was observed as a period of penitence characterized by waiting and preparation and as such could boast of a maximum number of participants in Holy Communion, but the very same season from the beginning of the 19th century on, under the influence of a spirit that robbed the church year of all meaning, became completely unimportant so far as participation in Holy Communion was concerned. For comparison the following Communion attendance figures at St. Nicholas for the Advent-Christmas season of 1820/21 are given:

First Sunday in Advent	41
Wednesday following	24
Second Sunday in Advent	20
Wednesday following	23
Third Sunday in Advent	21
Wednesday following	56
Fourth Sunday in Advent	19
First Christmas Day	20
Second Christmas Day	6
Third Christmas Day	0
Sunday after Christmas	0
New Year's Day 1821	0
Epiphany	0
First Sunday After Epiphany	4
Second Sunday After Epiphany	8

At the time of Johann Sebastian Bach in Leipzig it was still completely unthinkable that the main services on Sundays and festival days as well as the early services on Wednesdays and Thursdays had to be held without the Communion service because of a lack of communicants, but not infrequently in the 19th century this is what happened. The number of communicants declined further also after 1820/21. On the First and Second Christmas Days 1834 there were only five and three Communion guests in St. Nicholas, and on the same days in 1835 there were only one and six. This development finally had to lead to the result that the Communion service was detached from the main service more and more often. Nothing else but the figures provided can so clearly show to what an extent rationalism had a negative effect on the Leipzig liturgical practice and a disastrous influence that eventually—which means even now—led to a real "neglect of Communion." It is apparent that Lutheran orthodoxy is in no way to be blamed for this misfortune, but rationalism alone.

What this new spirit meant for the Leipzig church music has been pointed out in a few essential points by Arnold Schering in his description of musical life in Leipzig.[159] Schering describes the development of church music since Bach's death and occasionally also refers to a completely changed attitude of the successors of Bach in the St. Thomas cantorate concerning the essential nature of church music. Above all, since Hiller's term of office the music of the service now only is governed by an emotionalism that stresses feeling and solemnity, a kind of music that no longer stands in the employ of the proclamation of the Word and of the exposition of Scripture but desires only to beautify and adorn the service. It is no accident that shortly after Rosenmüller's induction into office in Leipzig the first "sacred concert" took place in a Leipzig church, when on 3 November 1786 Georg Friedrich Händel's *Messiah* was performed in the University Church. Since that time "this at first striking undertaking has often been repeated in the same place, as also in St. Thomas, St. Nicholas, and St. Peter" (*Bn*, p. 64).

We have to content ourselves here with these few indications regarding the later history of worship in Leipzig. The fundamental difference in liturgical practice as it remained completely under the influence of Lutheran orthodoxy in Leipzig up to the middle of the 18th century and then, especially since 1785, came entirely under the domination of rationalism is unmistakable. On the one hand there is an unconditional retention of the inherited legacy of the fathers, a self-evident faithfulness over against the Lutheran Reformation and its liturgical institutions; on the other hand there is a radical break with tradition, the unhesitating surrender of the liturgical treasures of faith. On the one hand there is an uncommonly great liturgical wealth and the employment of this liturgical treasure of forms according to the principle of variety; on the other hand there is a strong tendency toward simplification and abbreviation of the liturgical forms and of the entire service all the way to a complete disregard for outward organization. The liturgical practice that bore the imprint of orthodoxy was able to show a Communion piety, but this part of the liturgical practice that belonged to the essence of the Lutheran service wasted away so completely that the efforts at restoration begun in the 19th century and the new theological consciousness and practical endeavors in behalf of a revival of Communion piety have not been able to begin to make up for the harm done by rationalism. Precisely in this situation lies the best documentation for what the inroads of rationalism meant for the Leipzig liturgical practice: the dissolution and destruction of the liturgical tradition that had been in evidence in a most impressive way for 200 years and was principally informed by the spirit of Luther and the Lutheran reformers.

Of all of this process of dissolution that had long taken effect in other parts of Germany there was next to no sign in Leipzig at Bach's time, and the credit for this must unreservedly go to Lutheran orthodoxy, which simply did not grow rigid in death but made its appearance as a living and influential force. We may agree completely with Friedrich Kalb when he says: "As far as the teaching on worship and the life of worship is concerned, the adverse criticism which pronounced Orthodoxy ineffectual is certainly unjustified," and "we have every reason to acknowledge gratefully the zeal of the Orthodox fathers for the 'beautiful services of the Lord.' "[160] But with this statement also the question concerning the Bach cantata as a liturgical problem in the Leipzig service of that time is answered insofar that we cannot, not even with the best intentions, designate these cantatas as "products of secularization" (Keller), no, not even as a "welcome loosening up" of the service (Wallau). Only because the Leipzig service of that time represented a living phenomenon, still entirely nourished from the center of the Reformation, could also its church music achieve such a late flowering. We shall only be able to look on the Bach cantata as a product that grew up completely organically from the soil of a very lively liturgical tradition and therefore is a genuine liturgical achievement that fulfills its liturgical function in the same way and with the same intensity as the sermon.

Church music at the time of Bach (from the title page of J. Walther's *Musicalisches Lexicon*, Leipzig, 1732). Source: W. Neumann, *Bach: Eine Bildbiographie* (Munich, 1960), p. 33.

B.
Johann Sebastian Bach's Relationship to the Worship of His Time

We shall not be able to leave out of consideration the fact that the age of orthodoxy itself by no means idealized its worship. Numerous demands for reform in the age of orthodoxy that had to do with the liturgical life make us aware of the extent to which the critical function of theology also raised its voice in regard to worship. But it is very important to realize that these demands for reform are leveled not so much at worship itself, that is, at the essence and form of the Lutheran service. They are directed above all to the subject of worship, to *man* taking part in the service.[1] The "decisive theme of the demand for reform of the divine service" of orthodoxy was to emphasize "the harmony of heart and deed," and this expressed "a demand directed not to the divine service but to *man* taking part in it,"[2] for in this demand the right relation between "inner worship" and "outer worship" is being sought. In the age of orthodoxy people were well aware of the fact that the right attitude of the heart, the "inner devotion," is the presupposition for the external worship. But this "worship in spirit and in truth" demanded of the individual Christian in Lutheran orthodoxy entailed no tendency to disrupt the liturgy, for the "inner worship" was here thought of as in closest relation to the external worship—quite in contrast to the developing pietistic tendencies.

But if in the evaluation of the liturgical practice man and his personal, inner and outer, relation to the worship of his church is to be a part of the consideration, then the question of what the situation was in this respect in the case of Johann Sebastian Bach necessarily comes up in connection with our study. Did Bach have a positive inner relation to the worship of his time? Is there some reliable evidence, or at least some solid indication, to show that Bach was familiar with this "inner worship in spirit and in truth" and that he entered on his liturgical office in Leipzig and created his works for worship under the influence of this presupposition?

At least since the appearance of Philipp Spitta's 1873 volumes on Johann Sebastian Bach, this question was by and large considered to have been answered, and that in a positive way. A number of years ago, however, especially since the Bach anniversary year 1950, this question has come up anew and has meanwhile become a very serious problem. The well-known Bach scholar Friedrich Blume, in a paper[3] read at the International Bach Society's Bach Festival in Mainz, 1 June 1962, expressed his conviction that the composition of music for worship was not "an affair of the heart" for Bach, indeed that basically Bach had "a particular attachment" neither for the organ nor for his liturgical office in Leipzig (Blu, p. 217). Blume contended that "it was Bitter and then far more emphatically Spitta who turned Bach into the great Lutheran cantor, the retrospective champion of tradition, the orthodox preacher of the Bible and chorale, who still prevails in the popular imagination today. It was these two scholars and their descendants who established the conception of Bach as supremely the church musician, and the ascendancy of the churchman over the musician" (Blu, p. 216). In view of the numerous recasts [*Parodien*] to be found among Bach's compositions for worship, Blume comes to a conclusion of really basic importance, namely "that numerous works, oratorios, masses, and cantatas, which we have grown deeply to cherish as professions of Christian faith, works on the basis of which the Classical-Romantic tradition has taught us to revere the great churchman, the mighty Christian herald, have *a limine* nothing in common with such values and sentiments and were not written with the intention of proclaiming the composer's Christian faith, still less from a heartfelt need to do so" (Blu, p. 220).

Without presuming to respond in detail to Blume's numerous statements, we must still in connection with our own problem try to investigate the question whether it is really true that Bach had no heartfelt attachment to his liturgical office and commission. To be sure, the artistic value of the liturgical compositions of Johann Sebastian Bach in no way depends on the answer to this question, but certainly this answer will in no small way influence our response to the problem, whether these compositions are to be considered genuine liturgical works and whether even today they can fulfill any meaningful function in specified evangelical services.

1.

Bach's Decision to Work in Leipzig Seen in the Light of His Life and Calling

Until very recently the call inviting Johann Sebastian Bach to become cantor at St. Thomas Church in Leipzig was almost unanimously considered the crown of the life and career, the grand fulfillment of the real ambition, of this highly gifted musician. But Friedrich Blume has thoroughly shocked this conception with his thesis that at the time of his call to Leipzig in 1723 Bach "only with the greatest reluctance...resumed the cantor's gown," that according to contemporary concepts the transition from Köthen to Leipzig "meant a descent in social scale," and that in any case "Bach felt no inner compulsion to make the change" (Blu, pp. 218, 225). These theses are further undergirded by the supposition that long before this, most recently at his entry into the musical life of the court in Weimar in 1708, Bach presumably showed no special interest in an exclusively liturgical office. Under these circumstances the call to the St. Thomas cantorate in Leipzig must appear to have been a kind of emergency measure in the life of Bach, as Blume also quite frankly states when he says: "Bach had been a court musician for many years and had not thought of ever returning to the work of a church musician" (Blu, p. 219).

Now Friedrich Blume has been contradicted vigorously by professionals in all essential points of his statements,[4] but that does not relieve us of the responsibility to think about Bach's relation to the church and to the worship of his time, and above all to the liturgical office, to ascertain what impact this had on his view of life and profession.

a) Theological-Liturgical Education and Training

At first glance it may seem to be an overstatement to speak of a theological-liturgical education and training in the case of Johann Sebas-

173

tian Bach, especially since the extant biographical source material about Bach's childhood and youth must be described as rather scanty. And yet it is not out of place, as we shall presently want to demonstrate, to characterize the school days and the training period in Bach's life as a distinctly theological-liturgical education and training.

From earliest childhood Johann Sebastian Bach was most closely attached to the church, and that was the church of strictly orthodox Lutheranism, which at every turn in his childhood and youth confronted him in a rather impressive manner. The first 10 years of his life he spent in his native city of Eisenach, a Luther city whose very walls were in a position to transmit from generation to generation a long lively series of recollections from Reformation times. Here Bach "already as a child had to be conscious of the footsteps of the Reformer at every turn."[5] And here we must think not only of the Wartburg, the birthplace of the German Bible, and of St. George Church, where Luther had preached on his return from the Diet of Worms, but above all of Luther's school days, which must have left an especially lively impression with Johann Sebastian Bach, for after all, the home of his parents was located on the Lutherstraße, and he was enrolled in the lower classes of the old Latin school of St. George, from whose upper classes Luther had graduated almost 200 years earlier after going to school in Eisenach for three years. In this school, "which had a good reputation ever since Luther's day" and whose "teachers were all trained theologians, stood under church supervision, and in part later became pastors, the instruction in religion was the principal subject and occupied a good deal of time from Sexta to Prima."[6] The primarily theological orientation of even the earliest instruction can be estimated from the fact that already at the age of eight Bach had to learn "the Catechism, psalms, Bible history, writing and reading, particularly the Gospels and Epistles in German and Latin."[7]

The theological orientation continued in Ohrdruf. Here there was "a really exquisite school, the illustrious Lyceum,"[8] which "in its model arrangement of seven classes led all the way to preparation for the university" and "had a great tradition and a far-reaching reputation as a humanistic academy of the first rank, which guaranteed it an enrollment of many students from near and far."[9] For five years (1695—1700) Johann Sebastian Bach was privileged to be trained in this school, known and respected throughout Thuringia, and no doubt received "a schooling of a quality and thoroughness not often encountered at that time."[10] Already in Eisenach the then newly introduced textbook *Latinitatis vestibulum sive primi ad Latinam linguam aditus* (Threshold to Latin or first approaches to the Latin language) by the well-known pedagogue Johann Amos Comenius had taught young Johann Sebastian the first rudiments of Latin. And now this textbook "served even more decisively as the foundation of the instruction" in Ohrdruf, a book that pursued "the religious training for practical Christianity as the crown of all education."[11] For Comenius "the alpha and omega of the Christian school was the Bible." "The elementary school," beside other subjects, "had to teach at least a knowledge of the Catechism, of the most important stories and passages of Holy Scripture as well as the most commonly known psalms and church hymns," and the "higher schools" had included "beside science, arts, languages, and ethics, also Biblical theology in their curriculum."[12] The introduction to Biblical theology was taught through the strictly orthodox Lutheran dogmatics manual, the *Compendium locorum theologicorum* of Leonhard Hutter, which appeared first in 1610 and was still used at the St. Thomas School in Leipzig during Bach's cantorate, in fact, was published there in a new edition in 1736.

The last three years of his school days Johann Sebastian Bach spent in Lüneburg from 1700 to 1702. Like Electoral Saxony, so Lower Saxony was Lutheran territory. St. Michael School, which Bach attended there, had in the second half of the 17th century achieved "its highest prosperity ever," and when Bach went to school there, "it still enjoyed this prosperity."[13] Here in Lüneburg, too, a distinctly theological education formed the center of instruction. In addition to instruction in Latin, Greek, and even Hebrew, Bach now also penetrated to "the more complicated theological themes with the help of Hutter's *Compendium*," and so he was stationed "in the very center of Lutheran orthodoxy's field of influence."[14] Accordingly, Bach here became intimately acquainted with the most essential details of orthodox Lutheran theology.

Thus we may say without reservation that Johann Sebastian Bach's training in school was extensively carried out and determined theologically, predominately in the sense of strict Lutheran orthodoxy, and that he possessed a finished theological education when he left school. Bach was a very talented student and therefore was able to show correspondingly good accomplishments. There were reports of "quick apprehension" and "extraordinary understanding" when Bach graduated from Prima at the age of 15 years, whereas otherwise at this time the average age in this class was never less than 17 years.[15] When we consider these facts additionally, we may safely assume that Bach was able to reason out the individual theological problems, grasp their total depth, and in all of the critical questions of faith render theological judgments.

But Bach's training and education was also *liturgically* oriented, theoretically as well as practically, entirely in keeping with the convictions that the dogmaticians of orthodoxy had in their close affiliation with Luther concerning the essence and form of worship. Although terms like "liturgy" and "liturgics" were totally strange concepts to the Reformation era and to orthodoxy, still the matter of worship was at the center of all theological thought. Theological scholarship and worship were not divided into two expressions of the essence of the church more or less independent of each other but still formed a closely knit unit. To Friedrich Kalb belongs the honor of being the first to point out to what a degree worship was "the basic theme of all theology"[16] for the dogmaticians of orthodoxy and therefore pervades all of their theological systems from beginning to end. If therefore the theology of strictly Lutheran orthodoxy was the basis of Johann Sebastian Bach's entire education to a truly remarkable degree, we should have little doubt that Bach's training may in fact be described as theological-liturgical, because liturgics "had not yet been separated from dogmatics"[17] by the dogmaticians of Lutheran orthodoxy. The doctrine of faith and the doctrine of worship were one and the same thing for all of orthodoxy, so that a liturgical education and training was not to be separated at all from a specifically theological one.

And so there was no other way. Through his education in a strictly orthodox Lutheran sense, Johann Sebastian Bach now also in a practical way from early youth had to stand in close connection with the service and its liturgical riches. Although school choirs had already been known in the waning years of the Middle Ages, these choirs acquired a special importance for Lutheran worship since Reformation times at the urging of Luther particularly in this, that they took over the church music assignments that had thus far been taken care of by the choirs of priests in the chapters and cathedrals and thus at the same time became the chief representatives of musical culture until late in the 18th century.[18] And Eisenach, Ohrdruf, and Lüneburg were precisely places that enjoyed a rich tradition in this respect. It is true of course that all of Thuringia in those days was uncommonly given to the enjoyment of music and skillful in singing and "could therefore boast of a rich tradition in church music that echoed its way into the remotest villages."[19] And yet Eisenach itself seems to have stood at the peak of this musical development.[20] As in Luther's day, the St. George Latin School, which Johann Sebastian Bach attended from 1692 to 1695, provided the choir for the services at St. George Church, and additional responsibilities expected of the choir were singing at weddings and funerals and the regular singing for alms [Kurrendesingen] on the streets and squares of the city. "As a particularly gifted boy"[21] (his good voice and "manner of singing" were still praised by Philipp Emanuel Bach much later), Johann Sebastian Bach took part in the alms singing [Kurrende] under Cantor Andreas Christian Dedekind in Eisenach as well as later in Ohrdruf. In Ohrdruf Bach at first had "training in singing and choral directing as a choirboy" under Cantor Arnold and later under Elias Herda.[22] Here, too, "the choir appears to have been...an institution of great importance, under the leadership of the cantor," and the choir's sphere of activity included, as in Eisenach, "besides the church services on

Sundays and festivals, the performance of motets and concerted music at weddings and funerals, as well as perambulations with alms-singing, at fixed times, from door to door.''[23] Johann Sebastian Bach's talent and his industry and enthusiasm in school and as choir leader may well have been the deciding factor why Cantor Elias Herda, who himself had once been a student at St. Michael School in Lüneburg and probably still had connections there, was able to recommend 15-year-old Bach and his fellow student, Georg Erdmann, to the cantor of this school, August Braun, because there in Lüneburg "boys from Thuringia were in great favor, on account of their musical talents and proficiency." In any case, Bach and Erdmann "were at once admitted, on their proficiency, into the select group of *Mettenschüler* (Matins scholars) and immediately allowed the second grade salary given to the discantists at that time."[24] In Lüneburg, too, liturgical music had taken a preeminent position, and therefore it played an important role in the curriculum of the school. Johann Nikolaus Forkel was in Lüneburg more than half a century after Johann Sebastian Bach and described this city, alongside Augsburg, as "the actual cradle of figural music."[25] To be sure, about Bach's musical resposibilities in Lüneburg we are poorly informed. His participation in the choir as a singer could have been only of short duration because of the impending change of voice. Spitta conjectures that Bach's skill and talent as an instrumentalist may have made a longer stay at the school possible, indeed, that he may have become prefect of the choir and as such may have taken over certain duties as a conductor.[26] At any rate, the worship functions of the St. Michael choir were very extensive and various,[27] and Johann Sebastian Bach here learned to know anew the entire rich range of liturgical life as the Lutheran Church of that time still possessed it in remarkable measure.

Accordingly, also in a practical way Johann Sebastian Bach's training at school was liturgically oriented through and through, an education that was always closely connected with worship, and again and again in theory and practice pointed to worship as the core and center of Christian life. Lutheran orthodoxy, which in Eisenach, Ohrdruf, and Lüneburg guarded the Reformation heritage, still represented a very vigorous world of faith in 1700, just as it did in Leipzig. And when we consider what a close contact Bach had with the Lutheran Church and its worship throughout his life, as we shall see presently, we shall be able to say without hesitation that for him the Lutheran service with its riches of liturgy and church music became an abiding home already in his childhood—even though he soon lost his parental home in the relatively early death of his father and mother. In any case, there can be no doubt that Bach's school training and education involved strong theological-liturgical components. But it should be emphasized that thereby only one aspect of Bach's training and education is treated, although this is the decisive one.

b) Choice of Profession

Johann Sebastian Bach probably did not stay in Lüneburg longer than the customary two years to complete Prima, the senior class, and so he probably left St. Michael School at Easter 1702. Without doubt this school had provided him with "a thorough scholarly training for life's way, a comprehensive and well-rounded education" that his wishes could not have improved on, and also "in the area of music St. Michael Church with its rich tradition and its vigorous use of music was exactly the right place to bring his extraordinary gifts and abilities to early florescence," so that at his leave-taking from Lüneburg "he was well prepared for life and for his profession."[28] But to what kind of profession did he aspire?

Even to this day scholars have not been able to discover where Bach kept himself between Easter 1702 and Easter 1703. Because of his financial situation, study at the university was not open to him. Therefore, after completion of his education he now had to think seriously about a full-time professional appointment, especially because he had been completely on his own ever since leaving Ohrdruf, that is, ever since he was 15. It would have surprised no one if Bach, in keeping with his talents and abilities as an instrumentalist, had made efforts to gain employment outside the specific sphere of church life. The secular court profession of music making was in a flourishing state just at that time, while the civic church office was already declining in prestige by and large. Through certain contacts Bach was in a position to make approaches to the court music of Duke Georg Wilhelm of Hanover in Celle, where he had often visited while at Lüneburg. According to Friedrich Blume, it would even seem likely that Bach had temporarily played with the court orchestra of this "Little Versailles."[29] Bach's extensive acquaintance with French music may in no small measure have been due to these contacts with the court orchestra at Celle,[30] and these had to do not only with instrumental music but also with ballet and opera, so that we have reason to attach a good deal of importance to Blume's statement that "the new kinds of music making of an enlightened secular court must have opened up an entirely new world for Bach and conveyed a completely new kind of philosophy of music to him."[31] From Lüneburg Bach likewise made contacts in Hamburg, not only with the organist J. Adam Reinken, who was then almost 80 years old, but also with the opera, which had followed the Venetian and French pattern to arrive at independent importance and was in full bloom in Hamburg about 1700. Here "the brilliant appearance of R. Keiser provided a strong attraction."[32] In view of this variety of contacts, it certainly could not have been difficult for Bach to find a first appointment and a position that would guarantee a living.

However, the moment the question of choice of profession confronted him, his efforts were immediately directed toward procuring a church-related, liturgical office, namely that of an organist. We know that Bach already in August 1702, when 17 years old, applied for the position of organist at St. James Church in Sangerhausen and that he failed to get the appointment "only because of his youth."[33] His first position as violinist or violist in the orchestra of Duke Johann Ernst of Weimar in the spring of 1703 did not carry with it a decision concerning choice of profession but was thought of as a temporary solution, for only a few months later Bach again applied for a liturgical office, namely that of organist at St. Boniface Church in Arnstadt. Besides, concerning this first activity of Bach's in Weimar we certainly must assume that he vigorously supported the aged and overburdened court organist Johann Effler in his work, for in the minutes of the Arnstadt Consistory of 3 July 1703 Bach is referred to as "Court Organist of the Prince of Saxony at Weimar."[34] He also cultivated friendly relations with other church musicians in the city.[35] In any case, Bach must have established so good a reputation as an organist already during this short time of his first stay in Weimar that five years later he was called to be court organist there. Also, even at 18 he must have displayed surprising technical knowledge in the field of organ building,[36] for he had at first come to Arnstadt only in connection with his acting as organ expert at the acceptance of the newly built organ in St. Boniface Church in July 1703. Having thus revealed his technical knowledge in organ building, he also played the instrument at its dedication and here displayed his great art, and that must have been the reason why the position of organist was offered to him.[37] Bach must have been happy and eager to accept, especially since he was also attached to this city by family ties. At any rate, everything we know about Bach's first years of professional activity indicates beyond doubt that he resolutely strove toward the liturgical office of an organist and that "his keenest desire was for an organ of his own, and Arnstadt at length satisfied it."[38] Also, "the spirit of this city, which was influenced by Bach's superior in the church, Superintendent and Consistorial Junior Judge Johann Gottfried Olearius, in a strictly orthodox sense," must obviously have pleased young Johann Sebastian after an education that followed the same principles, for here he now found "his first sphere of professional activity of some duration as he took over the organist's position in Arnstadt."[39] In 1705 Bach left Arnstadt on an extended tour to visit Dietrich Buxtehude in Lübeck and overstayed his one-month vacation fourfold. This had some very uncomfortable consequences for him on his return, but we can hardly attribute this act to a lack of interest in his office as organist, for Bach had of course in an orderly way arranged for a substitute during his absence and knew that his duties were in good hands. We must rather think of this trip as the result of Bach's lively interest in the whole rich range of the art and practice of church music, for in his eagerness to learn he was obviously interested in adding more and more to his knowledge,[40] and Buxtehude was the only one of the great organists then living of whose musical art and practice Bach had no real conception as yet.

The variety of altercations in which Bach was involved with the church boards and individuals especially near the end of his Arnstadt term of office, which also very obviously contributed to his leaving Arnstadt, were not able to bring about a basic adverse decision against the career once decided on. This is proved by Bach's application for the desirable position as organist of St. Blasius Church in the free imperial city of Mühlhausen. This city had achieved a certain fame because of many important musicians—Joachim à Burck, Johann Eccard, Georg Neumark, Johann Rudolph Ahle.[41] The great prestige of the position now vacant here is indicated by the fact that "the able organist and composer," J. Rudolph Ahle, "had even as councillor been elected burgomaster" and that his son and successor, J. Georg Ahle, who had died 2 December 1706, "had been named the emperor's Poet Laureate for his skill in scholarship, poetry, and music." Now, too, a whole series of applications had come in again.[42] Without doubt even now other possible careers beside the specific work in the church would still have been open to Bach. During his time in Arnstadt he must certainly have kept up contacts with the court there and with Count Anton Günther, who was a great friend of music and was in a habit of spending considerable sums for theatrical productions and court concerts. Beside the duties of his calling, Bach may also occasionally have found employment there.[43] At that time the secular musical establishments at court showed a general upward trend, and the possibilities of a musical career were available in many other Thuringian noble residences; even the strictly orthodox and extremely pious Duke Wilhelm Ernst in Weimar had supported such an "opera house"—with opera performances on record since 1697—and even "court comedians."[44] Also in their salaries "the court musicians compared favorably with the higher clergy and with secular dignitaries."[45] But Bach's interest simply went in a different direction when the question of a career came up. He thinks of himself as dedicated to the worship of his Lutheran Church, and to it he offers his gifts and abilities. Here in Mühlhausen, in the resignation submitted after only a short time in office—less than one year—the expression "the final purpose" of his life and work turns up for the first time in Bach's life, a term that has been much discussed since then. This expression must remain completely incomprehensible if we should want to apply it *only* to Bach's assignments in Mühlhausen, as Waldemar Rosen has done.[46] It must almost surely mean essentially *more*, for "humanly speaking" in Mühlhausen Bach had certainly "drawn the long stick: an unusually good salary, a promise of an outstanding organ, a comfortable job, and an extensive field of work.''[47] Mühlhausen was the only city that during Bach's lifetime had two of his cantatas printed at public expense. Here the organ was completely rebuilt according to Bach's wishes. The esteem in which Bach was here permanently held is further attested by the fact that Johann Sebastian Bach's cousin succeeded him in Mühlhausen and that a quarter of a century later a son of Johann Sebastian Bach at the wish of his father became organist at St. Mary Church in Mühlhausen. Even after his leaving Mühlhausen, Bach on his part, too, kept up friendships with the well-known Pastor Eilmar and also certain other people there. For the baptism of his son Wilhelm Friedemann in November 1710 in Weimar Bach chose three persons from Mühlhausen as sponsors.[48] In more than one way Bach must have felt at home there. In his resignation addressed to the city council 25 June 1708 Bach clearly acknowledges the goodwill that was always tendered him there, and so the conjectures of Spitta and Bitter that Bach left there completely at odds with the council and the people of Mühlhausen are in error. The council regretted to let him leave and even asked him to continue as chief supervisor of the renovation of the organ. They also entrusted the composition of a cantata commissioned by the council for 1709, for the performance of which he then returned from Weimar.[49] But all these advantages as well as the appreciation expressed from all sides were not able to keep Bach from giving up his office again. He did this with the detailed explanation that he was striving for a "regulated church music to the glory of God" and that his goal, because of the open "opposition" [*Widrigkeiten*] and "annoyance of others" [*Verdrießlichkeiten anderer*], seemed unattainable in Mühlhausen but possible in Weimar, his new destination: "Thus God has shaped matters so that a change has unexpectedly been offered, in which, without annoyance of others, I see myself in more adequate living conditions and in the realization of my final purpose for a properly expressive church music" (*BD* 1:19—20; cf. *BR*, p. 60). The pulpit war between strictly Lutheran orthodoxy and the Pietism that had become more and more obtrusive for several decades was at this time carried forward in many areas of Germany. It was pursued in a crude manner also in Mühlhausen. The "opposition" and "annoyance of others" that Bach mentioned and from which he thought he might escape elsewhere were a heavy burden not only to him but also to "individual souls of this church," that is, to the whole congregation, and here we have to think of a serious split and unrest within the congregation.[50] The strong intrusion of Pietism in Mühlhausen and the confused situation in congregational life had to make Bach doubt "whether in the long run a regulated church music to the glory of God would be possible.''[51] For the Pietist, public worship and the church attendance of the individual Christian were by and large no longer necessary, and so also from this viewpoint the importance of church music was necessarily strongly downgraded, and the use of church music was mostly questioned altogether and declared superfluous. Therefore Bach already for the sake of his liturgical office could naturally take his stand in these controversies only on the side of Lutheran orthodoxy. But in Mühlhausen this entailed considerable difficulty, for in Bach's real sphere of activity, St. Blasius, Superintendent Frohne, of pietistic orientation, was the pastor, whereas the strictly orthodox Lutheran pastor, Georg Christian Eilmar, with whom Bach enjoyed a close friendship and remained firm in it even after his departure from Mühlhausen, officiated at St. Mary Church, and therefore close cooperation with him was not possible. It is therefore easy to understand why Bach withdrew from this unpleasant situation as soon as the opportunity presented itself. In any case, Frohne was the leading clergyman of the city, and as a result his views and decisions carried special weight. How intimately Bach was bound to Eilmar in friendship we can clearly see from the fact that even from Weimar Bach invited him to be a sponsor at the baptism of his first child (cf. *BD* 2:37).

As we therefore survey Bach's first professional years and with them his earliest applications for work, his striving for a specifically ecclesiastical-liturgical position was apparent from the beginning. His choice of profession, for the first time at age 17 and then repeated in the following years, favors a liturgical office in the Lutheran Church that had become near and dear to him in his earliest youth. We must agree totally with Christhard Mahrenholz when he says: "...this has become evident, how Bach's life from the very beginning of his professional activity was influenced by the idea of a regulated church music to the glory of God, but that means by the idea of proper Lutheran worship. As Bach himself says, this is the final purpose of his activity. From this aspect career decisions about accepting or declining calls are also influenced."[52]

Because it seemed to Johann Sebastian Bach that this office in Mühlhausen was losing its importance and prestige through the strong rise of Pietism and moreover because a dangerous countercurrent to his whole ambition was here appearing, one whose full effect could not even be anticipated as yet, he gave the Mühlhausen position up again as soon as a favorable opportunity to change to a new position presented itself. This can only be considered a logical decision. Bach must therefore have been fully aware of these initiatives, coming historically first from Pietism and leading to the process of dissolution appearing so ominously during the age of rationalism to cause the disintegration of the Lutheran liturgical tradition. No doubt in Mühlhausen he would have, according to his "slender ability, developed the church music as much as possible" and "would always have been happy to promote the final purpose, namely a regulated church music to the glory of God and in keeping with your [i.e., the city council's] wishes" (*BD* 1:19; cf. *BR*, p. 60).

c) Appointments in Weimar and Köthen

In the autumn of 1708, at the age of 23, Johann Sebastian Bach
entered the court service of Duke Wilhelm Ernst of Saxony-Weimar.
However, if we should from this fact draw the conclusion that Bach with
his transition from Mühlhausen to Weimar "resolutely turned his back on
the service of the church" (Blu, p. 218), we should indeed completely fail to
understand the office that Bach took over in Weimar in 1708 and at the
same time completely misinterpret the entire atmosphere into which Bach
came at his entry into the court service at Weimar.[53]

In Weimar Bach found exactly the external presuppositions for carrying out a "regulated church music" that he had sorely missed in the position he had left. In Weimar Pietism had, in spite of a variety of attempts,
not been able to gain and exercise a definite influence, so that here the entire liturgical life of the city was still clearly determined by Lutheran orthodoxy. Here Duke Wilhelm Ernst had strictly forbidden the pulpit war
between orthodoxy and Pietism and had repeatedly also taken other
measures that nipped the rise and spread of pietistic ideas in the bud.[54] He
was by no means moved by mere utilitarian considerations or thoughts of
church politics in the measures he employed against the Pietists, but he was
a deeply pious personality who took a lively interest in all theological controversies and in all engagements and contests clearly represented the position of orthodox Lutheran theology and piety. Charles Sanford Terry correctly described the duke as "conspicuous among the sovereigns of a period
remarkable neither for virtue, religion, nor philanthropic industry."[55]
Reinhold Jauernig, too, arrives at a similar conclusion in his characterization of the duke: "At a time when most of the German princes in the age of
Louis XIV aped that sovereign's court management and the license and excesses of the French court, the duke who ruled over the tiny dukedom of
Weimar, Wilhelm Ernst, stood among the rare exceptions. Unpretentious
in the conduct of his life, full of lively piety, of the Lutheran faith, he was
conscious of his responsibility for his country and administered his regency
in secular and ecclesiastical matters as 'government' according to Luther's
definition."[56]

The duke showed no hesitation in making much financial aid available
for the reconstruction of St. James Church in Weimar, for the erection of
an orphanage and the founding of a seminary for teachers and pastors, as
well as for the development of the *Gymnasium* in Weimar and for staffing
it with outstanding teachers, and otherwise too was in every way always at
pains in the best interest of the well-being of his subjects. In this way he
proved how closely a lively faith and active love belong together in the life

of a Christian and that his motto, *Alles mit Gott* (All things with God), was by no means a mere utterance of words or an empty phrase but represented a genuine profession of the heart confirmed by deeds.

Into the service of this duke, who again and again was expressly described as an exception among the princes of his time, came Johann Sebastian Bach in 1708. With the puritanical life of this court[57] Bach had to be very familiar from his first sojourn in Weimar in 1703, so that his decision to go to Weimar must have been even more deliberate than in the earlier applications. Here at the court of Duke Wilhelm Ernst, Bach had to be more closely involved with the Lutheran Church at every turn in his duties than was common otherwise at most of the courts of that time, for an essential part of the assignments of the court orchestra was regular participation in the musical presentations in the court chapel on Sundays and festival days. The duke, who in his younger years had kept a troupe of comedians at court but in later years no longer had any interest in opera and adopted a completely passive attitude over against all amusements and entertainments, but on the other hand had a remarkably fine understanding for art and learning and carried out various projects for their dissemination among the people, also had an open heart especially for the cultivation of church music and did whatever was in his power for its advancement. Not only in the city church but also in the court chapel of the duke regular liturgical presentations of cantatas were customary already long before Johann Sebastian Bach came to Weimar. For the relief of the court capellmeister, Johann Samuel Drese (1644—1716), who in the last years of his life was often ill, the duke had already in 1695 provided Vice-Capellmeister Georg Christoph Strattner. This was done with the special charge, as the official investiture specifies, that he should have "the direction of the whole band [*Capelle*] in the absence of the present capellmeister, Johann Samuel Drese, when, by reason of his well-known bodily infirmities, he could not be present, and in such cases to hold the usual examinations in the house of the said Drese; also nct at any time less than every fourth Sunday to conduct in the prince's castle-chapel a piece of his own composition, and at all times, whether he were conducting or not, to sing tenor."[58] For these cantata compositions the duke's house poet [*Hausdichter*], Oberconsistorial-Sekretär Salomon Franck (1659—1725), active in the Weimar Consistory since 1701, whose piety and extensive theological training made him a close friend of the duke, for many years customarily furnished the texts.[59] He did this by express commission of the duke: The texts were "prepared on the gracious Christian prince's commission" and then also "were to be performed musically by commission of the Most Serene Prince and Lord, LORD Wilhelm Ernst."[60] After the death of Drese in 1716 the duke at first tried to engage as the Weimar court capellmeister Georg Philipp Telemann, who had then already acquired a degree of fame.[61] This shows at what great pains the duke always was to provide a good and rich administration of music at court and in the services of the court chapel.

For a proper evaluation of Bach's change from Mühlhausen to Weimar in its full meaning, we must be aware of the Weimar court's close ties to the church in all areas in addition to the exceedingly pious personality of the duke and his vigorous attention to promoting the interests of art and scholarship. Bach entered the service of a prince from whom he could hope to receive the best support for advancing his own artistic development. And he was not disappointed in this prince, if we are willing for the moment to disregard Bach's departure and the accompanying circumstances in 1717. Proof for this are the continuous and very substantial raises in salary Bach received throughout his time of service in Weimar, and these suggest a continuing and growing appreciation of Bach at the court of the duke.[62] Bach entered the service of a prince with whose help he could above all entertain realistic hopes of achieving the goal of a "regulated church music," which he had so clearly expressed in his resignation in Mühlhausen. His sphere of activity at first was primarily the court chapel, which in the very year 1708 had received a new organ, and, as already in the case of his application in Arnstadt, this new instrument may not have been the last reason to induce him to become successor to the aged and sickly court organist Johann Effler. That Bach also took over still other functions in the court chapel cannot be proved in detail, but it is indeed likely if we consider especially his being titled *Konzertmeister* in 1714. But his main activity was no doubt that of the official court organist. Bach used to refer to himself in 1713 as *Fürstl[ich] Sächs[ischer] Hofforg[anist] u[nd] Camer Musicus* and in 1714 as *Concertmeister und Hofforganist*.[63] Spitta's statement that in the "Complete Treasury Accounts" Bach was at first entered only as "court organist" and only from 1714 on as "concertmaster and court organist"[64] has been confirmed by Jauernig.[65] Already on 14 July 1708 Bach was referred to as court organist, for at that time "the newly acquired court organist" was granted a subsidy for moving expenses. In the treasury accounts of 1712/13 Bach is for the first time called "chamber musician and court organist." In the Weimar church records, however, Bach is referred to as *F. S. Cammer Musicus und Hofforganist* already at the baptism of his first child on 29 December 1708.[66] Also the statement of the obituary, according to which Bach was always spurred on to his greatest performance by the interest of his duke in his organ playing,[67] as well as the fact that Bach research with great likelihood attributes a large part of the composer's works for organ to the Weimar years, confirms the fact that Bach's main assignment in Weimar was that of the official court organist.

But Johann Sebastian Bach was of course not able to realize immediately at his accession to his office in Weimar his desired implementation of a "regulated church music," which we must now understand to mean the regular composition and performance of cantatas in the service. The reasons for this are obvious. In the first place, the office of court capellmeister was still occupied. At Bach's entry into service at Weimar, Johann Samuel Drese was after all 64 years old and in addition constantly ill and unable to function, so that a change in the office of court capellmeister was certainly an approaching event. We could surmise that the duke, who because of the elimination of Johann Effler urgently needed a new court organist, was able to persuade Bach to take over the office of court organist temporarily by offering the prospect of a succession to Drese as court capellmeister within a few years.[68] Also the longer the problem lasted, the more urgently the duke may have intended to appoint an energetic composer and conductor for the Sunday cantatas [Kirchenmusiken] after the vice-capellmeister, Strattner, appointed in 1695 for the ailing Drese, died already in 1704 and when the very undistinguished son of Drese, who was then appointed vice-capellmeister, never was able to assist his father with great achievements in composition. But Bach was first appointed Konzertmeister on 2 March 1714 and in this capacity entrusted with only a part of the duties of the capellmeister by the duke, among them the obligation to compose and direct cantatas in the Sunday services at intervals of four weeks.[69] This limitation may have had something to do not only with Bach's trip to Halle[70] here under discussion but is probably to be attributed to the fact that from 1711 to 1714 a considerable series of building alterations were undertaken in the court chapel,[71] and thus conducting services and presenting cantatas were either not possible at all or were carried out with severe restrictions. In addition to a replacement of the church roof, these building alterations especially had to do with the organ area, which was considered obviously too small for larger presentations of church music and was then given a complete remodeling.[72] This remodeling of the organ area had a threefold goal: Situated under the unlighted framework of the roof, this area was to have daylight admitted; then also the acoustics both for organ music and for the cantata presentations were to be improved by the building changes; and finally space for the entire orchestra and the singers was to be guaranteed.[73] Earlier presentations of cantatas must accordingly have been restricted to a minimum so far as providing instrumentalists and singers is concerned. It would hardly be a mistake to assume that Bach may have suggested this remodeling to the duke in order to create the prerequisite conditions for the implementation of a "regulated church music" such as he was striving for. This assumption is confirmed by the fact that the crowning conclusion of all the work of renewal was a complete remodeling of the organ, then only six years old. The rededication took place on the Third Sunday After Trinity (17 June 1714), for which Bach created his Cantata BWV 21, a composition of grand proportions and rich instrumentation.[74] "In view of the thrifty business administration of Wilhelm Ernst,"[75] one would hardly assume that the duke could on his own initiative have decided so soon to undertake so costly a remodeling of an organ that was new in 1708. The cost of remodeling the organ was almost as much as the price of the new organ in 1708 had been.[76]

Bach had therefore in 1714 taken a definite step nearer to his goal to be able to implement a "regulated church music." First the preconditions for the actualization of this plan had to be created in Weimar. Once they had become reality in 1714, an entirely new chapter actually began in the cultivation of church music in the services of the court chapel. A purely external sign of this was the fact that from that time on the publication of cantata texts by court poet Franck began in a regular succession and in a volume not previously known.[77] Three weeks after Bach's appointment as Konzertmeister, a directive was issued on 23 March 1714 that all rehearsal activity by Bach was no longer to take place in the home of the capellmeister or the vice-capellmeister, as heretofore, but in the court chapel.[78] Before Palm Sunday, 25 March 1714, no cantata performance by Bach in Weimar can be documented with certainty, but on that day the first such performance after Bach's appointment as Konzertmeister took place. It was the grandly designed cantata *Himmelskönig, sei willkommen* (BWV 182), and it was followed by Cantata BWV 12 on 22 April and by Cantata BWV 172 on 20 May. In keeping with his commission, Bach then regularly for three years prepared and directed these liturgical presentations of cantatas.[79] Concerning this activity of Bach, Alfred Dürr correctly states: "For several years, therefore, Bach held to a strict plan, one which was not shaken either when one or more cantatas dropped out. The ideal of the 'regulated church music' here becomes reality for Bach for the first time!"[80] At the end of his *Studien über die frühen Kantaten J. S. Bachs* Dürr once more points out that Bach's statement about "the final purpose, namely a regulated church music to the glory of God," may by no means "be understood as a mere phrase" and that it is also not a "vague, general ideal expressed in rather strange words," but that it "represents the completely concrete plan that Bach then wanted to turn into reality."[81] For three years Bach was able to carry out this plan in Weimar, until at the death of the court capellmeister Drese on 1 December 1716 and the decision about succession precipitated by it, an entirely new situation, unexpected for Bach and finally also unacceptable to him, arose, a situation that induced him to leave Weimar as quickly as possible.[82]

In December 1717 Bach took up his new post as court capellmeister in Köthen. It may safely be assumed that Bach would never have applied for this office in Köthen if he had been spared the great disappointment in Weimar to see that the duke preferred someone else to him as court capellmeister. For three years Bach had already performed an essential part of the duties of the court capellmeister according to instructions, so that he would surely have had first claim to the office after the death of Court Capellmeister Drese. As the new court capellmeister he would then even more definitely and also without limitations have been able to strive to attain his goal of implementing "a regulated church music to the glory of God." In any case, it is worth noting that immediately after the death of Drese on 1 December 1716 Bach performed a cantata in the service of each of the three following Sundays, whereas before this he held strictly to the instruction to perform a cantata only every fourth week.[83] It must have been a very great disappointment for Bach when his justified hopes did not materialize. "The disregard of his accomplishments, heretofore acknowledged, and his being made inferior in rank behind the obviously insignificant son of Drese—these must have been a blow to Bach's legitimate confidence in himself and to his artistic self-respect," so that after this obvious slight on the part of the duke there was no other choice for Bach but to change to another post as fast as possible. "In this it may be assumed that Duke Ernst August and his wife supported him by paving the way for him to the court of Prince Leopold von Köthen, the brother of the duchess."[84] Duke Wilhelm Ernst obviously was not fully aware of the consequences of his decision, for it came as a complete surprise to the duke that Bach asked for his release from the service in Weimar after receiving the call to Köthen and that he pursued this request with great persistence. For several months the duke tried to block Bach's release. Bach's activity in Weimar finally ended with four weeks' incarceration and release from it as late as 2 December 1717 "because of his stubborn testimony and his insistence on forcing his release."[85]

The transfer from Weimar to Köthen was therefore not a desired change of position for Bach but rather a necessary release from a predicament with inner complications. In Köthen then the position of court capellmeister that had just eluded him in Weimar was offered to him, and with it a remarkably high salary was guaranteed. Bach's salary was then more than 120 Taler higher than that of his predecessor and "put him on a financial equality with the 'Hofmarschall,' second highest functionary of the princely Court."[86] This treatment may have felt like a great compensation for the disappointment experienced in Weimar, for Bach was no doubt ambitious for the title of *Hofkapellmeister*, as we also know from his life otherwise. The promptness with which Bach expected to leave Weimar is apparent from his official appointment as *Hochfürstlich Anhalt-Cöthenischer Kapellmeister* as early as 5 August 1717, but on account of the delayed dismissal on the part of the Weimar duke he was not able to enter this office until December 1717, in other words, after a delay of four months, even though his family had moved to Köthen already in August, and payment of his Köthen salary dated from the same time.[87] The removal from orthodox Lutheran Weimar to Reformed Köthen was relatively easy for Bach the Lutheran because his entry into the service of the Reformed Prince Leopold did not involve abandonment or impairment of his Lutheran faith. Prince Leopold came from a mixed marriage—the father was Calvinistic and the mother Lutheran[88]—and so already on account of his training in the parental home he must have inherited a certain tolerance for the Lutheran faith. His father "had promulgated a confessional edict of toleration immediately after his accession to rule,"[89] and his mother had seen to it that St. Agnes Church as well as a special school was built for the Lutheran faithful in Köthen.[90] Thus the guarantee was given to Bach and his family that they could live their Lutheran life without restraint also in Köthen. Accordingly, Bach sent his children to the Lutheran school there as a matter of course.[91] On the whole there was a good relationship between the Reformed and the Lutherans in Köthen. The Lutheran Kantorei, for instance, was customarily engaged for performances at certain festivals and other occasions at court and remunerated accordingly.[92] During Prince Leopold's reign "figural music had found a place in the Reformed Church in Köthen, not as a regular feature, but for certain festivals."[93] For Reformed liturgical practice of that time this was very unusual and therefore cannot be emphasized strongly enough here. Friedrich Smend has demonstrated that Johann Sebastian Bach composed and performed church cantatas for the services,[94] even if only in a restricted way, and so the view of Bach research down to the most recent times that the Köthen epoch was a time almost exclusively devoted to instrumental music is in need of revision. It is also interesting to observe that at Bach's time in Köthen "the capabilities of the Lutheran school Kantorei had improved considerably under the leadership of the court capellmeister."[95]

But even though Bach sought and found opportunity for liturgical music also in Köthen, yet the office and the responsibilities of the court capellmeister in Köthen were of course vastly different from those of the Weimar court capellmeister. At the Weimar court the regular church music presentations in the services, which at Bach's initiative at that time "without doubt experienced an essential intensification,"[96] had their place definitely in the very midst of the musical life of the court. In Köthen, on the other hand, Bach could implement his ideal of carrying out "a regulated church music to the glory of God" only in a very modest way. One cannot help getting the impression that, in spite of all the advantages and amenities, Johann Sebastian Bach himself thought of his Köthen career basically only as a transitional period, from which he would at the proper time be able to return to the area of Lutheran orthodoxy with its rich liturgical tradition and therefore to a specifically liturgical office. In any case, it is interesting to see that Bach within a mere five and one-half

189

years of service in Köthen twice directed his attention to another position, each time to a liturgical office in the Lutheran Church, and also took steps toward applying for the same. The first occasion took place in the autumn of 1720. After completing not even three full years at the Köthen court, Bach applied for the position of organist at St. James Church in Hamburg and spent four weeks in October and November in Hamburg for that purpose.[97] The second occasion in 1722, leading from Köthen to Leipzig, was Bach's application for the cantorate at St. Thomas Church, which eventually became successful and brought on the departure from Köthen. In connection with these applications of Bach's it is highly significant that both cities, Hamburg and Leipzig, at that time were unquestionably acknowledged as "the strongest citadels of Lutheran orthodoxy."[98] It can hardly be thought of as a matter of chance that Bach looked for a specifically liturgical position in just these two cities, for after all, the strictly Lutheran orthodoxy would be the most likely to guarantee that the realization of a "regulated church music" in the service would not come up against serious difficulties. The fact that Prince Leopold permitted his court capellmeister to travel to Hamburg in 1720 for about four weeks for purposes of applying for a position (Bach had after all already been absent from Köthen for some time in the months of May to July)[99] and that even after taking up the work in Leipzig Bach remained on friendly terms with Prince Leopold, indeed, even was accustomed to travel from Leipzig to the Köthen court to provide musical services, surely proves that there was always a close understanding between Bach and the prince and that the latter was not ill-disposed toward his court capellmeister's striving for advancement. In fact, the assumption is justified that the prince was from the very beginning aware that his court capellmeister's service at his court was of a transitional nature. It is not altogether impossible that Bach at his coming to Köthen had candidly presented his plans to the prince and had been given concessions in this matter by him. Otherwise Bach's application in 1720 in Hamburg, after hardly three years of service in Köthen, could easily have been understood as an unfriendly act.

In all these observations concerning Bach's service in Köthen the importance of these years for Bach's total work should in no way be disparaged or denied. Friedrich Smend has stated that "the fruit of the work at Köthen, even of that work that was not intended directly for church and worship, benefited his Leipzig vocal works, especially in the first years there," indeed that "without Köthen, the early Leipzig cantatas are not fully intelligible."[100] But if the question about Johann Sebastian Bach's real ambition is asked, on which tasks and offices in the course of his life he focused his attention particularly, certainly among the various services and duties he undertook in his lifetime his total love for the Lutheran Church and for a liturgical office in this church becomes evident again and again.

d) Application to Become Cantor of St. Thomas, Leipzig

Strictly speaking, we cannot refer to an application of Johann Sebastian Bach's for the cantorate of St. Thomas in Leipzig, for at that time the St. Thomas cantor as we know him today did not exist as yet. In those days it was a double office in the hands of a single person. It consisted of a town "musical director," who was at the head of the widely branched musical activity of the city and who above all was responsible for the very extensive musical service in the main churches, and of a "cantor," who under this title was the music teacher at St. Thomas School. Arnold Schering has correctly pointed out that the designation used for Bach again and again, "Cantor at St. Thomas," is wrong for him,[101] all the more since throughout Bach's time of office in Leipzig not St. Thomas Church but St. Nicholas Church was considered the primary church in the city, because at this church the superintendent of that time, Dr. Deyling, was the pastor, and Bach had to perform the cantata in the forenoon service on the first days of great festivals, as well as on all special festivals, in the church where the superintendent was active and customarily preached. If therefore Johann Sebastian Bach during his time of office in Leipzig rarely refers to himself as "Cantor" but almost always as "Director musices," this is not to be thought of as a disparagement of the title "Cantor," which today is used alone for the purely musical activity of a church musician. Actually, Bach had no interest in the title "Cantor" as a schoolteacher's title. But also technically the title "Director musices" best represented his work in Leipzig, namely as supreme city musical director to be responsible for the presentation of the church music in the main churches of the city as well as at other occasions. Since Bach in this capacity was also the leader of the town musicians [*Stadtpfeifer* and *Kunstgeiger*], there is nothing wrong about describing the position of the St. Thomas cantor at that time as the city's "general director of music," for "all the strands of a widely branched city music program in the last analysis converged in his hands."[102]

That Bach considered the duties and obligations connected with the "Director musices," but not those having to do with the school, as his main task is also confirmed by the fact that already shortly after beginning his Leipzig office he arranged for the Latin instruction to be given by the cantor in St. Thomas School to Magister Petzold of the St. Thomas School for an annual compensation. Since Bach as "Director musices" was required to compose and perform church music, his decision to come to Leipzig can only be understood as a new display of interest in a liturgical office in the Lutheran Church, indeed, as the last fulfillment of his struggle toward the "regulated church music." Friedrich Blume also adheres to this, "that during his first years in Leipzig he plunged with immense energy into the duties of his office in the church and in a quite inexplicable creative frenzy composed" his liturgical works, "which were deeply informed with the spirit of Lutheran piety and abound in all kinds of profound symbolism" (Blu, p. 225). In 1730, 22 years after he had clearly stated his life's goal in Mühlhausen concerning the "regulated church music," Bach took up this word anew and again placed the realization of this plan at the center of his striving and thinking by addressing the city council of Leipzig on 23 August 1730 in a memorial entitled *Kurtzer, iedoch höchstnöthiger Entwurff einer wohlbestallten Kirchen Music* (Short but most necessary draft for a well-appointed church music), in which he stated his views and proposals concerning the "well-appointed church music." If we consider that we possess authentic witnesses concerning Bach's views of life and vocation only in very sparse number, this twice-told word, spoken in two entirely different situations and phases of life, regarding the "regulated" or "well-appointed" church music could be doubly important. For here it becomes evident that in the use of this concept in two official written statements by Bach we obviously are not dealing with a declaration of Bach's that was hastily dashed off and not well thought out so far as its full consequences were concerned. Under these circumstances we also will not be able to agree with Friedrich Blume's hypothesis that Bach merely used this statement about the "regulated church music" as a pretext over against the council of the city of Mühlhausen to make his move to Weimar possible. We must rather agree with Christhard Mahrenholz, who says already regarding the Mühlhausen resignation that one "can sense from the resignation document how firmly Bach is resolved to subordinate everything else to the 'final purpose' of his life" and then again even more properly asserts about Bach's Leipzig memorial of 1730: "And again one perceives in this document that Bach is here touching the ultimate depth of his fundamental view of things."[103] Mahrenholz makes it clear that the expression " 'regulated, well-appointed church music' can be understood only in relation to the essence and the form of the worship of the Lutheran Church as it still flourished at that time."[104]

But now Friedrich Blume, to support his own thesis that Bach in 1723 "only with the greatest reluctance...resumed the cantor's gown...[and] outward circumstances alone were responsible," has tried to prove that for Bach the transition from Köthen to Leipzig according to contemporary concepts represented "a descent in the social scale," so that "Bach felt no inner compulsion to make the change" (Blu, pp. 218, 225).[105] As proof for this thesis Blume cites another document also dated 1730, the letter Bach wrote to the friend of his youth, Erdmann, on 28 October 1730, in which Bach candidly states that "at first...it did not seem at all proper to me to change my position of Capellmeister for that of Cantor" and that he had really "intended to spend the rest of his life" in Köthen (cf. *BR*, p. 125; *BD*

1:67). Since this letter has again and again been regarded as an especially important source for Bach's own view of himself and has been exploited as such, we shall present a rather detailed discussion of it here. [See also the editorial addition to note 46.—Ed.]

We must first of all take a careful look at the situation in which this Erdmann letter was written. Practically, it is very closely related to the memorial of 23 August mentioned above, for it was written only two months after that document. In both documents Bach expresses his great disappointment with the contemporary state of church music in Leipzig. But these complaints on Bach's part are fully understood only if we properly take into consideration the insult just heaped on Bach by the city council. The organist and musical director at New Church since 1729, Gerlach, had from the very beginning of his activity there enjoyed the goodwill of the city council. In May 1730 a considerable sum of money for new instruments for the performance of church music in New Church had been allocated and already a month later, 10 June 1730, Gerlach's salary was doubled.[106] It almost looked as if the city council was trying to create a new church music center at New Church, and this must have upset Bach tremendously, for he felt he was discriminated against. And when the council meeting of 2 August 1730 on top of it all decided "to restrict the Cantor's income" (cf. *BR*, p. 120; *BD* 1:69), Bach's anger rose to the boiling point. He wrote the very detailed, 10-page *Kurtzer, iedoch höchstnöthiger Entwurff einer wohlbestallten Kirchen Music; nebst einigem unvorgreiflichen Bedencken von dem Verfall derselben* (Short but most necessary draft for a well-appointed church music, plus some unpretentious reflections concerning its ruin) and submitted it to the city council on 23 August. Since this memorial of Bach's did not have the desired effect—we have no record of a comment on the part of the council—Bach then wrote the letter to his friend Erdmann in Danzig several weeks later. It is completely obvious that this letter of Bach's was written under the influence of the greatest vexation and disappointment, so that from the very beginning we should be warned against rating individual statements of the letter too highly. A detailed examination of these statements shows in more than one place how this letter carries a coarse tone and even contains inappropriate things. Already the bitter remark about "the authorities" being "odd and little interested in music" is factually unjustified and at least subjective and one-sided. The city council not only in 1730 provided considerable means for improving Gerlach's salary and the performance of cantatas in New Church, but also in later years it aided Gerlach financially again and again, so that the council cannot be accused of being devoid of all interest in encouraging church music. In at least one case the record shows that the city council also supported the cantatas of Bach. In 1747 Johann Christoph Altnickol belatedly received compensation for his three-year-long participation in the cantatas in the main churches, in connection with which the city council expressed the request regarding the participation of special instrumentalists and vocalists: "The cantor should always announce beforehand whom he intends to engage for this purpose" (cf. *BD* 1:148—49; see also *BR*, p. 176). But also the reason advanced by Bach himself as decisive for his leaving Köthen, namely that Prince Leopold's 1721 marriage to a princess described as "unmusical" [*amusa*] seemed to usher in a cooling of the prince's enthusiasm for music, does not hold water. In the first place, this so-called *amusa* died already before Bach's final agreement to go to Leipzig, and the prince was married to her for only one good year. Thus Bach had the opportunity to revoke his application for the position in Leipzig. But also the State Archives of Anhalt clearly indicate that no decline in the musical activity at the Köthen court was associated with the marriage of the prince.[107] And it would have been very strange too if the very musical prince, "who was not only a lover of music but also himself engaged in vocal and instrumental music,"[108] because of his marriage to a 19-year-old bride, of all people, had been affected adversely in his love for music and practice of the same. (The opposite is usually the case; the unmusical one usually learns to love and value music because of the musical partner.) The stated reason also fails to convince because Bach long before the marriage of the prince, as his application for the position in Hamburg in 1720 indicates, entertained the thought of leaving Köthen, and thus Bach's expressed intention to "spend the rest of his life" in Köthen may at best have been a first reaction to the great disappointment in Weimar in 1717. Even Bach's remark that he went to Leipzig so that he might more easily make university training possible for his sons hardly seems convincing, for in his bright financial position in Köthen Bach would easily have found it possible to finance the studies of his children.

Otherwise no further steps toward acquiring another position seem to have followed on this letter with its expressed interest in leaving Leipzig. If Bach really had been deeply interested in giving up his position in Leipzig, certainly still other evidences of his efforts to get away would have come down to us. It could not have been difficult for him to find another appointment, for he was known and highly thought of far and wide—it was not for nothing that he had an essentially higher salary than his predecessors and successors in all of his earlier positions. But in no case does the letter to Erdmann permit an interpretation that points to a lack of interest in the liturgical office and in church music on Bach's part. On the contrary, the request expressed in the letter that Erdmann might be on the lookout for "a suitable post in your city" can obviously be applied only to Danzig, and in keeping with conditions there that must then mean that Bach was looking for a new organist's or cantor's position. Also the scruples mentioned in the letter as bothering Bach already in Köthen and before his taking up the position in Leipzig, that of changing from capellmeister to cantor, cannot refer to the liturgical activity of the director of music, but only to the teaching duties of the cantor in the St. Thomas School, which obviously was less enticing or at least was felt to be a burden. For this reason the city council was prepared to release Telemann from this "instructing" if he should come to Leipzig.

But even aside from the fact that this letter of Bach's to Erdmann with its individual statements "must not be overrated or even weighed with the gold balance"[109] and therefore also cannot serve as the deciding source for a new impression of the Leipzig office of Johann Sebastian Bach, as Friedrich Blume has it, we must here still be concerned further about the problem whether the low estimate of Bach's office in Leipzig that Blume has expressed elsewhere too is really justified.

In connection with the solution of this problem, this fact must be thought of as especially worthy of mention, that the office Bach entered in Leipzig in 1723 was in his own time still an obviously very important office and one that was considered desirable even far beyond the boundaries of Saxony. This is proved already by the fact that within nine days after the death of Bach's predecessor, Johann Kuhnau, on 5 July 1722 the city council of Leipzig was confronted by no fewer than six applicants for the position that had here become vacant. Among these was no less a man than Georg Philipp Telemann, who at that time was a "world-renowned composer and the Hamburg city musical director"[110] and as such was since 1721 charged with supplying the five main churches of the city with church music regularly. This was a position that probably outranked the Leipzig office of musical director, so that even in Leipzig (for example, with Sicul) it excited some wonder "that Telemann thought of taking leave so soon from the well-paid and certainly honored Hamburg position to exchange it for the one in Leipzig."[111] Friedrich Blume says that in imperial cities such a position "already in Haßler's, Schütz's, and Förster's day was in high favor among musicians" of that time and that Bach, too, "probably would gladly have taken the kind of position Telemann had since 1721 as musical director of the five main churches of Hamburg."[112] But the fact that Telemann applied for the position in Leipzig, where he must have known the ups and downs of the position from his earlier Leipzig activity, now does not put the Leipzig office of musical director too far into the shade. Also the fact that the city council of Leipzig made a great effort to attract a distinguished, and possibly the best, musician for the vacant St. Thomas cantorate—and in this area Telemann certainly was the most distinguished, generally acclaimed phenomenon of the day—and the fact that the city council also for some time very firmly counted on Telemann's moving to Leipzig certainly demonstrate that the highly respected position of the

Leipzig musical director was conspicuous at that time. The city council in any case did not doubt the sincerity of Telemann's candidacy. Even when Telemann declined to accept the call passed by the city council, the Leipzig city fathers did not give up their effort to obtain "a famous man"[113] for their cantorate. The man next considered for the Leipzig position after Telemann had declined was Christoph Graupner. He was likewise a "highly regarded court capellmeister" in Darmstadt.[114] For many years he had studied in Leipzig under the St. Thomas cantors Schelle and Kuhnau and therefore also knew the conditions in Leipzig thoroughly, so that his readiness to follow the call to Leipzig and to exchange the office of a court capellmeister for that of the Leipzig musical director again let the highly respected position of the Leipzig musical director become very conspicuous. The plan miscarried only because of the opposition of the Landgrave of Hesse. And if we consider that Leipzig was at that time a "beautiful, rich, and proud city" and that "there was in all of Germany no other place, unless it was Hamburg, where modern life had more glamorously and impressively made its appearance in every direction,"[115] then it must surely have been an honored office to have the privilege of being the chief director at the head of the entire musical life of such a city. Under these circumstances it is difficult to understand that for Bach it should have been "a social comedown according to concepts of that time" to change from the office of court capellmeister to that of musical director. Friedrich Smend correctly pointed out "how remarkable" and yet how unaccountable the fact must appear "that immediately three court capellmeisters applied for this 'social comedown,' "[116] namely, beside Bach, the court capellmeisters Christoph Graupner in Darmstadt and Friedrich Fasch in Zerbst. After a detailed account of the current income of the St. Thomas cantor at that time, Schering comes to the conclusion: "All in all, Bach, after he had once obtained the highest German cantorate, was able to live in good comfort. The records of his estate show the respectable level of his assets."[117] For the "great reputation of the Leipzig position" then generally known, Friedrich Smend has referred to Johann Mattheson's 1728 statement about Johann Sebastian Bach, according to which Bach, after his call to Hamburg in 1720, sincerely desired by Mattheson, had failed, "has since then, as he deserves, been promoted to a respectable cantorate,"[118] and that in no way sounds like a "social comedown." Therefore the Leipzig position was also correctly described to Bach as "favorable," as his letter to Erdmann records.

Bach's application for the Leipzig position as musical director in 1723 was therefore an application for one "of the most distinguished positions of musical Germany," and in this office "he could not think of himself as much inferior to the Dresden court capellmeister."[119]

Even the applications for the St. Thomas cantorate in the second half of the 18th century indicate beyond any doubt that this position was still a desirable and highly regarded one after the death of Bach. Already the day after the death of Johann Sebastian Bach the city council had knowledge of four applicants who had sent in their applications in good time, looking forward to possible death for the 65-year-old cantor (two applications had come in on the very day of Bach's death). Among these applicants was no less a person than Philipp Emanuel Bach, the son of the now deceased St. Thomas cantor, who from his very own point of view and experience in the parental home certainly had to be most intimately acquainted with the advantages and disadvantages of the position of the St. Thomas cantor in Leipzig at that time, for he had also been a St. Thomas student in the years 1723—1730. Yet he considered it entirely worthwhile and respectable to apply for this office. Again after Harrer's death in 1755 Philipp Emanuel Bach applied for the St. Thomas cantorate, and at that time a special commendation for his candidacy was received in Leipzig from Telemann in Hamburg. Among the applicants for the St. Thomas cantorate in 1750 was Johann Ludwig Krebs, probably Johann Sebastian Bach's most eminent pupil, who was then court organist in Zeitz and who also applied again in 1755, when the position was once more vacant. The procedure at the time of Harrer's election to succeed Bach may clearly indicate how ardently the St. Thomas cantorate was still desired. When already in early summer 1749 the possibility of Bach's death seemed imminent, the Dresden secretary of state, a Count Brühl, was quick to approach Leipzig burgomaster Born by letter of 2 June 1749, calling on him "at the eventual death of Mr. Bach, when the position of Kapell-Director there will eventually be filled again," to be sure to let the election fall to his present Kapelldirektor Harrer.[120] Since Brühl even then awaited a binding promise from the Leipzig city council, Harrer duly appeared in Leipzig on 8 June 1749 "on order of the Honorable and Wise Council of this city, who were mostly present" to present a trial recital "for the future appointment as Cantor of St. Thomas, in case the capellmeister and cantor Herr Sebastian Bach should die," and he performed "with the greatest applause."[121]

In this connection we must contradict the common impression that Harrer possessed only very moderate musical talent. Harrer had been in charge of the private chapel of Count Brühl in Dresden for about 20 years and had year after year composed such musical works of both secular and sacred nature for home and festival as the count would order. Schering correctly reminds us that a person of inferior talent could hardly have held on for so long a time in the Dresden of that time, with its highly educated musicians and artists.[122] In comparison with Johann Sebastian Bach, however, Harrer had to seem inferior already for this reason, or at least he had to seem conspicuous, because "Harrer's whole nature, both as man and artist, revealed those compliant, soft, more Italian than German characteristics, which until then had been somewhat strange in the characterization of the St. Thomas cantors."[123]

Also Johann Sebastian Bach's second successor in the office in Leipzig, Johann Friedrich Doles (1756—1789), was a very accomplished musician and also a brilliant choral teacher. Already at age 15 he was offered the position of organist at Schmalkalden.[124] Under his leadership as the Leipzig cantor the accomplishments of the St. Thomas Choir rose to respectable heights, so that people in the middle of the 19th century still "believed that the unequaled heights of the singing at St. Thomas could be attributed to the activity of Doles."[125] The general "high esteem of contemporaries"[126] for Doles clearly indicates that in spite of the flourishing condition of the concert and theater professions in the second half of the 18th century the St. Thomas cantor was still the leading musical personality in the city of Leipzig. And it was not altogether different in the case of Bach's third successor, Johann Adam Hiller, who before becoming cantor at St. Thomas had already been active in Leipzig for years and had there "raised the concert profession to a high level of success."[127] Hiller is counted "among those musical professionals of the 18th century whose inexhaustible productivity excites wonder." His "comprehensive training, his far-reaching interests, and his strong musical endowment made it possible for him to excel as director, composer, organizer, pedagogue, and writer on musical subjects."[128] His services to voice pedagogy made him famous throughout Germany already during his lifetime.[129] He was likewise generally acknowledged among his contemporaries as an author on musical subjects and as a music critic, and "Hiller's composition of songs and *Singspiele* even more than his pedagogical and literary activity have guaranteed him an important place in the history of music."[130] Even before his call to become cantor at St. Thomas, Hiller had "about 1780 reached the highpoint of his fame."[131] The highest accolade his age could bestow was to call him "the Gellert of music." Thus when he was called to be cantor at St. Thomas in 1789, "an unbounded consciousness of responsibility for the proper guidance of minds" must have increased "in him, the born teacher of the people, in the thought that he had now become the absolute musical leader of a great religious city congregation."[132]

Hiller therefore also was a musician who was widely known, universally highly esteemed, and in Leipzig a musician established without a rival, who certainly had no need to apply for a position that was inferior to other musical offices. It was Hiller in fact who like no other applicant for the St. Thomas cantorate in the 18th century knew all about the circumstances in Leipzig because of his two decades of activity in this place, and his application for the St. Thomas cantorate could not have come about rashly. Shortly before his application for the cantorate, Hiller had applied to succeed Philipp Emanuel Bach (d. 14 December 1788) as city cantor in Hamburg and thus had also been in close competition with J. N. Forkel of Göttingen.

Accordingly, the thesis that Johann Sebastian Bach's call to Leipzig as cantor of St. Thomas was "a social comedown," which also was only reluctantly sought by Bach,[133] can only be emphatically contradicted also in the light of the Leipzig music history of the 18th century. Throughout the entire 18th century very distinguished musicians who were well known and highly thought of far beyond the boundaries of Saxony applied for the St. Thomas cantorate. The office of the St. Thomas cantor in Leipzig was by no means a position that was already destined for insignificance or one that was perceptibly losing its prestige. It is interesting anyhow to observe how much the two cities of Hamburg and Leipzig claimed the attention of the applicants for the St. Thomas cantorate throughout the 18th century. Already Telemann made application for the St. Thomas cantorate in Leipzig even when he was already city cantor in Hamburg. Johann Sebastian Bach had already in 1720, before his being called to Leipzig, sent in an application for a position as organist in Hamburg. Philipp Emanuel Bach had been able to succeed Telemann as city cantor in Hamburg in 1768 after both of his applications for the St. Thomas cantorate had failed in 1750 and 1755. And Hiller, too, shortly before his being called as cantor of St. Thomas in Leipzig, had sent an application to Hamburg for the office of city cantor that had become vacant at the death of Philipp Emanuel Bach.

Hamburg and Leipzig—these two "strongest citadels of Lutheran orthodoxy"[134] until far into the 18th century therefore also were the most likely to guarantee that the implementation of a "regulated church music" would not encounter basic difficulties there but would even be assisted and therefore seemed secured. In his five years of service in Köthen, which according to human considerations was possibly the happiest time of his life, Bach twice clearly and positively showed that for the sake of "the final purpose" of a "regulated church music" he was ready to exchange this good position for the liturgical office in one of the two cities, Leipzig and Hamburg. The application for Leipzig finally achieved his goal. Actually, for a musician whose goal was a "regulated church music," there could be no more beautiful position than to be able to work and create in a city in which Lutheran orthodoxy definitely still prevailed and church music therefore enjoyed the highest reputation. Thus we may understand Bach's application to Leipzig to be the final fulfillment of his aspirations. Bach entered the Leipzig office in the name of God, as he himself said in 1730 when he confesses that he was "risking it in the name of the Highest" and "was going to Leipzig." And he understood his call to this place as God's dispensation: "It pleased God that I should be called hither to be *Director Musices* and Cantor at the Thomas-Schule" (*BR*, p. 125; *BD* 1:67).

2.
Prolegomena
to Bach's Creativity

The question concerning Johann Sebastian Bach's attitude toward the worship of his time may in many respects be answered even by reference to his *way of life* alone. It is at all events worth noting that, with the exception of a little over five years of activity in Köthen, Bach's entire professional life was spent in cities in which the Lutheran Church and its worship still occupied a central position. If we consider that the number of cities of that kind, especially since the beginning of the 18th century, was declining rapidly, that Lutheran orthodoxy, except in the Thuringian-Saxon area, maintained itself longest in northern Germany, and that Bach's eyes again and again were turned toward Germany's North, the fact that Bach's life was spent in cities that bore the imprint of the spirit of Lutheran orthodoxy cannot be a matter of chance. Also Bach's brief activity in Mühlhausen, barely a year in extent, and his hasty effort to leave there seems to confirm the fact that Bach was fully aware of the importance of orthodoxy for the work of the church musician.

Not only Johann Sebastian Bach's way of life but also his *life's work* is able to inform us concerning his attitude toward the worship of his time, for by far the largest portion of Bach's works were composed for the Lutheran service and were performed there. And in view of our previous observations that the course of Bach's life conspicuously steered toward the liturgical office and work again and again and that Bach on his part also actually sought this liturgical work and sought it on the native soil of Lutheran orthodoxy, which was so ideal for realizing his "final purpose," all the efforts to think of Bach only as a self-centered musician who composed and performed his music only for its own sake must appear quite problematic from the very outset. In view of Bach's course of life, can one ever seriously consider it possible that Bach could create and work in his liturgical office and assignment without an inner personal tie to the liturgy and without any binding relation to the interests of the Gospel? We must ask this question so pointedly because Friedrich Blume has so clearly expressed his conviction that Bach wrote his liturgical works usually "not with the intention of proclaiming the composer's Christian faith, still less from a heartfelt need to do so" (cf. the discussion on p. 171—72).

We cannot of course discuss every angle and detail of this problem, but in view of the question whether Bach's cantatas may be classified as liturgical works and to what extent they can fulfill a meaningful function in today's evangelical service, we must still try to ascertain whether there are evidences and clues to show how Bach was accustomed to thinking of his liturgical assignment and office and how he usually approached the problems facing him. But this means that we must concern ourselves less with Bach's liturgical works themselves and more with the fundamental presuppositions for their origin and with a look at Bach's creativity. Without doubt, Bach research is still at the beginning of the investigation of these problems. Although a completely new examination of the sources has only now begun with the current edition of Bach's total output, an investigation that will only on completion of the Neue Bach-Ausgabe provide an exact survey concerning the origin of the liturgical works and therewith also a reliable insight into Bach's creativity, still the details so far examined already permit an answer to the question of what Bach's attitude to his liturgical office and therefore to Lutheran worship in general was.

a) Piety and Attitude of Mind

In reality "there has never been doubt," and "for all serious Bach research there is no question, that Bach's real spiritual home was orthodox Lutheranism."[1] But opinions vary widely concerning the meaning of this for Bach's life and work. To arrive at a clear picture in this area, we must strive again and again to try to understand Bach's life and work entirely from the viewpoint of his own time and to guard against approaching Bach with the problems of the 19th and 20th centuries. It is not at all surprising that Bach in Johann Nikolaus Forkel's report appears as "not at all the orthodox Lutheran, the preacher of the Word of God, but rather a sort of national hero, a guardian of the true German spirit. Above all, first and foremost, he is a musician" (Blu, p. 216), for this first biographer of Bach already totally represents the age of rationalism, which was introducing a thoroughgoing change in thought and perception, which could find no access to Bach's text-bound liturgical works because it was diametrically opposed to the theology contained in the texts as also against the Reformation and post-Reformation church hymns that seemed altogether too strange and then also against the "pompous" baroque poetry in general. What this new era stands for so far as the history of piety is concerned is plainly indicated in a revealing remark of Forkel's when with evident surprise he states that the forebears of Johann Sebastian Bach, "wholly consisted of cantors, organists, and town musicians, who had all to do with the church, and it was besides a general custom at the time to begin everything with religion," so that, for instance, at family gatherings, "the first thing they did...was to sing a chorale."[2] Now Johann Sebastian Bach is still entirely caught up in this tradition. In the family chronicle begun by him, "The Origin of the Family of Bach Musicians" of 1735 (cf. *BR*, pp. 203ff.; *BD* 1:255ff.), Bach professed loyalty to this tradition when beside the "home life" [*Heimwelt*] and the "professional life" [*Berufswelt*] he expressly "emphasizes the Lutheran faith life [*Glaubenswelt*] as a fundamental force in the life of the Bach clan."[3] This confession, expressed at age 50, therefore also forbids our taking as mere conventional florid embellishment his statements in the letter to Erdmann that he has moved to Leipzig "in the name of the Highest" and that he understands his call to the St. Thomas cantorate as "the will of God." Likewise already in the Mühlhausen resignation of 25 June 1708 Bach spoke of his call to Weimar as "the will of God." An especially impressive testimony of genuine piety is provided by a letter of Johann Sebastian Bach addressed to the Sangerhausen landlord of Bach's wayward son Johann Gottfried Bernhard, 24 May 1738, and touching matters relating to the son. There we read: "Since no admonition, nor even any loving care and assistance will suffice any more, I must bear my cross in patience and leave my unruly son to God's mercy alone, doubting not that He will hear my sorrowful pleading, and in the end so work on him, according to His Holy Will, that he will learn to acknowledge that the lesson is owing wholly and alone to Divine Goodness" (*BR*, p. 160; *BD* 1:107). This letter, whose sad occasion in a special way forbade all mere flourishes and phrases, permits the quoted words to let some of Bach's trusting prayer life shine through. He is in any case sure that his "sorrowful pleading" will be "heard." Under these circumstances we know that we may not regard the prayerful call "J. J." (*Jesu juva* [Jesus, help!]) at the beginning of his compositions and the doxology "SDG" (*Soli Deo gloria* [To God alone the glory!]) at the end of the same as mere formalities or craftsman's marks, but as genuine signs of his life of faith. Also Johann Sebastian Bach's attendance at Holy Communion, as shown by Albrecht Oepke, seems to have been more in his life than a purely conventional habit, for he was not in the habit of going to Communion a stereotyped number of times a year or at stated times in the church year, but attended in a definitely varied sequence. Thus beside regular attendance during the Trinity season in Bach's Leipzig time, attendance also in Lent (1724, 1726, 1734, 1736, 1738), between Easter and Pentecost (1728, 1732, 1733, 1743, 1747), in Advent (1727, 1729, 1732,

1741, 1742, 1743, 1745, 1746, 1748, 1749), and even in Epiphany (1727) are on record.[4] As a rule Bach went to Holy Communion twice a year, but an attendance of three times a year is recorded for Arnstadt in 1706 and for Leipzig in 1724, 1727, and 1732. Especially striking for the Leipzig times is the fact "that Bach frequently partook of Communion shortly after the death of a child"[5] and that in 1732 he attended Holy Communion twice in six weeks, on Jubilate Sunday and on the Thursday after Trinity. But this very record again and again brings up the question whether we should not be obliged—also in Bach's life—to reckon with more frequent attendance at Holy Communion (without previous confession), for the Communion registrations list only those by name who came to confession, and the number of these was always considerably smaller than the total number of Communion guests (cf. the statements on p. 140). We think it is also worth noting that in 1730, which brought great disappointments, Bach went to Holy Communion twice, namely on the Thursday after the First Sunday After Trinity and on the Thursday after the 24th Sunday After Trinity, so that the vexations of that year probably did not indicate any crisis of faith, as also that *Short but Most Necessary Draft for a Well-Appointed Church Music* and the letter to Erdmann do not in any way register any doubt about his call to the liturgical office.

Contrary to Oepke's exposition, regular participation in Holy Communion on the part of Johann Sebastian Bach is recorded at St. Thomas Church also after 1736. In the lists of communicants Bach's name always appears on Thursday after the following Sundays: Laetare and the 22d Sunday After Trinity 1738, the 23d Sunday After Trinity 1739, Trinity and the 22d Sunday After Trinity 1740, Trinity and the Second Sunday in Advent 1741, the Eighth Sunday After Trinity and the First Sunday in Advent 1742, Exaudi and the Third Sunday in Advent 1743, the 17th Sunday After Trinity 1744, Trinity and the Second Sunday in Advent 1745, the Sixth Sunday After Trinity and the First Sunday in Advent 1746, Exaudi and the 23d Sunday After Trinity 1747, Trinity and the Third Sunday in Advent 1748, and the Second Sunday After Trinity and the Third Sunday in Advent 1749. The entry in the communicant lists is given as follows: for 1738 *H. Bach, Cantor zu St. Thomas* and *H. Bach der Cantor*; for 1739 *H. Bach, Capellmeister* and *H. Capellmeister Bach*; for 1741—1746 *H. Bach, Capellmeister und Sohn* or also *H. Capellmeister Bach und Sohn*, and for the last three years *H. Capellmeister Bach und 2 Söhne* or *H. Bach, Capellmeister und 2 Söhne*. The fact that Bach's name is not found in the communicant list of 1737 is no doubt a result of the death in December 1736 of Dr. Christian Weiß, the head pastor for many years at St. Thomas and the father confessor of Johann Sebastian Bach in the first 14 years of his Leipzig activity. Bach now had to find a new father confessor, and that was obviously not easy for him, for whereas his name up to and including

1736 is always found in the first column, containing the names of those who came to confession with the head pastor, after that time his name no longer turns up in the first column of the communicant lists. In 1738 Bach had found a new father confessor in Subdeacon Teller, for in that year we find Bach's name in the fourth column of the communicant lists, among those coming to confession with the fourth clergyman of St. Thomas Church. After Teller in 1739 had moved up to deacon, we find Bach's name in the third column for 1739 and 1740, among those who came to confession with the third clergyman, until Teller in the summer of 1740 was moved to St. Peter and Bach again had to find a new father confessor. He found him for a short time in the newly called subdeacon of St. Thomas, for on the Thursdays after the 22nd Sunday After Trinity 1740 and after Trinity 1741 we again find Bach's name in the fourth column of the lists. When in 1741 several posts at St. Thomas again changed clergymen and in this connection the subdeacon, new the year before, left St. Thomas altogether, Bach again had to find a new father confessor. This time he found him in Archdeacon Wolle, who remained his confessor to the end of his days and to whom he also remained faithful when Teller came back to St. Thomas from St. Peter and became head pastor in 1745. Incidentally, with Bach stood *H. Prof. Gottsched Rect. Magnif.*, who, also among those coming to confession with the archdeacon since 1742, is usually listed twice a year in the second column of the lists, although he had previously also been among those who came to confession with Teller.[6]

Even this regular attendance at confession and Holy Communion, confirmed up to the last year of his life, makes it clear that Johann Sebastian Bach to the end of his life remained the same evangelical Christian, characterized by Lutheran faith and profound piety and always loyal to his church, just as we know him from the beginning of his life. When we in addition recall his really large theological library, consisting of Luther's works alone up to a fourth of the traceable total (and we should add that our knowledge of the list is incomplete, for after Bach's death his sons no doubt transferred to their own use books that seemed particularly valuable to them), and when we consider that the books proved to have been in this library were by no means "old pigskins of primarily historical and collectors' value" but that "most of them were in Bach's time still being disseminated and even brought out in new editions," indeed that Bach's library, as sample years indicate, "was enlarged up to the last years of the master's life,"[7] a real theological interest in the questions of faith of his church on the part of Bach and so an actual "matter of the heart" relation to the Gospel becomes evident. According to a handwritten auction sales receipt that begins with words that really say something, "These German and magnificent writings of the late D. M. Luther...," Bach as late as 1742 acquired an Altenburg edition of Luther's works at a respectable price.[8]

After Bach's death his library was also found to contain the earlier Jena German edition of Luther's works in addition to volumes of sermons by the Reformer.

A particularly convincing key to forming an estimate of the faith and piety of Johann Sebastian Bach finally are the last weeks of his life, which were governed by a clear premonition of approaching death. In view of that "utmost need" Bach on his sickbed produced an expanded version of the organ chorale "Wenn wir in höchsten Nöten sein," composed already in Weimar or Köthen, and he did this on the spur of the moment by dictating the notes, very likely to his son-in-law Johann Christoph Altnikol. Shortly before his death he had this organ chorale transferred in fair copy to the collection that already contained *Siebzehn Choräle* and the canonical composition "Vom Himmel hoch da komm ich her." In addition to a number of improvements undertaken at that time, a further characteristic of this fair copy is that Bach had the word *Choral* inserted in the soprano where the hymn tune entered.[9] But the most significant feature of this fair copy is the change of title from "Wenn wir in höchsten Nöten sein" to the text sung to the same tune, "Vor deinen Thron tret ich hiermit," to which Hans Klotz adds the remark: "Both titles—that of the original dictation and that of the fair copy—are obviously applied personally: 'Wenn wir in höchsten Nöten sein' is the prayer in the utmost need of sickness and blindness, and with 'Vor deinen Thron tret ich' Bach stood before his Maker."[10] Both titles finally are witnesses to Bach's genuine life of prayer; the last title points as it were to the last prayer of his life, at least to that which in his last days chiefly, perhaps even exclusively, occupied his attention—the transition from time to eternity. The celebration of Holy Communion for the sick in his home on Wednesday, 22 July 1750, finally shows that Johann Sebastian Bach as a Christian consciously prepared himself for this journey to his true home. The St. Thomas communicant registration of 1750 the week after the Eighth Sunday After Trinity carries the simple notice: "Private Communion: Cantor Bach at St. Thomas School." This last reception of Holy Communion in his life, six days before his death, makes it unmistakably clear that not even the statement of the obituary written in 1754 that Johann Sebastian Bach "quietly and peacefully, *by the merit of his Redeemer*, departed this life"[11] may be thought of as a mere flourish or phrase.

All these details from Johann Sebastian Bach's life of piety are of course only individual but very significant highlights that banish all doubt concerning Bach's undeviating confession to the Lutheran Church and his life of faith characterized by genuine piety. We must agree with Hans Arnold Metzger without reservation: "The importance of his really being *at home* in the worship of the congregation we must view as the central force for his creativity and for his piety. As ever since his school days he had grown up in the orthodox dogmatics of a person like Leonhard Hutter, so he self-evidently believed *with the church* and celebrated *with the church.*"[12]

This realization is everywhere confirmed in Bach's creativity, and more than ever in his late works. Although in the last 20 years of his creativity the number of liturgical works declined noticeably, this in no way indicates a lack of interest in the liturgical work itself. Walter Blankenburg has stated emphatically that "it is precisely the liturgical works of Bach's old age that come forward in the light of a conscious Christian affirmation of faith," indeed, that "studies of his works, above all in the *Christmas Oratorio*, the *Klavierübung*, Part III, and the *Mass in B-Minor*, in the research of recent times have made it absolutely clear that these creations in particular are motivated by a Christian faith and a Christian view of life," that "in them, beside the musical figures in the service of Biblical interpretation, the language of symbols, especially number symbolism, but also forms of rhythm, keys, instrumentation, organization of the composition, etc., emerge even more prominently and more on principle than in earlier years of Bach's activity."[13]

But the more influential orthodox Lutheranism and a heart-felt piety were for Bach's life and work, the more we ought to have the highest regard for a circumstance that is very informative for all of Bach's creativity, one that has been considered altogether too little in Bach research, and one that has not yet been recognized in its full effect. This is the fact that Bach lived and worked "in an existence that was not yet split into sacred and secular divisions but was internally united and nourished from the center of the faith of the Lutheran Reformation."[14] This is the same as saying that "Bach's ties to the Lutheran liturgy also signify the right and the duty to become active in the extraliturgical, the secular, area," obviously because "Martin Luther does not limit the concept 'worship' to the liturgical practice of a congregation gathered around Word and Sacrament but describes the entire life and activity of a Christian as an act of worship."[15] Much as we in connection with our project place the emphasis on Johann Sebastian Bach the *church* musician and on his positive attitude to the Lutheran service because that seems especially important to us, so we must at the same time oppose the misapprehension that we mean thereby to hide Bach's so-called "secular" creativity or the "secular" musician Bach. We consider the necessity to distinguish between Bach the "church" musician and Bach the "secular" musician altogether wrong, indeed, even illegitimate, since Bach was "neither the one nor the other in our modern sense," so that in the final analysis "the controversy whether Bach was a church musician or a secular musician is futile."[16] In any case, Bach did not know the contrast between the *church* musician and the *secular* musician, for the "sacred-secular antithesis with which the approach to Bach is made again and again

Leipzig order of service on the First Sunday in Advent (1723). Entry in Bach's hand on the score of Cantata 61 (See *BD* 1:248). Source: *Neue Ausgabe Sämtlicher Werke* (Kassel and Basel, 1954), 1:vi.

was not a problem of the Bach era," and accordingly we "stand in danger of looking at things from a perspective that is significant for *our* time but one from which the historical situation must appear distorted."[17] Not even in filing his works was it customary for Bach to undertake a division between the "secular" and the "sacred-ecclesiastical" ones.[18] We can understand Bach's attitude toward his offices and duties only from the view of his own time. It turns out that "the sacred-secular problem is such a difficult one for an interpretation of Bach that it does not find its way to the simplest thought of all, namely that one must not approach Bach in this way, but that for a presentation of Bach the unity of God and World [*Gott-Welt-Einsheit*] is the presupposition given by history."[19]

That Johann Sebastian Bach in his thinking and acting very consciously stood on the foundation of the orthodox Lutheran doctrine of faith, a foundation laid in his childhood and youth, is made clear in his course in figured bass. This must be considered a well-thought-out and therefore basic statement of Bach's, one that he dictated to his students. In its second chapter, which deals with "Definition," we read: "The figured bass is the most perfect foundation of music. It is played with both hands in this way, that the left hand plays the notes prescribed, but the right hand adds consonances and dissonances so that a sweet-sounding harmony may result to the glory of God and for an allowable delight of the heart. And as in the case of all music, so also the purpose and final goal of the figured bass should be nothing else but only the glory of God and the restoration of the heart [*Recreation des Gemüths*]. Where this is not observed, there you have no real music, only devilish bleating and harping."[20]

This juxtaposition of the glory of God and the "restoration of the heart" is, as Christhard Mahrenholz has pointed out, not an invention of Bach's. It is found, for instance, in Leonhard Hutter; indeed, "this statement of the object of music is already found in Luther's preface to the first evangelical hymnal of 1524, and in orthodoxy it again turns up in almost every commentary on the 15th article of the Augsburg Confession."[21] The same idea is also expressed in the wish of the preface to Gottfried Vopelius's *Leipziger Gesang-Buch* of 1693: "As for the rest, may our faithful GOD and the Father in heaven grant that this little book may be used to the glory of His most holy name and to the blessed edification of Christendom. Amen."

Even if the Bach quotation to begin with "contains no genuine Lutheran doctrine," because the juxtaposition of the glory of God and the delight of the heart "may be encountered in the early Middle Ages just as in the postorthodox era," yet the closing statement of the quotation itself, namely, that if music serves some other purpose, "it is not real music, only devilish bleating and harping," can undeniably indicate that Bach arrived at this formulation in the attitude of faith transmitted to him by Lutheran orthodoxy, for Lutheran orthodoxy, in agreement with Luther, was acquainted "with the demonic character of music that is not in the service of God."[22] In being able to dictate to his students such a clear direction for stating the purpose of music, Bach plainly confesses in what frame of mind he himself customarily thought of his office and his duties. This confession of Bach's in its entirety indicates an uncompromising renunciation of the spirit and creativity of the Enlightenment, in the eyes of which a statement of the purpose of music so formulated had to appear as an intolerant judgment. For the Enlightenment, it is true, still recognized music "as a factor devoted to God," but with the coming of the Enlightenment a thoroughgoing change had after all taken place, which Mahrenholz describes as follows: "The German Enlightenment provides greater emphasis for the divine origin of music, whereas orthodoxy more forcefully stresses music's being given for the glory of God. There is good reason for this. For orthodoxy there is no free area between God and Satan. Man with all his God-given powers and arts 'serves' either here or there. And every employment of music takes place either to the glory of God and so promotes the 'restoration' (rebirth) of man, or it takes place to the glory of Satan and so promotes the sinful entrapment of man. The necessity to combine 'to the glory of God' and the 'delight' of the heart is therefore not to be surrendered. The Enlightenment on the other hand creates for itself a free area between God and the devil, between the two fronts on the battlefield, where one may presumably in full freedom without commitment to the right or to the left exercise oneself. The art of music is of course not used to the glory of Satan but also not quite to the glory of God. It delights man on the 'neutral' field. The commitment of the delight of the heart to the divine origin of music is not given up, but the commitment to the purpose for the glory of God is lost. The vocable 'delight' [*Ergötzung*] now takes on a new connotation in the direction of a pleasant amusement of the senses. This valuation of music in the way of the Enlightenment therefore also no longer recognizes the 'instruction,' the training of man toward God as the consequence of the practice of music to the glory of God."[23]

Oskar Söhngen, too, interprets "restoration" [*Recreation*] very literally as "new creation, returning to the original definition of creation," so that "restoration of the heart" then means "fundamentally correcting the whole person," as indeed the concept "heart" [*Gemüt*] "was then more comprehensive than it is today, where it has been made to concentrate on denoting the emotional side of human mental life. Then it denoted 'the totality of mental powers and sensory implulses' and was used interchangeably with the concept *heart*, which denoted the real personal center of the human being."[24]

The statement found in the course in figured bass is evidently Bach's own formulation of a subscription to the Lutheran delineation of the purpose of music. This becomes evident from the fact that Bach again makes use of a formulation that tends in the same direction in his dedication of the *Orgelbüchlein*, namely, the confession that witnesses anew to his Lutheran stance of faith: "In praise of the Almighty's Will, And for my Neighbor's Greater Skill" [*Dem Höchsten Gott allein zu Ehren, Dem Nächsten, draus sich zu belehren*] (Cf. *BR*, p. 75; *BD* 1:214). Here, too, the "final purpose" of all composing and music making is summarized in the double purpose: Glory to God and service to the neighbor. Wolfgang Herbst has contrasted this formulation of the "final purpose" of Bach's creativity to the entirely different frame of mind of Christiane Mariane von Ziegler, a contemporary of Bach's in Leipzig. She, too, makes a statement regarding a "final purpose" of her poetical creativity in the preface to her book of poetry, *Versuch in gebundener Schreib-Art* (Essay in rhythmical style) (Leipzig, 1728). There we read that "the highest final purpose of all orators and poets is inherent in the awakening of pleasure."[25] In this formulation a totally different frame of mind is expressed, namely, that of the ethics of the Enlightenment as represented by the Deutsche Gesellschaft zu Leipzig of people like Johann Christoph Gottsched and Johann Adolph Scheibe, which definitely challenged Bach's "final purpose."[26]

This was very likely also the reason why a lasting cooperation with Christiane Mariane von Ziegler was impossible for Bach, for "Bach did not create his works to win the goodwill and recognition of the 'conceited' Leipzig churchgoers or his 'strange' city councilmen or his undisciplined St. Thomas students or his envious teacher colleagues, but to give the glory to God with them." For him "the valuation of music as a servant for the glory of God and from there as a teacher of mankind to promote a godly life stood firm and immovable."[27] Thus Bach clearly stood on the side of orthodox Lutheranism, but at a time in which even in Leipzig such a frame of mind and such a confession as it was expressed in the course in figured bass and in the *Orgelbüchlein* was for a long time no longer considered self-evident. Beside Christhard Mahrenholz, especially Hans Besch and Fred Hamel emphatically called attention to the agreement of Bach's own understanding of his creativity and the pedagogical foundation of Lutheran orthodoxy.[28]

Accordingly, in our evaluation of the creativity of Johann Sebastian Bach, we will have to consider his piety and frame of mind that carried a Lutheran imprint as a very central presupposition of this thinking and acting. Because Lutheran orthodoxy did not yet recognize the modern split of all being into sacred and secular areas, we also do not find in Bach the basic differentiation between church music and secular music, whereas characteristically in Christiane Mariane von Ziegler "in contrast to Bach, a curt and clear separation of the spiritual and the secular areas" is to be found.[29] In the course in figured bass Bach expressly speaks of *all music*.

When we thus realize that Bach with Luther and Lutheran orthodoxy was convinced that the whole area of music must serve "to the glory of God and for the restoration of the heart," we can understand that Bach could place at the head of his compositions, both those specifically intended for the church and for worship and also the "secular" works, the prayerful sign "J. J." (Jesus, help!) and could conclude all of these works with the song of praise "SDG" (To God alone the glory!). There could be no clearer documentation to show that for Johann Sebastian Bach his entire creativity and activity, no matter whether or not it was in the direct interest of the church and its liturgy, was in fact *worship* in the widest sense of the word, entirely in agreement with the admonition of the apostle Paul: "Whatever you do, in word and deed, do everything in the name of the Lord Jesus, giving thanks to God the Father through Him" (Colossians 3:17). This conviction, really to do *everything* "in the name of Jesus," we find confirmed in Johann Sebastian Bach down to this very formulation, for at the head of the *Clavier-Büchlein vor Wilhelm Friedemann Bach*, begun in Köthen, 22 January 1720, he wrote "In Nomine Jesu."[30] And that these signets at the beginning and end of Bach's works are by no means conventional flourishes can be seen unmistakably in this very *Clavierbüchlein* both at the end of the Sixth Sonata (BWV 1012) and at the end of the Inventions and Symphonies (BWV 772—801), for here the closing mark is not (as usually) abbreviated "SDG" but written out "Soli Deo Sit Gloria."[31]

b) The Will to Proclaim

People have never ceased to marvel that Johann Sebastian Bach and Johann Christoph Gottsched, without doubt the two most distinguished men of the city of Leipzig in the first half of the 18th century in their separate fields, lived side by side for almost three decades "without letting their interrelation develop beyond a respectful reserve," even though Gottsched himself wrote librettos for church [*geistliche*] cantatas and in fact "not only took an active practical part in writing texts for occasional cantatas but also devoted an entire chapter of his *Critische Dichtkunst* of 1729 to the theoretical requirements of cantata writing."[32] But this curious side-by-side immediately becomes intelligible when we realize the radically different mental attitudes of these two men and the consequences incidental to these differences and do not minimize these things. The spirit of the Enlightenment, which determined the life and work of Gottsched, certainly represents a radical upheaval for all intellectual life and endeavor, because the Enlightenment wants to liberate from ecclesiastic obligation and spiritual regimentation and thinks of the artist and his creativity as completely autonomous. Gottsched intensely deplored the fact that poets, to the detriment of poetry in their cantata librettos, let themselves become altogether too subservient to composers.[33] As in the case of his follower, Christiane Mariane von Ziegler, Gottsched, the leading spirit of the "German Society" [Deutsche Gesellschaft], embraced the notion that the autonomous art of poetry exists only for the sake of pleasing. For him the "final purpose" of all creating and activity is no longer the glory of God and service to the neighbor through proclamation and instruction, but the purpose of all poetry lies alone in this, to please the readers and, respectively, the hearers and spectators.[34] And even though spiritual poetry was still being written, it no longer represented a proclamation and attestation of Christian truth bound to the liturgy of the church and to Holy Scripture, but rather an uncommitted poetry with spiritual themes in which the poets now in general emphasized the factual content less than the formal and aesthetic structure of their words.

But with this aesthetical spirit of the Enlightenment, which was no longer especially interested in the real content of the poetry but compensated by emphasizing the artistic form of the poetry the more, Gottsched and the circle of followers going about their work in his spirit were not able to render any service at all to the St. Thomas cantor of that day in the fulfillment of his liturgical assignment, for Bach was rooted in a totally different but firm tradition, which was interested less in the formal-aesthetic structure of poetry and more in its spiritual declaration. Thus the Leipzig clergyman Carl Gottlob Hofmann, in the preface to his *Privilegirtes Vollständiges und Verbessertes Leipziger Gesangbuch* of 1737, stated that in his selection of about 1,000 hymns he had also included "a number of newer hymns" beside "the good old core hymns [*Kernlieder*]" and in the process had altered offensive passages, doing so for the following reason: "Though the rhyme and rhythm be ever so pure, purity and clarity of doctrine must be even more precious to us. And that is the reason why I have made occasional little changes in the newer hymns." These offending passages and the resulting changes of text therefore had to do with theological statements, which in Bach's time in Leipzig were still taken seriously, and for this reason also the hymns that were to be sung in the service and texts that were to be presented musically there required an ecclesiastical-theological censorship and authorization.[35] For Bach, too, the decisive criterion concerning texts he would set to music was the question about contents and truth. It is interesting to see that Bach adopted none of the rambling cantata texts of Christiane Mariane von Ziegler without shortening them. "They were all tightened up or altered, always to their advantage so far as the theological message is concerned."[36] Similar alterations are also found in the Bach cantata texts by Christian Friedrich Henrici and Salomon Franck.[37] Unfortunately we are familiar with only the smallest number of antecedent texts known to us and concerning the corrections and even alterations made in those texts Herbst feels entitled to say on the basis of a series of examples he produced that "Bach worried considerably more about the texts he set to music than many of his interpreters did. Above all, he attached the greatest importance to making the music's text also proclaim the Gospel as purely as possible. He would rather opt for an imperfect form, an infelicitous rhyme, or an uneven rhythm but retain instead the spiritual content that he wished for in the text and that was not watered down by rhetorical superfluity. Bach's procedure flies directly in the face of all aestheticism. Measured by the standard of the aesthetics of the Enlightenment, his corrections can frequently only be rejected, but for him the theological proclamation outweighs the aesthetic element."[38] But already the circumstance that for by far the larger number of Bach cantatas we do not know the author of the text can illuminate the fact that in all these texts the liturgical proclamation *alone* is the important element. Here, then, the name of the respective poet is naturally completely unimportant, whereas the poetic art of the "Deutsche Gesellschaft in Leipzig" was cultivated entirely "in order to please"[39] and thus moved the artistic achievement of a given poet definitely into the limelight.

The Bach cantata texts that have been much maligned and often adversely criticized, even called "inelegant" and "banal," and that must generally remain unintelligible in the primarily aesthetic point of view of the 19th and 20th centuries, immediately gain an understanding and a revaluation when we no longer view them in a formal and aesthetic way but take them for what they wanted to be: a proclamation of the Gospel.[40] It is therefore not accidental that the librettists as a rule were clergymen,[41] who used to compose the cantata texts in close connection with their sermons, and they did this with a view toward having these texts set to music and performed as cantatas in the services. Erdmann Neumeister clearly stated that his cantata texts, of which several annual sets were appointed for the polyphonic presentations in a number of churches in central Germany, regularly originated after his sermon preparation and that he always strove to express the central thoughts of his sermon in the poetry of the cantata, so that the cantata text could rightly be called a "sermon in poetical style."[42] Regarding Neumeister's poetry the remark has even been made that "in his tendency toward a pulpit tone he often runs into the danger of documenting the truth of any Christian teaching in a purely intellectual way.... That is not poetry but dogmatics."[43] These cantata texts, designed with a view toward the music, should certainly not, like purely literary exhibits, be judged from formal and aesthetic aspects, and that is why cantata poetry as a genus correctly is hardly given any attention in the history of literature. From the viewpoint of literary criticism, cantata poetry must constantly be subject to negative criticism already because among themselves they often (in the case of Johann Sebastian Bach, even always) completely lack uniformity in that they may combine very heterogeneous literary components from several centuries, especially hymns of the 16th and 17th centuries, plus Bible quotations in pure prose (Luther's German), and even the most dissimilar forms in a single section. We must agree with Brausch when he says: "The constant interruption of one form by another (hymn verse/recitative/hymn verse/recitative, etc.), which really disturbs reading, is the best proof that the author thought only of the music, where all things tend more toward an interlocking effect and such a combination of dissimilar elements often achieves a very good effect."[44] It was even possible in those days for cantors actually to make use of a number of lines of text from different authors or certain sentences from them in a single cantata.[45]

We cannot therefore do justice to the Bach cantata texts either if we treat them offhand only or principally from the viewpoint of literary criticism. These texts do not want to be inspected and judged in the first place, but they want to be *heard* together with the music and be taken seriously in their proclamation. What has been said about Neumeister's cantatas, that in them "the person of Christ...realistically comes to the fore, as if one saw the Savior Himself and spoke with Him,"[46] is basically true for all of Bach's cantata texts that are engaged in the service of liturgical proclamation. Like the sermon, they really want to *address* the hearer personally, and that always means to call him to repentance and to faith in the Lord, who in worship realistically confronts His congregation in the Word and Sacrament, so that the hearer summoned to a decision must necessarily answer and take a stand, and there cannot be a proclamation merely "for the sake of pleasing." This proclamation expressed in Bach's cantata music is a proclamation that was in every way strictly bound to the Sunday and festival day liturgy with its readings and can therefore be understood only from these close ties.

Only the texts that have a strong mystic cast clearly show to what an extent Bach's cantatas display a proclamation based centrally on Holy Scripture. Even though the old adage says: "Either mysticism *or* the Word,"[47] in the very work of Bach there is evidence to show how much "the *unio mystica* of Lutheranism is already a weakened and broken mysticism," for in Bach's cantatas the relationship to the Word of God plays a decisive role in spite of all the mysticism that is present, as also "the *unio mystica* of orthodoxy was already in its very first beginnings related strictly to Scripture and authenticated from it according to all the rules of the game."[48] Even "the mystic reminiscences in the texts are almost throughout somehow anchored in definite Bible passages," so that there can be no suggestion that "the basic meaning of the Word for the evangelical faith" is impaired or injured "because of the frequent mention of mystic thoughts."[49] Using Cantata BWV 186 as an example, Herbst demonstrates how definitely the second version, whose text in all probability can only have Bach as its source, "expresses the reference to the Word of God... partly by insertion into the old text, partly by new additions, and partly by chorale stanzas expressly chosen for this purpose."[50]

Another characteristic feature of Bach's cantata composition lies in this, that the *whole Bible* has been of basic importance for the origin and composition of the cantata texts. Consequently on hearing a cantata, only congregational members firmly rooted in the Bible (and that was still taken for granted among the worshipers at Bach's time) are able to comprehend the entire substance and meaning of the proclamation, and one of the reasons for the rejection of the cantata texts simply is to be found in this, that later generations no longer even remotely possessed that knowledge of the Bible, and therefore the appreciative access to the numerous references and allusions to the stories, pictures, and wording of the Bible had to remain a closed book to them. It has been said that "it is amazing how all of the so-called independent compositions of the recitatives and arias are from the images and the language of the Bible, and especially of the Old Testament" and that "with this renunciation of their own choice of words and their own formulations the cantata poets are walking in the footsteps of the hymn writers, who also regularly used the idioms and images of the Luther Bible as the basis of their hymns."[51] An example may clearly indicate how strong the linguistic influence of the Bible is in the Bach cantatas. The second movement (Tenor recitative) of Cantata BWV 109 in only 10 consecutive lines alludes to no less than five different passages of the Old Testament, namely, Numbers 11:23, Isaiah 31:20, Psalm 22:20, Isaiah 38:17, and Psalm 13:2-3.[52] But above all, also "the narratives of the Old Testament are taken up in the cantatas," but this is of course "never done for their own sake but always only because of the importance of the implications that accrue to them in addition to their simple worth as historical fact," for "all Old Testament material is simply and solely read from the viewpoint that salvation is actual and complete in Christ."[53] Bach (incidentally with Luther) had an especially strong preference for the Old Testament Psalms; 46 movements of his cantatas are settings of particular verses from the Psalms, and all of 26 cantatas begin with such verses. Beside these, the cantata texts contain additional quotations from the Psalms and clear allusions to definite Psalms in at least 58 cases.

In general, to have the pure Bible text set to music is a particular characteristic of Bach's liturgical works. This is already indicated by the fact that all of 128 movements in Bach's cantatas are musical settings of the pure Bible text. But further proof is furnished by a comparison of Bach's Passions with the works of his contemporaries, who are no longer familiar with the use of the pure Bible text but in its stead present the narrative part of the Passion in modern rhymes. Although Bach was familiar with Hamburg Ratsherr Brockes's libretto in such rhymes, *Der für die Sünden der Welt gemarterte und sterbende Jesus, aus den vier Evangelisten in gebundener Rede vorgestellt* (Jesus, tormented and dying for the sins of the world, presented in poetical style from the four evangelists), which Händel, Telemann, Keiser, and others set to music and Bach, too, drew on for his Passion music, "he adopted nothing as it was," in fact, "the decisive difference between his Passions and those of his contemporaries" lay in this, "that he completely ignored the rhymed narrative of the famous libretto and in its stead set the pure Word of the gospels to music, unadulterated and unshortened," and to that we can add with a perfect right: "What an advantage even purely artistically! Luther's classic language in place of the pompous rhymes of the poet from Hamburg! But Bach was concerned not only about the language, although he displayed a remarkable sensitivity in this matter, too, as his revisions of the parts he did adopt from Brockes prove. He was concerned about God's Word. Thus the Bible text becomes the main concern in this work, *The Passion According to St. John*."[54] This statement agrees with the observation that the cantata libretti, distributed among those who attended the service in Leipzig at Bach's time and furnished as an obligation on the part of the cantor of St. Thomas ever since Kuhnau's time, always display the Bible text in contrast to all other texts, also in contrast to the hymn stanzas quoted, in a particularly large and emphatically prominent typeface and thereby make it the supporting center of the whole printed text and its proclamation.[55] Bach definitely considered the Bible text the most important element in his liturgical composition. He makes this especially impressive in the fair copy of the *Passion According to St. Matthew*, where he "deliberately used red ink only for the Biblical text assigned to the evangelist and for the chorale *cantus firmus* (in the opening chorale fantasia for double chorus)."[56] Smend aptly comments on this fact: "Even he who only casually pages through this manuscript should, yes, must, again and again be impressed by the unique way in which this text is emphasized. Obviously Bach is interested in nothing but the Word of Scripture."[57]

In view of this clearly observable interest in the wording of the Bible and in the proclamation of the Word as bound to Scripture, we will always have to ask the question anew to what extent Johann Sebastian Bach created his own librettos or at least compiled them from available copy, in fact, even provided the direction for other librettists as they prepared such copy. For "it has meanwhile been thought of as a likelihood that Bach wrote some of his liturgical texts himself."[58] This suggestion has again and again been expressed in Bach research by very dissimilar authorities, and it has lately been supported again in a study devoted exclusively to the Bach texts by Luigi Ferdinando Tagliavini, who in a very detailed chapter treats the question concerning the texts originating from Bach himself and there ascribes about 30 cantata texts to Bach.[59] Even though Bach nowhere in his works expressly reveals himself as the author of a text and therefore all ascriptions in the final analysis must remain hypothetical, still, beside Tagliavini's arguments, above all Bach's great and lifelong ambition to dedicate his music to the service of the proclamation of the Word as well as his numerous corrections in the texts, undertaken in the interest of precise theological delineation, make the conjecture of Bach's authorship, now again heavily underscored and by Tagliavini convincingly presented (although with elimination of the theological question), at least very probable. In any case, it is very striking that Bach set to music only a few of the numerous Ziegler cantata texts, and of the eight annual sets by Neumeister he set only five cantatas completely and another incompletely, and of the many cantata texts that appeared in print everywhere and therefore were easily available he made use of none. Obviously numerous texts of his time must not have pleased him or at least must again and again have seemed unsuitable. If we consider that in his library Bach had an abundance of Bible commentaries and sermon collections for the Old and the New Testaments[60] and that almost all the hymnals of that time contained "summary meditations" on the Epistles and Gospels for Sundays and festival days, so that Bach was able "to penetrate as deeply and from as many sides as ever possible into the content and meaning of Holy Scripture,"[61] all the presuppositions for providing such texts, beside those attainments and skills already acquired in school, were given for Bach. Besides, as an author of texts for his own cantatas, Bach would take his place in a firm tradition, for concerning the predecessor in his Leipzig office, Kuhnau, we know for certain that he was accustomed to compile the texts for his cantatas himself at times,[62] as also Bach's contemporaries J. F. Fasch, Stölzel, Telemann, and others wrote poetry, and Stölzel even authored the majority of his numerous cantatas himself.[63]

But no matter how the question about Bach's authorship in regard to his cantata texts will be answered, it would seem to be firmly established that at least the choice and combination of texts for the cantatas was "invariably a theological activity."[64] This conclusion on the part of Wolfgang Herbst had previously been made manifest by Friedrich Smend when he compiled the source of the text for the *Passion According to St. John* as assembled by Bach himself, for in spite of his dependence on the libretto of Brockes, Bach adopted a "critical, selective, and remodeling approach," and this "not only in matters of language" but also and principally from a theological viewpoint.[65] Walter Blankenburg, too, in his studies of Bach's *Christmas Oratorio*, made the observation that Bach, "looking forward to planned parodies, already exerted an influence on the shaping of the text of the *Christmas Oratorio* and occasionally abstained from the use of parodies if these did not seem to promise to do justice to the new text."[66]

217

From all this a definite theological interest in the texts to be set to music becomes clear on Bach's part, so that there can be no doubt about his will to achieve a Christian proclamation. This emphasis would really not be necessary if it has become clear that that situation does not represent anything unusual at all. For Bach, as for every other musician firmly established in the Lutheran Kantorei tradition, it was self-evident, indeed, even professionally required, to cooperate in the service of the proclamation of the Word. The very fact that the wording of the cantata was made available to the congregation members in the service by means of specially printed librettos—and that was the case also in Weimar[67]—clearly indicates the interest in the text and its proclamation. But in Leipzig in Bach's time this proclamation was dogmatically still directed very strictly toward the center of Lutheran theology (cf. the discussion on p. 155). Smend makes the point, characteristic indeed for Bach, "that it is not accidental that the Passions are the towering pinnacles of Bach's works" and likewise that "the confession 'Crucifixus pro nobis' is not by mere chance also artistically and structurally the center of Bach's setting of the Nicene Creed," whereas in Christian art at that time "the Tormented, the Crucified is not placed at the center of things," but instead "the Victor, the Hero, Christ," for "the Conqueror of all distress, He who ascended to heaven, is more important for the artist than He who descends to the depths of the lost world, than He who drinks the bitterest cup, than He who is executed as a criminal."[68]

But we must of course also consider that the Leipzig theologians, with whom Bach had to share the ministry of proclamation in the liturgical service, were jointly responsible for the shape of the text of the liturgical works of Bach, for even if there are but few clues to that effect, there was without doubt some cooperation on the part of Bach with the clergymen who preached in the main churches. The authors of the cantata texts were as a rule clergymen, and it is without question to the credit of Lutheran orthodoxy that the writing of cantata texts flourished in the first half of the 18th century precisely in Saxony, where orthodoxy also was active longest.[69] In view of this fact, we are obliged to take a more thorough look at the repeated suggestion that certain Leipzig clergymen need to be considered as possible authors of Bach cantata texts, especially since the authors of three-fourths of the extant Bach cantatas are still unknown to us. The two chief pastors in Leipzig, Salomon Deyling and Christian Weiß, would be the first to come into consideration as possible authors of Bach cantata texts, for the largest number of Bach's cantatas were presented in the services in which these two clergymen regularly preached the sermons. Christian Weiß has often been thought of as an author of certain Bach cantata texts, but for some strange reason in all of Bach research Deyling has never been seriously considered as a writer of texts for Bach cantatas. This fact is all the more remarkable because already Friedrich Rochlitz, a student at St. Thomas under Doles, Bach's second successor in office, called attention to the regular collaboration of Deyling and Bach. Even though Rochlitz is not always considered reliable in his assertions, there can hardly be serious doubt concerning the credibility of his report according to which Bach "regularly at the beginning of the week sent" to the superintendent "several (usually three) texts of his church cantatas [*Kirchenstücke*] arranged for the day" and Deyling then chose one.[70] Bach's very office required harmonious cooperation with the chief pastors, and the specific choice of the right cantata is simply based on the fact that Bach's cantatas were composed in more or less close dependence on the Gospel for the Sunday and that also the sermons in the main services every year treated the Gospel for the Sunday, and so mutual checking was necessary. The report of Rochlitz pertains primarily to the last two decades of Bach's life when the latter had most of his cantatas in stock and frequently was content with repeat performances. But in Bach's first years in Leipzig Deyling's authorship of texts for Bach cantatas might certainly not seem unlikely. We do know in any case that "Deyling was also the writer of a number of hymns that found a place in the *Eisleber Gesangbuch*" (*Bn*, p. 50), that he therefore possessed poetic talents and also exercised them in this way. If we now compare, for example, the outline for the sermon preached by Deyling on the first festival day of the Reformation Festival in 1730 on Romans 1:16-17 with the text of the cantata presented in this service, we cannot deny that there is a certain relation between the purpose of the sermon and that of the cantata text, so that even the Leipzig poet Henrici, who wrote the cantata text in this case, must have been in contact with the Leipzig superintendent, or such contact must have been made through the cantor of St. Thomas, who regularly learned to know the purpose of the chief pastor. Deyling had preached a sermon in two parts: "The Testimony of the Apostle Paul Regarding the Pure Evangelical Doctrine of Faith, As He Testified (1) Regarding Its Saving Power; (2) Regarding Its Excellent Contents" (Sc*JL*, p. 161). The second section of the cantata, presented after the Sermon, immediately referred to the sermon, for at first the recitative sang the praises of the "excellent contents" of the "pure evangelical doctrine of faith": "LORD, if Thy Gospel, the heavenly doctrine, had not been our consolation, distress and death would have overwhelmed us completely. It is the Bread of life that brings strength to our spirit and refreshment to our soul and strengthens it with salvation. Here we have righteousness, the shield of faith that alone avails before God in heaven." And then followed an aria that took up especially the first part of the sermon: "Blest are we through the Word; blest are we through believing; blest are we here and there; blest if we remain faithful; blest if we are not hearers only, but also doers" (cf. Sc*JL*, pp. 125ff., and N*VT*, p. 333). Also the following move-

219

ment, a recitative we have to classify as a prayer, "And now, O God, to Thee we offer the fruit of our lips for this," can be characterized as taken from a request of the sermon, for Deyling had in his sermon exhorted his congregation "to pray all the more intensely for the preservation of it (the Gospel), the more the enemies seek to deprive us of this treasure." The first section of the cantata, presented after the reading of the Gospel and entirely given over to praise and thanksgiving, had likewise been taken up in Deyling's sermon, for "it had contained an admonition not to be ashamed of the Gospel but to be happy about it and to thank God heartily for the truth revealed." In this connection we should also refer to the Bach cantata presented at St. Thomas Church on the second day of the Reformation Festival in 1730, with text also by Henrici, and to the three-part sermon delivered in this service by Christian Weiß, which likewise corresponds to the cantata text so far as the contents and even largely the arrangement is concerned (cf. Sc*JL*, pp. 189—90, and N*VT*, pp. 333—34). Thus the third movement of the cantata presented after the Sermon took up the burden of the first two main sections of the sermon. Compare the words "Confess firmly and do not waver.... Remain in the confession of your hope" with the first part of the sermon, which according to its heading dealt with "the steadfast confession before men, which should be (a) fervent with heart and mouth, (b) durable, without wavering." The words given at the beginning and end of the third movement of the cantata, "Oh, beloved City of God, may God be with you further.... God is faithful, who has promised it," referred to the second part of the sermon, which dealt with "the constant trust in God's aid, which is based on (a) God's inner faithfulness, (b) His promised faithfulness." The appeal given in the fifth movement of the cantata, "All right, O holy congregation, then do according to the Word and stir up continuously to love and do good works," made reference to the third part of the sermon, which dealt with "the edifying walk in constant love" in which "we should (a) have regard for mutual edification, (b) grow in the fervency of love toward one another, (c) arouse one another with a good example." The stanza of the well-known Pentecost hymn by Martin Luther used in the final movement of the cantata, "Come, holy Fire, Comfort true, Grant us the will your work to do And in your service to abide," literally took up the thought of the main theme of the sermon: "The Holy Spirit Rousing Us to Abide in Jesus."

Thus we can hardly imagine adequately how close was Bach's actual regular cooperation with the Leipzig pastors in their common task, the proclamation of the Gospel, which self-evidently had to take place in agreement with the basic statements of Lutheran theology. The printed publication of the cantata texts alone must have prompted Bach again and again to seek the advice and guidance of his pastors, for in a confessional city like Leipzig, still strongly influenced by the spirit of strict Lutheran orthodoxy and boasting of a critical academic circle, no vague and ambiguous theological assertions would be permitted. The comparison between the statements of the cantata texts and the basic thoughts of the sermon in any case makes clear that the preacher and the St. Thomas cantor agreed on the proclamation within the service so far as the essential statements of the sermon were concerned.

For Bach's own self-understanding and for a proper appreciation of his liturgical music, it is also very revealing to see how on his part he tried to solve the given problems musically. Already Hans Besch pointed out to what an extent Bach in his cantata compositions again and again pursued the smallest details of the Bible text, and on the basis of this fact Besch established a close personal relation of Bach to Holy Scripture.[71] The research projects of the last decades have shown to an astonishing degree that this way of creating on Bach's part cannot be explained in a general way, as principally Albert Schweitzer has done it, by means of concepts of onomatopoeia or poetry, but that this compositional technique is strongly tradition bound and shows that Bach is completely dependent on the old Protestant motive technique [*Figurenlehre*] of the *Musica poetica*,[72] a technique that has also been described as "the theory of composition that approximates speech and interprets words"[73] and also as "a typically German phenomenon that emanated from the spirit of the Lutheran Reformation."[74] This "specifically Protestant development" therefore applied itself "directly to the musical treatment and handling of words,"[75] and in this process the association of *Musica poetica* with rhetoric became very important.[76] It was principally Arnold Schmitz who demonstrated the close connection between Bach's compositional method and the task, method, and goal of rhetoric.[77] Beyond that, the rules of the Protestant theory of preaching, which ever since the Reformation (Melanchthon) was most closely linked to rhetoric and which set down strictly codified rhetorical rules as binding for the sermon, were applied to the creation and arrangement of musical compositions. As a result, we can legitimately compare the composition of the cantata with that of the sermon, since both show great similarity in external construction and in purpose.[78]

With these newly acquired insights, "with the perception of composition as a musical rhetoric [*Redekunst*, 'art of speech'] subjected to very precise rules,"[79] the purpose of Bach's cantata composition now also becomes clear from its musical side, namely, as very consciously striving toward the goal of proclamation, an actual statement and address. Schmitz stresses the fact that ever since Flacius Illyricus (1520—1575) composers, too, had to give attention to the meaning [*sensus*] and the goal [*scopus*] of a text they wanted to set to music and that Johann Sebastian Bach, with his extensive acquaintance with the laws of speech and the motive technique [*Figurenlehre*], strives especially toward *docere* and *movere* among the three possibilities of rhetorical effect—*docere* (educating), *movere* (affecting), and *delectare* (delighting)—and among these two again principally toward *docere*.[80] That Johann Sebastian Bach's music was actually understood by his contemporaries as a species of rhetoric [*Redekunst*] we find confirmed in the words of a professor of rhetoric at the University of Leipzig, Master Johann Abraham Birnbaum, who wrote in 1739: "He so perfectly understood the resemblance which the performance of a musical piece has in common with rhetorical art that he was listened to with the utmost satisfaction and pleasure when he discoursed of the similarity and agreement between them; but we also wonder at the skillful use he made of this in his works."[81] Already the next generation after Johann Sebastian Bach was aware of the radical difference in the compositional manner of musicians when compared with those of the past epoch, when Philipp Emanuel Bach, for instance, in a letter to Forkel about 1775 made the point that his father, Johann Sebastian Bach, "had worked piously and according to the content in his ecclesiastical works."[82]

This intent to engage in Christian proclamation is likewise expressed in Bach's symbolic language, especially in his use of number symbolism. Here, too, Bach stands in an age-old tradition still alive in his time, but one that had been handed down to him above all by the Lutheran Church, for although number symbolism plays a certain role already in Luther's interpretation of the Bible, Lutheran orthodoxy had made incomparably stronger use of numbers as means of expression up to the authors whose works were found in Bach's library.[83] In Bach's works we find an almost inexhaustible abundance of possibilities so far as the musical application of the various types of symbolic numbers is concerned. And even if estimates disagree concerning the scope of what is actually present of this symbolism, still Schering's and Smend's researches have "proved that Bach was more familiar with the esoterica of symbolical relations than most of the composers of his time," but that this "indicates nothing else but that Bach tries by all available means, those that lie on the surface externally as well as those most hidden internally, to indicate what he wants to say, and surely no such exhaustive attempt at exploiting a text completely as in Bach's vocal music has ever again been made in the whole history of music."[84] Even in the Bach works of later years, in which the composition of vocal works of course recedes noticeably, a period that Friedrich Blume cites as proof for his contention that Bach's liturgical office and task presumably was not an "affair of the heart" with him, "there is still so much unambiguous symbolism transmitted that in these works the expression and testimony of a conscious Christian faith and an emphatic Christian way of thinking appears as the central artistic purpose."[85] Precisely the symbol of the symmetrical form used so frequently "makes the liturgical music of Bach's old age appear in the light of a consciously Christian confession of faith," for "in the musical symmetry of Bach compositions the life of the church and of the Christian is brought into relation with the Crucified."[86]

Thus we shall have to agree unreservedly with Alfred Dürr when he says concerning the compositions that grew out of Bach's liturgical office and task: "The Bach cantata seems to us to be the most successful and most consistent attempt of church music to have a part in the central concern of the evangelical service, the proclamation of the Word of God in the Sermon. No matter how we as theologians answer the question whether music can in any case be proclamation in the Lutheran sense, there can be no doubt that Bach's cantata actually *wants* to be proclamation. The sermon-like character of the texts, the up-to-dateness of the forms, the relation to real life situations of Bach's creative method, and the great effort to achieve exegesis of the text and intelligibility for the congregation are the means with which this goal is to be reached."[87]

c) The Problem of Parodies

The so-called parody technique of Johann Sebastian Bach is a compositional device that consists essentially of using existing musical works or musical movements as a basis for new compositions and so to make them useful for a purpose different from the original one. In this way Bach not infrequently used one and the same composition several times, and for his liturgical cantatas he even fell back on originally secular vocal and instrumental works of the most diverse kind. For Friedrich Blume this compositional method is further proof for the conception that Bach wrote his liturgical works not "with the intention of proclaiming the composer's Christian faith, still less from a heartfelt need to do so," because for Bach's self-understanding and so for our picture of Bach "it does make a tremendous difference whether a work was conceived from its own text or was merely rewritten to fit the new text" (Blu, p. 220). Although we must basically agree with this reasoning of Blume's, yet his entire argumentation in that connection shows that he does not do justice to Bach's parody work in its real meaning and therefore arrives at wrong conclusions. To begin with, his definition of "parody" is inadequate and in the total context of his discussions even misleading, for it is not true that "the term used by musicologists" only denotes "the adaptation of a secular vocal or instrumental work to a sacred text, the musical substance being either preserved or refashioned" (Blu, p. 219). By "parodying" we also understand—in Bach we find numerous examples—the exploitation of a secular vocal composition for another secular vocal composition, the recast of an instrumental composition for a secular creation with a text, and above all the use of sacred works in still other sacred compositions such as took place with almost the same frequency in Bach as parodying from the secular to the sacred realm. But what is the scope of Bach's creation by means of parody?

In the first place we must establish the fact that Johann Sebastian Bach represents no exception in this compositional technique but also in this matter stands in a firm tradition and that the other composers of his time also made use of the parody procedure. Still it is worth noting that "this procedure accounts for only a small area in the total Bach output" and that "only a very small number of compositions among his works for the church entirely or in part go back to nonliturgical musical compositions."[88] This emphasis is necessary because Blume maintains "that there are very many parodies among the cantatas of Bach's early years in Leipzig" and that "it is probable that there are many more than have so far been discovered" (Blu, p. 219). According to the new cantata chronology, which Blume characterizes as "fully established" (Blu, p. 222),[89] the vast majority of Bach's church cantatas belong to the first Leipzig years. Blume says: "There is evidence of a small number of cantatas in the years subsequent to 1726" (Blu, p. 219). From this the impression must be gained that a large proportion of the liturgical cantatas must be parodies, and as a result serious doubts about Bach's interest in Christian proclamation must arise. But now Smend has emphatically stated that among the approximately 190 church cantatas of Bach's "a total of only 14 reveal that the parody procedure was used, and then only in individual movements" and in addition that "in six cases both original and new texts are liturgical pieces and there is no evidence for the supposition that sacred prototypes go back to still earlier secular ones," so that "for the overwhelming preponderance of cantatas it is firmly established that they are original compositions."[90] Similar clarification is in order for Blume's statements about the parodies of the *Passion According to St. Matthew*, for when Blume speaks of the possibility "that the intactness of the *St. Matthew Passion* may be broken," and also of its "uncertain origins" (Blu, pp. 220, 225), we get the impression that the entire composition, or at least the larger part of it, is a parody. But even Blume can identify only nine of the 78 movements of the *St. Matthew Passion* as parodies, so that Dürr is right when he says: "Even if nine movements should prove to be parodies, we could hardly deny the remaining 69 movements, and therefore the whole composition, the purpose of Christian proclamation."[91] Blume's statement, "The *Christmas Oratorio* is, apart from the recitatives and the chorales, an adaptation or parody of earlier secular works" (Blu, p. 220), clearly indicates how easily a misleading picture of the actual total number of Bach's parodies arises. For apart from the fact that this statement is not even exact, because also the choir settings "Ehre sei Gott in der Höhe" (No. 21), "Lasset uns gehen gen Bethlehem" (No. 26), and very likely also "Ehre sei dir, Gott, gesungen"

(No. 43), as well as the Symphony (No. 10) and the aria "Schließe, mein Herze, dies selige Wunder" (No. 31) are new compositions,[92] "the major part" of the *Christmas Oratorio* is actually "original composition," because "of the 42 movements of Parts 1—4 no fewer than 32 are original compositions."[93]

Thus among Bach's vocal compositions presented in the Sermon section of the service the proportion of parodies in respect to the sum total is indeed minimal, even if we must reckon with the discovery of further examples. But in spite of that, the question remains how Bach's purpose of Christian proclamation is involved in these few cases and how we are to evaluate the parody process theologically in the first place.

It is interesting to note from the start that "parodies of complete works are frequent in Bach's secular compositions but scarce in his works for the church."[94] Bach must therefore obviously have adopted stricter standards than the usual ones in his parody work on sacred cantatas. In this connection a further observation is revealing, namely that Bach used the parody procedure going from secular to sacred but never from sacred to secular. Arnold Schering already realized this and commented: "This kind of inversion would have appeared to be a profanation and occurred only as a passing thing in moments of religious degeneration in German history throughout the times for which contrafacts are traceable on the German scene at all."[95] In spite of the fact that new parodies have been found in recent decades, up to the present time not a single case has come to our attention in which Bach parodied a sacred composition to form a secular one. Above all, certain details of the parody technique are significant. Studies of the *Christmas Oratorio* and its sources have shown to everybody's surprise how carefully also the work of creating a parody was approached by Bach on the basis of his liturgical commission and how everything was deliberately subordinated to purposes of proclamation. Thus this insight is important, "that Bach did not engage in parodies at all costs but always judged the suitability of the source involved from the viewpoint of the new text," and that on the whole "he already exerted an influence on the shaping of the text as he looked forward to planned parodies" and "occasionally abstained from the use of parodies if these did not seem to promise to do justice to the new text."[96] In the process itself "Bach in part drastically recast the voices to agree with the new text and possibly also changed the instrumentation for the sake of the new context," so that everywhere there is evidence of Bach's endeavor "in each case to provide the new text with a significant musical raiment."[97] By means of a long series of examples Blankenburg has illustrated "how Bach in his application of the parody technique provides such full justice for the new text, both as to meaning and expression, that the duplicate in comparison with the original sometimes experiences a marked diffraction and receives its own individual

Bach's autograph—opening of the *Credo* of the B Minor Mass (BWV 232), which dates from the last years of the composer's life. Bach quotes the intonation of the plainsong (see *LGB* 1682, p. 497—98). Source: Barbara Schwendowius and Wolfgang Dömling, *Johann Sebastian Bach: Life—Times—Influence* (Kassel, Basel, Tours, and London, 1977), p. 122.

character, and this is true to so marked a degree that the parody rises above its original artistically."[98] Blankenburg comes to the conclusion "that the use of the parody procedure did not prevent Bach from producing exceedingly significant, fully textual, and perfectly formed new creations absolutely possessing their own individual worth. A closer look at the prototypes of the parodies in the *Christmas Oratorio* shows that the latter exhibits a much greater conciseness and spiritual penetration than the secular cantatas displayed. This applies especially to the total plan of Parts 1—3, but also to many passages of the individual structures. But for Bach the inspiration to make these parodies rise above their prototypes without doubt flowed from the textual basis of the *Christmas Oratorio*, that is, in the first place from the Christmas Gospel. From this Bach's real inspiration for this oratorio arose."[99]

These important observations, however, apply not only to the *Christmas Oratorio* but also generally to all of Bach's parody work intended for the worship service. Already before Blankenburg, Smend had established the general fact that Bach "in his parody work made use of widely differing techniques, which, however, always had a practical foundation,"[100] that "at different times he used the parody procedure in ways that were different in scope and method," and that he thus "in time became ever more cautious." So, for example, he undertook parodying recitatives only until 1726, and the longer [he engaged in parodying] the more he was careful in using older materials "to derive these no longer from a single prototype but various prototypes and to choose his sources very deliberately so that he might really furnish the new texts with musical settings most suitable to them."[101] And even if it is true that not "all of Bach's parodies are to be described as in the last analysis completely successful, we may nevertheless say that in many cases only the recasting and the supplying of the new text involved in the process brought to full development the musical germ that lay dormant in the original, so that the parody by far surpasses its model in artistic quality."[102] Especially in his study of the parodies in the first three parts of the *Mass in B-Minor* (Kyrie, Gloria, and Credo), Smend "in each single case comes to the conclusion that Bach, both as to form and content, could not have chosen a more suitable model to achieve the result that the recast would not only equal the original in artistic value but even surpass it."[103]

Accordingly, those Bach parodies that are often judged to be accomplishments of lesser artistic quality need to be revaluated again and again, for the Bach parodies that are inferior in quality to their prototypes are few in number and therefore cannot materially detract from the total picture of Bach's parodied works as Smend and Blankenburg have outlined it by means of investigations and characterization of individual details. By and large, at least in respect to Bach's parodied works, it is objectively unwarranted to associate a derogatory sense with the term "parody."[104] Even if the parody technique is to be thought of only as a labor-saving device, that is, a time saver (Bach often had only pitifully little time at his disposal for the preparation of his works), still the main reason to be given for Bach's use of parody must be the opportunity to put to further use those compositions that were written for a single performance and yet displayed high quality. If this were not the case, it would be completely incomprehensible, for example, to recast purely instrumental pieces to produce vocal works, a process that presupposes the greatest mastery, in other words, to introduce vocal lines into a concerto or a suite, a project that requires very much work and time and not infrequently approximates an artistic new creation. One cannot but get the impression that Bach by all means wanted to let his church have the advantage of appropriating the best of his extraliturgical work. Here we should above all think of the instrumental movements of the church cantatas that are not at all required and in most cases represent borrowings from earlier instrumental concertos. Also the Soprano aria "Mein gläubiges Herze" of Cantata BWV 68 had no particular need for the attached instrumental movement. The reuse "evidently was undertaken only for the purpose of rescuing the movement from oblivion and of inserting it in a passage that would let the insertion appear appropriate because of the compatibility of its thematic material with the preceding aria."[105] Thus Dürr's question over against Blume is completely justified, whether Bach "may after all have been persuaded that music composed with the greatest concentration fulfills its noblest purpose only when it sounds forth to the honor not of the 'ruling gods of this world' but 'the' God," for "precisely for the later years, when Bach already was in possession of the bulk of his cantatas, we can hardly find any other reason for sacred parodies of secular congratulatory compositions than the one Blume subjected to doubt, 'the heartfelt need.' What else could have moved him to compose the *Christmas Oratorio*, the *Ascension Oratorio*, and many other cantatas? Or why does Bach in the 1730s revise a whole series of cantatas whose parodied versions from the first busy Leipzig years no longer pleased him . . . except because of the need to provide his best effort also in this type of composition?"[106]

The deciding prerequisite for the unhesitating, indeed, almost self-evident adoption of the parody precedure, however, is accounted for by the unitary style of the epoch. Bach was able to adopt the contemporary musical forms such as the recitative and aria without further ado and make them fruitful for the liturgical music, and in the process he did not simply imitate and "externally transpose, but he provided a new creation internally,"[107] so that the Bach recitative and the Bach aria in their very essence represent something entirely independent in music history, and therefore the common way of speaking of adopting recitative and aria from contemporary opera for church music is factually not quite adequate.[108] In the very same way Bach could also make his extraliturgical compositions fruitful for the liturgical service, especially when he did not permit himself to be tied down too much by the literal figures of speech in the original materials used, when in the parody of a secular original the same basic emotion was kept on, and when the theological situation [*Topos*] coincided with the literary and poetical one of the secular model.[109] The whole parody problem "usually clears up by the retention of the basic emotion or the same situation [*Topos*]."[110] Even if research is still caught in its beginnings in this matter, there can be no thought of changing the understanding that is eminently important for the theological consciousness and evaluation of Bach's cantatas, the inner unity of the totality of Bach's works, which knows no differentiation between the sacred and the secular and which in its understanding of the world as it is expressed there shows that it is genuinely Lutheran.

In this connection let us also make reference to a basic characteristic of Bach's way of working. This is important for the evaluation of the parody procedure and of the "occasional works," or the so-called "commissioned works," which (like the parodies) have often been criticized unfavorably.[111] Bach still follows the tradition of those musicians whose work "does not aim at timeless validity but seeks to exhaust the possibilities of the given situation and to fulfill its necessities."[112] This fact becomes most obvious when the autograph full scores of Bach's works, which are mere "director's sketches," generally giving no directions concerning articulation, tempo, dynamics, and instrumentation of the individual movements (because the composer stored all that in his memory when he studied the score and performed these works), are compared with the individual parts written out for the performance of those compositions. "The performance parts most often provide us with more information regarding Bach's intentions than the autograph full score," so that unmistakably "the substance of his compositions is essentially different from that of later epochs. The classical and Romantic artist works for 'eternity.' He strives hard for the validity of his works, for he does not want them to be dependent on the haphazardness of varying performances. He therefore sets down his intentions as clearly as possible. The composer of Bach's time, on the other hand, takes it into the bargain that his composition will be performed only a few times—if a congratulatory cantata, perhaps only a single time—but instead he tries his best by all means to do justice to each performance."[113] The presence of a whole series of Bach's works in several versions illustrates this way of composing, a procedure no longer intelligible for later generations. Dürr makes the observation that this method of working on the part of Bach, in which "every version of his work and each work itself has the purpose of doing justice to the situation at hand as far as ever possible, is precisely the situation of the Lutheran service, which lets the Word of God become an event 'here and now' [*hic et nunc*]," so that "this way of creating is much more appropriate to the sermon-like character of the cantata than the 'timeless' compositional method of classicism."[114]

Thus all these details concerning Bach's way of composing make it crystal clear that even Bach's parody procedure basically cannot provide us with any reasons for denying the St. Thomas cantor of that time an interest in Christian proclamation. On the contrary, Bach seems to have had the wish not to let single performances suffice for works that were composed for only a transitory purpose but "to transfer this music to a form that would make repeated use of it possible, namely, as music for the church year."[115] Bach actually considered composing liturgical cantatas his chief work. In its own way the list of Bach's works compiled after his death in his obituary shows this, for it lists the church cantatas at the head of all compositions. Even the obvious reduction in cantata composition beginning in 1728 cannot be cited as an argument for an increasing lack of interest on the part of Bach in his chief work. The reason for this reduction is that Bach already had in stock the better part of the cantatas based on the annually recurring liturgical texts, and these four or five deep for every Sunday. He could now apply himself more than in former years to the revision and reworking of these compositions.

d) Relation to the Hymn

Someone has made the interesting observation that the closer our studies in music history "approach the 18th century and actually cross the boundaries of the centuries, the more clearly we become aware of an obvious disregard for the chorale in cantata composition. This shows itself in various ways: either the chorale is dropped entirely, or it is dealt with in the most convenient way, in a four-part harmonization. To look for chorale cantatas in the Johann Sebastian Bach generation would be an unrewarding undertaking."[116]

Despite this fact, we cannot emphasize clearly enough that the Lutheran church hymn represents the critical foundation, "the heart and center,"[117] for the entire liturgical output of Johann Sebastian Bach in practically all phases of his life and activity. Aside from the fact "that Bach, altogether in distinction from his contemporaries, also built his course in composition on the chorale,"[118] he used the church hymn already in the very first cantatas positively verifiable for his Mühlhausen term of office, and then in the cantatas of his Weimar period, especially after 1715, "the use of the closing chorale became the norm" altogether. In fact, Bach's librettist Franck "probably complied with a wish of the composer" when he introduced church hymns into his cantata texts, "for his texts from the time before and after Bach's activity in Weimar do not show any chorales."[119]

Bach's interest in the church hymn becomes particularly clear at the beginning of his Leipzig term of office. Of the 44 cantatas of the first Leipzig cycle, 39 close with a simple setting of a church hymn, seven times cantatas with soloistic treatments of hymns turn up, 29 of a total of 30 choral cantatas begin with a chorus on a passage of the Bible, which in four instances is again combined with a hymn cantus firmus. A further distinguishing feature of the first year's cycle is the introduction of one or more simple hymn settings in eight one-movement cantatas. But above all, the second Leipzig annual cycle was notably given to the use of the hymn, and especially large is the number of soloistic hymn treatments (in 19 cantatas). Indeed, that type of cantata seems to be exclusively peculiar to Bach that has a church hymn as its foundation and then shows further paraphrases of stanzas of the hymn (41 among the 53 cantatas of the second annual cycle). According to Tagliavini, there can be no doubt that the recasts for these hymn or chorale cantatas were made at Bach's request.[120]

In the later years, too, Bach once more turned to the hymn in a special way to produce chorale cantatas that made use of pure hymn texts, especially between 1732 and 1735.[121] Also in the six parts of the *Christmas Oratorio*, which appeared at the end of 1734, the church hymn plays a role that is far from unessential. In the entire output of Bach cantatas there are only 11 completely preserved cantatas that have no relation to the hymn, namely, cantatas BWV 34, 35, 63, 82, 134, 150, 152, 170, 173, 181, and 196 (in this list no allowance is made for BWV 191, which cannot be called a cantata, and the unusual BWV 198, as well as the spurious and incomplete cantatas). This does not preclude that the presentation of one of these 11 cantatas could conclude with an appropriate hymn setting just available at the time. In all other cantatas the hymn in text and tune is a more or less standard ingredient of Bach's liturgical sermon music. The truly great importance of the hymn in Bach's cantatas really becomes evident when we consider in addition that the total cantata output contains, beside the 199 simple hymn harmonizations and 50 hymn arrangements, also 92 larger choral movements based on hymns (which here refers to compositions of grand design, essentially carried forward by an orchestral development or motet-like, polyphonic structures in choral settings dominated by the use of a cantus firmus). In the presentation of the cantata these larger choral movements generally demanded by far the most time as compared with the other movements of any given cantata. In addition, 186 other hymn settings of Johann Sebastian Bach have come down to us that do not originate from the liturgical works known to us but very likely belonged to lost cantatas and Passions.[122]

The extent to which even beyond cantata composition the Lutheran church hymn was a deciding factor in Bach's total output is clearly indicated not only in numerous organ compositions based on hymns or even the use of the opening line of the hymn "Komm, heiliger Geist, Herre Gott" in the Violin Sonata BWV 1005 but also in the interest Bach showed in the church hymn in the last years of his life, for instance, in a work of his last decade, the emendation and revision of the "Bach chorales handed down individually";[123] the recast (possibly as late as 1749) of the *Seventeen Chorales*;[124] the *Canonical Variations* on the hymn "Vom Himmel hoch da komm ich her," also originating from the last years of his life, a work that Bach in June 1747 presented at his being received into a restricted academy entitled Korrespondierende Sozietät der musikalischen Wissenschaften; and finally his last work, composed on his deathbed on the hymn "Vor deinen Thron tret ich hiermit." We should also indicate that Bach possibly developed the theme of the *Art of the Fugue* in its inversion from the first line of the hymn tune "Aus tiefer Not schrei ich zu dir."[125]

Only a comparison with the compositions of Bach's great contemporaries as well as his Leipzig predecessor can fully evaluate how much Johann Sebastian Bach raised the church hymn to high honor in his own compositions. For "in the church cantata of Johann Kuhnau...the chorale had receded almost entirely into the background," and from the Passion compositions of Telemann, Händel, and Keiser, who used the same libretto as Bach, namely, that of Brockes, Bach's work differed among other things in this, that for his compositions "he won back the Lutheran congregational and confessional hymn"[126] and that "the chorale, which for Brockes and his spiritual companions at best represents solemn embroidery, becomes an essential ingredient of the whole composition."[127] Treiber already had called attention to the "pregnant and artistic manner" of the "application" of the church hymn by Bach, as this master "went back to the artistic 17th-century treatment of the chorale" and "stands in close connection to similar works of the 17th century." Treiber had likewise pointed out "the great contrast between Bach and his contemporaries" in this area and had described the church hymn in the cantatas of Telemann, Römhild, and Freislich "as a second-class kind of composition," indeed, he had said regarding Telemann's relation to the church hymn: "He does not bring into play any kind of understanding and respect for it and sets lifeless four-part homophonic chorales with harmonizations that often haven't a thing to say."[128] But if in his frequent use of the church hymn Bach stood in barefaced contrast even to the predecessor in his office, Kuhnau, this situation clearly shows that the St. Thomas cantor of that time exercised an influence on the choice of the texts to be set to music and that we must conclude from Bach's interest in the church hymn that he had a very personal relation to the stock and store of his church's hymns. And still, in his interest in the hymn Bach stood within a certain tradition even in Leipzig, for about his predecessor Schelle we hear that in 1689, "stimulated by Carpzov, he turned to the composition of chorale cantatas and earned that man's special applause."[129]

The choice of hymns exercised by Bach, however, was everything but purely subjective. It was closely tied to the collection of hymns that was liturgically approved. Just as Bach in the well-known competency controversy regarding hymns with Master Gaudlitz in 1728 insisted on selecting the hymns for the Sunday and festival day services according to the hymn schedule established for the congregation, so he also used in his cantatas as much as possible the hymns appointed for a given Sunday. Conspicuously, Bach made no use worth mentioning of the hymns that at that time offered themselves to him in great abundance (though they were not familiar liturgically), that were available to him and demonstrably also studied by him in the eight-volume *Wagnersches Gesangbuch* (*WGB*) with its 5,000 hymns. This deserves to be emphasized especially because the Wagner hymnal itself had a volume entitled *Evangeliums- und Epistel-Lieder auf jeden Sonn-Fest- und Apostel-Tage gerichtet* (Gospel and Epistle hymns appointed for every Sunday, festival day, and apostle day), a volume, therefore, that could have provided enough material particularly suited for Bach's sermon music.

Bach's close attachment to the Lutheran service with its traditional hymns is already displayed in his Advent cantatas. "Nun komm der Heiden Heiland," the hymn consistently listed as hymn of the day [*Hauptlied*][130] for the First Sunday in Advent in the Kantorei schedules of the Lutheran Church and in the 1693 Leipzig hymnal of Gottfried Vopelius even as hymn of the day for all four Sundays in Advent,[131] was used in all three extant Bach cantatas for the First Sunday in Advent. Cantata BWV 61 begins with the first stanza of this hymn of the day; in Cantata BWV 62 this hymn is the basis for the entire cantata text, the first and last stanzas being retained literally as entrance and closing movements; and in Cantata BWV 36 with its eight movements, all of three movements have stanzas of this hymn of the day as their basic text. Beside this hymn of the day, these Advent cantatas make use of another hymn, namely, in the closing movement of Cantata BWV 61 the last stanza and at the end of Part I of Cantata BWV 36 the sixth stanza of the hymn "Wie schön leuchtet der Morgenstern." This hymn, too, belonged to the hymns appointed for this Sunday according to the various editions of the Dresden hymnals of 1725—1750.[132] The Bach cantatas composed before 1723 for the other three Sundays in Advent likewise contain stanzas from such hymns sung during Advent and expressly appointed for particular Sundays. "Herr Christ, der einig Gotts Sohn,"[133] used in the concluding movement of Cantata BWV 132, composed for the Fourth Sunday in Advent, was generally the hymn of the day for

233

this Sunday.[134] The hymn "Meinen Jesum laß ich nicht," used in Cantata BWV 70,[135] originally composed for the Second Sunday in Advent, is listed among the hymns sung on the Third Sunday in Advent in the *Privilegirtes Vollständiges und verbessertes Leipziger Gesangbuch* of 1737. For the same Sunday the hymn schedules of the Dresden hymnbooks appointed the hymn "Von Gott will ich nicht lassen," of which Bach had used stanza eight in Cantata BWV 186, originally composed for this Sunday.[136]

The same strict adherence to the hymn of the day and the other hymns customary for the services is also observable in Bach's cantatas for the Christmas festival days. The hymn of the day for this festival, Luther's "Gelobet seist du, Jesu Christ,"[137] not only served as the basis for Bach's Cantata BWV 91, composed for the First Festival Day, but it turns up in three further cantatas for this festival, namely, in the seventh movement of Part I of the *Christmas Oratorio*, assigned to this First Festival Day; in the second movement of Cantata BWV 64, assigned to the Third Festival Day; and in the fourth movement of Part III of the *Christmas Oratorio*, composed for the Third Festival Day. It need not be pure coincidence that this hymn does not appear in the cantatas written for the Second Festival Day. In the hymn schedules of the Dresden hymnbooks around 1750 this hymn is listed as the first among five appointed for the Third Festival Day, whereas it is not found at all among the five hymns assigned to the Second Festival Day. The other hymn stanzas used in the Christmas cantatas are practically all taken from well-known Christmas hymns. The Leipzig hymnal of 1693 had specified for all the festival days until the Sunday after Christmas: " 'Gelobet seist du, Jesu Christ' and other Christmas hymns," and the Dresden hymnbooks in a general way prescribed at least for the First Festival Day "The Hymns Concerning the Birth of Christ." But in his choice among the very plentiful Christmas hymns, Bach always stayed with the liturgical list as much as possible. The hymn used in Part I of the *Christmas Oratorio*, "Vom Himmel hoch da komm ich her," was among the hymns sung in Leipzig (cf. *LKA*, pp. 53ff.) and Weißenfels at Vespers on the First Festival Day. Also the hymn "Wir Christenleut habn jetzund Freud," which Bach used both in Cantata BWV 110 for the First Festival Day and also in Cantata BWV 40 for the Second Festival Day, generally had a firm position in the liturgical life of the Christmas days. In Weißenfels it was likewise sung at Vespers on the First Festival Day; in the Dresden hymnbooks it is listed among the hymns assigned to the Third Festival Day; and in the *Leipziger Kirchen-Andachten* it is assigned to the Second and Third Festival Days together with four other hymns and is there printed word for word.[138] Among these hymns we also find the hymn "Christum wir sollen loben schon," which Bach used in Cantata BWV 121 for the Second Festival Day, a hymn that in Weißenfels had its firm place in Vespers on the Second Festival Day and there also was assigned as the hymn of the day for the Sunday after Christmas. The hymn "Fröhlich soll mein Herze springen," used in Part III of the *Christmas Oratorio*, was at first also expressly listed by name in the hymn schedules of the Dresden hymnbooks in addition to the direction "The Hymns Concerning the Birth of Christ" for the First Festival Day. Obviously this recommendation of a hymn by Paul Gerhardt was necessary, for we know concerning Leipzig that the hymns of Gerhardt did not achieve general significance until Bach's time, that is, at the beginning of the thirties of the 18th century. Finally, our attention should be directed to the hymn "Lobt Gott, ihr Christen alle gleich," used by Bach in Cantata BWV 151, composed for the Third Festival Day. This hymn was sung in Weißenfels in the main service of the Third Festival Day, was listed in the second place among the five hymns appointed for the Third Festival Day in the Dresden hymnbooks, and in the *Leipziger Kirchen-Andachten* had its place among the five hymns assigned to the Second and Third Festival Days. But in spite of his restriction by tradition Bach was responsive to the newer body of hymns that certainly are not traceable in Leipzig hymnbooks before 1737: "Ermuntre dich, mein schwacher Geist" (in Part II of the *Christmas Oratorio*), "Ich freue mich in dir" (in BWV 197a and 133), and likewise the Gerhardt hymns now also first beginning to feel at home, "Schaut, schaut, was ist für Wunder dar" and "Wir singen dir, Immanuel" (both hymns used in Part II of the *Christmas Oratorio*; the former is the only hymn assigned for Christmas Eve in the Dresden hymnals around 1750). "Wie soll ich dich empfangen," the Gerhardt hymn included in Part I of the *Christmas Oratorio*, is already given in the Dresden hymnbook of around 1725 as the first hymn among those to be sung on the First Sunday in Advent. The stanzas used in Part III of the *Christmas Oratorio* and in Cantata BWV 40, "Seid froh dieweil" and "Jesu, nimm dich deiner Glieder," are derived from Leipzig Christmas hymns traceable to the Bach era. Only in three cases did Bach fail to use Christmas hymns in Christmas cantatas, but there were special reasons, for Cantatas BWV 40, 57, and 64, which come into consideration here, were presented on Second and Third Festival Days that celebrated not Christmas but St. Stephen's Day and St. John's Day. But also in these cantatas Bach made considerable effort to include Christmas hymn materials. His added use of stanzas from Christmas hymns in Cantatas BWV 40 and 64 show this. In Cantata BWV 57 for St. Stephen's Day Bach made very suggestive use of a stanza from a hymn listed in the Dresden hymnbooks under the heading "Hymns of Lament and Comfort in Cross and Trial" [*Klag- und Trost-Lieder in Creutz u. Anfechtung*]. Also consider the tune! Interesting in Cantata BWV 64 is the inclusion of a stanza from the non-Christmas hymn "Jesu, meine Freude," chosen by Bach as a substitute for the very similar hymn "Jesu, meines Herzens Freud," which is proposed, for example, among three hymns for the Third

Festival Day in the *Vollständiges und vermehrtes Leipziger Gesang-Buch* of 1730.

Also the cantatas for the turn of the year, that is, for the Sunday after Christmas and for New Year's Day, reveal close ties to the schedule of hymns determined liturgically. Thus the hymn schedules of the Dresden hymnbooks for the Sunday after Christmas suggest "Nun lob, mein Seel, den Herren," the hymn used by Bach in Cantata BWV 28. It is possible that also Cantata BWV 192, for which the liturgical use cannot be determined definitely, may belong to this time in the church year, for we learn from Weißenfels that the main services of the Sunday after Christmas and of New Year's Day concluded with the hymn "Nun danket alle Gott." The hymn "Helft mir Gotts Güte preisen," used in the final movements of Cantata BWV 28 and the New Year's Day Cantata BWV 16, commonly appears in the Leipzig and Dresden hymn schedules of the 17th and 18th centuries as one of the hymns suggested most often for New Year's Day; in the Leipzig hymnal of 1693 it is also additionally assigned for the Third and Fourth Sundays in Advent. The hymn "Das neugeborne Kindelein," which Bach used as the basis for the text of Cantata BWV 122, a hymn that in the Leipzig and Dresden hymnals was listed for New Year's Day, was among the hymns sung on New Year's Day in Leipzig for a long time. Bach's use of this hymn in a cantata the Sunday after Christmas probably is due to the fact that in keeping with an old liturgical tradition the hymn combines the celebration of Christmas and New Year's Day—see its first stanza—and thus in a special way was able to form a connecting link between Christmas and New Year's Day. For New Year's Day the Dresden hymnals about 1725 assigned hymn choices in a very general way from the three categories, "Hymns for New Year," "Jesus Hymns," and "Hymns of Praise and Thanksgiving," but in the Leipzig hymnals of Bach's time hymns only from the first and third of these categories were assigned. Beside the generally popular New Year's hymn "Helft mir Gotts Güte preisen,"[139] Bach in three further New Year's Day cantatas (BWV 41, 171, 190) used stanzas of the New Year's hymn so popular in Leipzig, "Jesu, nun sei gepreiset." In fact, this hymn, already printed among the few hymns for this festival in the *Leipziger Kirchen-Andachten* of 1694, was the basic text for Cantata BWV 41. The direction "Hymns of Praise and Thanksgiving" was taken into consideration in Cantatas BWV 16 and 190, for in these cantatas Bach used "Herr Gott, dich loben wir," the well-known Luther translation of the Te Deum laudamus, which was also sung in the main service at Weißenfels and in the Dresden hymnbooks was the first hymn given in the category "Hymns of Praise and Thanksgiving." The third suggestion, "Jesus Hymns," was also taken into consideration by Bach in Part IV of the *Christmas Oratorio*, the cantata for New Year's Day, for the hymn stanzas used in the third and fifth movements are from the hymn "Jesu, du mein liebstes Leben," which in the Dresden hymnbooks has the added heading "A Hymn of Praise Concerning the Tender Love and the Ineffable Benefactions of Our Lord and Savior Jesus Christ" and in the hymn lists there is assigned specifically to the Sunday After Christmas.

Additional illuminating details about Johann Sebastian Bach's hymn choices are found in the cantatas for the Sundays and festival days following New Year's Day. In a very general way the hymn lists of the various hymnbooks of that time specify again and again that up to the festival of the Purification of Mary [*Mariae Lichtmeß*] Christmas hymns are also to be sung. Thus, for example, for the First Sunday After Epiphany both the Leipzig hymnbook of 1693 and Volume I of the Wagner hymnbook simply gave the direction "Christmas Hymns." This suggestion was taken into consideration by Bach only in cantatas for the Sunday after New Year and for the Epiphany Festival. The Christmas hymn "Ihr Gestirn, ihr hohlen Lüfte" in Part V of the *Christmas Oratorio* is no longer found in the hymnbooks of the Bach era, but it is still contained in the Leipzig hymnbook of 1693 and in the Wagner hymnbook. In Cantata BWV 65 for Epiphany Bach used a stanza of the hymn "Puer natus in Bethlehem," a hymn that was regularly sung in Latin and German on this day and on the festival days preceding and is still to be found in the Leipzig and Dresden hymnbooks about 1750. The first stanza of the well-known Gerhardt Christmas hymn "Ich steh an deiner Krippen hier" Bach used in Part VI of the *Christmas Oratorio*, for the Epiphany Festival. Beside the general direction concerning the Christmas hymns to be sung at this time, every Sunday had specific hymns assigned to it. In the two cantatas for the Sunday After New Year (BWV 153 and 58) Bach used the hymn "Ach Gott, wie manches Herzeleid." In the Leipzig and Dresden hymnbooks of Bach's time this hymn was frequently assigned to the Sunday After Christmas. In the Leipzig hymnbook of 1693 it was listed among the hymns "Concerning the Cross, Persecution, and Tribulation," and it was well suited for the Sunday After New Year with its Gospel from Matthew 2:13-23 (Flight to Egypt). This hymn also forms the basis for Cantata BWV 3, composed for the Second Sunday After Epiphany. Also well suited for the settings of the Sunday After New Year and its Cantata BWV 153 is the Gerhardt hymn Bach used, "Befiehl du deine Wege." "Nun, liebe Seel, nun ist es Zeit," the hymn used in Part V of the *Christmas Oratorio* and composed for this Sunday, is given in the Leipzig and Dresden hymnbooks of Bach's time among the Epiphany hymns to be sung especially on the Epiphany Festival according to the hymn schedules. In Cantata BWV 65 for Epiphany Bach used the hymn "Ich hab in Gottes Herz und Sinn," which he also chose for Cantata BWV 92 for Septuagesima Sunday. In the Dresden hymnbooks of about 1750 this hymn is assigned to the Third Sunday After Epiphany. The hymn "Meinen Jesum laß ich nicht," which is the basis for Cantata BWV

124 for the First Sunday After Epiphany and besides is also used in Cantata BWV 154 for the same Sunday, is found in the hymn schedules of both the Leipzig and the Dresden hymnbooks for this Sunday; in fact, in the Leipzig hymnbooks of Bach's time it frequently appears as the first of the four hymns mentioned. In the concluding movement of Cantata BWV 155 for the Second Sunday After Epiphany a stanza of the hymn "Es ist das Heil uns kommen her" is used, a hymn that in the *Leipziger Kirchen-Andachten* is given as the first of the hymns to be sung on Septuagesima Sunday. The hymn "Zion klagt mit Angst und Schmerzen," used in Cantata BWV 13, likewise for the Second Sunday After Epiphany, is assigned to the First Sunday After Epiphany in the Dresden hymn schedules. The hymn of the concluding movement of the same cantata, "In allen meinen Taten," belonged to the Sunday After New Year according to the Dresden hymn schedules. On the Third Sunday After Epiphany the two hymns "Ich ruf zu dir, Herr Jesu Christ" and "Was mein Gott will, das gscheh allzeit" were sung in Leipzig from time immemorial. The latter hymn is the basis of Cantata BWV 111, composed for this Sunday. The hymn is used besides for Cantata BWV 72 for this Sunday and in Cantata BWV 144 for Septuagesima Sunday. In the Dresden hymnbooks, too, this hymn is assigned to the Third Sunday After Epiphany. In the other two cantatas for this Sunday, BWV 73 and 156, Bach used the first stanza of the hymn "Herr, wie du willt, so schicks mit mir," which directly alludes to the Sunday Gospel ("Lord, if you will, ..." Matthew 8:2). "Wär Gott nicht mit uns diese Zeit,"[140] which was generally considered the hymn of the day for the Fourth Sunday After Epiphany and was sung on this Sunday from time immemorial also in Leipzig, is the basis of Cantata BWV 14, composed for this Sunday. In the Dresden hymnbooks, too, this hymn is assigned to the Fourth Sunday After Epiphany, as is also the hymn "Jesu, meine Freude,"which Bach used in the final movement of Cantata BWV 81, composed for the same Sunday. The hymn generally considered the hymn of the day for the Purification of Mary, usually the concluding festival of the Epiphany season, Luther's "Mit Fried und Freud ich fahr dahin,"[141] which also appears as the hymn of the day for that festival in all the Leipzig and Dresden hymnbooks of the 17th and 18th centuries, is the basis for Cantata BWV 125, composed for that festival. In Cantata BWV 83, for the same festival, Bach likewise made use of that hymn in the final movement.

Cantata BWV 126, composed by Bach for Septuagesima Sunday, contains two different Luther hymns. In addition to several hymns mentioned specifically, the Dresden hymnbooks of about 1725 had often in a very general way suggested hymns "Concerning the Christian Church and the Word of God," and those Luther hymns used by Bach most often were listed among the hymns in that category in the hymnals.

In accordance with the hymn schedules of Leipzig and Dresden, the singing of Lenten hymns was begun already on Estomihi Sunday, the last Sunday before Lent [also called Quinquagesima]. Bach, too, followed this direction by incorporating such Lenten hymns in Cantatas BWV 23 and 159, composed for that Sunday. "Christe, du Lamm Gottes," the hymn used in Cantata BWV 23, is mentioned specifically in the Dresden hymn schedules for Estomihi Sunday in addition to the general suggestion "The Lenten Hymns." In Cantata BWV 22, likewise composed for this Sunday, Bach used the hymn "Herr Christ, der einig Gotts Sohn," which, for instance, in the Leipzig hymnbooks at the close of the 17th century appears as the hymn of the day for the Sixth Sunday After Epiphany[142] and is listed as the first among the three hymns appointed for the Second Sunday After Epiphany. In Cantata BWV 127, likewise composed for Estomihi Sunday, the hymn "Herr Jesu Christ, wahr' Mensch und Gott" forms the foundation for the text of the cantata. This hymn was in Weißenfels considered the hymn of the day for this Sunday, and in the Dresden hymnbooks it was assigned to Judica Sunday [Fifth Sunday in Lent], in the Leipzig hymnbook of 1693 even to the last three Sundays in Lent—Laetare, Judica, and Palmarum.

In connection with the Advent cantatas (p. 233), we have already indicated that Bach even before his time of office in Leipzig took into consideration the hymns assigned to given Sundays. Cantata BWV 80, originally composed for Oculi Sunday [Third Sunday in Lent], can serve as proof for this statement, for in this work, later revised in Leipzig for use at the Reformation Festival, Bach used the hymn "Ein feste Burg ist unser Gott," which was generally the hymn of the day for Oculi Sunday.[143] Cantata BWV 182, originally composed for Palm Sunday and also using a Lenten hymn, Bach was able to present in Leipzig only on the Festival of the Annunciation, which often occurred in Lent or when it was antedated to Palm Sunday. In Cantata BWV 1, also composed for this festival, the basic text is the hymn "Wie schön leuchtet der Morgenstern," which was assigned to this festival also in the hymn schedules of the Dresden hymnbooks.[144]

In his selection of hymns for the Easter cantatas Bach likewise maintained his connection with the familiar stock and store of hymns. The Luther hymn that frequently appeared as the first in the list of hymns assigned to Easter in the Leipzig and Dresden hymnbooks, "Christ lag in Todesbanden," was the hymn of the day for Easter in Leipzig from time immemorial. It was used as the basis of Cantata BWV 4, composed for the First Easter Day, and it was also used in Cantata BWV 158, presented on the Third Easter Day.[145] Also the hymn used in Cantata BWV 66, "Christ ist erstanden," was always sung before the Sermon on all Easter days in Leipzig and beyond that every Sunday throughout the Easter season (cf. the discussion on p. 124). In Cantata BWV 6, for the Second Easter Day,

Bach used the hymn "Ach bleib bei uns, Herr Jesu Christ," which in the Leipzig hymn schedules at Bach's time is listed among three hymns for this second festival day. In Cantata BWV 145, for the Third Easter Day, the hymn "Erschienen ist der herrlich Tag" is used. This hymn was not assigned particularly to the Second Easter Day in the Dresden hymn schedules until 1750, but it is listed in the *Leipziger Kirchen-Andachten* as early as 1694 as the first of three hymns assigned to the Second and Third Easter Days. The stanza of the hymn "Wenn mein Stündlein vorhanden ist" used in Cantata BWV 31 is not from an Easter hymn, it is true, but this stanza "Weil du vom Tod erstanden bist" was regularly sung "after the early Sermon" of the Second and Third Easter Days (*LKA*, p. 98). The stanza used in Cantata BWV 158, "Welt, ade! ich bin dein müde," is rather unusual for Easter; it becomes intelligible only if we consider that this cantata was also intended for the Purification of Mary, and the Dresden hymnbooks also suggest the hymn "Ich bin müde mehr zu leben" for this festival. Otherwise the hymn schedules of the Leipzig and Dresden hymnbooks for the Easter days also frequently contain the general direction "The Hymns of This Festival." Only in one case did Bach use an Easter hymn that was not so common and yet not unknown in certain Leipzig hymnbooks, namely, "Auf, mein Herz! Des Herren Tag" at the beginning of Cantata BWV 145.

For the Sundays following the Easter Festival the rule was "that until Quasimodogeniti [First Sunday After Easter] Easter hymns are still sung and that on the rest of the Sundays the hymns are chosen in accordance with the Gospel" (*LKS*, p. 36). Bach followed this direction too in his cantatas for the Easter season. Only Cantata BWV 67, for Quasimodogeniti Sunday, still uses an Easter hymn, namely, "Erschienen ist der herrlich Tag," which in Weißenfels was always sung at Vespers on this Sunday. The hymn used in the concluding movement of Cantata BWV 67, "Du Friedefürst, Herr Jesu Christ," also appears among the hymns for the Third Easter Day in the Dresden hymn schedules. In Cantata BWV 42, likewise composed for this Sunday, there is a stanza of the hymn "Verzage nicht, o Häuflein," which in the Dresden hymn schedules is mentioned among the hymns to be sung on Jubilate Sunday [Third Sunday After Easter]. The hymn generally customary for Misericordias Domini [Second Sunday After Easter], "Der Herr ist mein getreuer Hirt,"[146] which also in Leipzig appears as the hymn of the day for that Sunday in the various hymnbooks, Bach used in Cantatas BWV 85 and 104 for this Sunday. In Cantata BWV 112, also designated for this Sunday, Bach also used all five stanzas of another hymn paraphrasing Psalm 23 and beginning with the same words, a hymn assigned particularly to this Sunday in the Dresden hymn schedules. The hymn "Was Gott tut, das ist wohlgetan," used in Cantata BWV 12, composed for Jubilate Sunday, is nowhere in the hymn schedules mentioned as belonging to this Sunday; in the Dresden hymnbooks, for example, beside specific hymns, also hymns generally in the classification "Concerning Cross and Trial" are recommended, and among hymns of that category this hymn is often found. The concluding movement of Cantata BWV 108 for Cantate Sunday [Fourth Sunday After Easter] already contains an Ascension hymn, but one that is specifically assigned to this Sunday in the hymn schedules of the Dresden hymnbooks.

In choosing hymns for the cantatas of the Festival of the Ascension, Bach remained faithful to the direction given in the Leipzig and Dresden hymnbooks that on this day the hymns of the festival be sung, and accordingly he adopted such Ascension hymns for Cantatas BWV 11, 43, and 128. The Ascension hymn used in Cantata BWV 43 is also mentioned specifically in the hymn schedules of the Dresden hymnbooks of about 1750, even though this was superfluous in view of the earlier direction "The Hymns Concerning the Ascension." In Cantata BWV 183, composed for Exaudi Sunday [Sunday After the Ascension], Bach used a Pentecost hymn that is listed as the first of four hymns assigned to this Sunday in the Leipzig hymnbooks of Bach's time.

Also in his choice of hymns for the Pentecost cantatas, Bach followed the direction of the hymn schedules, which generally specified Pentecost hymns. The hymn of the day for the three festival days in Leipzig was Luther's "Komm, heiliger Geist, Herre Gott!" (LKS, p. 17). Beside the general direction "Pentecost Hymns," this hymn was additionally and specifically mentioned in the Leipzig hymnbook of 1693 among the hymns to be sung on this festival day, and we find it used vocally in Cantata BWV 59 and instrumentally in Cantata BWV 172, both composed for the First Pentecost Day. The hymn used additionally in Cantata BWV 172, "Wie schön leuchtet der Morgenstern," we find assigned also for the Second Pentecost Day in the hymn schedules of the Dresden hymnbooks. The hymn used in Cantata BWV 174, "Herzlich lieb hab ich dich, o Herr," was normally assigned to the First Sunday After Trinity in the Weißenfels service. The stanza used in Cantata BWV 184 is taken from a hymn usually found in the category "Concerning the Word of God and the Christian Church." The choice of a hymn from this category may have seemed especially apropos on "the birthday of the church." The stanzas set to music in Cantatas BWV 74 and 175 are taken from Pentecost hymns.

For the Festival of the Holy Trinity Bach chose all five stanzas of "Gelobet sei der Herr" as the textual foundation of Cantata BWV 129, a hymn found among those assigned for this festival. The Leipzig and Dresden hymn schedules had for this day in a general way recommended hymns for the Festival of the Holy Trinity but had in addition also named specific hymns. Among these, in the hymn schedules of both cities, was the Gerhardt hymn "Was alle Weisheit in der Welt," used by Bach in Cantata

BWV 176 for this festival day. In the Leipzig hymn schedules of Bach's time, this hymn is even the first among four to be named.

The same close ties to the liturgically approved list of hymns also becomes clearly evident in the cantatas of the Trinity season. The hymn used in Cantata BWV 20, for the First Sunday After Trinity, may also be found listed in the Dresden hymn schedules. Cantata BWV 76, later used also as the cantata for the Reformation Festival but originally designated for the Second Sunday After Trinity, contains two stanzas of the hymn "Es woll uns Gott genädig sein," which in the hymnbooks is generally given among the hymns "Concerning the Word of God and the Christian Church," but for this Sunday the Dresden hymn schedules contain, beside other hymns, the general direction "Concerning the Christian Church" and for the Reformation Festival even the memorandum "The Hymns Concerning the Word of God and the Christian Church." In this group of hymns also "Ach Gott, vom Himmel sieh darein" is frequently found, a hymn that from time immemorial was the hymn of the day in Leipzig for the Second Sunday After Trinity and one that Bach chose as the basis for Cantata BWV 2 for this Sunday. For the Third Sunday After Trinity the Leipzig and Dresden hymn schedules suggest in a general way, beside special hymns, "Hymns Concerning Repentance" or "And other hymns concerning confession and repentance," but in the Dresden hymnbooks the first among the hymns of confession and repentance frequently is "Ach Herr, mich armen Sünder," which Bach chose as the basis for Cantata BWV 135, composed for this Sunday. The hymn used in both cantatas for the Fourth Sunday After Trinity, Cantatas BWV 177 and 185, "Ich ruf zu dir, Herr Jesu Christ," is specifically assigned to this Sunday in the Leipzig and Dresden hymn schedules. In the older Leipzig hymnbooks this hymn is suggested for the Second and Fifth Sundays After Trinity. In Volume I of the Wagner hymnal it was additionally assigned to nine other Sundays. In Weißenfels it was the hymn of the day for the Third Sunday After Trinity. The hymn in Cantata BWV 24, also for the Fourth Sunday After Trinity, "O Gott, du frommer Gott," is attested in the Dresden hymn schedules and also in the Weißenfels services of this Sunday. In both cantatas for the Fifth Sunday After Trinity, BWV 88 and 93, Bach introduced the hymn "Wer nur den lieben Gott läßt walten," which in the Leipzig and Dresden hymn schedules of Bach's time as well as in Weißenfels was assigned to this Sunday. The hymn "Es ist das Heil uns kommen her," which forms the basis of the cantata for the Sixth Sunday After Trinity, BWV 9, is not only attested in the hymn schedules of Leipzig, Dresden, and Weißenfels but also generally acknowledged as the hymn of the day for the Sixth Sunday After Trinity.[147] Bach also used two stanzas of this hymn in Cantata BWV 186 for the Seventh Sunday After Trinity. In Cantata BWV 187, also for this Sunday, Bach used the hymn then generally known for its use as a table prayer, "Singen wir aus Herzensgrund," which in the Leipzig hymn schedules of Bach's time is the second of four hymns assigned to this Sunday.

An interesting choice is that of the hymn "Was willst du dich betrüben" for Canata BWV 107, composed in 1724 for the Seventh Sunday After Trinity. For his second annual series of cantatas, a series that featured church hymns, Bach obviously chose this less familiar hymn only because he had already chosen the hymn of the day of this Sunday, "Warum betrübst du dich, mein Herz," a hymn closely related in content, as the basic text of Cantata BWV 138, composed in 1723 for the 15th Sunday After Trinity; in the Leipzig hymnbook of 1693 both hymns are found under the heading "Concerning the Cross, Persecution, and Trial." This hymn appears not only in Weißenfels as well as in the Leipzig and Dresden hymn schedules of the 17th and 18th centuries but beyond that quite generally as the hymn of the day both for the Seventh and 15th Sundays After Trinity.[148]

Cantata BWV 45, composed for the Eighth Sunday After Trinity, contains a stanza of the hymn "O Gott, du frommer Gott," which in the Dresden hymn schedules and in Weißenfels was not scheduled until the Ninth Sunday After Trinity. The basic text for the cantata presented on the Eighth Sunday After Trinity in 1724, BWV 178, is the hymn "Wo Gott, der Herr, nicht bei uns hält," which is often listed in the hymnbooks under the heading "Concerning the Word of God and the Christian Church." In the Dresden hymn schedules the hymns of this hymnbook section were generally suggested for this Sunday in addition to specific suggestions. Bach made use of this suggestion, especially since he had in the same year, in the cantata for the Second Sunday After Trinity,[149] already used the widely known hymn of the day for this Sunday, also sung in Leipzig, Dresden, and Weißenfels, "Ach Gott, vom Himmel sieh darein." The substitute hymn, which in the contents of stanzas four and five shows a close relation to the thought of the hymn of the day, reveals Bach's discerning way of choosing hymns.

The hymn assigned for the Ninth Sunday After Trinity in the Dresden hymn schedules, "Was frag ich nach der Welt," is the basis for the cantata for this Sunday, BWV 94. The hymn used in the cantata for the 10th Sunday After Trinity, BWV 46, was the hymn of the day for this Sunday in Weißenfels. The Dresden hymn schedules for this Sunday prescribe, in addition to specific hymns, the general direction "Hymns Concerning Repentance." Bach chose such repentance hymns for the other two cantatas for this Sunday (BWV 101 and 102). The basic text of Cantata BWV 101 is the hymn specifically listed in the Leipzig and Dresden hymn schedules, "Nimm von uns, Herr, du treuer Gott." Also for the 11th Sunday After Trinity the Dresden hymn schedules prescribe repentance hymns

243

in addition to specific hymns by name. In the three cantatas for this Sunday such repentance hymns are present. The hymns used in Cantatas BWV 113 and 179 are also listed specifically in the Dresden hymn schedules of certain hymnbook editions, and the hymn in Cantata BWV 199 was the hymn of the day for this Sunday in Weißenfels. The cantata originally composed for the 12th Sunday After Trinity, BWV 69, in its original version contains a stanza of "Was Gott tut, das ist wohlgetan," the hymn assigned to this Sunday by the Leipzig and Dresden hymn schedules. Otherwise the Leipzig hymn schedules for this Sunday list primarily hymns of praise and thanksgiving, but they do not contain the relatively new hymn of the time used in Cantata BWV 137, "Lobe den Herren, den mächtigen König der Ehren." For the cantata for the 13th Sunday After Trinity, BWV 164, the hymn "Herr Christ, der einig Gotts Sohn" is used, which in the Dresden hymn schedules is listed first among the hymns to be sung. The concluding movement of the cantata for this same Sunday, whose text is not extant, Cantata BWV 77, contains the hymn "Ach Gott, vom Himmel sieh darein," which also is listed for this Sunday in the Dresden hymn schedules. In Cantata BWV 33, also composed for this Sunday, Bach chose the hymn "Allein zu dir, Herr Jesu Christ," which was sung in the Weißenfels services of this Sunday but in the older Leipzig hymnbooks was already assigned to the 11th Sunday After Trinity and in the Leipzig and Dresden hymn schedules of Bach's time was deferred until the 14th Sunday After Trinity. The cantata composed for the 14th Sunday After Trinity, BWV 25, closes with a stanza of the hymn "Treuer Gott, ich muß dir klagen," which in the Dresden and Leipzig hymn schedules of Bach's time was already assigned to the 13th Sunday After Trinity. In Cantata BWV 17, likewise composed for the 14th Sunday After Trinity, Bach introduced the hymn that was generally customary as hymn of the day for this Sunday and was sung on this Sunday also in Leipzig, Dresden, and Weißenfels. The additional stanzas of this hymn Bach used in the cantata for the 15th Sunday After Trinity, BWV 51. For the 16th Sunday After Trinity the Leipzig and Dresden hymn schedules, beside listing specific hymns, assigned "Hymns Concerning Death" as a very general direction, and Bach made use of such hymns in a variety of ways in all four cantatas for this Sunday. Consider the four different hymns in Cantata BWV 95. The hymn "Wenn mein Stündlein vorhanden ist" is sometimes even mentioned by name in the hymn schedules of the Dresden hymnbooks. The hymn assigned to this Sunday in the Leipzig and Dresden hymn schedules, "Ach, lieben Christen, seid getrost," Bach chose as the basis of Cantata BWV 114, composed for the 17th Sunday After Trinity. For the cantata composed for the 18th Sunday After Trinity, BWV 96, Bach determined to use the hymn "Herr Christ, der einig Gotts Sohn," which most often occupied the first or the second position in the Leipzig and Dresden hymn schedules and was also

Leipzig order of service on the First Sunday in Advent (1736). Entry in Bach's hand on the score of Cantata 62 *(See BD* 1:251). Source: *Neu Ausgabe Sämtlicher Werke* (Kassel and Basel, 1954), 1:vi.

sung in Weißenfels on this Sunday. In Cantatas BWV 5 and 48, composed for the 19th Sunday After Trinity, Bach gave consideration to the direction given in the Dresden hymn schedules for this Sunday, which specified "Hymns Concerning Repentance and Confession" in addition to listing specific hymns. In the first of these cantatas, the hymn of repentance "Wo soll ich fliehen hin" even becomes the basic text. Also the Leipzig hymn schedules list specific hymns of repentance among others for this Sunday. In the cantata composed for the 20th Sunday After Trinity Bach used the hymn "Wie schön leuchtet der Morgenstern," which in Leipzig was the hymn of the day for this Sunday and in the Dresden hymn schedules also enjoyed high priority. The hymn used in the cantata for the 21st Sunday After Trinity, BWV 188, is listed as the hymn of the day for this Sunday in the *Leipziger Kirchen-Andachten* of 1694. It is likewise still mentioned among the hymns for this Sunday in the Dresden hymn schedules around 1750. But the Dresden hymn schedules also in a general way suggest "Hymns of Lament and Comfort" for this Sunday. Among these we find the hymn used in Cantata BWV 188 and also the hymn "Was Gott tut, das ist wohlgetan," which Bach likewise used in Cantata BWV 98, also intended for this Sunday. Very likely also Cantata BWV 100 belongs to this Sunday. It is based on the same hymn but is not assigned liturgically. The hymn assigned to this Sunday in all the older Leipzig hymnbooks, "Aus tiefer Not schrei ich zu dir," which Bach used in Cantata BWV 38 for the same Sunday, was the hymn of the day in Weißenfels only on the 22d Sunday After Trinity. Also in the Dresden hymn schedules it appears only among the hymns of that Sunday. In Cantata BWV 89, composed for the 22d Sunday After Trinity, Bach made use of a stanza of the hymn of repentance "Wo soll ich fliehen hin." The Dresden hymn schedules for this Sunday had prescribed hymns of repentance in general but also, among other hymns, specific hymns of repentance, just as in the older Leipzig hymnbooks only hymns of repentance are assigned to this Sunday. The concluding stanza of the hymn "Wo soll ich fliehen hin" Bach employed in Cantata BWV 163 for the 23d Sunday After Trinity. For this Sunday, too, the hymn attested in the Dresden hymn schedules and in Weißenfels, "In dich hab ich gehoffet, Herr," was established, which Bach used in Cantata BWV 52, composed for this Sunday. In both cantatas written for the 24th Sunday After Trinity, BWV 26 and 60, Bach, in keeping with the direction of the Leipzig and Dresden hymn schedules to the effect that beside hymns specifically named, hymns "Concerning Death and Dying" should be used, exclusively chose hymns to be found in this classification in the hymnals. The hymns used by Bach in both cantatas for the 25th Sunday After Trinity, BWV 90 and 116, are found in the Dresden hymnbooks of that time among the "Hymns of Lament and Comfort," which in the Dresden hymn schedules were in general assigned to this Sunday beside those mentioned specifically by name. The hymn that forms the basis of Cantata BWV 116 is sometimes even mentioned specifically among the hymns to be sung on this Sunday. The hymn used in Cantata BWV 90 belonged to the hymns sung on this day in Weißenfels. For the single extant cantata for the 27th Sunday After Trinity, BWV 140, Bach chose the hymn "Wachet auf, ruft uns die Stimme," which had been especially assigned to this Sunday in the Leipzig and Dresden hymn schedules but in the Leipzig hymn schedules of Bach's time even occupies the principal position among the hymns to be sung on this day.

Also in the cantatas for the festival days occurring during the Trinity season we notice Bach's close adherence to his own time's known and liturgically organized treasury of hymns. In the cantata composed for the Festival of St. John the Baptist, BWV 7, the basis for the text is Luther's hymn "Christ unser Herr zum Jordan kam," which was quite generally considered the hymn of the day for this festival and in all Leipzig and Dresden hymn schedules usually heads the list of hymns to be sung on this day. Another hymn prescribed for this day in the hymn schedules of both cities, "Nun lob, mein Seel, den Herren," which was even the hymn of the day in Weißenfels, Bach took into consideration in Cantata BWV 167, also for this festival. Beside these the hymn schedules suggested more generally hymns "For the Festival of St. John the Baptist," of which one, "Tröstet, tröstet meine Lieben," to be found only in the later Leipzig hymnbooks (about 1740), was used in Cantata BWV 30, also composed for this festival. For the Festival of the Visitation of Mary, Bach in Cantata BWV 147 used stanzas of "Jesu, meiner Seelen Wonne," a hymn assigned to this day only in the Dresden hymn schedules. The universal hymn of the day for this festival, which also in all Leipzig and Dresden hymn schedules usually heads the list of hymns assigned to this day, was the well-known hymn of praise [the Magnificat], which the Leipzig hymnbooks presented also in hymn form, "Meine Seel erhebt den Herren," and this is the basis for Cantata BWV 10, written for this festival. Generally accepted as the hymn of the day for the Festival of St. Michael was "Herr Gott, dich loben alle wir," the hymn that in all the Leipzig and Dresden hymn schedules predominated as the festival hymn. This also is the basis of Cantata BWV 130, composed for this day. The other hymn attested for this festival in the hymn schedules of both cities as well as in Weißenfels, "Herzlich lieb hab ich dich, o Herr," Bach used in both of the other cantatas for this festival (BWV 19 and 149). For the Festival of the Reformation the Leipzig and Dresden hymn schedules very generally specify "Hymns Concerning the Word of God and the Christian Church." Of the hymns appearing under this heading, Bach used three for the cantatas for this festival and for the Reformation Jubilee in 1730: "Ein feste Burg ist unser Gott" in Cantata BWV 80 as well as "Es woll uns Gott genädig sein" and "Ach bleib bei uns,

Herr Jesu Christ" in two cantatas extant only in text (cf. N*VT*, pp. 180—81, 333—34). The hymn used in the Reformation Cantata BWV 79, "Nun danket alle Gott," was sung in the main service in Leipzig on Reformation Day after the Sermon (*LKS*, p. 30). The hymns suggested in the Dresden hymn schedules for the Festival of the Election of the Council, "Es woll uns Gott genädig sein" and "Verleih uns Frieden gnädiglich," are used in two cantatas by Bach for this festival (cf. N*VT*, pp. 171—72, 332, 382—83).

Everywhere, then, Bach's endeavor to draw into his cantatas, wherever possible, the familiar stock and store of hymns associated with the various Sundays and festival days becomes evident. But this adherence to the liturgically organized hymns of the church does not indicate a legalistic fixation, as his occasional adoption of newer hymns and above all also hymn materials not liturgically established clearly indicates. Considering the sources of the cantata texts, we cannot help noticing that Bach must often have lacked suitable stanzas in the Sunday hymns and therefore naturally had to be free to choose other hymns in each case and also to combine corresponding stanzas meaningfully. But also in such cases Bach strove to put the traditional hymnic materials to use as much as possible, and in this effort various collections of hymns must have inspired him to find the right stanzas. Thus it becomes conspicuous, for example, that in Volume III of the Wagner hymnbook the "Gospel hymn" for the 18th Sunday After Trinity begins with the stanza "HErr GOtt! erzeig uns deine Gunst, und zünd in unsern Hertzen an die innigliche Liebes Brunst, so keine Macht auslöschen kann" (Lord God, Thy grace on us bestow And set our heart's remotest trench With such a fire of love aglow Which earth's worst powers can never quench—*WGB* 3:191). In his Cantata BWV 169 for this Sunday Bach used the strikingly similar but in Leipzig well-known stanza by Luther: "Du süße Liebe, schenk uns deine Gunst, laß uns empfinden der Liebe Brunst, daß wir uns von Herzen einander lieben..." (O sweetest Love, your grace on us bestow; Set our hearts with sacred fire aglow That with hearts united we love each other...), a hymn that is nowhere in the hymn schedules assigned for this Sunday. The exceedingly meaningful choice of "Schmücke dich, o liebe Seele" for Cantata BWV 180 for the 20th Sunday After Trinity, likewise a hymn not to be found in the hymn schedules, was possibly also inspired by the Gospel hymn for this Sunday given in the Wagner hymnal, throughout extolling the mystery of the Sacrament of the Altar (*WGB* 3:199). The Gospel hymn for the 21st Sunday After Trinity in the Wagner hymnal begins with the stanza "WEr wolte nicht auf GOttes Treu all seine Hoffnung bauen? Es geht nie keine Stund vorbey, darinnen wir nicht schauen, wie er mit seiner Gegenwart genädiglich bey uns verharrt: Wer wolte GOtt nicht trauen?" (Who would not trust God's faithfulness And base all hope upon it? For not an hour of life will pass In which we do not con it How He with His own presence blest Among us in His grace does rest. Who would not trust His goodness?—*WGB* 3:202). With this we must compare the closing movement of the cantata for this Sunday, BWV 109, which does not make use of a Sunday hymn. This movement begins: "Wer hofft in Gott und dem vertraut, der wird nimmer zuschanden" (Whoever hopes and trusts in God, he will not be confounded). The Gospel hymn of the Wagner hymnal for the 24th Sunday After Trinity begins with "WAs ist der Mensch? ein Erdenstaub, ein welckes Graß, und fallend Laub, ein Rauch und Dampf, der gleich vergeht, wenn er entsteht, so fällt ein Mensch, der sich erhöht" (Just what is man? a speck of dust, Mere withered grass and fading leaf, All smoke and fume, soon bound to pass Where it began. Thus man exalts himself and falls.—*WGB* 3:214—15). As the basis of his Cantata BWV 26 for this Sunday Bach chose the hymn "Ach wie flüchtig, ach wie nichtig ist der Menschen Leben! Wie ein Nebel bald entstehet und auch wieder bald vergehet, so ist unser Leben, sehet" (How elusive, how diffusive Is the life of mortals! As when fog at first is sighted And as soon again is lighted, So man's life, behold, is blighted), again a hymn that is nowhere mentioned in the hymn schedules. Also the use of the hymn "Du Friedefürst, Herr Jesu Christ" in Cantata BWV 67 for Quasimodogeniti Sunday, a hymn not to be found in the hymn schedules for this Sunday, is probably influenced by the Wagner hymnal, which contains a Gospel hymn beginning with "DU Friedens-fürst, HErr JEsu Christ" (*WGB* 3:95). The choice of two hymns, "Zion klagt mit Angst und Schmerzen" and "Ach Gott, wie manches Herzeleid," for the cantatas for the Second Sunday After Epiphany, BWV 3 and 13, is possibly also to be credited to the Wagner hymnal. Both hymns are found among the hymns for "Cross and Solicitude" in the Leipzig hymnbooks of Bach's time. Both of the hymns here included are likewise influenced by thoughts "Concerning Patience and Hope in the Cross" (heading of one of the hymns, cf. *WGB* 3:35ff.) that do not do justice to the Gospel for that Sunday.

Other hymnbooks, too, must occasionally have stimulated Bach in the proper choice of hymns. It is worth noting that the *Geistreicher Lieder-Schatz oder Leipziger Gesangbuch* of 1717 contains no section of Epiphany hymns between New Year's Day and the Lenten hymns, but in their place 28 hymns under the heading "Jesus Hymns" are inserted. The hymns used by Bach in four cantatas for the Epiphany season (BWV 81, 123, 124, 154), "Liebster Immanuel, Herzog der Frommen," "Meinen Jesum laß ich nicht," "Jesu, meiner Seelen Wonne," and "Jesu, meine Freude," are, however, frequently found among the "Jesus Hymns" in the hymnbooks.

But the various ways in which Johann Sebastian Bach put to use and set to music the Lutheran church hymn, which is found to be associated with a hundred different tunes in the collection of Bach's cantatas, have been assembled by Werner Neumann in a systematic summary.[150] In view of the numerous forms of treatment given the hymns in the cantatas, Alfred Dürr has spoken of "idioms that are characteristic particularly for Bach's music" and on the basis of this fact has established in Bach "the close relation to the evangelical hymn" and has made the excellent statement about this hymn: "While in the first place it had no longer an abiding place at all in the Neumeister cantata and later, though taken up again, was by contemporaries usually furnished with a treatment that was inadequate and often did not even measure up to the most elementary rules of composition, Bach in his whole life cannot exhaust his possibilities in chorale treatments of the most diverse kinds. Not only in his works for organ but similarly also in those for voices, Bach is at pains to achieve a multiplicity of possibilities in the use of the chorale such as no master was likely to attain again. But the manner in which Bach uses the chorale in this effort definitely shows that he is interested not in a virtuoso dilettantism but here too in exegesis with the help of the church hymn that is generally understood by his hearers."[151] As especially Smend's investigations have always clearly demonstrated,[152] Bach's cantata compositions provide "a profusion of examples of the exegetical use of the chorale, which even in the most pretentious and musically intricate Passions and oratorios still invests them with the characteristic features of the parish."[153]

In this definitely great interest of Bach's in the evangelical church hymn and its proper musical use, Bach's clear determination to take part in the service of proclamation in Lutheran worship again becomes evident, for it was precisely the Lutheran hymn that from its beginning—in contrast to later times—was active in the service of Gospel proclamation, and that not infrequently with the acknowledged purpose of providing instruction. The preface to the *Neu Leipziger Gesangbuch* of Gottfried Vopelius in 1682 expresses this purpose unmistakably: "These beautiful hymns now have their special blessing. It goes without saying that we engage in welcome worship of God our Lord through them when we sing such hymns to honor Him and to present our needs to Him, but this, too, is a spendid benefit, that our articles of faith are very briefly and articulately stated in them, so that a simple Christian who otherwise has had no education and in many cases can neither read nor write will eventually at the same time grasp the articles of faith with the hymns and in this way become acquainted with them, if he by much repetition hears them in church or at home and sings along." When Bach established a close connection to the tested and tried collection of his church's hymns, he deliberately took his place in the tradition that even placed the church hymn in the service of the proclamation of the Gospel. And even if Bach took the hymns of the 16th and 17th centuries into consideration in the very same way, we cannot fail to recognize his preference for the hymn of the Reformation period, which preeminently "in its very essence is a hymn of proclamation."[154] This fact becomes most obvious when we compare the hymns appearing in the numerous classifications in the hymnbooks with Bach's choice. In no other group of hymns did Bach so much as approach the frequency of choice in the selection of his hymns as in the group under the heading "Concerning the Word of God and the Christian Church," which favored the hymns of the 16th century almost exclusively. In the *Geistreicher Lieder-Schatz oder Leipziger Gesangbuch* of 1717, for example, there are 12 hymns in this category, but nine of these are used in Bach's cantatas, most of them several times. This set of facts agrees with the observation that Bach had an especially positive interest in Luther's corpus of hymns, for the greater number of his hymns found a place in Bach's cantatas. In fact, in almost a fifth of the cantatas definitely attributable to Bach Luther's hymns play a more or less important role. Above all, the cantatas for the festival days, and especially the three principal festivals of the church year, are conspicuous in their use of Luther's hymns.

Bach's interest in Christian proclamation, as expressed in hymn materials, becomes most spectacular in those movements in which the church hymn is presented only in a purely instrumental medium. In the cantata for Jubilate Sunday (BWV 12), during the Tenor aria "Sei getreu, alle Pein wird doch nur ein Kleines sein" a trumpet plays the tune of the hymn "Jesu, meine Freude," a hymn otherwise not used at all in a vocal way in the cantata. In the duet of Cantata BWV 163, while the text "Nimm mich mir und gib mich dir..." is being sung, violins and a viola play the tune "Meinen Jesum laß ich nicht," which likewise is not used vocally otherwise in the cantata. Especially impressive are those movements in which one of the hymns of the day for a Sunday is used. In Cantata BWV 23 for Estomihi [Quinquagesima] Sunday, originally produced as an exhibit piece for the application for the Leipzig position, the hymn of the day for this Sunday, "Christe, du Lamm Gottes," is not reserved for the concluding movement, but already in the second movement (a Tenor recitative) the text "Ach, gehe nicht vorüber; du aller Menschen Heil, bist ja erschienen, die Kranken und nicht die Gesunden zu bedienen" (Oh, do not pass us by; for you, Savior of all people, have appeared to serve the sick and not those who are well) is interwoven with a four-part instrumental harmonization of that hymn. Also in the following choir number, "Aller Augen warten, Herr, du allmächtiger Gott, auf dich" (The eyes of all wait upon you, Lord, almighty God), the line of the basic voice in the tutti theme grew out of that hymn tune. Accordingly the entire cantata, consisting of four movements, is dominated by the church hymn. In the cantata for the First Easter Day, BWV 31, the Soprano aria with obbligato oboe on the text "Letzte Stunde, brich herein" is accompanied by violins and a viola playing the tune "Wenn mein Stündlein vorhanden ist," which is then also used in a vocal treatment in the last movement of the cantata. This longing for eternity is also developed impressively by means of an instrumental use of the hymns customary for the day in two further cantatas composed for the 16th Sunday After Trinity. In the first movement of Cantata BWV 161, while the Alto sings the text "Komm, du süße Todesstunde," the organ plays the tune of the hymn "Herzlich tut mich verlangen," which also receives vocal treatment in the concluding movement. In the middle of Cantata BWV 106, while the texts "Es ist der alte Bund: Mensch, du mußt sterben" (choir trio) as well as "Ja komm, Herr Jesu, komm" (Soprano) are sung, the tune "Ich hab mein Sach Gott heimgestellt" is heard in a three-voice setting for instruments (two flutes and gamba) built into the texture. This was the hymn of the day for that Sunday in Weißenfels and is also listed as the first among the Sunday's hymns in the Dresden hymnbooks. In the cantata for the Fourth Sunday After Trinity (BWV 185) the hymn particularly assigned to this Sunday, "Ich ruf zu dir, Herr Jesu Christ," is treated vocally only in the concluding movement but is used instrumentally already in the first movement in a duet for trumpet and oboe during the singing of the text "Barmherziges Herze der ewigen Liebe, errege, bewege mein Herze durch dich." The cantata composed for the First Day of Pentecost (BWV 172) does not use the text of the hymn of the day, "Komm, heiliger Geist, Herre Gott," but it does use its tune for obbligato organ (or two other instruments) during the duet "Komm, laß mich nicht länger warten." Also during the initial choral movement of the cantata for the 13th Sunday After Trinity, "Du sollst Gott, deinen Herrn, lieben..." (BWV 77), the hymn tune of "Dies sind die heilgen Zehn Gebot" is heard, the hymn chiefly assigned to this Sunday in the Leipzig and Dresden hymn schedules, but it is played only by a single trumpet, and that in 10 separate entrances for the five hymn lines. Equally significant is the use of the hymn "Es ist gewißlich an der Zeit" in Cantata BWV 70 for the 26th Sunday After Trinity. This hymn was sung in Leipzig and Dresden as the hymn of the day for this Sunday. In the cantata the hymn tune is heard only instrumentally, performed by a single trumpet during the singing of the Bass recitative: "Ach, soll nicht dieser große Tag, der Welt Verfall und der Posaunen Schall, der unerhörte letzte Schlag, des Richters ausgesprochne Worte, des Höllenrachens offne Pforte in meinem Sinn viel Zweifel, Furcht und Schrecken, der ich ein Kind der Sünden bin, erwecken?" (Ah, should not this alarming day, the world's demise, and the last trumpet's call, the final blow ne'er heard before, the Judge's words so clearly spoken, the yawning portals of the jaws of hell awaken doubt, much fear, and fright in my thoughts, since I am a child of sin?).

The melody of the penitential hymn "Herr Jesu Christ, du höchstes Gut" in the initial chorus of the cantata for the 19th Sunday After Trinity, "Ich elender Mensch, wer wird mich erlösen vom Leibe dieses Todes"

(BWV 48)—and penitential hymns were customarily assigned to this Sunday—is also presented only instrumentally by one trumpet. The degree to which Bach took for granted among the hearers a proper understanding for his instrumental use of hymns is clearly demonstrated by his use of "Herzlich lieb hab ich dich, o Herr," a favorite hymn for the Festival of St. Michael, in Cantata BWV 19, composed for this festival, for while the Tenor sings the text "Bleibt, ihr Engel, bleibt bei mir! Führet mich auf beiden Seiten, daß mein Fuß nicht möge gleiten" (Stay, O angels, stay with me! Take my hands and gently lead me, that my feet may never slip), the tune of this hymn, played by a single trumpet and otherwise not used in the cantata, could be understood only as referring to its third stanza: "Ach Herr, laß dein lieb' Engelein an meinem End die Seele mein in Abrahams Schoß tragen" (Lord, let at last your angels come, To Abram's bosom bear me home).

We will without hesitation be able to establish the fact that in his use of the hymn Bach himself was definitely interested "in confronting his hearer with the living Word of God."[155] The very fact that Bach so frequently specified the penetrating sound of the trumpet for the cantus firmus indicates that he was really concerned about making the proclamation expressed in the composition as audible and clear as possible. In the cantus firmus of the duet of Cantata BWV 10 this is achieved by means of a trumpet and two oboes in unison. Since the same cantus firmus also occurs as an instrumental strain in the movement "Suscepit Israel" in Bach's *Magnificat,* Dürr rightly, especially in view of the history of this movement, points to the necessity to "deromanticize" the interpretation of this movement. It seems to him that "instead of the conventional romantic rendition with murmuring oboes in the background rather the impression of radiating exaltation, of the upward look (without doubt inspired by the text *suscepit,* for which Luther has *hilft auf*) would have to be substituted."[156] Actually we will do justice to the work of Bach and to his interpretation only if we carefully study the theological meaning of the hymn Bach uses at any given point and so ascertain the purpose of his proclamation and then take the knowledge we have gained into consideration in our performance techniques. At any rate, for Bach in his entire liturgical work the life-giving and life-preserving Word of God was at stake, the *viva vox evangelii* that was to be heard in the sermon as well as in sermon music and in the church hymn. Bach's liturgical cantatas "do not want to be works of music or art in their own right; they want to advance the work of Luther, the preaching of the Word and always only the Word, with their own materials."[157] But as "the tonal language of Luther's church is the evangelical chorale," because Luther "is the creator of this precious treasure of our church," so also for Johann Sebastian Bach the hymn of his church became "the preeminent medium for interpreting the Word."[158] The high respect he had for this inherited treasure of faith bequeathed by the fathers is apparent in this, that for him above all the church hymn that had proved itself liturgically is in its basic statement unassailable. In dealing with his proposed texts, he is well aware of "the differentiation between religious poetry in general and hymn writing authorized as it were through hymnbook publication," insofar as he "very rarely makes changes in a text from a hymnbook but otherwise exercises his blue pencil copiously."[159]

This respect for the liturgical heritage of the fathers again shows Bach's firm roots in the Lutheran tradition and his loyalty to the church that had from the beginning sung the good news of the Gospel into the hearts of its congregations precisely through the evangelical hymn and had through it captured people's hearts. Because Bach was acquainted with this available power of the evangelical hymn through personal experience from his early youth, the more he was influenced by the unconditional resolve to proclaim the Gospel, the more strongly his method of composing had to lead to the evangelical hymn and remain fixed on it, and "no one else in the centuries since Luther's day made this task his own as well as Johann Sebastian Bach."[160]

e) Conclusions

Once we have seen how deeply Johann Sebastian Bach's music and musical thought was rooted in the Lutheran theology and piety in which he was reared and grew up, the question about Bach's relationship to the worship of his time practically provides its own answer, for the Lutheran piety was primarily a *liturgical* piety. As even from a purely theoretical view "worship plainly appears as the basic theme of all theology" for Lutheran orthodoxy, and " 'worship' embraced the totality of the Christian life and did not mean only the liturgical area," and Lutheran orthodoxy in practice, too, "displayed great faithfulness in understanding, retaining, and celebrating the divine service as 'the real spiritual occurrence,' "[161] so there was no other way but that for Johann Sebastian Bach, a person firmly rooted in this theology and church from an early age and also professing his loyalty to it, "worship and the praise of God incorporated in it should become the basis of all of his creative work."[162] Neither were things different in Köthen. When Bach here, too, remained loyal to the Lutheran Church, he confessed his loyalty to the Lutheran service, and so his creative work in this place also has to be looked on as worship in the wider sense of the word. It is true, it must have bothered him that he could contribute only very little to the actual worship service of his Lutheran Church in this place, and so his going to Leipzig in 1723 can only be characterized as a logical decision. Gurlitt has hit it exactly right when he writes concerning this decision of Bach's: "This fateful decision, to place his daily labors definitely and entirely into the service of the church of the Word and to devote himself to the proclamation of the Word, is one that Bach arrived at in a most notable manner. He was not moved by considerations of what would serve some immediate 'practical' purpose, nor by cool, rational deliberations, nor by some willful impulse, nor, for that matter, by purely personal motives of any kind. Instead, he was prompted entirely by reasons of conscience. His attitude represented a victory that he had won by habitual faithfulness on the one hand and by indifference on the other, an attitude giving heed only to the genuineness of the assigned task and of the required confession."[163] In Leipzig Bach set foot on ground on which the realization of what he had 15 years earlier on leaving Mühlhausen called his "final purpose" seemed a splendid possibility. Because the Lutheran service still made great demands on the musicians of that time, Bach was able with undivided attention and with his entire artistic creativity to devote himself to the worship service of his church. In view of the very manner in which Bach in his first Leipzig years threw himself into the round of liturgical tasks and duties—just think of his presenting six two-section cantatas in the first quarter year or two cantatas in a single service[164]—there can be no doubt about the sincerity of his serious intent. Thus we may consider Bach's clearly stated purpose of 1708 and 1730 to achieve a "regulated" or "well-ordered church music" the very aim of his life and calling, just as we may view the whole path of his life and calling only as a path that was indeed beset by detours but in the last analysis proceeded with the goal in mind of always aiming at the liturgical office and task in the Lutheran Church.

This conclusion can in no way be altered by the variety of controversies in which Bach was involved during his time of office in Leipzig; on the contrary, in the final analysis they are to be understood in the light of his struggle toward the "final purpose" of his creative work. Mahrenholz has aptly described this situation: "Whenever we examine the questionable cases, we find that in the final analysis almost always the possibility of achieving the final purpose of a regulated church music was at stake. For whether the controversy had to do with university services, the reception of new dormitory students, the choice of the choir prefect, the school discipline, or other contested cases in which the irascible and sensitive St. Thomas cantor often gives the impression of a quarrelsome person constantly thinking of his own civic reputation, always not the church music as such but a regulated, ordered, liturgically organized church music conducted according to a plan is at stake. Bach was contending...not for the musical products of his creative efforts but for the final purpose of his creative efforts."[165] Bach very obviously was of the opinion that in the Leipzig of his time it was still worthwhile to carry on the fight "so that both for his own church music and that of other masters a place corresponding to the beginning made by the Lutheran Reformation might remain guaranteed in a well-ordered worship service."[166]

With this interest of Bach's in the worship of his church, proved by his struggle and contention for proper church music, his way of creating, to be understood from the viewpoint of his liturgical commission, was in perfect harmony. There can be no doubt that a true interest of the heart for the liturgical office and task and an accompanying positive attitude toward and a genuine commitment to Lutheran worship is revealed in Bach's compositional technique, which had a high regard for the proper interpretation of Scripture, and in his effort to dedicate his best compositions to the worship service of the church as well as to make the church hymn the center of his liturgical work and so to provide the most intimate union with the stock and store of hymns that had proved themselves liturgically. From the liturgical service Johann Sebastian Bach had received his commission to compose cantatas regularly, and his creating and composing always drew him back to that liturgical service.

And finally, on the basis of the fact that Johann Sebastian Bach felt a real inner attachment to the liturgical service of his time, we may on the one hand arrive at the conclusion that the liturgical life at the time of orthodoxy enjoyed a high vitality—for which artist would offer his creative talent to a liturgy that is moribund and destined to end in meaninglessness? On the other hand we may characterize Bach's cantatas as genuine liturgical works, for here the presupposition described by Söhngen is present: "Only when music combines with faith and beauty with truth does it receive the full authority to serve in the sanctuary."[167]

Appendix of Sources

1.

Leipzig, 17 June 1732

On the 13th of this month 800 Salzburg emigrants arrived in this city, and on the following day, at two in the afternoon, over 800 more of them in excellent order. Because the citizens now registered with the magistrate to have him assign to each as many as he could lodge and this was immediately granted them, they really competed with one another for these emigrants. As a result, many a citizen who really wanted to accommodate more people, and also could have done so, could hardly lodge 10 persons in his home. In the first group there were many who had a strong desire for Holy Communion. Accordingly, these were divided into three groups for St. Thomas, St. Nicholas, and New Church and were there examined and instructed by the clergy, went to confession, and received absolution. On the following Sunday, amid great manifestation of devotion, they partook of Holy Communion with the other communicants. In all the churches very comforting sermons were preached for these people, who were obviously eager to hear the Word of God. Also, they were encouraged to remain steadfast in the faith. In addition, God filled the hearts of all the citizens with sympathy for them, so that they were well supplied with money, clothing, food, and drink. Yesterday morning at eight o'clock the first, and today the rest, left again for Duben, most of them being brought there on wagons. At the Halle gate the city council ordered three large booths erected, one for the council, one for the university, and one for the representatives of the business community. Here each of these groups doled out additional money for the journey for all, from the greatest to the least. The businessmen's group gave them 16 groschen a head, and there is no doubt that the magistrate did even better. Also the head of every host house provided according to his means. Then, amid many tears, these emigrants were accompanied by a large number of local citizens until they had proceeded a good way beyond the city limits. After the second detachment of these dear people had enthusiastically attended the local worship service on Sunday, over 100 persons declared at the close of the service that they wished to partake of Holy Communion, and yesterday, after the early service, the Sacrament was offered to them. The local clergy, according as they had room, had 30 to 40 of them come into their homes and delighted them with spiritual and material benefactions. These good people honestly insisted that they had been told that in Saxony, and especially in this city, they would find very few compassionate people, if any; but now they openly state that they have nowhere else been treated so well and that they will never in their lives forget these deeds of kindness. From the representatives of the businessmen's group the pregnant women each received one florin on behalf of their unborn child.

257

Two women gave birth here, and their children were baptized. These were also amply supplied with layettes and clothes. Two wealthy widows each had 1,000 florins distributed among the people, and a certain physician similarly provided 800 florins. On the 14th of this month also all the stores presented them with all kinds of goods, clothes, linens, books, etc. Even the young craftsmen, we were also told, collected together what they were able to provide and gave this money to these people. (*Derer Saltzburgischen Emigrations-ACten*, compiled by Johann Jacob Moser, 1 [Frankfurt and Leipzig, 1732]: 689)

2.

Order for Saturday Vespers: "At 1:30 the bells are rung, and the officiant immediately opens with the responsory 'Deus in adjutorium meum intende' (Make haste, O God, to deliver me), to which the choir responds 'Domine ad adjuvandum me festina' (Make haste to help me, O Lord) and forthwith continues with the Gloria Patri....In addition, in St. Thomas Church a few motets are sung; in St. Nicholas Church (and during Advent and Lent in both churches) the responsory and antiphons assigned in ancient times to the following Sunday, together with an added German hymn, are sung. After this a penitential text is expounded for those who go to confession, and the appointed prayers for the church are read. After the Sermon the Magnificat is sung, and then the Collect and Benediction close the service." (*LKS*, p. 42; cf. also *LKA*, pp. 83—84)

3.

For comparison, the order of Vespers on Sundays and festival days is given here. On ordinary Sundays the service was begun "with organ and the singing of a motet....After that, in accordance with the season and the Gospel, a hymn is sung. At its conclusion the officiant proceeds to the lectern and reads a psalm, then prays the Lord's Prayer aloud, and continues with the customary hours' prayers....After that another German hymn is sung, at the last stanza of which the officiant enters the pulpit, approximately at two o'clock. After his introductory statements, the hymn 'Herr Jesu Christ, dich zu uns wend' is sung as in the early service, and the Lord's Prayer is prayed silently. After that the Epistle is read or whatever else serves as text for the Sermon according to the season....At three o'clock the officiant customarily concludes, and after the close of the Sermon the prayers are read in order, just as in the early service, but with the omission of the general confession. The intercessions and thanksgivings are offered as in the early service, but there are no announcements....When the officiant leaves the pulpit, the Magnificat, Mary's hymn of praise, is sung in German after a suitable introduction [*praeambulo*] by the organ...or it is performed polyphonically in Latin. After the conclusion of this hymn of praise, the choir boys intone a responsory suitable for the season. Then the officiant chants a collect before the altar. Then follows the Benediction, and the Vespers service concludes with the hymn 'Nun dancket alle Gott' " (*LKS*, pp. 12ff.).

4.

The order of the Sunday Catechism instruction in Leipzig in Bach's time:
"(1) As soon as the hymn 'Nun dancket alle GOtt' after the Collect for Vespers has come to its close, there is a single sounding of the bell as for the hour of prayer.

(2) After that the precentor in the choir begins to sing the hymn chosen by the officiant who leads the instruction. (3) During the last stanza of the hymn indicated, the officiant, accompanied by the sexton, goes to the pulpit as in the prayer service (but without surplice), reads the text (with which the lesson is to deal) together with Luther's explanation in the Catechism, then prays the Lord's Prayer, and (4) immediately proceeds to his place below the pulpit, very briefly recalls [the past instruction], and so begins the present lesson, which he will continue no longer than half an hour and finally close with good wishes and benediction. (5) Again the precentor begins the singing, this time of 'Sey Lob und Ehr mit hohem Preiß' '' (*LKA*, pp. 50—51; *LKS*, pp. 14—15). For the Catechism instruction during the week the same liturgical order obtains in principle.

5.

To provide a practical example of the scope and content of such prayers, we present the ''Prayer Before the Sermon, During the Cantata'':

''I will sing to the Lord, because He has dealt bountifully with me. Here in the tents of the righteous I will pay my vows with singing and praying and tell of the Lord's praise with an eloquent mouth and a loud voice. My glory shall be in singing devoutly to You, O God, and not remaining silent but praising Your power and Your wonders and benefactions. O my Stronghold, I will thank You publicly in the congregation, for You are my protection in distress; my poor song shall praise You and sing of Your mercy forever. Behold, in this assembly of the church I will sing psalms, spiritual songs, and hymns of praise in the spirit, that is, with devotion, and at the same time with understanding, that is, deliberately and with discernment. Indeed, it is our purpose to comfort one another in psalms and so to sing and make melody to You, our God, with all our heart.— Therefore sing to the Lord a new song; sing to the Lord, all the earth; tell of His salvation from day to day. Sing praises, all peoples; sing praises to God; sing praises with understanding. Let your voice of praise and thanksgiving resound; indeed, let us, with united heart and voice and holy rapture singing, proclaim the wonders God has done. Then He will again give power to His thunder, that is, to the Word that is preached, and will again let the sugar-sweet voice of His Gospel, the voice of His Word, be heard among us with a loud report. Come before His countenance with exultation. Sing to God, who is our strength; make a joyful noise to the God of Jacob with melodious voice.—O God, highly praised forever, be pleased to accept our poor though well-meant church hymns, now in this time until we enter the church in heaven with its angelic music and become members of the heavenly Jerusalem, where alleluias will be sung in every nook and corner. There we will sing to You, O God the Father, 'All Glory Be to God on High'; to You, O God the Son, eternal 'Hosanna'; to You, O God the Holy Spirit, 'Holy, Holy, Holy'; to You, O triune God, one Te Deum laudamus after another. There, there, where sweetest hymns your saints forever raise to You, I too shall praise You with a hymn of thanks and offer my Maker a better musical offering. In Christ Jesus. Amen. Amen'' (*LKS*, pp. 83—84).

6.

The Prayer section proceeded according to the following order, an order strictly observed: ''At the conclusion (end of the Sermon) the publishing of the banns takes place for persons who intend to enter the estate of holy matrimony, and then the prayers of the church are read according to the following sequence: (1) The general confession of the church, (2) the general prayer of the church, beginning 'Almighty and eternal God and Father...' (3) another prayer, beginning 'Almighty and righteous God....' When these prayers have been concluded, the following prayers are offered according to the order in which they are found noted on the special bulletin board in the sacristy: (A) Intercessions. (1) For the sick, children, boys, girls, young ladies, young gentlemen, matrons, women (women under the mighty hand of God), men (men under the mighty hand of God); (2) for the afflicted, married couples with dangerous family crosses, persons with temptations; (3) for pregnant women and honorable pregnant women, women in childbirth (in difficult and dangerous deliveries); (4) for marital problems and engagements; (5) for matters known only to God; (6) for matters in litigation; (7) for scholars and other people making journeys; (8) for those who desire prayers for them to God; (9) for favorable weather for the harvest, for rain and sunshine. During this time the people can read the 'Prayer During the Officiant's Reading of the Intercessions.' (B) Thanksgivings. (1) For those whom God has restored to their former health; (2) for wives who have had a successful delivery; (3) after a completed harvest, also for rain and sunshine granted; (4) when God the Lord has graciously averted dangerous thunderstorms, conflagrations, etc.; (5) for those whom God has saved from great misfortunes, floods and fires, dangerous falls, etc., etc. During these prayers one can read the 'Prayer During the Officiant's Reading of the Various Thanksgivings.' (C) Announcements. (1) Of those to be ordained (Note: takes place only on workdays and weekdays); (2) of funerals and the deceased (with the time of the funerals); (3) of the festival days and apostles' days; (4) of the quarterly offerings and those for the university; (5) of the Lenten and Catechism services; (6) of collections for all sorts of things; (7) of charities; (8) of those who have been converted from the Catholic and the Jewish faiths; (9) of poor sinners, together with an intercession; (10) of suicides and violent deaths. During the officiant's reading of the list of the deceased, one can read the 'Prayerful Sigh While the Officiant Announces the List of the Deceased' " (*LKS*, pp. 7ff.). But of course since 3 August 1710 a slight change had been incorporated at the beginning of this comprehensive Prayer section. For since that time "the banns, which up to that time had been read before the general confession of the church and the prayers, for the first time followed these items" (*Bn*, p. 46). Also we should add to this order of events that "at the three high festivals, Easter, Pentecost, and Christmas, no banns were published on the First Festival Day but always only on the Second Festival Day," and likewise "no list of funerals was read on the First Festival Day but only on the Second" (Ro, pp. 1—2, 47, 77).

7.

For better visualization we here present the figures of Communion attendance in the two main churches for the church years 1728/29 and 1742/43 side by side:

	1728/29		1742/43	
	St. Nich.	St. Thom.	St. Nich.	St. Thom.
Advent 1	317	345	316	269
Wed., resp. Thurs.	161	176	289	200
Advent 2	274	210	236	212
Wed., resp. Thurs.	195	177	215	191
Advent 3	260	216	337	212
Wed., resp. Thurs.	171	200	296	157

Advent 4	233	254	96	68
Christmas Day 1	93	98	64	46
Christmas Day 2	132	111	136	95
Christmas Day 3	98	84	70	46
Sun. after Christmas	(omitted)		28	11
New Year's Day	51	50	49	42
Sun. after N. Year	60	44	(omitted)	
Epiphany	10	32	80	51
Epiphany 1	31	46	79	71
Wed., resp. Thurs.	—	—	77	91
Epiphany 2	68	44	130	147
Wed., resp. Thurs.	51	39	143	161
Epiphany 3	82	66	186	148
Wed., resp. Thurs. (1729)	94	115		
Purification (1743)			124	112
Epiphany 4	154	132	340	191
Purification (1729)	108	90		
Wed., resp. Thurs. (1743)			158	162
Epiphany 5	162	184	(omitted)	
Wed., resp. Thurs.	127	171	(omitted)	
Septuagesima	147	159	136	137
Wed., resp. Thurs.	100	87	162	121
Sexagesima	122	123	138	157
Wed., resp. Thurs.	102	97	140	141
Estomihi	153	165	152	112
Wed., resp. Thurs.	99	125	86	126
Invocavit	153	154	98	113
Wed., resp. Thurs.	(omitted; Day of Repentance)		144	174
Reminiscere	185	177	149	175
Wed., resp. Thurs.	147	203	163	264
Oculi	248	253	156	175
Annunciation	125	111		
Wed., resp. Thurs.			246	258
Laetare	225	218	192	193
Wed., resp. Thurs.	161	207		
Annunciation			208	194
Judica	302	298	287	208
Wed., resp. Thurs.	236	218	265	260
Palm Sunday	320	250	296	230
Maundy Thursday	261	349	263	221
Good Friday	226	147	230	166
Easter Day 1	249	223	206	217
Easter Day 2	237	203	286	210
Easter Day 3	127	121	119	113
Quasimodogeniti	197	173	149	140
Wed., resp. Thurs.	149	142	147	171
Misericordias Domini	215	226	156	172
Wed., resp. Thurs.	140	113	132	125
Jubilate	95	60	40	49
Cantate	60	43	49	33

Rogate	86	52	58	51
Ascension	89	71	79	74
Exaudi	130	123	111	109
Wed., resp. Thurs.	77	80	80	122
Pentecost Day 1	137	152	130	125
Pentecost Day 2	141	108	129	138
Pentecost Day 3	57	50	58	59
Trinity Sunday	136	143	106	125
Wed., resp. Thurs.	140	170	128	176
Trinity 1	212	202	162	182
St. John's Day	94	128		
Wed., resp. Thurs.			149	202
Trinity 2	158	143	142	158
Visitation	97	159		
St. John's Day			134	165
Trinity 3	142	168	116	167
Wed., resp. Thurs.	138	167		
Visitation			120	108
Trinity 4	201	216	147	144
Wed., resp. Thurs.	128	152	237	294
Trinity 5	313	223	210	211
Wed., resp. Thurs.	140	173	(omitted;	
			Day of Repentance)	
Trinity 6	319	272	259	212
Wed., resp. Thurs.	(omitted;		254	222
	Day of Repentance			
Trinity 7	421	364	244	261
Wed., resp. Thurs.	254	227	214	320
Trinity 8	276	272	196	282
Wed. resp. Thurs.	191	127	176	233
Trinity 9	279	214	214	269
Wed., resp. Thurs.	149	115	141	143
Trinity 10	170	185	158	187
Wed., resp. Thurs.	171	169	143	171
Trinity 11	216	265	208	260
Wed., resp. Thurs.	163	186	156	189
Trinity 12	265	227	178	239
Wed., resp. Thurs.	120	128	134	170
Trinity 13	182	179	196	169
Wed., resp. Thurs.	114	137	189	163
Trinity 14	187	208	153	169
Wed., resp. Thurs.	135	147	157	158
Trinity 15	193	162	217	195
St. Michael's	89	89		
Wed., resp. Thurs.			156	143
Trinity 16	49	43		
resp. St. Michael's			169	183
Wed., resp. Thurs.	(omitted)		87	51
Trinity 17	45	41	53	38
Trinity 18	94	78	52	50
Wed., resp. Thurs.	74	64	(omitted)	

Trinity 19	164	175	56	73
Wed., resp. Thurs.	106	121	59	78
Trinity 20	209	209	137	146
Reformation	84	70	126	155
Trinity 21	239	206	168	189
Wed., resp. Thurs.	158	168	(omitted; Day of Repentance)	
Trinity 22	312	255	254	268
Wed., resp. Thurs.	(omitted; Day of Repentance)		206	271
Trinity 23	363	298	211	239
Wed., resp. Thurs.	246	207	194	236
Trinity 24	(omitted)		222	250
Wed., resp. Thurs.	(omitted)		185	227

8.

We present two documents by Gerber that express this high regard for Holy Communion observable generally in Saxony in the first half of the 18th century:

"At Holy Communion, when the Consecration takes place, all communicants kneel before the altar, and when they have received the Sacrament, each again kneels at the altar and offers a prayer of thanksgiving for the precious meal of mercy he has tasted. This is all very commendable and a credit to our worship service"(Gb, p. 396).

"Before we approach the Holy Supper, we first make our confession in the confessional, and after receiving the absolution we proceed to the Holy Table of our most bountiful Savior. This most sacred Supper...we celebrate according to the order and institution of our Lord with the greatest devotion and reverence, and during it the servants of God exercise the greatest care so that in the distribution of it neither any of the consecrated bread nor any of the wine is dropped or falls to earth. In the ancient church the priest addressed the communicants as they approached the Holy Supper with this thought-provoking formula: 'Lift up your hearts to God,' a formula even today still in use in various places at Holy Communion. After this, the Lord's Prayer...and the Words of Institution are read or sung....Throughout the reception of Holy Communion the congregation keeps on praising and glorifying the Lord our God with spiritual and devotional hymns and songs of praise. In most localitites also wax candles are lit in this celebration, and the officiants who distribute this most worthy meal are clad in white surplices and beautiful chasubles" (Gb, pp. 754—55).

9.

People are not satisfied with one organ. In many a church there have to be two of them, so that a person is inclined to say: "What is the use of this rubbish?" I am fully aware that he will receive little thanks who makes a remark about unnecessarily large and expensive organs and likewise about church music, for people are so used to these things that they think worship cannot exist without them or that it at least suffers great damage when organs and instrumental music are omitted. Indeed, many people think of these things as no less than an essential or indispensable ingredient of the service, but they are not that at all, for worship consists of praying, singing, praising, and hearing or considering the Word of God, and for that organs and other musical instruments are not necessary, and the first Christian church did not use them for two or three hundred years. (Gb, p. 279)

10.

But when a great deal of money is spent for the works of a large organ and the organists produce so loud and raucous a sound on them in the church that one is in danger of becoming deaf and the singing can be understood little or not at all because of the sound of the pipes, that certainly is an abuse that ought to cease. Many organists make it a habit to let their artistry be heard by playing long preludes, but this is not only an annoyance to hear, but it also is a waste of time, and the service is prolonged. And many an organist and schoolmaster is so headstrong and obstinate that he insists on his own way and will let no one tell him anything. If the pastor is a peaceloving man, he must let this mad fellow have his way and patiently bear the annoyance; but at times there is likely to be a quarrel, or at least a complaint, when the organist or schoolmaster in defiance of the pastor plays a long prelude, and that surely is annoying. It would be better if such a disagreeable nut [*widerwärtiger Kopff*] had no organ to play. (Gb, p. 280)

11.

But even if music kept in modest bounds may achieve a lasting place in the church, especially since blessed Dr. Dannhauer considers it a decorative element of the service [*eine Zierde des Gottesdienstes*], though it is not endorsed by all theologians, it is certainly well known that it is practiced with excess, so that a person may feel inclined to say with Moses, Numbers 16:7, "You have gone too far, sons of Levi," for it often sounds so very worldly and theatrical, like music that would be more suitable for the dance floor or the opera. Least of all does the music in the view of many pious hearts seem proper when sung for the Passion. Fifty or more years ago it was customary for the organ in church to have to be silent on Palm Sunday, and on such days no music was presented, because that was the beginning of the week of suffering and torture. Since then the Passion story, which formerly was sung in such a simple and plain, homely and devotional way, has begun to be presented musically with a variety of instruments and in a most elaborate style, and occasionally a snippet of a Passion hymn is introduced at which the whole congregation sings along, and then the instruments again are heard in great numbers. When this Passion music was performed for the first time in one of our great cities with 12 violins, many oboes and bassoons, and other instruments, many people were shocked and didn't know what to make of it. In a certain court chapel many honored government officials and ladies of noble birth were gathered and sang the first Passion hymn from their books with great devotion, but when this theatrical music commenced, all these people were filled with the greatest amazement, looked at one another, and said, "May God preserve us, children. It's as if a person were at the opera or the theater." But all of the people thoroughly disapproved of the music and registered justified complaints about it. But of course there were also such spirits as take pleasure in such vain aberrations, especially if they are of a sanguine temperament and are given to voluptuousness. Such people defend the long musical presentations in the church to the best of their ability and regard others as cranks and melancholy spirits or ill-humored, just as if they alone possessed the wisdom of Solomon and others had no understanding. Oh, what a blessing it would be in the Christian church if we still had the simplicity of the first Christians in our services so far as preaching, praying, and singing are concerned. Unfortunately we have

264

departed from that by a long way. If some of those first Christians should rise, visit our assemblies, and hear such a roaring organ together with so many instruments, I do not believe that they would recognize us as Christians and their successors. Of course, I am well aware that I will be subjected to much criticism on account of this statement, but I am used to that and have not died from it. It is enough that many sensible people are of the same mind with me. I also know that a number of cantors, too, recognize that the loud, vain musical presentations are unedifying and annoying. (Gb, pp. 283—84) [Cf. *BR*, pp. 229—30, 442, for another translation of most of the quotation—Ed.]

12.

Naturally, church music should be kept within modest bounds, but the cantors take these great liberties for themselves to provide a hearing for their artistry, as they employ as many instruments as ever they can assemble and put on long theatrical musical presentations to suit their own phantasies and pleasures, which would certainly be more suitable for an opera or a theater than for a worship service. And the only cantors who act this way are generally good drinking companions and carnal and lascivious fellows. Therefore all sensible Christian hearts detest their music making, for they know that the great musician is not an instrument of the Holy Spirit. But one is surprised to see how many concessions are made for such people by those who have the rule over them, just as if they were lords and regents to preside over the service. Preachers are told how long they are to preach, and they must be guided by that. In an important city there was a preacher who could never find the conclusion and always preached two hours and even longer. But those who had the supervision over him put a stop to his lengthy sermon several times and finally forbade it altogether under threat of fines. For cantors, however, there is no law so far as I know. But those who are Christian and pious cantors know their place and manage to keep within bounds. (Gb, p. 225)

13.

Just let someone tell me what such prayers are for. To speak a prayer as one enters the church is right, and one can do that. But what are the rest of the prayers for? When the Kyrie is sung, we should sing along and not pray by ourselves alone. Yet in the cities the Kyrie is sung polyphonically with instruments. When I in my boyhood went to school in the town of Borna, I remember that there the Kyrie was presented polyphonically every Sunday with violins, two trombones, and one cornet.... Because of this din of the instruments the voices of the singers could be heard only imperfectly or not at all, and for that reason many people took refuge in their prayer books. But what kind of devotion can you expect when the ears are filled with such a loud sound of instruments and various voices? And what is music for if no one wants to listen to it? (Gb, pp. 243—44)

14.

Characteristic of Rosenmüller's conception of confession are the following statements, which at the same time give some insight into the practice of private confession:

"Private confession in the strictest sense, in which each penitent must recite his confession and the preacher must speak the absolution to each individually, brings with it great inconvenience and basically has no advantage.... For the preacher it is

265

veritable torture when he must spend most of the hours of the day on which he should study his Sunday sermon in hearing confession and pronouncing the absolution and thus must keep on speaking until he is practically ready to faint. Let us say he has a hundred or even more penitents. Either he must repeat the same thing over and over 30 or 50 times or, if he wants to say something different to each one, he will in the end really say nothing at all, unless he is a genius [*divinum ingenium*].... *General confession* has a great advantage over the private confession.... The preacher can more carefully prepare himself for an edifying and moving address. Each penitent has the advantage of hearing a complete and edifying message, whereas in the few minutes that can be allotted to the private confession practically nothing is said. The solemnity of the rite and the exhortations and admonitions of the preacher addressed to an entire assembly make more of an impression and are accepted more willingly than the personal reproofs in the confessional. Many people ... who heretofore were either kept from Holy Communion entirely by the irksome procedures of private confession or at least turned up only very seldom, would attend more diligently if general Confession were allowed for them'' (Rm, pp. 165ff.).

Notes

Editor's Introduction

1. For a review of much of the literature, see W. E. Buszin, "Lutheran Theology as Reflected in the Life and Works of J. S. Bach," *Concordia Theological Monthly* 21 (December 1950): 896—923.
2. See *BJ*, 1973, 99.
3. R. Nestle, "Das Bachschrifttum 1968—1972," *BJ*, 1976, 95— 161, and "Das Bachschrifttum 1873—1977," *BJ*, 1980, 87—145; and W. Blankenburg, "Die Bachforschung seit etwa 1965: Ergebnisse— Probleme—Aufgaben," *Acta Musicologica* 50 (1978): 93—154; ibid. 54 (1982): 162—207; and ibid. 55 (1983): 1—58.
4. W. Emery, C. Wolff, and N. Temperley, *The New Grove Dictionary of Music and Musicians* 1 (London, 1980): 785—840 (also in *The New Grove Bach Family* [London, 1983], pp. 44—237); and W. Blankenburg, *Theologische Realenzyklopädie* 5 (Berlin and New York, 1976): 90—94.
5. W. E. Buszin, "The Chorale in the Baroque era and J. S. Bach's Contribution to It," *Studies in Eighteenth-Century Music: A Tribute to Karl Gieringer on His Seventieth Birthday*, ed. H. C. Robbins Landon (London, 1970), pp. 108—16; J. Tolonen, *Protestanttinen Koraali ja Bachin fuugateemat teoksessa Das Wohltemperierte Klavier I* (Helsinki, 1971); M. Petzoldt, "Die theologische Bedeutung der Choräle in Bachs Matthäus-Passion," *MuK* 53 (1983): 53—63; and R. Ganzhorn-Burkhardt, "Zur Bedeutung der Choräle in Bachs Johannespassion," ibid., 64—73.
6. P. Brainard, "Bach's Parody Procedure and the St. Matthew Passion," *Journal of the American Musicological Society* 22 (1969): 241—60; and R. L. Marshall, *The Compositional Process of J. S. Bach: A Study of the Autograph Scores of the Vocal Works* (2 vols.; Princeton, 1972).
7. J. Birke, *Christian Wolffs Metaphysik und die zeitgenössische Literatur- und Musiktheorie: Gotsched, Scheibe, Mizler* (Berlin, 1966); K. Geiringer, "Der Einfluß der Aufklärung auf J. S. Bachs kunstlerisches Denken," *Studia Musicologica* 2 (1969): 201—06; M. Petzoldt, "Zwischen Orthodoxie, Pietismus und Aufklärung: Überlegungen zum theologiegeschichtlichen Kontext Johann Sebastian Bach," in R. Szeskus, ed., *Bach-Studien 7*: Johann Sebastian Bach und die Aufklärung (Leipzig, 1982), pp. 66—108; and the latter work as a whole.
8. P. S. Minear, "J. S. Bach and J. A. Ernesti: A Case Study in Exegetical and Theological Conflict," *Our Common History as Christians: Essays in Honor of Albert C. Outler*, ed. J. Deschner, L. T. Howe, and K. Penzel (New York, 1975), pp. 131— 55; see also R. M. Stevenson, "Bach's Quarrel with the Rector of St. Thomas School," *Patterns of Protestant Church Music* (Durham, NC, 1953), pp. 67—77.
9. W. Blankenburg, "Johann Sebastian Bach," *Orthodoxie und Pietismus*, ed. M. Greschat (Stuttgart, 1982), pp. 301—15; W. Zeller, "Vom Abbild zum Sinnbild—J. S. Bach und das Symbol," *Theologie und Frömmigkeit: Gesammelte Aufsätze*, ed. B. Jaspert, 1 (Marburg, 1971): 165—77; H. L. Holborn, "Bach and Pietism: The Relationship of the Church Music of Johann Sebastian Bach to Eighteenth-Century Lutheran Or-

thodoxy and Pietism'' (doctoral diss., School of Theology at Claremont, 1976); U. Siegele, *Bachs theologischer Formbegriff und das Duett F-Dur* (Stuttgart, 1978), and ''Bachs Ort in Orthodoxie und Aufklärung,'' *MuK* 51 (1981): 3—14; U. Meyer, *J. S. Bach als theonome Kunst* (Wiesbaden, 1979); L. Prautzsch, *Vor Deinen Thron tret ich hiermit: Figuren und Symbol in den letzten Werken Johann Sebastian Bachs* (Stuttgart, 1980); R. A. Leaver, ''Bach's *Clavierübung III*: Some Historical and Theological Considerations,'' *The Organ Yearbook* 6 (1975): 17—32; R. A. Leaver, ''Number Associations in the Structure of Bach's *Credo, BWV 232*,'' *Bach: The Quarterly Journal of the Riemenschneider Bach Institute* (hereafter cited as *Bach*), 7, no. 3 (1976): 17—24; R. A. Leaver, ''Bach und die Lutherschriften seiner Bibliothek,'' *BJ*, 1976, 124—32 (expanded English version in *Bach* 9, no. 3 [1978]: 9—12, 25—32); R. A. Leaver, *Music as Preaching: Bach, Passions, and Music in Worship* (Oxford, 1982); G. Stiller, ''Beicht- und Abendmahlsgang Johann Sebastian Bachs im Lichte der Familiengendenktage des Thomaskantors,'' *MuK* 43 (1973): 182—86; G. Stiller, ''Johann Sebastian Bach und Johann Christoph Gottsched—eine beachtliche Gemeinsamkeit,'' *MuK* 46 (1976): 166—72; G. Stiller, ''Bachkantate und liturgische Tradition,'' *Bachfestbuch* (Berlin, 1976), pp. 17—29.

10. G. Herz, ''Toward a New Image of Bach,'' *Bach* 1, no. 4 (1970): 9—27; ibid. 2, no. 1 (1971): 7—28.

11. C. Trautmann, '' 'Calovii Schrifften 3. Bände' aus Johann Sebastian Bachs Nachlaß and ihre Bedeutung für das Bild des lutherischen Kantors Bach,'' *MuK* 39 (1969): 145—60 (abridged English translation by H. C. Oswald in *Concordia Theological Monthly* 42 [1971]: 88—99); R. A. Leaver, ''The Calov Bible from Bach's Library,'' *Bach* 7, no. 4 (1976): 16—22; see also the forthcoming book edited by R. A. Leaver.

12. Herz, ''New Image,'' pp. 26—27: ''Bach's relation to his professional service as organist and cantor was indeed a relation of the heart. In contrast to Blume, we may now state that there is no split between Bach, the man, and Bach, the church musician.''

13. F. Blume, *Two Centuries of Bach: An Account of Changing Taste*, trans. S. Godman (London, 1950), p. 84.

14. Cf. p. 20.

15. C. S. Terry, *John. Seb. Bach: Cantata Texts Sacred and Secular, with a Reconstruction of the Leipzig Liturgy of His Period* (London, 1926).

16. Cf. p. 34.

17. Terry, *Cantata Texts*, p. ix. These handwritten transcripts are to be found with the rest of his library, which Terry bequeathed to The Royal College of Music, London.

18. Ibid.

19. Ibid., pp. ix, 5.

20. Quoted in R. D. Preus, *The Theology of Post-Reformation Lutheranism: A Study of Theological Prolegomena* (St. Louis, 1970), pp. 199—200, 197—98.

21. Ibid., pp. 406—07.

22. Vols. 2, 9, 13—14, 23—24.

23. Vols. 6, 10—11, 15—20, 25, 28.

24. See note 11 above.

Author's Preface

1. W. Blankenburg, ''Theologische und geistesgeschichtliche Probleme der gegenwärtigen Bachforschung,'' *Theologische Literaturzeitung* 78 (1953): 396.

2. ''Individualismus und Gemeindebewußtsein in Johann Sebastian Bachs Passionen,'' *Archiv für Reformationsgeschichte* 41 (1948): 132—54.

3. ''Johann Sebastian Bach und der Gottesdienst seiner Zeit,'' *MuK* 20 (1950): 145—58; also in *ML*, pp. 205—20.

4. We list the following essays by this author: (a) ''Johann Sebastian Bach und die Aufklärung,'' *BG*, pp. 25—34; (b) ''Bach—geistlich und weltlich,'' *MuK* 20 (1950): 36—46; (c) ''Das Parodieverfahren im Weihnachtsoratorium Johann Sebastian Bachs,'' *WF*, pp. 493—506.

5. ''Bachs Kantaten als Auslegung des Wortes Gottes,'' *MuK* 30 (1960): 81—94.

6. *Johann Sebastian Bach und die lutherische Mystik*, inaugural dissertation presented to the theological faculty of Erlangen University, 1958.
7. *Die Bedeutung der alttestamentlichen Historien in Johann Sebastian Bachs Kantaten* (Tübingen, 1960).
8. In 1965 Walter Blankenburg offered an excellent report on the literature, together with all problems under discussion, in his essay, "Zwölf Jahre Bachforschung," *Acta Musicologica* 37 (1965): 95—158.

The Problem

1. Printed, for example, in the *Fest- und Programmbuch* of the third German Bach festival in Eisenach, 1907, p. 8. This goal of the Neue Bach-Gesellschaft has been reprinted also in the printed programs of subsequent Bach festivals.
2. H. Keller, "Johann Sebastian Bach und die Säkularisation der Kirchenmusik," *Universitas: Zeitschrift für Wissenschaft, Kunst und Literatur* 2 (1947): 1425—34.
3. G. Ramin, "Johann Sebastian Bachs Kantaten in heutiger Sicht," *Universitas* 3 (1948): 1159—63.
4. See the summary of this essay under the title "Die kirchliche Bedeutung der Bachschen Musik," *Kongreßbericht Lüneburg 1950* (Kassel and Basel, 1950), pp. 107-11.

A. Liturgical Life in Leipzig
During the First Half of the 18th Century

1. So, for example, W. von Loewenich, *Die Geschichte der Kirche* (Witten, 1954), p. 321.
2. Cf. F. Hamel, *Johann Sebastian Bach: Geistige Welt* (Göttingen, 1951), pp. 126—27.
3. G. Rietschel, *Lehrbuch der Liturgik*, 2d, newly revised edition by P. Graff, 1 (Göttingen, 1951): 385.
4. C. Mahrenholz, "Johann Sebastian Bach und der Gottesdienst seiner Zeit," *ML*, p. 5.
5. Cf. O. Kirn, *Die Leipziger Theologische Fakultät in fünf Jahrhunderten* (Leipzig, 1909), p. 143.
6. Ibid., pp. 147ff.
7. Ibid., pp. 145—146.
8. Ibid.
9. Hamel, p. 116.

1. Description of Liturgical Life in Leipzig

10. Cf. Spi, 2:263ff.
11. Cf. Sch*ML*, pp. 24ff., 103—04.
12. Cf. C. S. Terry, *Joh. Seb. Bach: Cantata Texts, Sacred and Secular* (London, 1926). Incomprehensibly, in his references to hymns he constantly cites the *Unverfälschter Liedersegen: Gesangbuch für Kirchen, Schulen und Häuser* (Berlin, 1851 [!]), while the Dresden hymnbook used in Leipzig in the time of Johann Sebastian Bach is not utilized at all in this study. In listing the graduals, Terry often appeals to the work of Paul Graff (*Geschichte der Auflösung der alten gottesdienstlichen Formen in der evangelischen Kirche Deutschlands bis zum Eintritt der Aufklärung und des Rationalismus* [Göttingen, 1921]), which presents the *de tempore* hymn plan of that time, although this by no means proves that these selections were sung on the respective Sundays as gradual hymns also in Leipzig. The handwritten notations of the St. Thomas sexton, Rost, were later kept current, supplemented, and corrected down to the 19th century, so that in the use of this source one must be careful to observe whether the citation really applies to the time of Johann Sebastian Bach. Terry often disregarded this state of affairs, e.g., on pages 206, 208, and 512 of his book. There is not one word that the reported citations with regard to the announcements on Maundy Thursday and Good Friday, as well as the hymns to be sung during Communion on the Festival of the Reformation, were written by a successor of Sexton Rost.
13. This theme will be dealt with in a second part, which is already in manuscript.

269

a) The Sources

14. I owe this information to Hans-Joachim Schulze of the Bach-Archiv in Leipzig.
15. *BR*, p. 114.
16. Cf. W. Neumann, "Zur Frage der Gesangbücher Johann Sebastian Bachs," *BJ*, 1956, 114.
17. In spite of having many things in common, the individual cities had their own peculiarities, as a comparison between the Leipzig and the Dresden hymn traditions shows.
18. Only a second edition, 1730, is available, but it was probably unchanged over against the first edition, 1729. Not until 1734 was there an edition revised and enlarged by Carl Gottlob Hoffmann, deacon at St. Nicholas.
19. Terry gained this information merely by a cursory comparison of tables of contents, and a number of hymn verses in Bach's cantatas could not have been taken from this Leipzig hymnbook of 1729 because of considerably revised texts (cf. Werner Neumann's objection, "Gesangbücher," p. 122). But this does not alter the fact that those hymns were part of the familiar store in Leipzig.
20. In this source, strictly speaking, we are dealing with the forerunner of the *Leipziger Addreßbuch*, so titled only since 1823. The oldest city directory, called *Das ietz lebende Leipzig*, is from the year 1701 (cf. E. Kroker, *Aufsätze zur Stadtgeschichte und Reformationsgeschichte* [Leipzig, 1929], p. 135). The titles of the annual editions during Bach's stay in Leipzig are not uniform (cf. the abbreviations of frequently cited sources and bibliography for listed editions).

b) The Intensification of Liturgical Life at the Beginning of the Century

21. Graff, p. 16.
22. Rietschel, p. 385.
23. Cf. Lh, pp. 254—55. For additional comparison we mention also the population in 1789, which was 32,144, and that of 1797, which was 31,847.
24. Cf. P. Kaiser, "Die Geschichte der Matthäikirche," *Unsere Matthäikirche in 4 Jahrhunderten, 1494—1894* (Leipzig, 1894), p. 16.
25. Cf. the summary of the documents in Spi, 3:303—04 (given in full in the original German edition, 2:853ff.), as well as A. Schering, *Musikgeschichte Leipzigs* 2 (Leipzig, 1926): 195ff.
26. In detail in Lh, pp. 633—46.
27. Cf. B. Hartung, *Die alte und die neue Peterskirche in Leipzig* (Leipzig, 1885), p. 10.
28. Ibid., pp. 9ff. The *Catecheticum* was continued until 1876.
29. Cf. *Bn*, pp. 41—42.
30. This becomes clear when the relevant report in Lh, pp. 412ff., is compared. Accordingly only the following deviations must be recorded: The Thursday Catechism instruction at St. Peter had meanwhile been transferred to Tuesday at 2:00 p.m., and the Sunday instruction at St. George was shifted to one hour later. Otherwise Leonhardi says nothing about Catechism instruction at St. James.

c) Sunday Services

31. The word "beforehand" refers to the main service immediately following.
32. The same time span is indicated as early as 1694: The service "lasts until ten or eleven o'clock and even beyond, since there are many communicants" (*LKA*, p. 42). Even at the end of the 18th century the duration of the main service in New Church is given as three hours (Lh, p. 420).
33. Cf. Ro, pp. 1, 26, 30 (with regard to the three high festivals), as well as Ro, pp. 1, 3, 7, 14—15, 32, 34—36, 46 (with regard to the special festivals occurring on weekdays).
34. Cf. Hartung, pp. 9—10. Not until 1812 was "the petition of the catechists to interrupt the sequence on festival days granted" (p. 10).
35. Also E. H. Albrecht, *Sächsische evangelisch-luther'sche Kirchen- und*

Predigergeschichte von ihrem Ursprunge an bis auf gegenwärtige Zeiten (Leipzig, 1799), presents an exact overview of the worship life in Leipzig at the end of the 18th century (pp. 30ff.). This presentation, which is largely in verbatim agreement with the report in Lh, confirms the state of affairs that throughout the 18th century nothing was changed in the worship life of the city as far as the numerical wealth of services and devotions is concerned.

d) Weekday Services

36. Sicul lists the beginning of this service as well as the other weekly early services at St. Nicholas and St. Thomas as at 6:45. It was probably done in this way, that, as Lh still attests, the "bells were rung at 6:30," and the service proper was begun at 6:45 (Lh, pp. 413, 417).
37. Sicul calls this devotional service an *Examen Biblicum* (Sc*NA*, p. 580).
38. The starting time for this devotion changed according to the season of the year, from 5:00 to 4:00 p.m. and in winter even to 3:00 p.m. (cf. LA 1723, p. 83; Sc*NA*, p. 588).
39. Sicul calls this devotional service a "catechization" (Sc*NA*, p. 583).
40. The starting time for this service appears to have been changed occasionally. Whereas LA 1723 mentions only the time of 3:00 p.m., Sicul can report a starting time of two and of three (Sc*NA*, pp. 584, 587).
41. This devotional service is also called the prayer service, as is also the devotion on Tuesday, 5:00 p.m., at St. George (cf. LA 1723, p. 83). Here, too, the starting time for this devotion changed from 5:00 to 4:00 and 3:00 p.m. according to the time of year.

e) The Church Year

42. In the cantata BWV 64, performed on the third Christmas day 1723, "the thought of the evangelist John, the apostle of love, dominates the whole work," and thus this day was observed as St. John's Day (F. Smend, *Johann Sebastian Bach: Kirchen-Kantaten* 5 [Berlin, 1950]: 46). This would mean that in a given year the second and third Christmas days were observed respectively as St. Stephen's Day and St. John's Day, and in the following year all three days were observed as Christmas festival days. This is supported by the fact that numbers 2 and 3 of the *Christmas Oratorio*, performed at Christmas 1734, contain no reference to St. Stephen's Day or St. John's Day, because in this year the second and third festival days were in the rotation not observed as St. Stephen's or St. John's Day. For the chronology of Bach's cantatas, cf. A. Dürr, *Zur Chronologie der Leipziger Vokalwerke J. S. Bachs* (2d ed.; Kassel, 1976).
43. Also *LKS* confirms this usage and adds expressly that this was done in all three chief churches (*LKS*, p. 29—here New Church is improperly counted as a chief church!). With regard to the provision for the ringing of the bells it should be said that on the three high festivals the first festival day was always inaugurated with the ringing of bells both at 4:00 a.m. and at 6:00 a.m., and all the bells were rung (Ro, pp. 26, 30, 47); furthermore, that on all special festival days of the church year, including the First Sunday in Advent and Palm Sunday, the day was inaugurated with the ringing of bells at 6:00 a.m., and on all ordinary Sundays, in which the third days of the high festivals, apostles' days, and even Maundy Thursday were included, the bells were customarily rung at 6:30 (cf. Ro, pp. 3, 15, 17, 21, 23, 27, 32, 36, 44, 49).
44. We learn this quite incidentally from Rost (Ro, p. 36). According to his report, from 1715 on the bells were always "rung for confession" at eight o'clock the previous day. This practice was otherwise customary on Saturdays and days preceding Communion services.
45. Cf. Graff, p. 127.
46. Cf. *Hoch-Fürstliches-Sachsen-Weißenfelsisches Vollständiges Gesang- und Kirchenbuch*, 1714, which reports the orders of worship for the following apostles' days: The apostle Thomas (21 December), Conversion of the apostle Paul (25 January), the apostle Matthias (24 February, or in a leap year 25 February), the apostles Philip and James (1 May), the apostles Peter and Paul (29 June), the apostle James the Elder (25 July), the

271

apostle Bartholomew (24 August), the apostle and evangelist Matthew (21 September), and the apostles Simon and Jude (28 October).

47. Cf. the facsimile reprint of this document in NBA, I/1:vi; see also *BD* 1:248.

f) The Clergy

48. Cf. the roster, by name, of the "Saturday-preachers" in *ChV*, pp. 15ff., 37ff. This schedule, prepared in the middle of the 18th century and continued to 1864, lists in chronological sequence all of the clergymen of the city since the time of the Reformation, together with important details of their professional careers. Unless otherwise noted, also the subsequent personal references come from this list.

49. Cf. Albrecht, pp. 94—95. [Deyling was appointed pastor of St. Nicholas in April 1721 and four months later, on 13 August, he was invested as superintendent minister in Leipzig by Dr. Heinrich Pipping, Oberhofprediger in Dresden (cf. K. G. Dietmann, *Die gesamte der ungeänderten Augsp. Confession zugethane Priesterschaft in dem Churfürstenthum Sachsen und denen einverleibten Landen* I/2 [Dresden and Leipzig, 1753]: 31). A cantata, presumably by Johann Kuhnau, Bach's predecessor in Leipzig, was performed at this investiture: *Erschallt, Gott zu loben, ihr freudigen Lieder.* Neither score nor parts are extant, but copies of the printed text are known: *Texte Der Kirchen-Music zu S. Nicolai, in Leipzig, Bey der Den XIII. Augusti MDCCXXI. Angestellten Investitur Des Herrn Superintendentens daselbst, Seiner Magnificenz Herrn D. Salomon Deylings* (Leipzig, 1721).—Ed.]

50. Cf. F. Hudson in NBA, *KB* I/33:12ff., where a list, complete with names and dates of all "full bridal masses" conducted at St. Thomas in the years 1723 to 1750, is given.

51. This statement applies in principle also to the burials to be performed. Concerning the university church, which held a unique place in the worship life of the city, it is distinctly emphasized: "Also in this church funeral services are held by the priests of the ministerium of the city" (LA 1723, p. 32). The number of the "deceased" between 1723 and 1730 totaled in successive years 928, 961, 807, 1,065, 1,014, 1,269, 1,194, and 1,127 (cf. Lh, p. 262).

g) The Church Music

52. Cf. A. Werner, *Vier Jahrhunderte im Dienste der Kirchenmusik* (Leipzig, 1933), p. 122.

53. Cf. F. W. Riedel, "Kuhnau," *MGG* 7 (1958): 1878ff.

54. Cf. besides Bach's *Kurtzer, iedoch höchstnöthiger Entwurff einer wohlbestallten Kirchen Music (BD* 1:60ff.; *BR*, pp. 120ff.) also Sch*BLKM*, pp. 18ff.; Spi, 2:239ff.

55. Cf. facsimile of the libretto in NBA, *KB* II/6:156.

56. Cf. the following booklets of librettos: (1) *Texte zur Leipziger Kirchen-Music, Auf das Heil. Oster-Fest, Und die beyden Nachfolgenden Sonntage, Anno 1731* (containing the text for cantatas BWV 31, 66, 134, 42, 112); (2) *Texte zur Leipziger Kirchen-Music, Auf die Heiligen Pfingst-Feyertage, Und das Fest Der H. H. Dreyfaltigkeit, Anno 1731* (containing the text for cantatas BWV 172, 173, 184, 194); (3) *Oratorium, welches die heilige Weyhnacht über in beyden Haupt-Kirchen zu Leipzig musiciret wurde, Anno 1734* (containing the text of the six cantatas of the *Christmas Oratorio,* BWV 248). See facsimiles in N*VT*, pp. 438—55.

57. Cf. facsimile in NBA, I/1:vi; see also *BD* 1:248.

58. Cf. Dürr, pp. 42, 57ff.

59. See note 57 above.

60. Cf. Dürr, p. 63.

61. Cf. H. Preuß, *Die Geschichte der Abendmahlsfrömmigkeit in Zeugnissen und Berichten* (Gütersloh, 1949), p. 19.

62. Cf. B. F. Richter, "Über die Schicksale der der Thomasschule zu Leipzig angehörenden Kantaten Johann Sebastian Bachs," *BJ*, 1906, 56.

63. Cf. Dürr, p. 75.

64. The numbers in parentheses refer to the movements of the respective cantatas.

65. Sch*BLKM*, pp. 10—11; cf. also Sch*ML*, p. 95.

66. Cf. Spi, 3:39ff.
67. Cf. F. Smend in NBA, *KB* II/1:186—87.
68. Cf. Spi, 2:268. For other reasons Alfred Dürr, too, feels that the presentation of the second section of this cantata in the service on the Festival of the Trinity in 1731, perhaps *sub communione*, is not precluded (Dürr, p. 104). In any case, Bach had to present some *Music* during Communion on this Sunday, for it was considered a festival day.
69. Sch*ML*, pp. 647ff.
70. Cf. comments by Bach and Kuhnau, reprinted in Spi, 2:220; and German edition, 2:864, which is not translated in the English edition.
71. Sch*BLKM*, p. 121.
72. Cf. Sch*BLKM*, p. 122.
73. Cf. Sch*BLKM*, p. 122.
74. Cf. Spi, 2:266—67.
75. Cf. Christhard Mahrenholz' preface to the outline of *Agende für evangelisch-lutherische Kirchen und Gemeinden*, ed. Lutheran Liturgical Conference of Germany and Liturgical Commission of the United Ev. Luth. Church of Germany, I/1 (Berlin, 1951): 45.
76. Cf. Sch*ML*, p. 216.
77. C. Mahrenholz, "Orgel und Liturgie," *ML*, pp. 16, 27.
78. Cf. besides Bach's notes on the liturgy for the first Sunday in Advent (cf. note 57 above) and the various orders of service for the three days of the Reformation anniversary of 1730, which indeed do not always mention the entry of the organ (Sch*JL*, pp. 117—24), primarily Rost, who furnishes a wealth of pertinent data (Ro, pp. 26ff., 30, 32, 47, et al.). Of some significance is his note concerning the first Good Friday Vesper service at St. Paul, of which he reports, among other things: "Musical instruments besides the organ were played during the German hymns" (Ro, p. 25).
79. Cf. Spi, 3:29.
80. Sch*BLKM*, p. 13.
81. Cf. F. Hudson in NBA, *KB* I/33:11ff., or also the libretto of the five cantatas in N*VT*, pp. 174ff.
82. Cf. K. Ameln in NBA, *KB* III/1:13ff., 181ff. Cantata BWV 157 was originally composed for a service of mourning (cf. Dürr, p. 95). In general, with reference to the whole subject see Sch*BLKM*, p. 12; Sch*ML*, pp. 51ff.
83. Sch*ML*, p. 54. Cf. further details in Sch*BLKM*, pp. 13ff.

2. An Evaluation of Liturgical Life in Leipzig

a) Worship and Piety

1. We must leave unresolved the question whether or not it is completely justified to characterize Gerber as a Pietist, as do both P. Graff (*Geschichte der Auflösung der alten gottesdienstlichen Formen in der evangelischen Kirche Deutschlands bis zum Eintritt der Aufklärung und des Rationalismus* [Göttingen, 1921], p. 81) and F. Smend (*Bach in Köthen* [Berlin, 1951], p. 137). Although Gerber was obviously "counted among the Pietists by his contemporaries, and without question correctly too" (Smend, p. 137), Graff already recognized the fact that Gerber's views regarding worship were "not implicitly those of Pietism." In his statements and views in *Historie der Kirchen-Ceremonien in Sachsen* Gerber again and again appealed to Philipp Jakob Spener, who was considered the father of Pietism but in spite of that presumably always held to Lutheran theology and to the Lutheran Church.
2. Cf. Leu*Ref*, pp. 59—60, 73, 83ff., 102, 105, 113, 115, 123—24, etc.
3. Cf. Leu*Ref*, pp. 42, 45—61.
4. Cf. Leu*Gsch*, pp. 9—10.
5. Cf. Leu*Gsch*, pp. 94, 96.
6. H. Kretzschmar, *Bachkolleg: Vorlesungen über J. S. Bach* (Leipzig, 1922), p. 34. H. Besch, *Johann Sebastian Bach: Frömmigkeit und Glaube* (Kassel and Basel, 1950), pp. 177ff., shows how often this view was repeated or basically maintained in somewhat varied form.

7. Thus possibly still in F. Hamel, *Johann Sebastian Bach: Geistige Welt* (Göttingen, 1951), p. 137, who, like others before, has come to this conclusion solely on the basis of the so-called "pietistic" cantata texts credited to the elder Weiß.
8. E. H. Albrecht, *Sächsische evangelisch-luther'sche Kirchen-und Predigergeschichte von ihrem Ursprunge an bis auf gegenwärtige Zeiten* (Leipzig, 1799), p. 323.
9. Cf. Leu*Gsch*, pp. 58, 64, 89—90, 94, 102.
10. Leu*Ref*, p. 134.
11. Ibid., p. 133.
12. Cf. Leu*Gsch*, pp. 7ff.; also Leu*Ref*, p. 63. Leube correctly calls attention to the fact that the large number of 17th-century writings expressing lamentation and calling for repentance are in no small degree attributable to the catastrophes of the Thirty Years' War and its consequences, which were looked upon as the vengeance of God. Yet one may "never assume that the number of lamentations is directly proportionate to the frequency and seriousness of the corruption in the Lutheran Church" (Leu*Ref*, pp. 151—52). Cf. in general the very reasonable statements of Leube about the fact that such a gloomy picture of these conditions could develop in the age of Lutheran orthodoxy (Leu*Ref*, pp. 140ff.).
13. Hamel, pp. 93—94.
14. Stated repeatedly in Hamel, pp. 96, 101, 108, 117. [Pfeiffer was Bach's *second* favorite author after Luther; see R. A. Leaver, *Bachs theologische Bibliothek* (Stuttgart, 1983), p. 25 and Nos. 14—18, 37—39.—Ed.]
15. Leu*Gsch*, pp. 15, 19—20.
16. Cited in accordance with Leu*Ref*, p. 56.
17. Cf. Leu*Gsch*, p. 11.
18. *BD* 2:200.
19. J. von Walter, *Die Geschichte des Christentums* II/2 (Gütersloh, 1950): 652.
20. Cf. also what Leube writes about Heinrich Höpfner, Johann Hülsemann, Friedrich Rappolt, Johann Höpner, Johann Benedikt Carpzov II, Johann Adam Scherzer, Johann Olearius, Martin Geier, and Christian Lange (Leu*Ref*, pp. 42, 56—63).
21. Cf. Leu*Gsch*, pp. 103ff.
22. Leu*Gsch*, p. 13.
23. Besch, p. 220.
24. Cf. Hamel, pp. 94—111. [Cf. also Leaver, passim—Ed.]
25. Hamel, p. 103.
26. Cf. Graff, p. 114.
27. Leu*Ref*, p. 141.
28. Rm, p. 179; cf. also especially pp. 125—82. Further details at the end of this chapter.
29. F. Kalb, *Theology of Worship in 17th-Century Lutheranism*, tr. H. P. A. Hamann (St. Louis, 1965), pp. xi, 187.

b) Worship and Liturgical Order

30. Spi, 2:264.
31. Cf. H. Goltzen, "Der tägliche Gottesdienst," *L* 3:193ff.
32. Cf. ibid., p. 192.
33. Ibid., pp. 193, 197.
34. Cf. ibid., p. 202.
35. Cf. ibid.
36. E. Weismann, "Der Predigtgottesdienst und die verwandten Formen," *L* 3:85—86.
37. Graff, p. 317.
38. Cf. ibid.
39. Kalb, p. 187.
40. In the conjecture here presented, we base our argument on the supposition that Cantata BWV 61, composed already in Weimar in 1714, was first performed in Leipzig on the First Sunday in Advent, 28 November 1723. Werner Neumann has already labeled as highly unlikely a performance of this cantata, assumed frequently years ago, as taking place in Leipzig as early as 1722 (in connection with Bach's candidacy for the cantorship at St. Thomas). Cf. NBA, *KB* I/1:11. Our supposition gains support especially from the

consideration that in Leipzig no other Sunday in the church year had such a conflicting significance as this Advent Sunday did, which on the one hand was counted among the special festivals but on the other did not show that special hallmark of the festival ser-vices—the Latin Preface. This inconsistency in the celebration of this Sunday (cf. the discussion on p. 58) may well have prompted Bach's noting down the liturgy of the ser-vice, especially since he had up to that time in Leipzig experienced only ordinary Sunday services or such as were expressly festival services. For the same reason also the second sketch of the liturgy for this Sunday on the back of the title page of Cantata BWV 62 may have been made, particularly if we are to accept Neumann's conjecture that Bach, because of a trip to Dresden, had to entrust the second performance of this cantata on the First Sunday in Advent 1736 to a substitute (cf. NBA, KB I/1:68), who would of course have to be provided with specific directions concerning the course of the service on that day.

41. C. Mahrenholz, *Agende für evangelisch-lutherische Kirchen und Gemeinden,* Preface, I/1 (Berlin, 1951): 13, 15.
42. O. Brodde, "Evangelische Choralkunde," *L* 4:377.
43. F. Smend, *Joh. Seb. Bach: Kirchen-Kantaten* (Berlin, 1950), part 1, p. 8.
44. Cf. Graff, pp. 157—58.
45. For the entire subject, especially for the musical presentation of the Gloria, cf. the discus-sion on pp. 89—90; also in the same place the determination that the occurrence side by side of "Et in terra pax" and the German Gloria hymn in one and the same service in Leipzig is confirmed only for Lent and the apostles' days. This suggests that the "Et in terra pax" was chanted in this season and on these days. The occurrence side by side of a concerted arrangement of "Et in terra pax" and the German Gloria hymn in one and the same service, as this is re-recorded in the *Hoch-Fürstliches Sachsen-Weißenfelsisches Vollständiges Gesang- und Kirchenbuch* (cf. *L* 4:631), is unknown in the Leipzig sources.
46. C. S. Terry, *J. S. Bach: Cantata Texts, Sacred and Secular* (London, 1926), p. 34.
47. M. Luther, *The German Mass and Order of Service,* Preface, trans. A. Steimle and U. S. Leupold; ed. Helmut T. Lehmann, *Luther's Works,* American Edition, 53 (Philadelphia, 1965): 63.
48. Cf. *ML,* p. 157 (especially Luther's words quoted from "Vermahnung zum Sakrament").
49. Cf. Graff, p. 158.
50. So referred to by C. Mahrenholz, *Agende* I/1:34.
51. R. Stählin, "Die Geschichte des christlichen Gottesdienstes," *L* 1:55.
52. Cf. the various lectionary tones for both readings in the Agenda of 1712 (*Ag*, pp. 100ff.). In Leipzig no attacks were made on the old traditional stock and store of pericopes before the beginning of the 19th century. At the time of Bach signs of a breakup in this matter were already observable in many places. Cf. Graff, pp. 161ff.
53. Compare the study by C. Bunners, *Kirchenmusik und Seelenmusik* (Berlin, 1956).
54. O. Söhngen, "Theologische Grundlagen der Kirchenmusik," *L* 4:138. Söhngen correctly emphasizes that "in looking over the church music map of Germany, one cannot overlook the fact that the most fruitful areas lie in Silesia, Saxony, Thuringia, Franconia, and northern Germany" (p. 137), where the *Lutheran* Reformation was especially active and where a liturgical richness of the services was characteristic for a long time.
55. K. F. Müller, "Das Ordinarium Missae," *L* 2:34. For the whole subject, cf. Graff, pp. 164ff.
56. Cf. the facsimile in Smend, *Kirchen-Kantaten,* p. 9. In the repeated outline of the liturgy for this Sunday on the reverse of the title page of Cantata BWV 62, Bach also seems to be in doubt whether or not the Creed was really "intoned," for at first he omitted the note, then cued it in, and finally crossed it out (cf. W. Newmann, NBA, *KB* I/1:51).
57. Cf. Graff, pp. 171—72.
58. Cf. the discussion on p. 81. In addition we should note that also in other places the hymn "after the Sermon" was sung not immediately after the Sermon but only after the whole pulpit section of the service had been concluded (cf. Graff, p. 175).
59. Cf. Mahrenholz, *Agende* [see note 41 above], p. 58.
60. Stählin, p. 60.

61. Cf. T. Knolle, "Luthers Reform der Abendmahlsfeier in ihrer konstitutiven Bedeutung," *Schrift und Bekenntnis: Zeugnisse lutherischer Theologie* (Hamburg and Berlin, n.d.), p. 104. Cf. also W. Reindell, "Die Präfation," *L* 2:496ff.
62. Cf. Reindell, pp. 498ff. [Luther's paraphrase of the Lord's Prayer and admonition to Communion are part of the *Deutsche Messe*; cf. Luther, "German Mass," *Luther's Works* 53 (Philadelphia, 1965): 78ff.—Ed.]
63. Cf. Reindell, pp. 498ff., who cites 10 different forms of Communion liturgies, all of which, however, date back to the two basic types confirmed as present with Luther.
64. Kalb, p. 187.

c) Worship and Holy Communion

65. Cf. T. Knolle, "Erneuerung der Ordnung des heiligen Abendmahls," in *Vom Sakrament des Altars: Lutherische Beiträge zur Frage des heiligen Abendmahls*, ed. H. Sasse (Leipzig, 1941), p. 271.
66. A. Oepke, "Johann Sebastian Bach als Abendmahlsgast," *MuK* 24 (1954): 202—08. This theme, however, is in need of an urgent reworking, for Oepke's article contains too many errors. Concerning assertions about matters in Leipzig it needs to be said that it is not true that there were no name lists of Communion registration available for St. Nicholas and that also those of St. Thomas were presumably kept in a very incomplete manner. Both main churches are in possession of communicant lists going back to the 17th century, at St. Thomas a complete set since 1961 [NOTE: This date is in the German original, but it must surely be a printing error for 1661—Ed.], at St. Nicholas with a few lacunae for the first half of the 18th century. The lists are carefully entered in both main churches, and this obviously in the manner customary at that time, namely that only the men (except at Communion for the sick when also the women) were entered by name. Incorrect, too, is Oepke's observation that the documentation of Bach's participation in Communion "suddenly discontinued" at the year 1736 and that Bach's father confessor presumably was Subdeacon Weise. Up to the year 1736 Bach went to confession with the regular pastor of St. Thomas, Dr. Christian Weiß, two to three times annually, and because this man died in December 1736, Bach had to look for a new father confessor, most often then the archdeacon of St. Thomas. But those who went to Confession with the archdeacon are registered in the second column of the Communion register, and from 1737 on Bach's name can be found also in the other columns of the Communion register, mostly in the second column, whereas up to 1736 it always appears in the first column. Also Oepke's observation that the figures of the Communion registration at St. Thomas in Bach's time show a tendency toward decline is in error. The total number of communicants Oepke reports for 1727 (which also is incorrect because Oepke forgot about the Communion celebrations for the sick) is unfortunate in that it is actually the lowest figure in the entire first half of the 18th century and so represents an exception.
67. The identical total entered for St. Thomas in 1725 and 1726 needs to be verified.
68. J. B. Rüling, *Die Johanniskirche zu Leipzig in 7 Jahrhunderten* (Leipzig, 1916), p. 19.
69. Thus again recently in C. Albrecht, *Einführung in die Liturgik* (Berlin, 1964), p. 32. The procedures that are without doubt correctly criticized, according to which "failure to attend worship is to be punished with fines and police penalties (iron collars)," do not by any means apply only to the age of orthodoxy. Albrecht himself refers to an ordinance of Saxony of 1557, that is, immediately after the Reformation. No, these procedures have remained an inglorious accompaniment to the church government exercised by secular princes all the way into the 20th century. Just consider the severe interference the king of Prussia, Friedrich Wilhelm III, exercised in the 19th century with his orders affecting the church and especially the liturgical practice of his time!
70. Cf. Kalb, p. 91.
71. Besch, pp. 263—64.
72. Kalb, p. 92.
73. H. Preuß, *Die Geschichte der Abendmahlsfrömmigkeit in Zeugnissen und Berichten* (Gütersloh, 1949), pp. 18—19. Cf. in detail the evidences Preuß produces on pp. 118—38.

74. Ibid., p. 19.
75. W. Herbst, *Johann Sebastian Bach und die lutherische Mystik* (Dissertation, Erlangen, 1958), p. 74.
76. Knolle, "Erneuerung," p. 276. Cf. especially the note there in which Knolle mentions a large number of such hymn stanzas.
77. J. Gerhard, cited in Preuß, p. 118.
78. Cf. Graff, p. 177.
79. On the various disintegrating tendencies cf. ibid., pp. 177ff.
80. Cf. ibid., pp. 372—73.
81. Cf. ibid., pp. 372ff.
82. Cf. ibid., pp. 383—84.
83. Cf. Kalb, p. 123.
84. Knolle, "Erneuerung," pp. 277, 281.
85. Ibid., p. 280.
86. A. Schweitzer, *J. S. Bach,* trans. E. Newman (London, 1962), 2:373.
87. Ibid., 2:374.
88. Smend, *Kirchen-Kantaten,* part 4, p. 28.
89. Preuß, pp. 21—22.
90. Ibid., p. 22.
91. Leu*Gsch*, p. 114; cf. also pp. 96, 103.
92. Cf. Preuß, pp. 22—23.
93. The statements of Gerber concerning Communion piety otherwise make it clear that he is to be labeled "Pietist" only conditionally. Like his great model, Philipp Jakob Spener, he doubtlessly represents genuine Lutheran views.
94. S. Schöffel, "Orthodoxie," in *Aus Hamburgs Kirche* (Hamburg, 1929), p. 25. Cf. also in the same publication, in the contribution of Chief Pastor Dubbels, "Pietismus und Rationalismus," the observation (p. 28) that Pietism "in Hamburg was restricted to a short intermezzo" (1684—1693) and, as in Leipzig, this could doubtlessly be credited to the influence of orthodoxy.

d) Worship and Music

95. Kalb, p. 149.
96. Cf. *WF*, p. 281.
97. Cf. ibid., pp. 273, 281.
98. Smend, *Bach in Köthen,* p. 139.
99. Ibid., p. 133.
100. Cf. P. Brausch, *Die Kantate: Ein Beitrag zur Geschichte der deutschen Dichtungsgattung* (Dissertation, Heidelberg, 1921), pp. 51ff., 64; G. Feder, "Die protestantische Kirchenkantate," *MGG* 7:581ff., especially 599ff.
101. Brausch, p. 89.
102. *ML*, p. 218.
103. Kalb, p. 149. No change in this state of affairs is occasioned by the fact that "until far into the 18th century there was heavy controversy in an extensive polemical theological literature concerning the nature of church music" (Bunners, p. 77).
104. Cf. Kalb, pp. 142ff.; also Bunners, pp. 57ff.
105. Cf. Kalb, p. 145; also Leu*Ref*, p. 108. For Dannhauer's conception of music, cf. a detailed discussion in Bunners, pp. 15ff. Cf. also what Leube writes about the two Rostock theologians, Quistorp and and Großgebauer, who can be considered forerunners of Pietism, and also about Johann Brunnemann (Leu*Ref*, pp. 73, 76, 137; cf. also Leu*Ref*, pp. 72, 108, 119, 124). Among these theologians the introduction of instrumental music into the service, including also organ music, met with the stiffest resistance. Großgebauer was filled with "a downright fanatic hatred of the organ" (Leu*Ref*, p. 76). Quistorp did not want to tolerate instrumental music even during the reception of the Sacrament.
106. Cf. Bunners, pp. 81ff.
107. Söhngen, p. 46.

108. Cf. Hamel, pp. 49—50, 56ff.

109. Smend, *Bach in Köthen*, p. 137. Another positive evaluation of church music is found very near the end of the extensive treatise of Gerber (Gb, p. 756).

110. Smend, *Bach in Köthen*, p. 137.

111. Cf. the result of Leube's research (Leu*Ref*).

112. Smend, *Bach in Köthen*, p. 138. Also see the statements of Gerber in the Appendix of Sources, No. 11, which again and again have been made to refer to the premier performance of Bach's *St. Matthew Passion* in 1729 but in all probability do not have the Leipzig circumstances in mind (cf. ibid., pp. 136—37).

113. Hamel, p. 116. W. Gurlitt also calls Leipzig central Germany's, and Hamburg northern Germany's, "citadel of Lutheran orthodoxy" (*Johann Sebastian Bach: The Master and His Work*, trans. O. C. Rupprecht [St. Louis, 1957], pp. 100, 101).

114. Cf. Söhngen, pp. 69ff., as well as W. Blankenburg, "Der mehrstimmige Gesang und die konzertierende Musik im evangelischen Gottesdienst," *L* 4:664.

115. Smend, *Bach in Köthen*, p. 142.

116. Cf. Eggebrecht, pp. 282—83, as well as F. Blume, "Barock," *MGG* 1:1302.

117. Spi (German edition), 1:489; cf. Spi, 1:495. H. Melchert has confirmed this judgment of Spitta's in a special study ("Das Rezitativ der Kirchenkantaten J. S. Bachs," partial reprint of the dissertation of the same title, *BJ*, 1958, 5—83).

118. W. Gurlitt, "Johann Sebastian Bach in seiner Zeit und heute," *Bericht über die Wissenschaftliche Bachtagung der Gesellschaft für Musikforschung, Leipzig, 23—26 Juli 1950*, ed. W. Vetter and E. H. Meyer (Leipzig, 1951), p. 54. Cf. there also the insight expressed that "the age of Johann Sebastian Bach... may have been the last era in which the traditions and the prestige of the *Res publica christiana*, the Christian community of Europe, were still strong enough and unquestioned enough to guarantee the unity and security of a great style in life and art. If Germany at the time of Bach among all the European countries remained the most medieval country, then the old Lutheran lands, specifically Electoral Saxony—the land of the Reformation, the home of Bach and his kindred—retained its medieval nature longest by far" (p. 53).

119. The discussion concerning the question whether Bach's cantatas are able to serve a significant liturgical purpose in today's service has been carried on for more than a century, but it has generally ended in frustration because people simply would not take the Bach cantata seriously as a complete liturgical and musical work of art and because they were ever and again satisfied with purely formal and aesthetic, and therefore completely one-sided and inadequate, explanations of the Bach cantata, and this necessarily had to lead to adverse judgments on the Bach cantata as worship music. [Two more recent discussions of the question are J. Stalmann, "Bach im Gottesdienst heute: Zur Integration seines Vokalschaffens in gegenwärtige liturgische Praxis," in *Bachiana et alia Musicologica: Festschrift Alfred Dürr zum 65. Geburtstag am 3. März 1983*, ed. W. Rehm (Kassel and New York, 1983), pp. 267—74; and R. A. Leaver, *Music as Preaching: Bach, Passions, and Music in Worship* (St. Louis, 1984).—Ed.]

120. In this connection W. Blankenburg speaks of a "specifically Protestant development" (p. 672). Eggebrecht expresses himself in the same way (pp. 263ff.).

121. The musicological studies of recent decades that have to do with the relationship between music and rhetoric (espcially from the 16th to the 18th centuries) have a fundamental significance for the understanding of Lutheran church music up to 1750 (cf. Blankenburg, pp. 672—73).

122. Söhngen, p. 104.

123. Ibid., p. 79.

124. Cf. Blankenburg, p. 670.

125. Stählin, p. 55.

126. Söhngen, p. 164.

127. A. Schmitz, *Die Bildlichkeit der wortgebundenen Musik Johann Sebastian Bachs* (Mainz, 1950), p. 67.

128. Herbst, p. 145. Following Gurlitt, "Bach judged his own work not by the standard of the human inner world or his own estimate of his humanity and artistry, not by the emotion of the heart, but by an order of being that transcends human possibilities. His music does

not become enmeshed in the flood tide of experiences and emotions, not in the description of frames of mind, but it conducts itself as a kind of structuring that *builds objectively in the midst of the order of creation and represents a reflection and likeness of it.* Thus the master builds, arranges, molds, and combines everything from the first note to the last, the smallest rhythmic figure, the minutest turn of melody, every charm of harmony and timbre into the artwork's tectonic unity: a maximum of coordination and subordination of the most fanciful multiplicity into an architectural unity. And all this from purely musical means" (cf. "Bach in seiner Zeit," p. 75). Eggebrecht contradicts Heinrich Besseler, who in his effort to determine Bach's place in history recognizes in Bach's art a new start in history, namely, a breakthrough of "individualism," "emotionalism," "experientialism," and "expressivity" (in the sense of "unburdening oneself"). For details cf. pp. 251ff.

129. W. Ehmann, "Die *Kleinen geistlichen Konzerte* von Heinrich Schütz und unsere musikalische Praxis," *MuK* 33 (1963): 12.

130. Söhngen, p. 165.

131. In connection with this problem we refer the reader especially also to the instructive article of M. Dibelius, "Individualismus und Gemeindebewußtsein in Johann Sebastian Bachs Passionen," *Archiv für Reformationsgeschichte* 41 (1948): 132—54. There Dibelius defends the thesis that "the tension between individualism and congregational consciousness is an endowment of Protestantism from its very beginning," that this "duality of thought, congregational consciousness and individualism, shows itself especially impressively in the very appearance of Lutheran orthodoxy," and that "this same orthodoxy numbers among its own the greatest hymn writer of old Protestant individualism, Paul Gerhardt." Dibelius closes his article with the words: "No proclamation without appropriation for the individual; no subjective piety without reference to the common faith in the proclaimed Word—if that is Protestantism, then Bach is one of its mightiest proclaimers."

132. Söhngen, p. 133.

133. Söhngen sets up this differentiation to define genuine liturgical music (p. 133).

134. Smend, *Bach in Köthen*, p. 120. Even though Smend states that in his discussions "he has in no sense presented a complete characterization of baroque style," he has nevertheless in few and telling words outlined the spirit of the time and milieu of Bach. One has only to think of Bach's great contemporary Georg Friedrich Händel, who in his operas and oratorios treated these subjects in such varied ways. In this connection we should recall Bach's lack of interest in these musical devices: "The civic opera and the civic concert hall—institutions open to his famous contemporaries—did not exist at all for Bach as a composer" (G. Feder, *Bachs Werke in ihren Bearbeitern 1750—1950* [Dissertation, Kiel, 1955], p. 1).

135. Smend, *Bach in Köthen*, p. 121.

136. Herbst, p. 154.

137. Cf. I. Röbbelen, *Theologie und Frömmigkeit im deutschen evangelisch-lutherischen Gesangbuch des 17. und frühen 18. Jahrhunderts* (Berlin and Göttingen, 1957), pp. 194ff.

138. Herbst, p. 137.

139. Ibid.

140. Röbbelen, p. 196.

141. H. Werthemann, in her study *Die Bedeutung der alttestamentlichen Historien in Johann Sebastian Bachs Kantaten* (Tübingen, 1960), has demonstrated to what a degree the whole Old Testament (indeed, the whole Bible in general in the Lutheran interpretation) is of the highest importance for the cantata texts.

142. For the whole subject, cf. pp. 211—23.

143. Söhngen, p. 172.

144. Thus the cathedral chapter at Naumburg, for instance, in 1708 debated the question "whether it might not be better to omit polyphonic music before and after the Sermon" (A. Werner, *Vier Jahrhunderte im Dienste der Kirchenmusik* (Leipzig, 1933), p. 20, which see for details).

145. Blankenburg, p. 667.

146. Werthemann, p. 4.
147. Bach's cantata music of course also expresses adoration, praise, and thanksgiving in rich measure. In the final analysis we cannot thematically divide the whole liturgy into parts of pure adoration and those of pure proclamation (cf. Blankenburg, p. 668).
148. Söhngen, "Bach und die Liturgie," *Der Kirchenmusiker* 1 (1950): 126.

e) Outcome and Outlook

149. Cf. J. G. Rosenmüller, *Einige Predigten, gehalten in der Thomaskirche zu Leipzig* (Leipzig, 1786), pp. 95ff.
150. Cf. Rm, pp. 165ff.
151. Rm, p. 154.
152. Rm, p. 140.
153. Rm, pp. 150ff.
154. Rm, p. 178.
155. Cf. Rm, pp. 170ff.
156. Rm, p. 178. Cf. also Rosenmüller's views concerning "wax candles, chasubles, and other vestments" on p. 108 above!
157. G. Rietschel, *Lehrbuch der Liturgik*, 2d, newly revised edition by P. Graff (Göttingen, 1951), 1:385.
158. C. F. Enke, *Über den Werth des neuen für die Leipziger Stadtkirchen bestimmten Gesangbuches: Eine Predigt am 3. Adventssonntage* (1796), p. 18.
159. Cf. Sch*ML*, pp. 335ff., 362ff., 624ff., esp. 645ff.
160. Kalb, pp. 171, 187.

B. Johann Sebastian Bach's Relationship to the Worship of His Time

1. Cf. F. Kalb, *Theology of Worship in 17th-Century Lutheranism*, trans. H. P. A. Hamann (St. Louis, 1965), pp. 155ff.
2. Ibid., p. 159.
3. Published under the title "Outlines of a New Picture of Bach," *Music and Letters* 44 (1963): 214—27 [Hereafter identified as Blu].

1. Bach's Decision to Work in Leipzig Seen in the Light of His Life and Calling

4. Cf. among the large number of publications pertinent to this subject the following contributions: (a) A. Dürr, "Zum Wandel des Bach-Bildes," *MuK* 32 (1962): 145—52; (b) F. Smend, "Was bleibt? Zu Friedrich Blumes Bach-Bild," *Der Kirchenmusiker* 13 (1962): 178—88; (c) J. G. Mehl, "Johann Sebastian Bach—liberaler Humanist oder lutherischer Christ? Zum 'neuen Bachbild' Friedrich Blumes," *Gottesdienst und Kirchenmusik*, 1962, pp. 203—18; (d) M. Mezger, "Ein 'neues' Bach-Bild?" *Die Welt*, No. 162, 14 July 1962.

a) Theological-Liturgical Education and Training

5. F. Hamel, *Johann Sebastian Bach: Geistige Welt* (Göttingen, 1951), p. 14.
6. H. Helmbold, "Junge Bache auf dem Eisenacher Gymnasium," *JSBiThü*, p. 20.
7. C. S. Terry, *Bach: A Biography*, 2d ed. (London, 1933), p. 21.
8. F. Reinhold, "Die Bache in Ohrdruf," *BiThü*, p. 120.
9. Hamel, p. 21.
10. Reinhold, p. 120.
11. Hamel, pp. 21, 23.
12. Ibid., p. 23.
13. G. Fock, *Der junge Bach in Lüneburg* (Hamburg, 1950), p. 62.
14. Hamel, p. 29.

15. Cf. Terry, pp. 28, 30, etc.; cf. also G. Kühn, "Johann Sebastian Bach in Eisenach," *BiThü*, p. 64; A. Örtel, "Johann Sebastian Bach in Ohrdruf," *BiThü*, p. 68.
16. Kalb, p. 14; cf. in general pp. 10ff.
17. Ibid., p. 16.
18. Cf. the article "Chor" by W. Blankenburg, *MGG* 2:1230— 65.
19. R. Herrmann, "Die Thüringer und die Bache," *BiThü*, p. 100 (cf. the entire contribution beginning at p. 97, and especially p. 99).
20. Cf. the statement of an Eisenach chronicler in 1698: "Claruit semper urbs nostra musica" (Our musical town has always been famous), Spi, 1:183. Georg Philipp Telemann, who worked in Eisenach four years, describes this town as "the high school of music" and maintains that the Eisenach court orchestra was superior to the Paris opera orchestra (cf. W. Greiner, "Bach in Thüringen," *BiThü*, pp. 32—33).
21. F. Blume, "Bach, Johann Sebastian," *MGG* 1:963.
22. Örtel, p. 186.
23. Spi, 1:187—88.
24. Ibid., pp. 189—90.
25. Cf. Terry, p. 34.
26. Spi, 1:190—91. Fock, however, considers Bach's activity as a prefect very unlikely but agrees with Spitta in the assumption that Bach is likely to have functioned as an instrumentalist (pp. 51ff.).
27. Cf. for detail Spi, 1:191—92, and Terry, pp. 35ff.; also cf. above all Fock, who describes the rich church music tradition in Lüneburg in detail, pp. 9ff. Worth noting is the fact that in Lüneburg people were "in the habit of going to Communion once every three months" and that during these frequently very long celebrations of Holy Communion in Lüneburg very often (at least every three weeks) "a musical presentation was made" [*ein Stück musiciret*]. Among these presentations also vocal and instrumental solos are to be considered. Fock tells us that in certain north German cities special emphasis was given to good music for the Sacrament, in fact, that "also Bach's famous Chaconne for Solo Violin was intended to be played 'during the Distribution' [*sub communione*], as its title indicates" (pp. 24—25).

b) Choice of Profession

28. Fock, p. 100.
29. Blume, *MGG* 1:967.
30. According to Fock, "Bach encountered French music already everywhere in Lüneburg, so that the reputation of having introduced him to French music belongs not only to Celle, as has been assumed heretofore on the basis of the obituary, but in the same measure also to Lüneburg" (p. 47).
31. Blume, *MGG* 1:967.
32. Ibid.
33. R. Jauernig, "Bachs erster Aufenthalt in Weimar," *BiThü*, p. 69. Terry (p. 56) reports that Bach "despite his youth so impressed the electors that he was voted the appointment," but Bach's application came to grief because of the negative attitude of the ruler of the land, Duke Johann Georg of Saxony-Weißenfels.
34. Cf. K. Müller, *Arnstädter Bachbuch: Johann Sebastian Bach und seine Verwandten in Arnstadt*, ed. K. Müller and F. Wiegand (Arnstadt, 1957), p. 65; cf. also there p. 89 and *BD* 2:10.
35. Thus Bach "was a friend, perhaps even a relative," of the organist at the City Church, Samuel Heintze. The wife of this organist was a sponsor at the baptism of one of Bach's children. There is also a report about Bach's relation to "the important cantor at the City Church and teacher at the Weimar Latin School, Georg Theodor Reineccius, who had published a collection of church cantatas that Bach learned to know at that time" (cf. Jauernig, p. 69).
36. Jauernig conjectures that Bach may have acquired his outstanding knowledge of organ building from the Weimar court organist Effler, who was known "far beyond the borders of the Dukedom of Saxony-Weimar as a master in building, maintaining, and

repairing organ mechanisms'' (p. 70). But we must also consider all of Bach's childhood and youth, during which numerous organs were built and projected. Besides, there are records of organ builders of that time who were near relatives of Bach's (cf. G. Kraft, "Johann Sebastian Bach und Ohrdruf," *JSBiThü*, pp. 26ff.).

37. It is striking that Bach received the appointment as organist on 9 August 1703 from the Arnstadt Consistory and on 14 August 1703 with a handshake bound himself to the appointment and was installed in his office, even though St. Boniface Church had an organist, albeit a very mediocre one, who had to yield the office when Bach began his service. Cf. Terry, pp. 59—60, and Spi, 1:222ff. The esteem then accorded Bach in Arnstadt is discernible from this fact alone, that no other organist before or after him received so high a salary as Bach did (cf. Müller, p. 95).

38. Terry, p. 58. Hamel, too, sees Bach's first Weimar appointment only as a "transitional position," in fact, he even describes it as "an emergency solution, which he left again as soon as possible in order now finally to follow his inclination toward church music in general and toward organ in particular" (p. 41).

39. Hamel, p. 41.

40. Cf. the minutes of 21 February 1706 of the Consistory of Arnstadt, in which Bach himself apparently explained his overstaying his vacation in this way: "...to comprehend one thing and another about his art" (*BR*, p. 51; *BD* 2:19).

41. Cf. Spi, 1:335, 340.

42. Cf. Müller, p. 116. According to Ernst Brinkmann, the organist of St. Blasius "was according to ancient tradition considered the representative of the highest musical honor in the entire area of the imperial city" ("Die Mühlhäuser Bache," *JSBiThü*, p. 222).

43. Cf. Müller, pp. 68—69, 77—78; also Terry, p. 64.

44. Cf. Spi, 1:228.

45. Müller, p. 68.

46. W. Rosen, *Johann Sebastian Bach: Leben und Werk* (Leipzig, 1935), p. 28. [For a more recent discussion, see W. H. Scheide, "Bach vs. Bach: Mühlhausen Dismissal Request vs. Erdmann Letter," *Bachiana et alia Musicologica: Festschrift Alfred Dürr zum 65. Geburtstag am 3 März 1983*, ed. W. Rehm (Kassel and New York, 1983), pp. 234—42.—Ed.]

47. *ML*, p. 206. Both the predecessor and the successor of Bach received a smaller income than Bach (cf. Müller, p. 117, and Terry, p. 81).

48. *BD* 2:43.

49. Cf. W. Baumgarten, "Johann Sebastian Bach in Mühlhausen," *BiThü*, p. 76; Brinkmann, p. 224.

50. Cf. the detailed report of the clashes, above all the heavy altercations between the two leading clergymen of the city, Frohne and Eilmar, in Spi, 1:358ff., and Terry, pp. 81ff. Cf. also Hamel, pp. 50ff.

51. *ML*, p. 213.

52. *ML*, pp. 218—19.

c) Appointments in Weimar and Köthen

53. According to Blume, Bach presumably "turned his back on service to the church" even "with the express purpose of taking up court assignments," which, in the whole trend of Blume's thesis, is tantamount to a definitely announced departure from the ecclesiastical-liturgical office. Yet we know of no source in which this "express purpose" of Bach's is definitely stated. On the contrary, Bach's Mühlhausen resignation, which can most easily be thought of as an "express purpose" of Bach's, says very definitely that he is interested in carrying out "a regulated church music" and that he is moving to Weimar in the hope of being able to achieve this projected goal there. Whether Bach was able to reach this projected goal there is another question. But if we want to speak of an unqualified "express purpose" of Bach's, it will not do to disregard the Mühlhausen resignation as an authentic source or to give it a completely unsatisfactory interpretation, as Blume has done in his answer to Alfred Dürr (*MuK* 32 [1962]: 153—56. Blume calls Bach's demand for a "regulated church music" a "subterfuge that he uses over against

the council there"). The unsatisfactory interpretation of this resignation by Blume becomes even more problematic because of the fact that Blume also is not able to advance any reasons for Bach's departure from Mühlhausen.

54. Cf. the measures and countermeasures employed by the duke against the inroads of Pietism as given in Spi, 1:376—77.

55. Terry, p. 85.

56. Jau. I, p. 82. Cf. also Hamel, according to whom Salomon Franck described the duke as "the Nurse of churches, the Patron of godliness, and the Shield of pure doctrine" (p. 65).

57. For the *Sabbatmandaten* of Duke Wilhelm Ernst, which were to contribute to the improvement of the liturgical life, cf. G. Kraft, "Thüringer Stadtpfeiferfamilien um Bach," *JSBiThü*, pp. 155—56.

58. Quoted in Spi, 1:391—92.

59. Franck had already in 1694 dedicated to Duke Wilhelm Ernst his first cycle of cantata texts, *Evangelische Seelen-Lust über die Sonn- und Festtage durchs gantze Jahr*, and thus recommended himself as a cantata librettist long before coming to Weimar. His cantata texts were set to music also by other composers of his time beside J. S. Bach (cf. the article "Franck" by Dürr, *MGG* 4:681—83.).

60. Cf. the exact title page and foreword to the Franck cantata cycle, *Evangelisches Andachts-Opfer*, Spi, 1:540—41, following German text.

61. Cf. Spi, 1:586—87.

62. Cf. especially Jau. I, pp. 77—78. According to this, "Bach's income rose from 158 Gulden to at least double that, to 316 Gulden," a figure we must compare with the highest salary of court capellmeister Drese, who until his death customarily received only 200 Gulden, and also with the final salary of court organist Effler, who received only 130 Gulden. Bach therefore from the very beginning of his activity in Weimar was in relatively good circumstances. Cf. also Jau. II, pp. 56—57.

63. *BD* 1:213 and 24.

64. Cf. the detailed sources in Spi, 1:379—80, and German edition, 1:513.

65. Jau. II, p. 55.

66. *BD* 2:37.

67. Cf. the words of the obituary: "The pleasure His Grace took in his playing fired him with the desire to try every possible artistry in his treatment of the organ. Here, too, he wrote most of his organ works" (*BR*, p. 218).

68. Drese had also been court organist for the Duke of Saxony-Jena (Spi, 1:391) before he was called as court capellmeister to Weimar in 1683, and Bach's disappointment in 1717, when Drese died and the succession was not decided in his favor, seems to confirm the supposition here stated.

69. Cf. beside Jau. II, p. 57, A. Dürr, *Studien über die frühen Kantaten J. S. Bachs* (Leipzig, 1951), pp. 52—53.

70. Cf. the details in Spi, 1:515ff. It is incidentally interesting here, too, that Bach again held out for a new organ, this time one with 63 stops.

71. Cf. Jau. II, pp. 63ff.; also Jau. I, pp. 78—79.

72. Cf. the description of the inside of the chapel in Terry, pp. 96—97, and Jau. II, pp. 58ff; cf *BD* 4:93. According to Terry, "Accommodation for singers and players can have been found [only] with difficulty."

73. Jau. I, p. 78.

74. Cf. Jau. I, p. 79, and Dürr, *Studien*, p. 54.

75. Jau. II, p. 68.

76. Jau. I, pp. 77, 79.

77. Cf. Dürr, "Zum Wandel," p. 146; also Dürr, "Franck," *MGG* 4:681 (chronological list of Franck's publications; the last volume of cantatas was published in 1718, a short time after Bach's departure).

78. Cf. Jau. II, p. 57.

79. Cf. the exact lineup of cantatas that achieved performance in 1714—1716 in Dürr, *Studien*, pp. 54—55.

80. Ibid., p. 53. It is also worth noting that at Bach's application for the office of organist in Our Lady's Church in Halle in 1713 an office was involved in which "part of the

organist's duties consisted in composing music and conducting church music" (Spi, 1:515). At the application itself the presentation of a cantata was demanded, and Bach met this demand (according to Dürr, Bach presented a cantata of his in Halle in November or December 1713. Cf. *Studien*, p. 51). Thus Bach could have realized his plan of implementing a "regulated church music" also in Halle.

81. Dürr, *Studien,* p. 212. Dürr has called attention to the fact that the word "regulated" becomes clear from the character of Bach's Mühlhausen cantatas, of which none were intended for an ordinary Sunday, but all were designed for special occasions. Dürr's explanation of this term is very plausible: "In the usual Sunday services obviously no cantatas were presented, and that was what Bach saw as his final purpose, namely to provide *regular* presentations of cantatas within the main services" (p. 212).

82. The real reasons for Bach's being passed over by the duke and Bach's departure from Weimar on that account remain unclear in detail. Terry conjectures that Bach was drawn into the tensions existing between Duke Wilhelm Ernst and his nephew Duke Ernst August and that the failure of Bach's endeavors to get the appointment as capellmeister may have to be traced back to this quarrel between uncle and nephew (pp. 113—14). Bach had certainly maintained good contacts with both dukes and in any case was on such good terms with Duke Ernst August that the duchess—a sister of Prince Leopold of Köthen—stood as sponsor at the baptism of Bach's son Leopold August (born 15 November 1718 in Köthen), who died early (cf. *BD* 2:73). For the whole matter, cf. Jau. I, pp. 49—106, as well as Jau. II, pp. 98ff. Jauernig supports Terry's conjecture and almost lets it become certainty.

83. Cf. the listing of Bach's cantatas performed in Weimar in Dürr, *Studien,* pp. 54—55.

84. Jau. II, p. 101.

85. Cf. the report of Court Secretary Theodor Benedict Bormann in Jau. II, p. 98.

86. Cf. Terry, p. 121.

87. F. Smend, *Bach in Köthen* (Berlin, 1951), p. 13.

88. Terry, p. 118.

89. Smend, *Bach in Köthen*, p. 28.

90. Terry, p. 118.

91. Smend, *Bach in Köthen,* p. 28.

92. Ibid., p. 21.

93. Ibid., p. 28.

94. Cf. ibid., pp. 68ff.

95. Ibid., p. 95.

96. Dürr, "Zum Wandel," p. 146.

97. The details of the application cannot be produced exactly. Friedrich Blume of course thinks that this application on the part of Bach is "very unlikely" (cf. the answer to Alfred Dürr in *MuK* 32:155). But it is certain that Bach was in Hamburg in October and November 1720 and performed there as an organist. Neumeister and other Hamburg citizens later lamented about the fact that Bach's application in Hamburg did not lead to the desired goal.

98. Hamel, p. 116.

99. Cf. Bach's trip to Karlsbad with Prince Leopold (Terry, p. 130).

100. Smend, *Bach in Köthen*, p. 169.

d) Application to Become Cantor of St. Thomas, Leipzig

101. Sch*ML*, p. 24. Cf. also A. Schering, *Musikgeschichte Leipzigs* 2 (Leipzig, 1926): 43.

102. Cf. Schering, *Musikgeschichte Leipzigs*, p. 43; also Sch*ML*, p. 622.

103. *ML*, p. 206.

104. *ML*, pp. 206ff.

105. Smend correctly called attention to the fact that Bach in 1723 "did not in any case don the cantor's gown 'again,' for he had never worn one before" ("Was bleibt?" pp. 186—87).

106. Cf. the detailed treatment in Sch*ML*, pp. 68ff.

107. Cf. Smend, *Bach in Köthen*, pp. 74—75.

108. Jau. II, p. 101.

109. Smend, *Bach in Köthen*, p. 74. Walter Blankenburg also remarks that this letter "is irrelevant in every direction" (cf. his article "Zwölf Jahre Bachforschung," *Acta Musicologica* 37 [1965]: 126).

110. Sch*ML*, p. 10.

111. Cf. ibid., p. 10.

112. Blume, "Antwort" to Alfred Dürr, *MuK* 32:155.

113. Cf. the statement of "Dominus Consul Regens" Dr. Lange at the council meeting of 22 April 1723: "It was necessary to be sure to get a famous man, in order to inspire the [university] students" (*BR*, p. 90; *BD* 2:95).

114. Sch*ML*, p. 12.

115. Ibid., pp. 6, 9.

116. Smend, "Was bleibt?" p. 187.

117. Sch*ML*, p. 24. For details of the estate see *BR*, pp. 191— 97; *BD* 2:490—97.

118. *BD* 2:186—87; cf. *BR*, p. 81.

119. Sch*ML*, p. 80.

120. Cf. ibid., p. 326.

121. J. S. Riemer, *Handschriftliche Chronik Leipzigs* (cited after Sch*ML*, p. 327). Cf. facsimile in W. Neumann, *Auf den Lebenswegen Johann Sebastian Bachs* (Berlin, 1953), p. 295.

122. Sch*ML*, p. 335.

123. Ibid., p. 341.

124. F. Blume, "Doles," *MGG* 3:628.

125. Sch*ML*, p. 359.

126. Blume, "Doles," col. 635.

127. L. Hoffmann-Erbrecht, "Hiller," *MGG* 6:410ff.

128. Ibid., col. 415.

129. Schering concludes: "No one in Germany at that time contested his position as the musical pedagogue" (Sch*ML*, p. 402).

130. Hoffmann-Erbrecht, col. 419.

131. Ibid., col. 412.

132. Sch*ML*, pp. 401, 645. Otherwise, too, Schering is not sparing in his positive statements about Hiller: "Leipzig was to be congratulated to have found such a man" (Sch*ML*, p. 402), and he "was the tutelary spirit of music in Leipzig," and "his talent was able further to guarantee Leipzig the reputation of being an outstanding musical city. For whoever came here as a friend of the arts in the second half of the 18th century first mentioned the name Hiller when the conversation turned toward music" (Sch*ML*, p. 400).

133. Beside the theory that Bach in 1723 "only with the greatest reluctance...resumed the cantor's gown," Blume is bold to make the even more problematic assertion that "the Passions and oratorios were, as Bach himself once said, an 'onus,' a task which he performed with considerable reluctance" (Blu, pp. 218—19). Cf. the critical remarks of Dürr ("Zum Wandel," p. 151) and Smend (*Bach in Köthen*, pp. 187—88).

134. Hamel, p. 116.

2. Prolegomena to Bach's Creativity

a) Piety and Attitude of Mind

1. W. Blankenburg, "Theologische und geistesgeschichtliche Probleme der gegenwärtigen Bachforschung," *Theologische Literaturzeitung* 78 (1958): 396.

2. *BR*, pp. 300—01.

3. W. Gurlitt, *Johann Sebastian Bach: The Master and His Work,* trans. O. C. Rupprecht (St. Louis, 1957), pp. 9—10.

4. Cf. A. Oepke, "Johann Sebastian Bach als Abendmahlsgast," *MuK* 24 (1954): 202—08. [Stiller's discussion of the frequency of Bach's attendance at confession and Communion should be compared with his subsequent essays: "Beicht- und Abendmahlsgang Johann Sebastian Bachs im Lichte der Familiengedenktage des Thomaskantors," *MuK* 43 (1973): 182—86; "Johann Sebastian Bach und Johann Christoph Gottsched: Eine

beachtliche Gemeinsamkeit," *MuK* 46 (1976): 166—72.—Ed.].

5. Oepke, p. 207.

6. The deliberate choice of a father confessor on the part of Bach incidentally makes it clear that for Bach and for many of his contemporaries confession was by no means a perfunctory affair, but a lively experience that presupposed a mutual relation of confidence between father confessor and penitent.

7. F. Hamel, *Johann Sebastian Bach: Geistige Welt* (Göttingen, 1951), p. 111. Cf. for the whole subject H. Preuß, *J. S. Bachs Bibliothek* (Leipzig, 1928), and Hamel, pp. 109ff. [also R. A. Leaver, *Bachs theologische Bibliothek* (Stuttgart, 1983)— Ed.].

8. Cf. H. Besch, "Eine Auktions-Quittung J. S. Bachs," *Festschrift für Friedrich Smend* (Berlin, 1963), pp. 74—79 [also Leaver, p. 42 and No. 2—Ed.].

9. Cf. for the whole subject H. Klotz, NBA, *KB* IV/2:102, 106.

10. Ibid., p. 106.

11. Italics not in the original! *BR*, p. 220.

12. H. A. Metzger, "Joh. Seb. Bach und der evangelische Gottesdienst seiner Zeit," *MuK* 20 (1950): 52.

13. W. Blankenburg, "Zwölf Jahre Bachforschung," *Acta Musicologica* 37 (1965): 131—32, 134.

14. F. Smend, *Bach in Köthen* (Berlin, 1951), p. 142.

15. *ML*, p. 217.

16. Ibid.

17. H. H. Eggebrecht, "Zur Antithese Geistlich-Weltlich," *Musica* 4 (1950): 249.

18. Cf. Smend, p. 116.

19. Eggebrecht, p. 250.

20. New translation; cf. Spi, 3:318.

21. *ML*, pp. 211—12.

22. Ibid., p. 212.

23. Ibid.

24. Söhngen, "Theologische Grundlagen der Kirchenmusik," *L* 4:207. The quotation in the statement of Söhngen is from F. Kluge and A. Götze, *Etymologisches Wörterbuch der deutschen Sprache*, 16th ed. (Berlin, 1953), p. 256.

25. W. Herbst, *Johann Sebastian Bach und die lutherische Mystik* (Dissertation, Erlangen, 1958), pp. 56ff.

26. Cf. the weekly periodical edited by Scheibe from 1737, *Critischer Musikus*. In it an entirely different conception of the meaning of music is expressed. Scheibe saw the "chief purpose of church music" principally in this, "to edify the hearers, to rouse them for devotion in order to awaken in them a quiet, holy awe over against the divine Being" (quoted from W. Gurlitt, "Johann Sebastian Bach in seiner Zeit und heute," *Bericht über die Wissenschaftliche Bachtagung der Gesellschaft für Musikforschung, Leipzig, 23—26 Juli 1950*, ed. W. Vetter and E. H. Meyer [Leipzig, 1951], p. 73). The conception of the second successor to Bach as cantor of St. Thomas, Johann Friedrich Doles, is also worth mentioning. He summarized the purpose "of true church music" still more in the direction of the emotion and edification of the hearer by saying that the purpose is "as in all music, to move the heart" (cf. ibid., p. 73).

27. *ML*, p. 213.

28. Cf. H. Besch, *Johann Sebastian Bach: Frömmigkeit und Glaube* (Kassel and Basel, 1950), pp. 267ff.; Hamel, pp. 58ff.

29. Herbst, p. 56.

30. Cf. W. Plath, NBA, *KB* V/5:13.

31. Ibid., p. 32.

b) The Will to Proclaim

32. Hamel, pp. 129, 176. Concerning Gottsched's *Dichtkunst*, cf. P. Brausch, *Die Kantate: Ein Beitrag zur Geschichte der deutschen Dichtungsgattung* (Dissertation, Heidelberg, 1921), pp. 222ff.

33. Cf. Brausch, p. 223.

34. Cf. Herbst, pp. 54ff.

35. Cf. Spi, 2:230—31.
36. Herbst, p. 66.
37. Cf. ibid., pp. 52, 65ff., 108. Cf. also Brausch, p. 190. Brausch is also of the opinion that the editing of the Henrici texts provided "improvement and added depth" for them. Concerning the radical revision of the text for Cantata BWV 84, Brausch states that Henrici's "Philistine conception of contentedness has been revised on the basis of a genuine, heartfelt spirit of being resigned to the will of God."
38. Herbst, p. 68; also cf. the discussions beginning on p. 63.
39. Ibid., p. 55
40. Cf. the distinguished publication by Helene Werthemann, *Die Bedeutung der alttestamentlichen Historien in Johann Sebastian Bachs Kantaten* (Tübingen, 1960), in its entirety.
41. Brausch, p. 89.
42. Cf. W. Blankenburg, "Der mehrstimmige Gesang und die konzertierende Musik im evangelischen Gottesdienst," *L* 4:678—79.
43. Brausch, p. 72.
44. Ibid., p. 89.
45. Cf. ibid., pp. 232—33, on this point.
46. Ibid., p. 71. Cf. Luther's well-known definition of the liturgical happening in his dedication sermon at Torgau in 1544, according to which the service is statement and counterstatement, Word of God and response of the believer (cf. "Sermon at the Dedication of Castle Church, Torgau, 1544," *Sermons I,* ed. and tr. John W. Doberstein, *Luther's Works,* American Edition, 51 [Philadephia, 1959]: 342ff.).
47. E. Brunner, *Die Mystik und das Wort* (Tübingen, 1924), p. 89.
48. Herbst, p. 139.
49. Ibid., pp. 141ff.
50. Ibid., pp. 141—42.
51. Werthemann, p. 4. In this connection we should also think of Rudolf Alexander Schröder's hymn writing, which was also bound to the substance and language of the Bible, in fact, even saturated with Biblical treasures. It is interesting to note that Schröder "in the midst of choosing baroque lyricism was himself summoned to be a spiritual poet and to take up new creation" (cf. G. Thürer, "Vom Wortkunstwerk im deutschen Barock," *Die Kunstformen des Barockzeitalters,* ed. R. Stamm [Bern, 1956], p. 380).
52. Cf. Werthemann, p. 5.
53. Ibid., pp. 6ff.
54. F. Smend, "Luther and Bach," *Bach-Studien: Gesammelte Reden und Aufsätze,* ed. C. Wolff (Kassel, 1969), p. 158. Also Bach's librettist Henrici in 1725 "imitates Brockes's free recitative-like and metrical recast of the words of the Bible" (Brausch, p. 105).
55. Cf. the facsimiles in the second part of N*VT.*
56. Gurlitt, *Master,* p. 116.
57. Smend, "Luther und Bach," p. 158.
58. Herbst, p. 64.
59. L. F. Tagliavini, *Studi sui Testi delle Cantate sacre di J. S. Bach,* (Padua, et al., 1956), pp. 135—223.
60. Cf. Hamel, pp. 100ff., and Smend, pp. 156—57 [also Leaver, passim; Bach had 11 volumes containing Bible commentaries and a further 23 volumes of sermons on Biblical texts—Ed.].
61. Hamel, p. 102. [See also R. A. Leaver, "Bach's Understanding and Use of the Epistles and Gospels of the Church Year," *Bach: The Quarterly Journal of the Riemenschneider Bach Institute* 6, no. 4 (1975): 4—13.—Ed.]
62. Cf. "Johann Kuhnaus Entwurf der Grundsätze einer Kantatenkomposition," newly reprinted in *St. Thomas zu Leipzig: Schule und Chor, Stätte des Wirkens von Johann Sebastian Bach, Bilder und Dokumente der Geschichte der Thomasschule und des Thomanerchores mit ihren zeitgeschichtlichen Beziehunge,* ed. B. Knick, with an introduction by M. Mezger (Wiesbaden, 1963), pp. 120—21.
63. Cf. Brausch, pp. 116, 172. Cf. also G. Feder, "Die protestantische Kirchenkantate," *MGG* 7:583.

64. Herbst, p. 3.
65. Cf. Smend, *Bach in Köthen*, pp. 123—34.
66. W. Blankenburg, "Das Parodieverfahren im Weihnachtsoratorium Johann Sebastian Bachs," *WF*, p. 505.
67. Cf. Jau. II, pp. 93ff.
68. Smend, *Bach in Köthen*, pp. 120—21. Cf. also pp. 132—33. Cf. further Smend, "Luther und Bach," pp. 169ff.
69. Cf. Brausch, p. 153.
70. Cf. *Wege zu Bach: Drei Abhandlungen von Friedrich Rochlitz, 1749—1842*, ed. J. M. Müller-Blattau (Augsburg, 1926), pp. 37— 38.
71. Besch, *Frömmigkeit*, pp. 231ff. Herbst (pp. 140ff.) also agrees with this interpretation.
72. The name *Musica poetica* for this theory of composition is obviously found only in the Protestant area. For this statement and for the whole development of this theory, cf. H. H. Eggebrecht, "Über Bachs geschichtlichen Ort," *WF*, pp. 247— 89.
73. H. Zenck, "Grundformen deutscher Musikanschauung," *Jahrbuch der Akademie der Wissenschaft in Göttingen*, 1941/42, p. 28.
74. Blankenburg, "Zwölf Jahre," p. 136.
75. Blankenburg, "Der mehrstimmige Gesang," p. 672.
76. It is interesting to observe that the close connection between the *Musica poetica* and rhetoric is traceable especially in Protestantism, whereas the Italian theory of music of that time obviously has "no connection to rhetoric (the theory of writing a speech), but essentially only to oratory" (cf. Eggebrecht, "Über Bachs geschichtlichen Ort," *WF* p. 281).
77. A. Schmitz, *Die Bildlichkeit der wortgebundenen Musik Johann Sebastian Bachs* (Mainz, 1950), and "Die oratorische Kunst J. S. Bachs: Grundlagen und Grundfragen," *Kongreßbericht Lüneburg 1950* (Kassel and Basel), pp. 33—49.
78. Cf. Herbst, p. 144. For the entire development, cf. Blankenburg, "Der mehrstimmige Gesang," pp. 672ff.
79. Blankenburg, "Der mehrstimmige Gesang," p. 672.
80. Cf. Schmitz, *Bildlichkeit*, pp. 12, 26, 86.
81. Cited according to Spi, 2:238.
82. Cf. F. Hamel, "Bach als geistesgeschichtliche Erscheinung," *Kongreß-Bericht: Internationale Gesellschaft für Musikwissenschaft Utrecht, 1952* (Amsterdam, 1953), pp. 218—23.
83. Cf. Smend, "Luther und Bach," pp. 158ff.
84. A. Dürr, "Johann Sebastian Bachs Kirchenmusik in seiner Zeit und heute," *WF*, p. 301.
85. Blankenburg, "Zwölf Jahre," p. 132.
86. Cf. ibid., p. 134.
87. Dürr, p. 302.

c) The Problem of Parodies

88. F. Smend, *Joh. Seb. Bach: Kirchen-Kantaten*, pt. 5 (Berlin, 1950): 15.
89. Smend rejects the new chronology of the cantatas ("Was bleibt? Zu Friedrich Blumes Bach-Bild," *Der Kirchenmusiker* 13 [1962]: 179ff.). Also Blankenburg in his contribution "Zwölf Jahre Bachforschung" repeatedly hints that he does not consider the new chronology as finally established.
90. Smend, "Was bleibt?" pp. 181—82.
91. A. Dürr, "Zum Wandel des Bach-Bildes," *MuK* 32 (1962): 150. Anyway, if Blume should be right in this matter, the parodies of the *St. Matthew Passion* would originate in a liturgical work, namely in Cantata BWV 244a, composed for a funeral service.
92. Cf. NBA, *KB* II/6:167.
93. Blankenburg, "Zwölf Jahre," p. 124.
94. Cf. Smend, *Kirchen-Kantaten*, pt. 5:25.
95. A. Schering, "Kleine Bachstudien," *BJ*, 1933, p. 37.
96. Blankenburg, *WF*, p. 505.
97. Ibid.

98. Ibid., pp. 504—05. Cf. the examples beginning on p. 495.
99. Ibid., pp. 505—06.
100. Smend, *Kirchen-Kantaten*, pt. 5:19.
101. Smend, *Bach in Köthen*, pp. 118—19.
102. Ibid., p. 118.
103. Smend, *Kirchen-Kantaten*, pt. 5:25.
104. Blume's expositions, too, are not entirely free of such views that do not fully evaluate the parodies artistically. Cf. Smend's critical remark on this subject ("Was bleibt?" pp. 182—83).
105. A. Dürr, NBA, *KB* I/35:47.
106. Dürr, "Zum Wandel," pp. 149—50.
107. Spi, 1:495 [following the German text].
108. Cf., for example, Hermann Melchert's conclusion in his study of the Bach recitative: "Even if outward appearance can point to many a similarity between Bach's recitative and other products of that time, this can not delude us concerning the fact that here we have a form that has its own character" ("Das Rezitativ der Kirchenkantaten J. S. Bachs," *BJ*, 1958, p. 78). In the same connection Melchert points out that "the situation is similar in the other musical forms: There, too, Bach makes use of the materials his time offers him to create works of unique significance with their help." For the theological reflection concerning the essence of the Bach recitative and the Bach aria, this musicological perception, that is, that compositional technique that did not "transpose" but actually "provided a new creation," seems to me to be of decisive importance.
109. For this series of problems, cf. Schmitz, "Die oratorische Kunst," pp. 47—48. There Schmitz makes the point "that church music and secular music did not give rise to separate emotions," and he adduces a number of examples from the *Christmas Oratorio* to show how the same situation [*Topos*] was retained in the parody.
110. Ibid., p. 47.
111. Smend has expressed the criticism that Blume, too, is not entirely free of evaluating the "occasional works" adversely ("Was Bleibt?" pp. 185—86).
112. Dürr, "Kirchenmusik," p. 298.
113. Ibid., pp. 298—99.
114. Ibid., p. 299.
115. Dürr, "Zum Wandel," p. 149.

d) Relation to the Hymn

116. F. Treiber, "Die thüringisch-sächsische Kirchenkantate zur Zeit des jungen J. S. Bach (etwa 1700—1723)," *Archiv für Musikforschung* 2 (1937): 137.
117. Smend, "Was bleibt?" p. 188.
118. Ibid.
119. K. Gudewill, "Über Formen und Texte der Kirchenkantaten Johann Sebastian Bachs," *Festschrift Friedrich Blume zum 70. Geburtstag* (Kassel et al., 1963), pp. 169—70.
120. Cf. Tagliavini, p. 247.
121. Cf. Gudewill, p. 174.
122. Cf. Blankenburg, "Zwölf Jahre," p. 106.
123. Cf. H. Klotz, NBA, *KB* IV/3:11, 14—15.
124. Cf. ibid., p. 13.
125. Cf. Blankenburg, "Zwölf Jahre," p. 139.
126. Gurlitt, *Master*, p. 112.
127. Smend, *Bach in Köthen*, p. 123.
128. Treiber, pp. 137, 140. Berndt Baselt, it is true, has pointed out that Telemann's attitude to the congregational hymn is in need of a new investigation ("Georg Philipp Telemann und die protestantische Kirchenmusik," *MuK* 37 [1967]: 205).
129. P. Hauschild, "Schelle," *MGG* 11:1659.
130. Here and in the discussions following, cf. the hymn schedule set up for this purpose for all Sundays and festival days of the church year in P. Graff, *Geschichte der Auflösung der alten gottesdienstlichen Formen in der evangelischen Kirche Deutschlands bis zum*

Eintritt der Aufklärung und des Rationalismus (Göttingen, 1921), pp. 132ff. [See also the more recent study, D. Gojowy, "Lied und Sonntag in Gesangbüchern der Bach-Zeit: Zur Frage des 'Detempore' bei Chorälen in Bachs Kantaten," *BJ*, 1972, pp. 24—60.—Ed.]

131. Cf. in that source the first list in the Appendix: *Kirchen-Ordnung dieser christlichen Lieder... auf die Jahrs-Fest und Sontage gerichtet.*

132. The hymn schedules in these hymnbooks of about 1725 as a rule contained only three or four hymns for each Sunday and festival, but the number of these hymns in the hymn schedules of about 1750 already increased to 8—10 or more.

133. Even though this movement is not in the original score, the supplementation undertaken is justified because that stanza of the hymn is expressly mentioned in the libretto. Cf. A. Dürr NBA, *KB* I/1:104.

134. Graff, p. 133. The hymn is, for instance, given as the hymn of the day in the *Hoch-Fürstliches Sachsen-Weißenfelsisches Vollständiges Gesang- und Kirchenbuch* of 1714. The statements about Weißenfels that follow are made on the basis of this source.

135. Cf. the text of the first edition in N*VT*, pp. 290—91.

136. Cf. N*VT*, p. 291.

137. Cf. *LKA*, pp. 53ff., as well as the indexes in *WGB* and in the *Leipziger Gesangbuch*, 1693; also Graff, p. 133. In Weißenfels this hymn is the hymn of the day for all three festival days.

138. *LKA* does not contain a special hymn schedule, but in the order of the church year the complete listing of the hymns sung on the individual Sundays and festival days is given.

139. Cf. Graff, p. 133. In Weißenfels the hymn was firmly established in Vespers for New Year's Day.

140. Cf. ibid., p. 133.

141. Cf. ibid., p. 134.

142. The hymn was generally considered the hymn of the day for this Sunday (ibid., p. 133).

143. Cf. ibid., p. 133, and N*VT*, p. 278. The hymn was the hymn of the day for this Sunday also in Weißenfels. It also appears in the hymn schedules of the Leipzig and Dresden hymnbooks for this Sunday.

144. In the *LKA* a single hymn, "Herr Christ, der einig Gotts Sohn," is assigned to this festival and given verbatim. The hymn, in addition to two others, had been suggested for the Purification of Mary.

145. The hymn was the hymn of the day for all three Easter days also in Weißenfels.

146. Graff, p. 133. In Weißenfels this hymn was sung at the beginning of the main service on this Sunday.

147. Ibid., p. 134.

148. Ibid. For the presentation of Cantatas BWV 107 and 138, cf. A. Dürr, *Zur Chronologie der Leipziger Vokalwerke J. S. Bachs*, 2d ed. (Kassel, 1976), pp. 61, 73.

149. For the chronology of the cantatas, cf. ibid., pp. 72— 73.

150. W. Neumann, *Handbuch der Kantaten Joh. Seb. Bachs* (Leipzig, 1953), p. 207.

151. Dürr, "Kirchenmusik," p. 300.

152. Cf. above all Smend, *Bach in Köthen*, pp. 112, 121—22, 123—34; as well as Smend, "Luther und Bach," pp. 162—63.

153. Dürr, "Kirchenmusik," p. 300.

154. W. Blankenburg, "Der gottesdienstliche Liedgesang der Gemeinde," *L* 4:571.

155. Dürr, "Kirchenmusik," p. 303. The author concluded his essay with these words.

156. A. Dürr, NBA, *KB* II/3:40.

157. Smend, "Luther und Bach," p. 163.

158. Ibid.

159. Herbst, p. 35.

160. Smend, "Luther und Bach," p. 163.

e) Conclusions

161. F. Kalb, *Theology of Worship in 17th-Century Lutheranism*, trans. H. P. A. Hamann (St. Louis: Concordia Publishing House, 1965), pp. 14, 39, 187.

162. *ML*, p. 218.
163. Gurlitt, *Master*, pp. 100—01.
164. Cf. Dürr, *Chronologie,* pp. 57ff.
165. *ML*, p. 219.
166. Ibid.
167. Söhngen, p. 170.

Bibliography

(See also Abbreviations of Frequently Cited Sources on p. 7—9.)

1. Sources

Albrecht, E. H. *Sächsische evangelish-luther'sche Kirchen- und Predigergeschichte von ihrem Ursprunge an bis auf gegenwärtige Zeiten*. Leipzig, 1799.

The Book of Concord: The Confessions of the Evangelical Lutheran Church. Trans. and ed. T. G. Tappert. Philadelphia, 1959.

Enke, C. F. *Über den Werth des neuen für die Leipziger Stadtkirchen bestimmten Gesangbuches: Eine Predigt am 3. Adventssontage*. Leipzig, 1796.

Das jetzt lebende und florirende Leipzig. Leipzig, 1723.

Luther's Works, American Edition. Ed. J. Pelikan and H. T. Lehmann. St. Louis and Philadelphia, 1955—.

Mitzler, L. C. *Neu eröffnete musikalische Bibliothek*. 4 vols. Leipzig, 1739—1754.

Moser, J. J., ed. *Derer Saltzburgischen Emigrations-ACten*. Vol. 1. Frankfurt and Leipzig, 1732.

Register of Communicants at St. Nicholas Church (from 1652).

Register of Communicants at St. Thomas Church (from 1691).

Register of Communicants at the New Church, 1729—1740.

Rosenmüller, J. G. *Einige Predigten, gehalten in der Thomaskirche zu Leipzig*. Leipzig, 1786.

Vollständiges Kirchen-Buch: Darinnen die Evangelia und Episteln auf alle Fest-Sonn- und Apostel-Tage durchs gantze Jahr...die Kirchen-Agenda, Ehe-Ordnung und allgemeinen Gebete, die in den Chur-Sächs. Ländern gebraucht werden, enthalten. Leipzig, 1743.

2. Hymn Books (arranged chronologically)

(See also *LGB* 1682, *LGB* 1717, *LKA*, and *WGB*.)

Vopelius, G. *Leipziger Gesang-Buch, Welches Anno 1682 in octavo mit derer Lieder Melodeyen von 4—5 biß 6 Stimmen: Jetzo aber ohne dieselben, mit vielen Liedern vermehret*. Ed. J. Günther. Leipzig, 1693.

Unfehlbare Engel-Freude oder Geistliches Gesang-Buch. Leipzig, 1710 [second part of *LKS*].

Hoch-Fürstliches Sachsen-Weißenfelsisches Vollständiges Gesang- und Kirchen-buch. Weißenfels, 1714.

Das Privilegirte Ordentliche und Vermehrte Dreßdnische Gesang-Buch. Leipzig and Dresden, 1725.

Das Vollständige und vermehrte Leipziger Gesang-Buch, Worinnen Die auser-

lesensten Lieder, welche in der Evangelischen Kirche gebräuchlich, an der Zahl 856. Ed. F. Werner, Leipzig, 1730.

Privilegirtes Vollständiges und verbessertes Leipziger Gesangbuch. Ed. C. G. Hofmann, Leipzig, 1737.

Auserlesenes und vollständiges Gesang-Buch, worinnen 804 der besten und geistreichsten Lieder, welche in denen Chur-Sächß. Kirchen pflegen gesungen zu werden, enthalten. Dresden, 1750.

3. Literature

Albrecht, C. *Einführung in die Liturgik.* Berlin, 1964.

Baselt, B. "Georg Phillip Telemann und die protestantische Kirchenmusik." *MuK* 37 (1967): 196—207.

Baumgarten, W. "Johann Sebastian Bach in Mühlhausen." *BiThü,* pp. 73—77.

Besch, H. "Eine Auktions-Quittung J. S. Bachs." In *Festschrift für Friedrich Smend,* pp. 74—79. Berlin, 1963.

———. *Johann Sebastian Bach: Frömmigkeit und Glaube.* 2d ed. Kassel and Basel, 1959.

Blankenburg, W. "Bach—geistlich und weltlich." *MuK* 20 (1950): 36—46.

———. "Chor." *MGG* 2:1230—65. Cf. *KM,* pp. 11—16.

———. "Johann Sebastian Bach und die Aufklärung." In *BG,* pp. 25—34; also in *KM,* pp. 163—73, and *WF,* pp. 100—10.

———. "Der mehrstimmige Gesang und die konzertierende Musik im evangelischen Gottesdienst." *L* 4:661—719.

———. "Das Parodieverfahren im Weinachtsoratorium Johann Sebastian Bachs." In *WF,* pp. 493—506.

———. "Theologische und geistesgeschichtliche Probleme der gegenwärtigen Bachforschung." *Theologische Literaturzeitung* 78 (1953): 391—410.

———. "Zwölf Jahre Bachforschung." *Acta Musicologica* 37 (1965): 95—158.

(For other works by Blankenburg, see also *KM, L,* and *WF.*)

Blume, F. "Antwort" [to Alfred Dürr]. *MuK* 32 (1962): 153—56.

———. "Bach, Johann Sebastian." *MGG* 1:962—1047; also in *SM,* pp. 363—412, 895ff.

———. "Barock." *MGG* 1:1275—1338.

———. "Doles." *MGG* 3:627—39.

———. *Renaissance and Baroque Music: A Comprehensive Survey.* Tr. M. D. Herter Norton. New York. 1967.

———. *Two Centuries of Bach: An Account of Changing Taste.* Tr. S. Godman. London, 1950.

(For other works by Blume, see also Blu and *SM.*)

Brausch, P. *Die Kantate: Ein Beitrag zur Geschichte der deutschen Dichtungsgattung.* Dissertation, Heidelberg, 1921.

Brinkmann, E. "Die Mühlhäuser Bache." *JSBiThü,* pp. 220—28.

Brodde, O. "Evangelische Choralkunde." *L* 4:343—557.

Brunner, E. *Die Mystik und das Wort.* Tübingen, 1924.

Bunners, C. *Kirchenmusik und Seelenmusik: Studien zu Frömmigkeit und Musik im Lutherthum des 17. Jahrhunderts.* Berlin, 1966.

Dibelius, M. "Individualismus und Gemeindebewußtsein in Johann Sebastian Bachs Passionen." *Archiv für Reformationsgeschichte* 41 (1948): 132—54.

Dubbels (*Hauptpastor*). "Pietismus und Rationalismus." In *Aus Hamburgs Kirche.* Hamburg, 1929.

Dürr, A. "Franck." *MGG* 4:681—83.

————. "Johann Sebastian Bachs Kirchenmusik in seiner Zeit und heute." In *WF*, pp. 290—303.

————. *Studien über die frühen Kantaten J. S. Bachs.* Leipzig, 1951.

————. "Zum Wandel des Bach-Bildes." *MuK* 32 (1962): 145—52.

————. *Zur Chronologie der Leipziger Vokalwerke J. S. Bachs.* 2d ed. Kassel, 1976.

Eggebrecht, H. H. "Über Bachs geschichtlichen Ort." In *WF*, pp. 247—89.

————. "Zur Antithese Geistlich-Weltlich." *Musica: Zweimonatschrift für alle Gebiete des Musiklebens* 4 (1950): 247—50.

Ehmann, W. "Die *Kleinen geistlichen Konzerte* von Heinrich Schütz und unsere musikalische Praxis." *MuK* 33 (1963): 9— 23.

Feder, G. *Bachs Werke in ihren Bearbeitern 1750—1950.* Dissertation, Kiel, 1955.

————. "Die protestantische Kirchenkantate." *MGG* 7:581— 608.

Fest- und Programmbuch des dritten Deutschen Bachfestes. Eisenach, 1907.

Fock, G. *Der junge Bach in Lüneburg.* Hamburg, 1950.

Forkel, J. N. "On Johann Sebastian Bach's Life, Genius, and Works" (1802). *BR*, pp. 293—356.

Goltzen, H. "Der tägliche Gottesdienst." *L* 3:99—296.

Graff, P. *Geschichte der Auflösung der alten gottesdienstlichen Formen in der evangelischen Kirche Deutschlands bis zum Eintritt der Aufklärung und des Rationalismus.* Göttingen, 1921.

Greiner, W. "Bach in Thüringen." *BiThü*, pp. 22—56.

Gudewill, K. "Über Formen und Texte der Kirchenkantaten Johann Sebastian Bachs." In *Festschrift Friedrich Blume zum 70. Geburtstag*, pp. 162—75. Kassel, 1963.

Gurlitt, W. "Johann Sebastian Bach in seiner Zeit und heute." *Bericht über die Wissenschaftliche Bachtagung der Gesellschaft für Musikforschung, Leipzig, 23—26 Juli 1950*, ed. W. Vetter and E. H. Meyer, pp. 51—80. Leipzig, 1951.

————. *Johann Sebastian Bach: The Master and His Work.* Trans. O. C. Rupprecht. St. Louis, 1957.

Hamel, F. "Bach als geistesgeschichtliche Erscheinung." *Kongreß-Bericht: Internationale Gesellschaft für Musikwissenschaft, Utrecht, 1952.* Amsterdam, 1953.

————. *Johann Sebastian Bach: Geistige Welt.* Göttingen, 1951.

Hartung, B. *Die alte und die neue Peterskirche in Leipzig.* Leipzig, 1885.

Hauschild, P. "Schelle." *MGG* 11:1658—61.

Helmbold, H. "Junge Bache auf dem Eisenacher Gymnasium." *JSBiThü*, pp. 19—24.

Herbst, W. *Johann Sebastian Bach und die lutherische Mystik.* Dissertation, Erlangen, 1958.

Herrmann, R. "Die Thüringer und die Bache." *BiThü*, pp. 97— 103.

Hoffmann-Erbrecht, L. "Hiller." *MGG* 6:409—19.

Jauernig, R. "Bachs erster Aufenthalt in Weimar." *BiThü*, pp. 69—70. (For other works by Jauernig, see also Jau. I and Jau. II.)

Kaiser, P. "Die Geschichte der Matthäikirche." In *Unsere Matthäikirche in vier Jahrhunderten, 1494—1894.* Leipzig, 1894.

Kalb, F. *Theology of Worship in 17th-Century Lutheranism.* Trans. H. P. A. Hamann. St. Louis, 1965.

Keller, H. "Johann Sebastian Bach und die Säkularisation der Kirchenmusik." *Universitas: Zeitschrift für Wissenschaft, Kunst und Literatur* 2 (1947):1425—34.

Kirn, O. *Die Leipziger Theologische Fakultät in fünf Jahrhunderten.* Leipzig, 1909.

Knick, B., ed. *St. Thomas zu Leipzig: Schule und Chor, Stätte des Wirkens von Johann Sebastian Bach, Bilder und Dokumente zur Geschichte der Thomasschule und des Thomanerchores mit ihren zeitgeschichtlichen Beziehungen.* Introduction by M. Mezger. Wiesbaden, 1963.

Knolle, T. "Erneuerung der Ordnung des heiligen Abendmahls." In *Vom Sakrament des Altars: Lutherische Beiträge zur Frage des heiligen Abendmahls*, ed. H. Sasse, pp. 270—92. Leipzig, 1941.

———. "Luthers Reform der Abendmahlsfeier in ihrer konstitutiven Bedeutung." In *Schrift und Bekenntnis: Zeugnisse lutherischer Theologie*, pp. 88—105. Hamburg and Berlin, n.d.

Kraft, G. "Johann Sebastian Bach und Ohrdruf." *JSBiThü*, pp. 26ff.

———. "Thüringer Stadtpfeiferfamilien um Bach." *JSBiThü*, pp. 145—69.

Kretzschmar, H. *Bachkolleg: Vorlesungen über J. S. Bach.* Leipzig, 1922.

Kroker, E. *Aufsätze zur Stadtgeschichte und Reformationsgeschichte.* Leipzig, 1929.

Kühn, G. "Johann Sebastian Bach in Eisenach." *BiThü*, pp. 63—67.

Loewenich, W. von. *Die Geschichte der Kirche.* Witten, 1954.

Mahrenholz, C. Preface to *Agende für evangelisch-lutherische Kirchen und Gemeinden.* Vol. 1, Part 1. Berlin, 1951.

———. "Zur musikalischen Gestaltung von Luthers Gottesdienstreform." *ML*, pp. 154—68.

(For other works by Mahrenholz, see also *ML*).

Mehl, J. G. "Johann Sebastian Bach—liberaler Humanist oder lutherischer Christ? Zum 'neuen Bachbild' Friedrich Blumes." *Gottesdienst und Kirchenmusik*, 1962, pp. 203—18.

Melchert, H. "Das Rezitativ der Kirchenkantaten J. S. Bachs." *BJ*, 1958, pp. 5—83.

Metzger, H. A. "Joh. Seb. Bach und der evangelische Gottesdienst seiner Zeit." *MuK* 20 (1950): 49—54.

Mezger, M. "Ein 'neues' Bach-Bild?" *Die Welt*, No. 126, 14 July 1962.

Müller, F. "Das Ordinarium Missae." *L* 2:1—45.

Müller, K. "Der junge Bach." In *Arnstädter Bachbuch: Johann Sebastian Bach und seine Verwandten in Arnstadt*, ed. K. Müller and F. Wiegand, pp. 58—130. Arnstadt, 1957.

(For other works by F. Müller, see also *L*.)

Müller-Schwefe, H.-R. "Bachs Kantaten als Auslegung des Wortes Gottes." *MuK* 30 (1960): 81—94.

Neumann, W. *Auf den Lebenswegen Johann Sebastian Bachs.* Berlin, 1953.

———. *Handbuch der Kantaten Joh. Seb. Bachs.* Leipzig, 1953.

———. "Zur Frage der Gesangbücher Johann Sebastian Bachs." *BJ*, 1956, pp. 112—23.

(For other works by W. Neumann, see also *BD* and N*VT*.)

Oepke, A. "Johann Sebastian Bach als Abendmahlsgast." *MuK* 24 (1954): 202—08.

Örtel, A. "Johann Sebastian Bach in Ohrdruf." *BiThü*, pp. 67—68.

Preuß, H. *Die Geschichte der Abendmahlsfrömmigkeit in Zeugnissen und Berichten.* Gütersloh, 1949.

———. *Johann Sebastian Bach—der Lutheraner.* 2d ed. Erlangen and Würzburg, 1950.

———. *Johann Sebastian Bachs Bibliothek.* Leipzig, 1928.

Ramin, G. "Johann Sebastian Bachs Kantaten in heutiger Sicht." *Universitas: Zeitschrift für Wissenschaft, Kunst und Literatur* 3 (1948): 1159—63.

Reindell, W. "Die Präfation." *L* 2:453—521.

Reinhold, F. "Die Bache in Ohrdruf." *BiThü*, pp. 119—26.

Richter, B. F. "Über die Schicksale der der Thomasschule zu Leipzig angehörenden Kantaten Joh. Seb. Bachs." *BJ*, 1906, pp. 43—73.

Riedel, F. W. "Kuhnau." *MGG* 7:1878—87.

Rietschel, G. *Lehrbuch der Liturgik.* 2d ed., ed. P. Graff. Vol. 1. Göttingen, 1951.

Röbbelen, I. *Theologie und Frömmigkeit im deutschen evangelisch-lutherischen Gesangbuch des 17. und frühen 18. Jahrhunderts.* Göttingen and Berlin, 1957.

Rochlitz, F. *Wege zu Bach: Drei Abhandlungen von Friedrich Rochlitz, 1749—1842.* Ed. J. M. Müller-Blattau. Augsburg, 1926.

Rosen, W. *Johann Sebastian Bach: Leben und Werk.* Leipzig, 1935.

Rüling, J. B. *Die Johanniskirche zu Leipzig in 7 Jahrhunderten.* Leipzig, 1916.

Scheide, W. H. "Johann Sebastian Bachs Sammlung von Kantaten seines Vetters Johann Ludwig Bach." *BJ*, 1959, pp. 52—94, and 1961, pp. 5—24.

Schering, A. "Kleine Bachstudien." *BJ*, 1933, pp. 30—70.

———. *Musikgeschichte Leipzigs.* Vol. 2. Leipzig, 1926.

(For other works by A. Schering, see also Sch*BLKM* and Sch*ML*.)

Schmitz, A. *Die Bildlichkeit der wortgebundenen Musik Johann Sebastian Bachs.* Mainz, 1950.

———. "Die oratorische Kunst J. S. Bachs: Grundlagen und Grundfragen." In *Kongreßbericht: Gesellschaft für Musikforschung, Lüneburg 1950*, pp. 33—49. Kassel and Basel. 1950.

Schöffel, S. "Orthodoxie." In *Aus Hamburgs Kirche.* Hamburg, 1929.

Schweitzer, A. *J. S. Bach.* Trans. E. Newman, with a preface by C. M. Widor. 2 vols. London, 1962.

Smend, F. *Bach in Köthen.* Berlin, 1951.

———. *Joh. Seb. Bach: Kirchen-Kantaten.* 2d ed. Berlin, 1950.

———. "Luther und Bach." *Bach-Studien: Gesammelte Reden und Aufsätze,* ed. C. Wolff, pp. 153—75. Kassel, 1969. Partially translated in *The Lutheran Quarterly* 1 (1949): 399—410.

———. "Was bleibt? Zu Friedrich Blumes Bach-Bild." *Der Kirchenmusiker* 13 (1962): 178—88.

Söhngen, O. "Bach und die Liturgie." *Der Kirchenmusiker* 1 (1950): 124—27.

———. "Theologische Grundlagen der Kirchenmusik." *L* 4:1— 267.

Spitta, P. *Die Passionsmusiken von Johann Sebastian Bach und Heinrich Schütz.* Hamburg, 1893.

(For another work by Spitta, see also Spi.)

Stählin, R. "Die Geschichte des christlichen Gottesdienstes von der Urkirche bis zur Gegenwart." *L* 1:1—81.

Tagliavini, L. F. *Studi sui Testi delle Cantate sacre di J. S. Bach.* Padua, 1956.

Terry, C. S. *Bach: A Biography.* 2d ed. London, 1933.

———. *Johann Sebastian Bach: Cantata Texts, Sacred and Secular.* London, 1926.

Thürer, G. "Vom Wortkunstwerk im Deutschen Barock." In *Die Kunstformen des Barockzeitalters,* ed. R. Stamm, pp. 354—82. Bern, 1956.

Treiber, F. "Die thüringisch-sächsische Kirchenkantate zur Zeit des jungen J. S. Bach (etwa 1700—1723)." *Archiv für Musikforschung* 2 (1937): 129—59.

Wallau, R. "Die kirchliche Bedeutung der Bachschen Musik." In *Kongreßbericht Lüneburg 1950*, pp. 107—11. Kassel and Basel, 1950.

Walter, J. von. *Die Geschichte des Christentums*. Vol. 2/2. Gütersloh, 1950.

Weismann, E. "Der Predigtgottesdienst und die verwandten Formen." *L* 3:1—97.

Werner, A. *Vier Jahrhunderte im Dienste der Kirchenmusik*. Leipzig, 1933.

Werthemann, H. *Die Bedeutung der alttestamentlichen Historien in Johann Sebastian Bachs Kantaten*. Tübingen, 1960.

Zenck, H. "Grundformen deutscher Musikanschauung." *Jahrbuch der Akademie der Wissenschaften in Göttingen,* 1941/1942. Göttingen, 1942.

Index

Justification, 156

Kalb, Friedrich, 131, 167, 176
Kantorei, use of in churches, 75—80, 82,
    86—87, 89—91, 95, 117—18,
    123
Kantorei tradition, 143—44, 149—51, 218
Keiser, Reinhard, 232
Keller, Hermann, 25—26
Klausing, Heinrich, 32
Klavierübung, 206
Klotz, Hans, 205
Konzertmeister, 185—87
Korrespondierende Sozietät der
    musikalischen Wissenschaften,
    232
Köthen, 183, 187—90, 192, 194,
    199—200, 205, 211, 254
    court music, 194
    Lutheran Kantorei, 189
    Reformed Church, 189
    St. Agnes Church, 189
Krantz, Friedrich Gottlieb, 100
Krebs, Johann Ludwig, 197
Kretzschmar, Hermann, 99
Kuhnau, Johann, 28, 41, 74, 77, 79, 81,
    195—96, 216—17, 232
Kurrendesingen, 95, 176

Latin, use of in worship, 112, 118—20,
    123—28, 159—61
Lazareth Church, baptisms at, 71
    renovation of, 43—44
    worship schedule, 73
Leipzig. *See also names of individual
    churches*
    archives and libraries, 34—35
    charitable activity, 103—04, 257—58
    city council, 195—97, 257
    city council, Bach's memorial to,
        192—93
    Consistory, 33
    concert music, 198
    directories, 38
    Gymnasium, 74
    hymnbook, 1682, 36
    hymnbook, 1693, 234, 236—37, 239,
        241, 243
    hymnbook, 1717, 42, 47, 249, 251
    hymnbook, 1730, 236
    hymnbook, 1735, 159
    hymnbook, 1737, 212, 234
    hymnbook, 1796, 159
    intellectual life, 31
    Latin School, 74
    musical director, 191, 195—96

order of service at, 108—31
population, 39—40
publishing in, 104
St. John's Hospital, 49
town musicians, 191
University of, 31—33, 64, 97
use of Dresden hymnbooks at,
    37—38
Leipziger Kirchen-Andachten, 35, 105
Leipziger Kirchen-Staat, 35, 36, 104, 109
Lent, 58—60, 62, 65—66, 80, 84, 86—93,
    100, 106, 122—24, 127—29, 159,
    239, 249, 258
Leopold, Prince of Anhalt-Köthen,
    188—90, 194
Library, Bach's, 102, 104, 140, 204—05,
    217
Librettos, cantata, 79, 81, 121, 143, 216
    printed, 218, 220
    used by Bach, 216, 232
Lüneburg, 175—78
    St. Michael School, 177—78
Luther, Martin, 142, 144, 148—50,
    155—56, 204, 206, 208—09, 211,
    214—16, 220, 222, 234, 236,
    238—39, 241, 247—48, 251,
    253—54
    works, 204—05

Magnificat (BWV 243), 253
Mahrenholz, Christhard, 182, 192,
    208—10, 255
Main service, 116—29, 131, 138—39
Marian festivals, 56
Mass, order of the, 116
Mass bell, 106, 160
Mass in B Minor (BWV 232), 77, 84, 86,
    206, 226 (illustration), 227
Matins, 49, 100—01, 104, 110—12, 116
Mattheson, Johann, 196
Maundy Thursday, 56, 60, 62—63, 65, 163
Memorial sermons, 94
Metzger, Hans Arnold, 205
Mizler, Lorenz Christoph, 31, 80
Motet, 75, 81—82, 84—88, 92—94, 231
Mühlhausen, 180—83, 185, 200, 230
    organ, 181
    resignation from, 143—44, 180, 192,
        202, 255
    St. Blasius Church, 182
    St. Mary Church, 181—82
Music, 62, 71, 75—79, 81—82, 84—86,
    88, 91, 94
Music, purpose of, 150, 208—10
    theological evaluation of, 144
Musica poetica, 221
Mysticism, 20, 99, 154—56, 214

Sangerhausen, 179
Scheibe, Johann Adolph, 210
Schein, Johann Herman, 93
Schelle, Johann, 88, 196, 233
Schering, Arnold, 34, 84—85, 94—95,
    166, 191, 196—97, 222, 225
Schmitz, Arnold, 151, 221
Schöffel, Simon, 142
Schott, Georg Balthasar, 91
Schütz, Friedrich Wilhelm, 67
Schweitzer, Albert, 141, 221
Scriver, Christian, 104
Secular compositions, Bach's, 206, 208,
    225
Secularization of the Lutheran Church,
    25—26, 31, 142—43, 149, 158,
    167
Separatism, 100, 102
Sermon, length of, 124, 265
    prominence of, 111
Sermon music, 150—52, 155—57, 231,
    233, 253
Seventeen Chorales, 232
Sick, Communion of, 135, 164
Sicul, Christoph Ernst, 35—36, 42, 47, 51
Sieber, Urban Gottfried, 67, 70
Singspiele, 198
Smend, Friedrich, 20, 84, 117, 141, 146,
    189—90, 196, 216—18, 222, 224,
    227, 250
Söhngen, Oskar, 209, 256
Spener, Philipp Jakob, 45, 99, 101—02,
    146
Spitta, Philip, 11, 20, 34, 84, 88, 109,
    171—72, 177, 181, 185
Steinbach, Johann Friedrich, 45, 132
Steinert, Johann Michael, 91
Stemler (superintendent at Leipzig), 45
Stölzel, Gottfried Heinrich, 217
Strattner, Georg Christoph, 184, 186
Students of theology, 52
Subdeacon, 62, 67—70, 72, 204
Sunday, observance of, 106
Sunday services, 48—51
Superintendent, 66—67, 72, 108, 191

Tagliavini, Luigi Ferdinando, 216—17,
    231
Telemann, Georg Philipp, 41, 74, 184,
    195—97, 199, 216—17, 232
Teller, Romanus, 42, 67—68, 204
Terry, Charles Sanford, 34—35, 38, 119,
    183
Thiry Years' War, 26
Thomasius, Christian, 31
Tostleben, Christoph, 99

Traffic, public, halting during worship, 63
Treiber, Fritz, 232
Tune books, 159

University Church. See St. Paul Church

Vesper sermon, 50
Vespers, 56—57, 59—60, 62—66, 68—70,
    72—74, 76—77, 79, 85, 87,
    91—94, 100—01, 110—13, 116,
    128—29, 131, 158, 163—64, 258
Vestments, 58, 64, 107—08
Vocal solo, 142, 151
Vopelius, Gottfried, 36, 38, 208, 233, 250

Wagnersches Gesangbuch, 137, 233
Wallau, Rene, 25—26
Walter, Johann, 60
Weddings, 58—59, 71, 93—94
Weekday sermons, 53
Weekday services, 51, 100, 110—14, 116
    decrease in, 163
Weigel, Johann Christoph, 44
Weimar, 179—89, 192, 194, 202, 205, 218,
    230—31
    court chapel, 184—86
    court orchestra, 184
    St. James Church, 183
    worship practices, 106
Weiß, Christian, 67, 99, 203, 218, 220
Weißenfels, hymn schedule, 234—36,
    239—44, 246—47, 252
    observance of apostles' days in, 57
Weiz, Anton, 38, 46
Well-appointed church music, 192—93
Werner (Vespers preacher at New
    Church), 45, 65, 132
Werthemann, Helene, 20
Wilhelm Ernst, Duke of Saxony-Weimar,
    180, 183—84, 187—88
Wittenberg University, 32, 97
Wolff, Christian, 31—32
Wolle, Christoph, 204
Worship, attendance at, 97, 106, 164
    Bach's attitude toward, 200—11
    length of service, 49—50, 53, 163
    purpose of, 164, 175—76, 254
    relation to theology, 175—76
    theological evaluation of, 171
Worship schedule, 48—55
    later changes, 163
Wünschet Jerusalem Glück (BWV Anh.
    4), 79—81

Ziegler, Christiane Mariane von, 210, 212,
    217